GIVING VOTERS A VOICE

GIVING
VOTERS
A VOICE

The Origins of the Initiative
and Referendum in America

STEVEN L. PIOTT

UNIVERSITY OF MISSOURI PRESS
COLUMBIA AND LONDON

Copyright © 2003 by
The Curators of the University of Missouri
University of Missouri Press, Columbia, Missouri 65201
Printed and bound in the United States of America
5 4 3 2 1   07 06 05 04 03

Library of Congress Cataloging-in-Publication Data

Piott, Steven L.
    Giving voters a voice : the origins of the initiative and
referendum in America / Steven L. Piott.
        p. cm.
Includes bibliographical references and index.
    ISBN 0-8262-1457-6
    1. Referendum—United States—History.   I. Title.

JF494 .P556 2003
328.273—dc21

                                        2002151760

∞ This paper meets the requirements of the
American National Standard for Permanence of Paper
for Printed Library Materials, Z39.48, 1984.

Text Designer: Stephanie Foley
Jacket Designer: Susan Ferber
Typesetter: The Composing Room of Michigan, Inc.
Printer and Binder: The Maple-Vail Book Manufacturing Group
Typefaces: ITC Giovanni and Palatino

To Laura and Amy

Contents

Acknowledgments

The author of every historical monograph accrues a debt of gratitude in the process of researching his or her topic, and that is certainly the case here. General thanks and credit should be given to the staffs of the reference, newspaper, and special collections departments of the University of Arkansas Libraries, Special Collections, Fayetteville; the Arkansas History Commission, Little Rock; the University of Arkansas Newspaper Library, Little Rock; the University of California Research Library, Special Collections, Los Angeles; the John Randolph Haynes and Dora Haynes Foundation, Los Angeles; the University of Colorado, Western Historical Collections, Boulder; the Colorado Historical Society, Denver; the University of Missouri, Western Historical Manuscript Collection, Columbia; the State Historical Society of Missouri, Columbia; the North Dakota State University, North Dakota Institute for Regional Studies, Fargo; the North Dakota Historical Society, Bismarck; the Ohio Historical Society, Columbus; the Historical and Philosophical Society of Ohio, Cincinnati; the University of Oklahoma, Western History Manuscripts, Norman; the Oklahoma Historical Society, Oklahoma City; the South Dakota Historical Society, Pierre; and the Library of Congress, Manuscripts Division, Washington, D.C.

I would also like to thank Nicole Merriman of the State Library of Ohio, Columbus; Melanie Sturgeon and Jeff Malcomson of the History and Archives Division, Arizona Department of Library Archives and Public Records, Phoenix; Susan Searcy of the Nevada State Library and Archives, Carson City; Tracey Kimball of the New Mexico Legislative Council Service, Santa Fe; Alyssa Williams of the Maryland State Archives, Annapolis; John A. Heldt of the Montana State Library, Helena; Rosalind Libbey of the New Jersey Historical Society, Newark; James Stuart Osbourn of the Newark Public Library; Rebecca B. Colesar of the New Jersey State Library, Trenton; Jan Blodgett of the Dickenson College Library, Carlisle, Pennsylvania; and Theresa M. Kostka of the Cumberland County Historical Society, Carlisle, Pennsylvania, for responding to either written or e-mailed queries. Charles A. Braithwaite of the University of Nebraska, Roger D. Bridges of the Rutherford B. Hayes Presidential Center, and Josh Stevens of the Missouri Historical Society in St. Louis kindly granted permission to publish material that appeared in the *Great Plains Quarterly*, the *Hayes Historical Journal*, and *Gateway Heritage*, respectively. Several Faculty Development grants from the College of Arts and Sciences at Clarion University made travel to various collections possible.

I would also like to give special mention to Lana McClune, History Department secretary, for her technical and clerical assistance. Similar appreciation should go to Judy Bowser and Geraldine Ortz of the Inter-Library Loan Office of the Clarion University Library for tirelessly tracking down hard-to-find but invaluable sources. This project would have ground to a halt long ago without their knowledgeable assistance and professional and friendly manner. Three other individuals played important parts in the preparation of this book. Cynthia Kennedy took time from her own work to read portions of the manuscript and offer valuable comments and suggestions. Christopher Gibbs read most of the chapters and offered, as he has done since graduate school, the kind of trusted, solid criticism that is hard to come by. Larry Gragg read the entire manuscript and offered helpful suggestions. As in the past, his willingness to respond to endless interpretive and organizational questions helped to keep the topic in focus. To all three, as wordsmiths, critics, and confidants, I am grateful. The voices of F. Alan Coombs and David Thelen are in here somewhere, even though they have not read a word of what is written. Thanks.

GIVING VOTERS A VOICE

1

The Intellectual and Political Origins of the Initiative and Referendum

In the late nineteenth century Americans struggled with the harsh economic transformations of an emerging industrial society. Workers, farmers, consumers, and taxpayers increasingly felt ignored as participants in the political system. In their minds, policy makers identified issues and set priorities within a political environment ever more susceptible to the influence of economic power. The special or privileged interests, and the professional politicians they controlled, had precluded any discussion of vital social, economic, and political issues. Workers looked in vain for a serious discussion of protective labor legislation, antistrikebreaking ordinances, or limits on court injunctions. Farmers felt powerless to challenge federal monetary policies or to obtain assistance against falling farm prices and unregulated transportation charges. Consumers expressed dismay over the power that corporations exerted over utility rates and felt stymied in their demands for municipal ownership of those utilities. Frustrated taxpayers complained of tax inequities and onerous tax burdens. Exacerbating these problems was a political system in which important issues and fundamental social problems were easily subverted or ignored by the political party, the party caucus, or the corporate lobby. Concluding that their elected representatives no longer represented their interests, many Americans became discontented and increasingly dissatisfied with governmental policies, party agendas, and a system of governance that rewarded organized power at the expense of the needs of the people. Popular democracy appeared to be a sham. At stake were fundamental questions of economic and political democracy.

Many well-known nineteenth-century commentators, such as Edward Bellamy in his popular novel *Looking Backward* (1888), underscored this general theme. During a conversation between Bellamy's characters Dr. Leete and Julian West, Leete reminds his nineteenth-century guest that "the organization of [your] society . . . was such that officials were under a con-

1

stant temptation to misuse their power for the private profit of themselves or others. Under such circumstances it seems almost strange that you dared entrust them with any of your affairs." In a similar vein, British observer James Bryce suggests in *The American Commonwealth* (1888) that U.S. democracy had become perverted by the power of wealth, and that this power had been frequently used to corrupt voters, jurors, legislators, and parties. Special interests used legislative privilege to monopolize wealth and opportunity and to act against the public interest. Consequently, Americans were "neither well served nor well led." Joining these two critics was Eltweed Pomeroy, president of the National Direct Legislation League, who, in 1896, linked the growing demand for expanding the bounds of popular democracy to "conditions that have been growing progressively worse for the last quarter century." To Pomeroy, those conditions were economic, caused by "the irresponsibility, corruption, and imbecility of legislative action" that allowed legislatures to "smother, dodge, and avoid vital questions."[1]

Beginning in the late 1880s many frustrated individuals began to suggest ways to improve the existing situation. Some sought to create new political organizations and new political parties. Others sought to capture control of existing parties. Still others suggested reforming existing voting procedures by creating a secret ballot, passing direct primary laws, establishing nonpartisan state and local elections, granting the vote to women, allowing for the direct election of U.S. senators, and reducing the influence of money in political campaigns through the enactment of corrupt-practices acts. A growing number, however, began to reach the conclusion that the political structure itself needed to be opened up. They argued it would be better if voters were allowed to bypass unresponsive or irresponsible political bodies and directly legislate for themselves using the initiative and referendum. Under the initiative a given percentage of voters could propose a law, which then must be approved at the polls. Under the referendum a given percentage of voters could request that a law passed by a lawmaking body be submitted for popular approval. Ideally, legislation could then reflect human need rather than corporate power, and minority opinions could be allowed a hearing. Special interest legislation could be curbed and political accountability encouraged. If voters had the power to make and veto law, they could control their institutions of government and reaffirm the social contract heralded in the Declaration of Independence.

American reformers learned about direct legislation from the Swiss. Eu-

---

1. Bellamy, *Looking Backward*, 45; Bryce, *The American Commonwealth*, 591 (see also 609 and 614 for relevant commentary); Pomeroy, "The Direct Legislation Movement and Its Leaders," 43; Pomeroy, "Direct Legislation," *Arena* 22 (July 1899): 102.

ropean revolutions in the 1830s directed political change along democratic lines in Switzerland and elsewhere. In Switzerland such changes drew on the democratic habits and customs that had been developed in the Landsgemeinden (open-air assemblies) of some of the mountain cantons, and on the Volksanfragen (popular consultations) established in Zurich and Berne during the fifteenth and sixteenth centuries. According to W. D. McCrackan, "it was a magnificent movement, bearing a striking likeness to the revival of political thought amongst the farmers of the United States in the Grange and Alliance. There were the same wrongs of special privilege to redress, . . . and the same political tyranny of the politicians to break." The first step toward direct government involved an assault on reactionary, almost feudal political administrations in the cantons. In 1844 the Canton of Valais established a "referendum"—no laws could take effect until a majority of voters had adopted them. Twenty-five years later, Zurich adopted a constitution that took legislative powers away from its Grand Council, allowing it only to frame laws before referring them to the people for final acceptance. Within five years the referendum became a permanent part of the Federal Constitution of Switzerland. In 1891 the people accepted an amendment allowing for the initiative.[2]

British and American observers began to write about the Swiss experiment in the late 1880s, and a variety of books and articles appeared in the United States in the last two decades of the century.[3] J. W. Sullivan's *Direct Legislation by the Citizenship through the Initiative and Referendum* had the greatest influence. Sullivan, originally from Carlisle, Pennsylvania, had dropped out of high school to become a printer's apprentice. After working for a variety of newspapers in various cities, he moved to New York City around 1882 and gained employment as foreman of the proofroom of the *New York Times*. He joined the Typographical Union and soon became editor of the *Union Printer*, the official organ of Typographical Union no. 6. Active among labor reform groups, Sullivan became a follower of Henry George and the single-tax idea and worked as labor editor of the Georgist

---

2. McCrackan, *The Rise of the Swiss Republic*, 325 (see also 338–40). See also Pomeroy, "Direct Legislation Movement and Leaders," 29–30; and Simon Deploige, *The Referendum in Switzerland*, 68–123.

3. See A. V. Dicey, "Democracy in Switzerland," *Nation* 43 (November 18, 1886): 410–12; A. V. Dicey, "Democracy in Switzerland II," *Nation* 43 (December 16, 1886): 494–96; Boyd Winchester, *The Swiss Republic*; Bernard Moses, *The Federal Government of Switzerland*; Sir Francis Ottiwell Adams, *The Swiss Confederation*; W. D. McCrackan, "The Swiss Referendum," *Arena* 3 (March 1891): 458–64; W. D. McCrackan, "The Initiative in Switzerland," *Arena* 7 (April 1893): 548–53; W. D. McCrackan, "How to Introduce the Initiative and Referendum," *Arena* 7 (May 1893): 696–701; McCrackan, *Rise of Swiss Republic*; John Martin Vincent, *State and Federal Government in Switzerland*; and Nathan Cree, *Direct Legislation by the People.*

weekly *Standard* from 1887 to 1889. He had begun to collect material relating to direct legislation in 1883 after learning of the experiment in Switzerland. As Sullivan recalled some years later, "as exchange editor of a social reform weekly journal, I gathered such facts bearing on the subject as were passing about in the American newspaper world, and through the magazine indexes . . . I gained access to whatever pertaining to Switzerland had gone on record in the monthlies and quarterlies."[4] In 1888 he took a leave of absence from his editorial duties to observe things firsthand in Switzerland. Upon his return, he vigorously advocated the initiative and referendum as instruments for governing labor unions, as well as being of value at the state and municipal levels.[5]

Sullivan wrote tirelessly on the subject, including a special section in *Twentieth Century,* a series of letters to the *New York Times* in 1889, and an essay that same year in *Chautauquan Magazine* titled "The Referendum in Switzerland." In 1892 he published his book *Direct Legislation.* As a journeyman printer, he set the type himself. He kept the length to 120 pages; wrote in a clear, simple style; and held the cost to a quarter (later, ten cents). *Direct Legislation,* the first book to argue the relevancy of direct legislation for the United States, sold between ten and fifteen thousand copies a year for the first three years. As one reformer later said: "It has done more in this country to crystallize and give definiteness of aim to the sentiment of the really democratic leaders . . . than any other one thing. It made converts, and they spread its circulation." According to William Dwight Porter Bliss, a crusading Christian socialist and advocate of direct legislation, "Few books have done more good in this century."[6]

Sullivan detailed how the Swiss disposed by vote "all questions of taxation, public finance, executive acts, state employment, corporation grants, public works, and similar operations of government commonly, even in republican states, left to legislators and other officials." As for those officials, they had to rest content with the power of stewardship of communal lands, the postal system, and banking. The Swiss had discovered a direct, simple way to adjust their social contract, and in so doing had initiated a political

---

4. Sullivan, *Direct Legislation,* ii.

5. See *Dictionary of American Biography,* s.v. "Sullivan, J. W."; Edwin S. Potter, "Letting the People Rule," 121–22; W. S. Rood, "James W. Sullivan: The Father of the Initiative and Referendum in the United States," 5–6; and *New York Times,* September 29, 1938.

6. Pomeroy, "Direct Legislation Movement and Leaders," 32, 34; Bliss quoted in ibid., 34. Sullivan's book made quite an impact. According to Pomeroy, "A thousand copies were sold in one lump in Oregon, three hundred went to Montana, five hundred to Kansas, and many in hundreds to clubs and individuals. Mr. Wayland of the *Coming Nation* sold a thousand, and another person paid for the free distribution of two thousand" (34). See also Sullivan, *Direct Legislation,* ii; and Potter, "Letting the People Rule," 122.

revolution. By banishing special privilege and divisive partisanship and eliminating autocratic legislative power and self-interested bureaucracy, they had made their system more accountable and more responsive. Sullivan observed that "they have written their laws in language so plain that a layman may be judge in the highest court. They have forestalled monopolies, improved and reduced taxation, avoided incurring heavy public debts, and made a better distribution of their land than any other European country. They have practically given home rule in local affairs to every community."[7]

Sullivan believed that direct legislation would work in the United States and that it could cure the nation's political ills. Direct legislation, he concluded, stood firmly rooted in the American tradition of town meetings and the constitutional amendment process. The town meeting, like the Swiss communal meeting, sought to enact local statutes, elect local officials, set local taxes, and establish local appropriations. Any citizen could propose a measure, and the majority would agree to accept or reject any proposal—initiative and referendum. Both required open conduct of political affairs and free expression of opinions. Finally, both meetings implemented the theory that sovereignty lay with the people. Sullivan generalized in his description of the nature of the New England town meeting tradition. Recent studies of seventeenth-century New England town life have shown a strong desire for consensus and a willingness to allow local elites to control the political agenda. In the eighteenth century, however, the town meeting asserted its independence, expressed a growing lack of confidence in governing elites, and became more like Sullivan imagined. Sullivan included a detailed example of the political activities in the town of Rockland, Massachusetts, to show that the town meeting tradition was still vibrant in 1891.[8]

Sullivan also suggested that in the process of revising state constitutions every ten or twenty years (a process that in every state but Delaware required approval by popular vote), the definition of admissible subject matter had broadened. The people now used the amendment process much as popular legislators. As one observer noted: "Some recent state constitutions have come almost to resemble bodies of statutes."[9] The trend would continue. Between 1900 and 1920 more than fifteen hundred amendments to state constitutions were proposed, and three-fifths of them were adopted. Constitutional amendments requiring popular referenda in many states included determining the location of state capitals, locating state universi-

7. Sullivan, *Direct Legislation*, 23–24, 71 (see also 5–71).
8. See ibid., 72–82; and Kenneth A. Lockridge, *The New England Town: The First Hundred Years*, 37–56, 119–38.
9. John Fiske, *Civil Government in the United States*, 196.

ties and correctional institutions, raising state debt levels or rates of taxation on property for state purposes, chartering banks, extending the franchise, and controlling the manufacture and sale of alcoholic beverages. In
addition, many state constitutions prior to 1900 mandated referenda to determine local boundary questions, select county seats, or approve municipal charters. Sullivan believed that voters, especially in the newer western
states, were moving toward popular declaration of the right to direct con-
sultation in the making of constitutional law. He favored the natural national development of these state and local forms.[10]

Sullivan concluded that direct legislation would precipitate peaceful political revolution. By using this practical tool, citizens could regain the legislative and fiscal powers they had delegated to bodies that, by the late
nineteenth century, either seemed committed to avoiding controversial issues or were actually determined to abuse the public trust. "Were legislation direct," he insisted, "the sphere of every citizen would be enlarged;
each would consequently acquire education in his role, and develop a lively interest in the public affairs in part under his own management." Adoption of direct legislation might renew hope in those who had given up on
political reform. Third-party advocates could discover a mutuality of interest and a starting point for further reforms, such as prohibition, the single tax, or municipal ownership. It offered organized wageworkers the opportunity to transform the power they exerted in their unions into political
power. There they could finally win the eight-hour day, antistrikebreaking
ordinances, police neutrality in strikes, and limits on court injunctions. An
end to the "lawmaking monopoly" meant an end to class legislation, machine rule, fiscal extravagance, nepotism, and the spoils system. Simple acceptance of the natural process of direct legislation would work these
changes.[11]

The expanding literary discussion of direct legislation coincided with
practical efforts to apply the idea to real life. In early 1892, in Newark, New
Jersey, a few friends organized the People's Power League, with Henry L.
Beckmeyer, a well-known local labor leader, as president. Within weeks,
several hundred of the state's leading reformers had joined.[12] On June 17,

10. See Harold Underwood Faulkner, *The Quest for Social Justice, 1898–1914,* 84; and
Sullivan, *Direct Legislation,* 82–86. Sullivan took his information on the historical de-
velopment of the referendum in the United States from E. P. Oberholtzer, "Law-Making
by Popular Vote," *Annals of the American Academy* 2 (November 1891): 324–44. See also
Bryce, *The American Commonwealth,* 470–71. The most detailed account can be found in
Ellis Paxson Oberholtzer, *The Referendum in America,* 118–19, 173–240, 335–67.

11. Sullivan, *Direct Legislation,* 93. For an expanded argument, see 90–120.

12. Actually, a political footnote predated this. During the election campaign of 1882,
Benjamin Urner of Elizabeth, New Jersey, ran for Congress on the Greenback Party tick-
et and lost. Feeling he had suffered severely from the bribery methods of his opponents,
Urner started to publish a short-lived newspaper that actively agitated for the initiative

1892, delegates from eleven state industrial and reform organizations held a convention in New Brunswick and decided to merge the People's Power League with the reformist People's Union. The new organization included labor reformers and Farmers' Alliancemen, as currency contraction and falling commodity prices convinced many farmers that they faced ruin. According to one New Jersey member of the alliance, the farmer "is now tormented with the horrible conviction that he has been duped and deceived, in some way, and by somebody, all these years, to vote against himself; consequently he is looking for a way out of his present unfortunate condition. He has gone so far as to decide that hereafter he will do his own thinking, vote independently, and pay less heed to his political bosses."[13]

The People's Union adopted the *Star Spangled Banner*, edited by William Farr Goodwin of Middlesex County, as its official newspaper, endorsed the Populist Party's St. Louis platform, and elected delegates to attend the party's convention in Omaha. However, they declined to join the new party in order to retain at least the appearance of nonpartisanship. Those in attendance clearly sympathized with the Populists but preferred to keep direct legislation as their highest priority. They pledged to work only for the election of candidates who would endorse the following statement: "The people should have the power to propose law by mandatory petition, and to vote direct upon any act passed by legislative bodies for the purpose of accepting or rejecting, as by the people shall be deemed best." They elected J. W. Arrowsmith of Orange president. Arrowsmith was politically associated with the Prohibition Party, but when a major petition drive by that party in 1890 had no effect upon the New Jersey legislature, he turned his attention to the referendum movement. Influenced further by reading Boyd Winchester's book, *The Swiss Republic*, he was instrumental in organizing the People's Power League and the People's Union. Supporting Arrowsmith were twenty-one members of the State Executive Committee. This committee worked hard to get the "direct legislation" principle written into the platforms of the Democratic and Republican Parties in 1892, but failed.[14]

---

and referendum. The idea of direct legislation was thus known to some reformers in New Jersey prior to the literary movement of the late 1880s and early 1890s. Prior to 1892 the only organized political agitation for direct legislation came from a plank in the platform of the Socialist Labor Party, which met in convention in Chicago on October 12, 1889. See J. W. Arrowsmith, "Direct Legislation Movement in New Jersey," 2.

13. "Address by Rev. H. D. Opdyke," *Direct Legislation Record* 1 (May 1894): 10.

14. Arrowsmith, "Direct Legislation Movement," 2. Arrowsmith abandoned his business interests in the mid-1890s and assumed the editorship of the *Bloomfield (N.J.) Record*. He remained active in both the Direct Legislation League of New Jersey and the National Direct Legislation League. See George W. Hopping, "J. W. Arrowsmith," *Direct Legislation Record* 4 (June 1897): 35–36; Arrowsmith, "Direct Legislation Movement," 2; Pomeroy, "Direct Legislation Movement and Leaders," 36–37; and *Newark Evening News*, June 20, 1892.

In January 1893 the People's Union transformed itself again, this time into a new organization called the Direct Legislation League of New Jersey in an apparent effort to capitalize on the popularity of Sullivan's book. Many years later, J. W. Arrowsmith regretted that the name "Referendum League" had not been chosen instead, and suggested that the movement (in New Jersey) might have been more popular at the time if it had. Ironically, from the vantage point of 1911, Arrowsmith concluded that perhaps the best name for both active propaganda and educational effect might have been the original People's Power League. Sullivan, then living in Montclair, New Jersey, and lecturing nationally on the initiative and referendum for the American Federation of Labor (AFL), joined this new group and helped draft a proposed amendment to the New Jersey State Constitution. The amendment guaranteed voters the right to initiate and reject legislation that affected either the entire state or any municipal division of the state (county, city, town, township, borough, or village). It allowed for 5 percent of the voters of the state or locale to petition either to initiate or to refer a law. Members planned a state convention to give their new organization permanent status and issued several documents publicizing their work to reformers in other states. They looked toward passage of their amendment at the next legislative session.[15]

The convention met in Newark on July 22, 1893, and elected William A. Cotter, a Flemington lawyer, as president and J. W. Arrowsmith as vice president. Eltweed Pomeroy, president of Pomeroy Bros. Company, a small, cooperatively run manufacturing firm that produced ink, served as secretary. The league continued to reject identification with any party, and included among its members Republicans, Democrats, Populists, and Prohibitionists. Labor and farm groups lent solid support. The Essex Trade Council, the state's Typographical Union, and the New Jersey branch of the American Federation of Labor all endorsed the league's principles. Joseph P. McDonnell of the *Paterson Labor Standard* and John G. McCormick of the *Trenton Potter's Journal* supported the cause in their newspapers. The Reverend H. D. Opdyke, state secretary of the New Jersey Farmers' Alliance and editor of the *Farmers' Voice*, maintained a special referendum section in his publication and spoke for thousands of New Jersey farmers.[16]

15. See *Equity* 13 (October 1911): 147; "Amendment to Article IV," *Direct Legislation Record* 1 (May 1894): 4; and Rood, "James W. Sullivan," 5. The referendum provision of the amendment did not apply to measures classified as being "for public peace, health and safety" (*Direct Legislation Record* 1 [May 1894]: 4).

16. Samuel Gompers dates his own formal endorsement of direct legislation to the AFL's Twelfth Annual Convention in Philadelphia in December 1892. At that meeting, Henry Wiseman of the Bakers' International Union introduced a resolution framed by himself and Gompers that emphatically endorsed the principle of direct legislation, recommended that the affiliated bodies carefully consider the principle and begin to agi-

The Direct Legislation League of New Jersey lobbied through the winter of 1893–1894 and managed to get its amendment introduced in the state assembly. J. W. Sullivan provided key testimony at special hearings in Trenton on March 12. He reminded his listeners that the league asked only for that which Article 1, Section 2, of the state constitution already guaranteed: "All political power is inherent in the people. Government is instituted for the protection, security, and benefit of the people, and they have the right at all times to alter or reform the same whenever the public good may require it." Sullivan provided examples of New Jersey citizens voting on public libraries, prohibition, licenses, charters, bonds, and appropriations. He noted the successful experience of the Swiss with direct legislation, and closed with a plea to reconstruct the legislative mechanisms then in use. "Unrestricted representative government is an antiquated machine. Reform it, improve it, simplify it, by direct legislation." The efforts of Sullivan and the league failed to achieve passage of the amendment: it lost, thirty-two votes to twenty-eight. All Republicans voted against it, and all but two Democrats voted in favor. Eltweed Pomeroy concluded that it failed because "the bosses in power had seen that it would overthrow them."[17]

Defeat in the New Jersey legislature underscored the need for the league to expand their efforts in publicity and education. To that end Sullivan began, in May 1894, the *Direct Legislation Record*, which he described as "A Non-Partisan Advocate of Pure Democracy." He hoped that the *Record*, published monthly in New York City, would aid in introducing direct legislation amendments in other state legislatures, help to keep the issue before the public, and serve as a bulletin for news on the subject nationwide. Sullivan ran the *Record* until October 1894. In January 1895, Eltweed Pomeroy took over. Pomeroy, an earnest single taxer, a follower of Edward Bellamy, and a member of the Nationalist Party, also wrote extensively on direct legislation for various reform periodicals and became a spokesperson for the cause. B. O. Flower, editor of the *Arena*, remembered Pomeroy as an "apostle" of direct legislation:

> [He] traveled over the United States in the promotion of his business, and wherever he went he hunted up the Single-Taxers and other advanced thinkers on political and economic problems, and presented Di-

---

tate for its incorporation into state law, and called attention to "the mode of procedure adopted by the Direct Legislation League of New Jersey in carrying on this agitation as one worthy of emulation." See Gompers, "The Initiative, Referendum, and Recall," in *American Federationist*, George Judson King Papers, Library of Congress, Manuscripts Division, Washington, D.C.; and Arrowsmith, "Direct Legislation Movement," 2–3.

17. Sullivan, "Address," *Direct Legislation Record* 1 (May 1894): 4–10; Pomeroy, "Direct Legislation Movement and Leaders," 37–38. See also *Direct Legislation Record* 1 (May 1894): 2–16.

rect Legislation, thus performing a work that entitles him to live in the affection of all lovers of fundamental democracy. I often remarked to my friends that Eltweed Pomeroy reminded me of the apostles in the days of early Christianity, only his evangel was political emancipation. Wherever he went he gave the little band of workers all the latest news of progress and interest throughout the country, and brought workers far removed into touch one with the other.[18]

Pomeroy redesigned the *Direct Legislation Record* as a quarterly, moved it to Newark, and made it the organ of the Direct Legislation League of New Jersey. Under Pomeroy, the *Record* gave stability, vitality, and focus to the direct legislation movement, providing a medium for sharing ideas, viewpoints, correspondence, and information on pending legislation.[19]

Pomeroy used the *Direct Legislation Record* to overcome a virtual "blackout" of direct legislation activities by "mainstream" newspapers. During the late nineteenth century the newspaper served as the most important vehicle by which an interested citizenry could follow politics. Both Democrats and Republicans sensed this dependency and established a spirited journalistic competition. In the style of reporting, fact and prejudice seemed to coexist in a manner that suited the sensibilities of a highly partisan electorate. Voters received a full record of what was said in the political arena as well as a party-biased position on issues. The tendency to link politics with newspaper reporting had its drawbacks. Access to either the Democratic or the Republican press could be difficult for political minorities. In areas in which one of the major political parties predominated, a forum for new ideas or dissenting views might not be possible. In Republican-controlled North Dakota in 1900, for example, there were reportedly 163 newspapers of which 146 were Republican.[20]

The blackout ignored growing activity on direct legislation. By 1894 groups acting independently of the New Jersey league had started initiative and referendum leagues in South Dakota, Oregon, and Kansas. In 1895 Michigan, Nebraska, Washington, and Colorado groups joined the movement, and league activists introduced constitutional amendments in each of these states. Municipalities embraced direct legislation as well. In Seattle citizens cooperating with the Western Central Labor Union took advantage of a flexible charter provision and adopted the initiative and referendum by popular vote. When Denver's Common Council refused to

18. Flower, *Progressive Men, Women, and Movements of the Past Twenty-five Years,* 64.
19. See Pomeroy, "Direct Legislation Movement and Leaders," 34; *Direct Legislation Record* 1 (May 1894): 1; and Gompers, "Initiative, Referendum, and Recall," in *American Federationist,* King Papers, Library of Congress, 695.
20. See Thomas C. Leonard, *The Power of the Press: The Birth of American Political Reporting,* 132; and Elwyn B. Robinson, *History of North Dakota,* 230.

honor campaign pledges to reduce water rates, taxpayers organized a formal association, drew up their own political platform, and nominated candidates. At its convention the association passed a resolution that stated, in part:

> Our city is controlled by bribed and perjured agents of corporation greed, our county treasury looted, our citizens intimidated by an army of irresponsible deputies. . . . We are promised reform at every recurring election. As a vote-catcher, these promises have succeeded, but the elected have refused to redeem their pledges. A public office has become a public distrust, a curse which a community already overburdened by taxation has been compelled to support, a channel through which robbery by a few powerful corporations is legalized, and is used by them to escape their just share of taxation.

The third plank of the association platform favored "[t]he securement of the people of a larger share in their own government by Direct Legislation."[21]

The New Jersey league, encouraged by this news, looked for a renewal of its own campaign to bring about a direct legislation amendment and for an opportunity to lead a growing national movement. League members believed that a combination of exhortation, lobbying, and publicity could win a favorable vote for their amendment in the legislature during the winter session. In the meantime, the second annual convention of the Direct Legislation League of New Jersey took place on August 21, 1894, in Asbury Park. Representatives of every political party and every social reform organization in the state attended. Speakers encouraged those present to find common ground behind the initiative and referendum movement. The titles of their addresses included "Republicanism and Direct Legislation," "Democracy and Direct Legislation," "The Socialist Labor Movement and Direct Legislation," "The People's Party and Direct Legislation," "Prohibition and Direct Legislation," "Laborers and Direct Legislation," and "The Farmers and Direct Legislation." Each speaker added criticism of the existing system. It failed to produce leaders, irresponsibility and partisanship plagued it, and it failed to do the will of the people. Moreover, it diffused the force of real issues, replacing them with false ones instead. Finally, it made only token attempts to deal with fundamental social problems. Direct legislation, on the other hand, would work swiftly, producing decision

---

21. The Denver story is recounted in *Direct Legislation Record* 2 (December 1895): 29. See also *Direct Legislation Record* 1 (June 1894): 17; W. G. Armstrong, "Seattle Adopts Direct Legislation," ibid., 22; and Pomeroy, "Direct Legislation Movement and Leaders," 38–41.

in every instance. It would respond to the people, not the party, the caucus, or the lobby. In addition, it promised to bring representative government into conformity with popular sovereignty.

Aware that they met in the midst of a severe economic depression, and that much of the public was becoming increasingly convinced that its interests were not being served by the government, Democratic state senator Robert Adrain of New Brunswick challenged the delegates: "What more appropriate time than the present to urge this great agitation? Times of general calamity and confusion have ever been productive of the greatest results; the purest ore is produced from the hottest furnace, and the brightest thunderbolt is elicited from the darkest storm; the very air is permeated with sickening stories of perfidy and dishonor." In response, the league began a series of Sunday afternoon public meetings, circulated an official league letter interrogating political candidates as to their position on direct legislation, and organized a speaker's bureau of fifteen to twenty individuals who would speak anywhere in the state.[22]

Despite all this, the second legislative campaign for a direct legislation amendment in New Jersey fared worse than the first. This time considerable opposition developed toward the initiative, that part of the package most threatening to the prerogatives of legislators. Sensing defeat, the league decided to remove the initiative from its proposed amendment in hopes that the referendum would survive. Proponents introduced the modified amendment in the House and Senate on January 21, where it was immediately referred to the respective judiciary committees. The Senate committee issued a favorable report too late in the session for further consideration. The House committee did not report it at all. Chairman Charles B. Storrs commented that "the amendment has blown out of the window and we don't know where it is." Clearly, the Republican-dominated legislature would smother even a modified referendum bill.[23]

The state's leading newspapers and most leaders of the two main parties still dismissed advocates of direct legislation as a fringe element and regarded the initiative and referendum as a Populist and labor plank. This confirmed Sullivan's fear of having the movement linked to a single party or interest. Pomeroy, however, believed a change in tactics could correct the situation. Stymied at the state level, Pomeroy and others wanted to call a national gathering on direct legislation and sought cooperation with the Populists to achieve it. In addition to his duties as editor of the *Direct Legislation Record* and secretary of the New Jersey league, Pomeroy also edit-

22. Adrain quoted in *Direct Legislation Record* 1 (August 1894): 54. See also *Direct Legislation Record* 1 (July 1894): 39–40; 1 (August 1894): 45–57, 59–60; 1 (October 1894): 77; and 2 (March 1895): 1.

23. Storrs quoted in *Direct Legislation Record* 2 (March 1895): 1. See also *Direct Legislation Record* 2 (June 1895): 10.

ed a weekly column in the *Coming Nation* and in the rapidly growing *Appeal to Reason*. Both of these socialist publications strongly supported the Populists and direct legislation.[24]

As the following chapters will show, direct legislation had a natural affinity with the democratic nature of the Populist movement, and direct legislationists and Populists could find much common ground in their critiques of the political economy. Although Populists could philosophically embrace the principle of direct democracy and their political challenge eventually did much to popularize the idea, they nonetheless had to be prodded before making a formal commitment. Most textbook authors note that the 1892 Populist Party platform included the initiative and referendum. A closer reading of that document, however, shows that those reforms were not called for as "demands" or even classified as "planks." Instead, the initiative and referendum were added to the "Expressions of Sentiments" section (a list of resolutions) at the end of that document. Moreover, as the Committee on Platform and Resolutions pointed out, the items were "not a part of the platform of the People's Party, but as resolutions expressive of the sentiment of this convention." Resolution no. 7 merely stated: "We commend to the favorable consideration of the people and the reform press the legislative system known as the initiative and referendum." Historian Eric F. Goldman notes that the direct legislation proposals appeared "so radical in 1892 that their chief advocate at Omaha, a representative of a New Jersey workingman's organization [Joseph R. Buchanan], had to argue vigorously for including them in the platform, but he was ultimately successful."[25]

By 1896 the Populists' lukewarm commitment had strengthened, as three-fourths of the Populist state platforms included direct legislation planks. General James B. Weaver's newspaper, the *Farmer's Tribune*, had endorsed the principle editorially, and the venerable Ignatius Donnelly had reportedly proposed that direct legislation be made the dominant issue of the Populist Party. Obviously encouraged by these developments, the advocates of "fusion" with the Populists issued a call for a national conference on direct legislation to be held in St. Louis on July 21, 1896, the day before the Populist convention in that city. They hoped to organize the Direct Legislation League on a national basis and to secure the strongest possible direct legislation statement in the Populist platform.[26]

24. See Elliott Shore, *Talkin' Socialism: J. A. Wayland and the Role of the Press in American Radicalism, 1890–1912*, 76.

25. Goldman, *Rendezvous with Destiny*, 40. See also Richard D. Hefner, ed., *A Documentary History of the United States*, 200–201; and Chester McArthur Destler, *American Radicalism, 1865–1901*, 24 n. 63.

26. See *Direct Legislation Record* 3 (January 1896): 2, 8; 3 (June 1896): 24; and Potter, "Letting the People Rule," 122–23.

At the St. Louis meeting, delegates elected Eltweed Pomeroy as president of the National Direct Legislation League. They also chose fifty-six delegates to represent the league in every state and territory. Some states obviously had multiple representatives, and the list of names indicates that some were selected to be everyday organizers, whereas others were chosen to lend their names and influence and to underscore the league's broad appeal. Among the latter were Edward Bellamy, utopian socialist and author of *Looking Backward;* Eugene V. Debs, labor leader and socialist; Samuel Gompers, president of the American Federation of Labor; B. O. Flower, crusading editor of the *Arena;* Ignatius Donnelly, Populist orator and author of the 1892 preamble to the Populist Party platform; J. A. Wayland, socialist editor of the *Appeal to Reason;* William Jennings Bryan; J. W. Sullivan; Jacob S. Coxey, Populist protester and leader of the celebrated "industrial army" of 1894; Annie L. Diggs, Populist journalist and party organizer; William S. U'Ren, father of the initiative and referendum in Oregon; and Henry L. Loucks, Populist leader and editor of the *Dakota Ruralist.* Delegates adopted a constitution, designated the *Direct Legislation Record* as their official organ, and passed the following simple resolution: "We demand the restoration of Direct Legislation to the people by vesting in the voters the power to propose laws, whether municipal, state or national and to enact or veto them." After much debate, they withdrew a motion to include the "Imperative Mandate" (the recall) as part of direct legislation. Looking to secure national endorsement and more deeply infuse their reforms into the broader reform culture, they also selected a special committee, which included Ignatius Donnelly, Annie Diggs, Jacob Coxey, and Eltweed Pomeroy, to advocate direct legislation before the Populist convention. This time the People's Party went beyond merely "commending" the initiative and referendum as they had done four years earlier and adopted a plank formally endorsing the measures. No other major party went so far.[27]

The defeat of the Populists in 1896 did not deter Pomeroy and the Direct Legislation League. In December Pomeroy, aware that almost every state legislature would soon assemble, urged that they adopt direct legislation measures. The propaganda value of such efforts, he believed, would win adherents to direct legislation by proving it to be a "clear, definite and practical" program. Pomeroy urged supporters to join or create direct legislation leagues, draw up constitutional amendments, and submit them. He suggested that a sympathetic legislator from each house should introduce and push the measure, backed by all forces favorable to direct legislation.

27. *Direct Legislation Record* 3 (September 1896): 25–30. It is worth noting that even though direct legislationists and Populists were kindred spirits and political allies, there were limits to their cooperation. Populists ultimately sought salvation through a new political party. Direct legislationists sought salvation through direct voting, not party.

Boards of trade, municipal and civic leagues, farmers' alliances, granges, and trade unions should pass resolutions in favor of the idea and have copies of the resolutions sent to each member of the legislature and to the press. Pomeroy advocated circulating petitions and, if possible, hiring lobbyists to work for the measures. Organization, mobilization, and political savvy, Pomeroy promised, would yield success. His rally cry foreshadowed an increased determination on the part of those involved with the movement and a heightened receptivity to direct legislation nationally.[28]

During the 1890s a much overlooked political movement for direct democracy developed. A theoretical discussion of the initiative and referendum as practiced in Switzerland quickly became a discussion of the practical application of those forms of citizen initiatives in the United States. J. W. Sullivan argued that direct legislation could greatly enhance the process of representative government in this country. It could revive voter interest in the political system and increase popular debate of political issues. Citizens could regain a sense of direct participation in the modern political system. Government could be made more responsive and more accountable.

The publication of Sullivan's book *Direct Legislation through the Citizenship* in 1892 triggered the political forms of the movement. Reformers in New Jersey—ironically, a state that never passed the initiative and referendum—organized and then mobilized behind a proposed direct legislation amendment to the New Jersey Constitution. Defeat in 1894 only intensified efforts to educate the people and publicize their program. Creation of the *Direct Legislation Record* in 1894 under the editorship of J. W. Sullivan and then Eltweed Pomeroy did just that. The *Record* served as a clearinghouse for information, an alternative to the "establishment" press, and a link to political activities in other states.

By 1894, the movement had generated its own momentum. Direct action through public meetings, petitions, speaker's bureaus, the interrogation of political candidates, the appointment of state and territorial organizers, the publication of pamphlets and model legislative bills, and the general exchange of information all contributed to expanding the horizons of the reformers. Formation of the National Direct Legislation League and cooperation with various agrarian associations, municipal and civic leagues, and trade union organizations created a basis for an ever widening belief in their ability to achieve social and political change.

28. *Direct Legislation Record* 3 (December 1896): 37–39.

2

South Dakota and Oregon

SOUTH DAKOTA

In 1898 South Dakota became the first state to amend its constitution to give its citizens the option of the initiative and referendum. Exactly what impetus propelled South Dakota to enact these reforms at this time, however, has been a matter of some discussion among historians. One scholar has suggested that the accepted explanation for the enactment of the initiative and referendum in South Dakota—that they were Populist reforms—is too simplistic. Instead, he emphasizes the impact of the depression of the 1890s and the broadening of the reform base to include consumers and taxpayers. According to this argument hard times in the late 1880s triggered farmer protest and the organization of the Farmers' Alliance. Then, in 1890, as economic turmoil spread to the cities as well as the farms, discontented urban and rural citizens joined to establish the Independent (later Populist) Party and broadened the political discussion to include the initiative and referendum. As economic conditions worsened in the early 1890s, the popularity of the initiative and referendum increased. The depression of the 1890s brought more suffering and injustice and united disaffected farmers and workers with angry consumers and taxpayers behind a successful crusade for the passage of the initiative and referendum at the state level in 1898. This movement provided both the popular base and the democratic focus for the later Progressive movement in South Dakota.[1]

This interpretation owes an intellectual debt to historian David P. Thelen, who had previously suggested a framework for understanding the origins of Progressivism in his influential book, *The New Citizenship: The Origins of Progressivism in Wisconsin*. In his study of Wisconsin, Thelen per-

---

1. H. Roger Grant, "The Origins of a Progressive Reform: The Initiative and Referendum Movement in South Dakota."

16

suasively argues that consumers and taxpayers (primarily in an emerging urban-industrial environment), frightened and angry at the apparent failure of industrial capitalism during the depression of the 1890s, came together in search of solutions to problems that the existing political system seemed incapable of addressing. The result was a mass-based, cross-class movement that placed direct democracy at the center of its reform vision and provided the impetus for turn-of-the-century Progressivism.

Although Thelen's model goes a long way toward discerning the genesis of reform in the United States during the Progressive Era, it does not adequately explain the origins of the initiative and referendum in South Dakota. Economic conditions were certainly important, but so too were political circumstances. If farmers felt economically dependent during the late 1880s and early 1890s, they also felt politically impotent. When they complained of monopoly-controlled transportation, warehouse, and marketing agencies, they also complained of partisan politics, one-party domination, and a state legislature that ignored farmer demands. Eventually, farmers believed that changes to the political economy could come about only through political empowerment. In 1890 farmers and workers formed the Independent Party and actively took up the discussion of direct legislation. South Dakota Independents added the initiative and referendum to their platform in 1892. The depression of the 1890s did not appear to have a dramatic effect on the popularity of direct legislation, as economic conditions had been depressed in South Dakota for nearly a decade. Populist victory in South Dakota in 1896 brought the passage of a proposed constitutional amendment for the initiative and referendum, whereas Populist failure in 1898 convinced a majority of voters that they should ratify it. There was a growing sense that the way to improve partisan representative government, with all its seemingly inherent deficiencies, was to adopt a process that enabled people to control the political agenda. Political experience, as much as economic dislocation, provided the impetus for the adoption of the initiative and referendum in South Dakota.

Dakota Territory in the 1880s, like many states in the agrarian Midwest, was passing through various stages of what might best be described as a boom-and-bust economy. During the early 1880s Dakotans witnessed a surge in the number of immigrants coming into the territory, a rapid expansion in wheat production, generally good harvests, a boom in town construction, and the advance of the first railroads into the territory. ("Dakota, the Land of Promise" was the slogan of the Chicago, Milwaukee, and St. Paul Railroad.) Encouraged by these developments, many in the territory began to talk of statehood. However, this upward cycle was not to last. As early as 1884 Dakota farmers began to complain that the price for wheat was 20 percent below what it cost them to produce it and that buyers unfairly graded their grain. When drought pinched Dakotans that same year, few realized the danger in their growing dependence on wheat or the lack of crop diversification and livestock. Markets continued to be depressed, and farmers increasingly talked of abuses in grain grading and transportation rates. By 1885 the peak of the Great Dakota Boom had passed. Farmers who had only recently been convinced of unbounded opportunity and the potential for success were now confronted with the specter of distress and possible failure.[2]

Farmers looking for an explanation increasingly blamed monopolistic transportation, warehouse, and marketing agencies and a territorial legislature that allowed such abuses to exist. Many of these farmers joined the newly created Farmers' Protective Union, or "Farmers' Club," a nonpolitical organization that held territory-wide meetings to discuss questions of farm economics. Others joined the Northern Farmers' Alliance, organized in April 1880 by Milton George, owner and editor of the Chicago-based farm magazine *Western Rural*. A chapter of the Northern Alliance first appeared in Dakota Territory in February 1881. The organization was envisioned as aiding farmers in their struggle against monopolistic and discriminatory railroad rates and grain elevator charges. In December 1884 representatives from the Farmers' Protective Union and the Northern Farmers' Alliance met in Huron and laid the groundwork for the Dakota Territorial Alliance.[3]

At that meeting they agreed to demand the equal taxation of property, the end of free railroad passes for public officials, the regulation of transportation rates, and the enactment of legislation in the interest of farmers. Representatives met for a second time in Huron in February 1885 to formalize the organization, select a slate of officers, and draw up a constitution. The key individual in the new organization was Henry L. Loucks, a recent homesteader from Canada and organizer of the territory's first farmers' club in Deuel County in 1884. Loucks, a born leader, was elected president of the Dakota Territorial Alliance at its convention in January 1886. He also edited the alliance newspaper, the *Dakota Ruralist*. The alliance sponsored numerous cooperative warehouses and grain elevators. After incorporating as a joint-stock cooperative agency, it sold binding twine, coal, barbed wire, farm machinery, and household items at reduced prices and underwrote fire, hail, and life insurance protection.[4]

---

2. See Doane Robinson, *History of South Dakota*, 1:294–325; Hallie Farmer, "The Economic Background of Frontier Populism"; and Terrence J. Lindell, "South Dakota Populism," 16–24.

3. See Herbert S. Schell, *History of South Dakota*, 224.

4. Loucks became president of the National Farmers' Alliance and Industrial Union in 1892. He also authored numerous works: *The New Monetary System* (1893); *Govern-*

The Republican Party had controlled Dakota politics from the organization of the territory in 1861. Although farmers made up the majority of the population and predominated in the party, businessmen, lawyers, land speculators, and professional politicians controlled the party. The economic dependence of farmers made them increasingly aware of their political impotence. When local Republican machines refused to put forth farm candidates, farmers ran as independents and farmers' clubs backed candidates who pledged to bring their demands to the floor of the territorial legislature. Farmers hoped to have a strong enough antirailroad and antimonopoly bloc to present a persuasive case for some type of regulatory legislation when the legislature met in Bismarck in January 1885, but they were only partially successful. The legislature passed a bill to create the Territorial Board of Railroad Commissioners, but the bill was weakened by an amendment that deprived the commission of any power to control freight rates. Two years later, in 1887, with even stronger farmer pressure, the legislature passed an elevator and warehouse law empowering the railroad commissioners to license and bond companies engaged in the business of grain storage and to regulate the weighing and grading of grain. However, this law also had a loophole exempting so-called private elevators, almost half the elevators in the territory, many of them large enough to control the grain storage business in their respective areas. Politically inexperienced Dakota farmers had been given painful lessons in their inability to prevent corporate-influenced legislators from either preventing or amending effective regulatory legislation.[5]

Some who were disenchanted with the existing economic and political situation in the territory advocated another form of insurgency. In 1885 W. H. Lyon of Sioux Falls, later an attorney and member of the South Dakota legislature, petitioned the constitutional convention of the Dakota Territory to establish a statewide referendum. He specifically requested that the

---

ment *Ownership of Railroads and Telegraphs* (1894); *The Great Conspiracy of the House of Morgan and How to Defeat It* (1916); and *"Our Daily Bread" Must Be Freed from the Greed of Private Monopoly* (1919). See *Dictionary of American Biography*, s.v. "Loucks, Henry L."; *The National Cyclopedia of American Biography*, s.v. "Loucks, Henry L."; Alden Whitman, ed., *American Reformers*, 540–41; D. Robinson, *History of South Dakota*, 1:319–25; Schell, *History of South Dakota*, 223–25; Kenneth E. Hendrickson Jr., "Some Political Aspects of the Populist Movement in South Dakota," 78; Lawrence Goodwyn, *Democratic Promise: The Populist Moment in America*, 155–56; Robert C. McMath Jr., *Populist Vanguard*, 84–85; and Lindell, "South Dakota Populism," 28–49. For an analysis of what types of farmers joined the Farmers' Alliance in Marshall County, South Dakota, see John Dibbern, "Who Were the Populists? A Study of Grass-Roots Alliancemen in Dakota."

5. See Larry Remele, "'God Helps Those Who Help Themselves': The Farmers' Alliance and Dakota Statehood"; Schell, *History of South Dakota*, 225; and Hendrickson, "Some Political Aspects," 78–79. For the context of territorial politics in Dakota, see Howard R. Lamar, *Dakota Territory, 1861–1889*.

convention "incorporate a provision in this constitution that all appropriation bills . . . and all laws of general interest to the people should be drafted by the Legislature and submitted for the people to enact or reject." Lyon
later stated that his proposal was "too novel and experimental at that time"
to be immediately incorporated into the design for a new constitution, but
he undoubtedly started others thinking about the concept of direct legislation.[6]

The individual who is given most credit for conceiving and formulating
the idea of direct legislation in South Dakota, however, was Father Robert
W. Haire, a Roman Catholic priest from Aberdeen, South Dakota. Active in
politics, Father Haire was a member of the Knights of Labor and, later, a
Populist and Socialist. He spent three years at the University of Louvain in
Belgium in the early 1870s and may have learned something of the Swiss
referendum while studying there. He was ordained to the priesthood in
Michigan in 1874. Six years later he moved to Dakota Territory and held a
parish that extended along the North-Western Railroad line from Springfield, Minnesota, to Jamestown, North Dakota. By the mid-1880s his parish
had been reduced to Aberdeen, South Dakota, and the surrounding area. It
was at that time, in 1885 or 1886, that Father Haire began to discuss a variation of direct legislation. His original proposal was for the creation of what
he termed the "People's Legislature," which included the principles of the
initiative and referendum. Each county in the territory would elect one
state representative to this legislature, which would formally draft bills
suggested by voters in their respective counties. When more than 25 percent of the counties supported any one bill, copies of the measure would
be printed and circulated in pamphlet form to voters who would accept or
reject the proposals at the general election. Father Haire thought his plan
could bypass both the domineering party caucus and the deceptive legislative committee system. Active in the Knights of Labor, Father Haire continued to promote his views in their publication in Aberdeen and as a delegate to their state assembly. Though nothing immediately resulted from
his suggestions, both he and Lyon had enlivened the political debate and
suggested a new political direction.[7]

6. "South Dakota Constitutional Convention of 1885"; H. L. Loucks, George A. Silsby, and W. H. Lyon, "The Initiative and Referendum: A Symposium," 72. See also Burton Ellsworth Tiffany, "The Initiative and Referendum in South Dakota," 14:331, 351;
and Grant, "Origins of Progressive Reform," 394.

7. Father Haire's political activities ultimately brought him into conflict with Bishop
Martin Marty of the Sioux Falls diocese, and he was relieved of his parish (newspaper
clipping, March 4, 1916, Haire folder in Doane Robinson Papers, South Dakota Historical Society, Pierre). For additional information on Haire, see William C. Pratt, "Socialism on the Northern Plains, 1900–1924," 11–12; Tiffany, "Initiative and Referendum,"
331–32; Grant, "Origins of Progressive Reform," 394–95; C. B. Galbreath, "Provisions

The initiative and referendum did not immediately catch fire in the territory. One possible explanation, aside from the novelty of the proposals, was that even sympathetic listeners, such as Henry L. Loucks, were reluctant to break with the traditional two-party culture and abandon any possible political future in the dominant Republican Party. The energetic, reform-minded Loucks hoped that continued lobbying could wrest reforms from the final session of the territorial legislature in 1889 without having to resort to a more fundamental political challenge. Claiming the support of twenty-eight of forty-eight members in the lower house and seven of twenty-eight members in the upper house, the alliance looked to have an influence strong enough to overcome the legislative disappointments of 1885 and 1887.

Once again, though, the inability of the alliance to organize effectively as a pressure group, coupled with apparent Republican unwillingness to alter the status quo, resulted in the failure of significant reform legislation for Dakota farmers. The following summer's severe drought drove many homesteaders, debt-ridden or destitute, to leave the state. Demoralized farmers and frustrated reformers saw an economic and political emergency that demanded resourceful and responsive political action, but politicians ignored alliance suggestions. Neither major party nominated candidates endorsed by the alliance, and the Republicans spurned their suggestions for candidates to the United States Senate. The South Dakota Alliance, echoing the demands of the national Farmers' Alliance, called for a graduated income tax, governmental ownership and operation of railroads, free and unlimited coinage of silver, and direct election of U.S. senators, but the inaugural South Dakota legislature of 1890 ignored their demands. The defeat of an alliance-sponsored bill to tax mortgages held by nonresidents exhausted the patience of members of the South Dakota Alliance, who soon met in Pierre and passed a resolution that condemned the legislature for being unresponsive to farmer—that is, alliance—demands.[8]

Having been consistently ignored within the framework of partisan politics in South Dakota, Henry Loucks and other Republicans in the alliance decided to abandon their role as a pressure group and resort to direct political action. On June 6, 1890, representatives of the Dakota Territorial Alliance and the Knights of Labor met in Huron and founded the Independent Party. A month later they reconvened in the same city to nominate a

for State-Wide Initiative and Referendum," *Annals of the American Academy* 43 (September 1912): 84; *Equity* 12 (October 1910): 159; Doane Robinson to Henry L. Loucks, December 1, 1911, folder 119, Robinson Papers, South Dakota Historical Society; and Edwin C. Torrey, *Early Days in Dakota Territory,* 199.

8. See Hendrickson, "Some Political Aspects," 80–83; D. Robinson, *History of South Dakota,* 1:335–37; and Remele, "'God Helps,'" 29, 32.

slate of candidates and embrace the principles of the national Farmers' Alliance. Henry L. Loucks was the party's unanimous choice for governor. One historian of the period has described the Independent movement as "one of principle—one against the abuses of the old parties—one that demanded better terms and conditions for farmers and other laborers—one that was warranted by the vagaries of politicians and the gag rule of party bosses."[9]

In the November election, Loucks ran a strong second to Republican A. C. Mellette in a three-party race, carrying thirteen counties and polling more than twenty-four thousand votes (32 percent). The Republicans enjoyed a one-vote majority in both the House and the Senate over the combined votes of the Independents and Democrats, but the minority felt strong enough to challenge Republican dominance for the first time. When the South Dakota legislature convened in January 1891, a coalition of Independents and Democrats adopted an Australian ballot law and a corrupt-practices act, but failed to enact any of the far-reaching reforms for which the alliance and the Independent movement had worked so diligently.[10]

Supporters of the newly formed Independent Party realized that before the party could ever become a controlling force in South Dakota politics, they would have to educate and persuade voters. Accordingly, the editors of approximately forty newspapers in the state agreed to form the Reform Press Association that would espouse the Independent platform, urge the dissemination of reform literature through the creation of local circulating libraries, and offer selected books and pamphlets at low cost to readers.

The beacon of the agrarian-reform press was the *Dakota Ruralist*. The editors of the *Ruralist* claimed to have the largest circulation of any newspaper in South Dakota in 1891, reaching more than four hundred South Dakota post offices and averaging publication of twelve thousand copies a week. The *Ruralist* published a myriad of reform ideas ranging from Loucks's own theories on monetary reform to Lyon and Haire's initiative and referendum. Loucks even made Haire a regular contributor to his newspaper. On August 8, 1891, the radical priest reiterated his proposal to place the lawmaking power into the hands of the "organic electorate" of the state. Allowing voters to confirm or reject laws would eliminate what he called legislative "humbugging" and "secret skullduggery." Father Haire reminded the readers of the *Ruralist* that Swiss voters could veto laws made by their legislature through a referendum. South Dakotans, on the other hand, did not possess this power, and the "people seldom get any law

---

9. George Martin Smith, *South Dakota: Its History and Its People*, 3:658.
10. See Schell, *History of South Dakota*, 227–29; Hendrickson, "Some Political Aspects," 83–85; and D. Robinson, *History of South Dakota*, 1:343–46.

passed they want." On September 5, 1891, the *Ruralist* announced that the Swiss had modified their constitution to include the initiative. It seemed that Father Haire's ideas could indeed have practical application.[11]

In May and June 1892, the *Dakota Ruralist* ran three full pages explaining the initiative and referendum and promoting those reforms as the "latest and fullest development of popular government." The editors reminded readers that the initiative and referendum were not strange devices but merely the logical extension of referring school levies or constitutional amendments to the voters. Direct legislation would make legislators truly responsible to their constituents, place government directly into the hands of the people, eliminate bribery and boodling, and save tax dollars. It could also be the necessary first step toward other reforms such as the nationalization of telegraphs, railroads, and mines and the municipalization of street railways and water, gas, electric, and telephone works. Direct legislation would enable voters to control monopolies and prevent class legislation and special privileges.

After selling the idea, the *Dakota Ruralist* offered an organizational plan. Every newspaper in the state would be supplied with printed matter pertaining to the initiative and referendum, a few thousand pamphlets would be printed for private distribution, and workers for the cause would be recruited in every school district and voting precinct. The *Ruralist* recommended that the Fourth of July be designated as the date to organize initiative and referendum leagues in every county. It likened the popularity of the initiative and referendum to that of the Australian ballot, which, in a short span of five years, had been adopted in thirty-one states. The *Ruralist* requested the names of all those interested in direct legislation and asked for a membership fee of twenty-five cents.[12]

Advocacy of the initiative and referendum in the columns of the *Dakota Ruralist* did much to publicize the merits of those reforms, but direct democracy also gained immeasurable support from organized labor. The principal workingman's affiliation in a state with many railroad workers, coal and metal miners, and telegraph, printing, and construction workers was the Knights of Labor. Although the Knights were declining nationally by the late 1880s, members were still organizing local assemblies throughout South Dakota. Eleven Knights of Labor assemblies were organized in the state between 1883 and 1887, and thirteen more appeared between 1888 and 1896.[13]

11. See Lindell, "South Dakota Populism," 91–92; and *American Newspaper Annual*, 1270.

12. *Dakota Ruralist*, May 19, June 2, 1892.

13. See Jonathan Ezra Garlock, "A Structural Analysis of the Knights of Labor: A Prolegomenon to the History of the Producing Classes," 235.

The Knights supported a broadly based reform program that included the eight-hour day, factory and mine inspection, anti-Pinkerton (that is, antistrikebreaking) legislation, child labor laws, government ownership of quasi-public corporations, and an end to land speculation. Their platform made them close allies of the alliance and Independent movement and enthusiastic supporters of direct legislation. The general assembly of the Knights of Labor formally endorsed the idea, and Grand Master Workman Terence V. Powderly repeatedly spoke in favor of the initiative and referendum. He also recommended a little book titled *Direct Legislation by the Citizenship through the Initiative and Referendum*, recently published by J. W. Sullivan, to the readers of the *Dakota Ruralist*. The popular volume became one of the titles on the *Ruralist's* periodic lists of recommended reform literature.[14]

Labor's real involvement with the initiative and referendum, however, occurred at the local level. Assembly 545 of the Knights of Labor at Milbank, in Grant County, is credited with organizing the first Initiative and Referendum League in South Dakota in 1892. A variety of reform types—advocates of woman suffrage, single taxers, Bellamy Nationalists, and Christian socialists—joined farmers and workers in the ranks of the league. Prohibitionists did not figure prominently in the South Dakota league because South Dakota's constitution, approved along with statehood in 1889, included a prohibition amendment, which was repealed, however, by the voters in 1896.[15]

W. H. Kaufman, chapter member of the Milbank Knights of Labor, became the first secretary of the league. An active speaker and organizer, he provided firsthand accounts of an emerging grassroots movement. On June 9, 1892, Kaufman reported in the *Dakota Ruralist*:

> Never before have I known so much enthusiasm for a reform movement. I went out twelve miles; had an audience of fifteen for no one knew what the referendum was; but everyone present signed the petition, and gave me so much silver that I asked the president to bring it to town himself. Another audience of eighteen sent me back with $8.00. Out at Vernon the little school house was filled with bright, thinking people. Every voter signed the petition, and they gave me $9.25. . . . Mr. L. Shampine, who drove me to the next town said, "when I first heard of this movement I thought it a good thing. When I learned a little more about it I said 'that is just what we want.' When I heard the matter explained last night I could not go to sleep till 2 o'clock."

14. See Grant, "Origins of Progressive Reform," 398–99. Powderly's comments can be found in the *Dakota Ruralist*, June 21, 1892.
15. See Grant, "Origins of Progressive Reform," 397; and Smith, *South Dakota,* 655, 675.

Kaufman encouraged everyone interested in the initiative and referendum to ask for a petition blank. Completed petitions would be sent to delegates to the Independent State Convention requesting that they incorporate the initiative and referendum into the state platform.

It was impossible for direct legislation not to become linked to the third-party movement in South Dakota and to the emerging People's Party at the national level. Independents, who held their state convention in Redfield on June 21, 1892, recognized the rising popularity of the initiative and referendum in South Dakota and added those reforms to their party demands for the first time. Reflecting on this early period from the vantage point of 1915, Henry Loucks remembered clearly what triggered the Independent revolt and how direct legislation became central to that party's program:

> Our experience was that the railroad and allied corporations controlled the political machines of both political parties, and thru them our conventions and legislatures. We were discouraged by the failure of our representatives to do the will of the people even when promised in platform pledges. The legislative sins of ommission [*sic*] and commission were many. We were helpless and almost hopeless until Rev. R. W. Haire suggested The Initiative, Referendum and Imperative Mandate (Recall) as the most efficient and effective remedy.[16]

To secure direct legislation the Independents placed principles above party. Doing so required breaking up both political parties and the organization of a new one to obtain results.[17]

The 1892 campaign in South Dakota was bitterly contested. The Independents-Populists intensified their attacks on the "standpat" Republican administration, whereas the Republicans severely denounced the Populist challenge. The Initiative and Referendum League of South Dakota made one last nonpartisan attempt to get the Republican and Democratic Parties to declare themselves, as the Independents had done, in favor of a constitutional amendment, but both of the old parties remained silent on the subject. It appeared that direct legislation had, in fact, become so much a part of partisan politics that an amendment would be possible only when the Populists gained control of the legislature. That was not to happen in 1892. Republican C. H. Sheldon tallied more than thirty-three thousand votes for governor, a margin of eleven thousand votes over the Independent-Populist candidate, A. L. Van Osdel, and nineteen thousand votes more

16. Letter from Loucks to Judson King, February 6, 1915, George Judson King Papers, Library of Congress, Manuscripts Division, Washington, D.C.

17. See Tiffany, "Initiative and Referendum," 346; Schell, *History of South Dakota*, 229–30; *Dakota Ruralist*, July 21, 1892; and Grant, "Origins of Progressive Reform," 399.

than Democrat Peter Couchman. The Republicans secured all the state of-fices, and only seventeen Independents were elected to the legislature.[18]

The reform record of the 1893 South Dakota legislature was a dismal one. Reformers introduced bills for equal taxation of real property and for more effective regulation of railroad rates, but the legislative majority was indif-ferent to both measures. The only sop to reformers was the passage of a bill requiring the popular election of railroad commissioners. State senator Louis N. Crill of Union County introduced a referendum bill that, for the first time in South Dakota, received a committee hearing. The proposal pro-vided that after a bill had passed the legislature and before it had gone into effect, 10 percent of the voters could petition for a vote on the measure. Only "a half hour's argument was made upon the merits of the bill, which fell upon ears which had no receptacle for independent doctrines." Al-though many apparently spoke in favor of the measure, once party lines were drawn the vote stood at seven for and thirty-one against. The *Dakota Ruralist* could do no more than remind its readers: "[L]et the people re-member that the Referendum can only be obtained by electing an Inde-pendent [Populist] Legislature."[19]

As the Populists sought to rally their forces for the upcoming political campaign of 1894, Henry Loucks continued to advocate direct legislation in the *Dakota Ruralist*. In the fall of 1893, as the nation slipped into economic depression, the *Ruralist* charged that special or class legislation was the pri-mary curse of governments. Corruption, bribery, and boodling made truly representative government impossible, and corruption, bribery, and bood-ling exacted a price. Voters were left powerless politically and exploited economically. "We are paying $5 more than we ought for each ton of hard coal, 7 cents more than we ought for each gallon of kerosene or gasoline, 25 to 90 cents more than we ought for each telegram, three times as much as we ought for express and easily double a reasonable charge for freight. Why? Simply because we do not have direct legislation by the initiative and referendum in state and nation." To make the same point in more humor-ous fashion, the *Ruralist* reprinted a jingle by T. H. Porter called "Let the People Rule":

> A Government of the people should the people's right protect,
> But this cannot be done unless we legislate direct.
> While we elect our Congressmen and give them all the power,
> Our liberties are endangered—they are not safe one hour. . . .

18. See Tiffany, "Initiative and Referendum," 346–47; Smith, *South Dakota*, 665; Schell, *History of South Dakota*, 232; and Hendrickson, "Some Political Aspects," 86.

19. *Dakota Ruralist*, February 23, June 15, 1893, latter cited in Grant, "Origins of Pro-gressive Reform," 400. See also Tiffany, "Initiative and Referendum," 352; and Hen-drickson, "Some Political Aspects," 86–87.

Now, have we lost all common sense? Are we a lot of fools?
Haven't we—the people—got the power to change these silly rules?
Ain't we the Government ourselves? And is it not quite true?
That we can make the laws direct, without trusting this boodle crew?[20]

To the *Ruralist* the solution was simple. Adoption of the initiative and referendum would end bribery, logrolling, and legislative "dealing," and citizens could regain their rightful sovereignty.

The 1894 campaign was a repeat of 1892. The Populists, at their party convention in the Corn Palace in Mitchell on June 12, added a strong direct legislation plank to their state platform: "Believing that all laws should emanate from the people and that they alone should have the veto power, we demand that the voters of South Dakota be given the absolute control of all legislation by means of the initiative and referendum at the earliest possible date." In the election the Populists ran well ahead of the Democrats but were again defeated by the Republicans. Populist Isaac Howe collected more than twenty-six thousand votes (35 percent) for governor but still trailed incumbent Sheldon by almost fourteen thousand votes. Only twenty-four Populists were elected to the legislature. In the 1895 session, reformers reintroduced and again lost a bill to give the railway commissioners real power to regulate passenger and freight rates. This time the indifference of the legislative majority to the railroad rate bill sparked criticism even within Republican ranks. A referendum bill was reintroduced, but it once again failed in committee. Adding insult to arrogance, the Republican Party further embarrassed itself when W. W. Taylor, retiring state treasurer, was found guilty of embezzling $367,000 from the state. It was beginning to look as if the Republicans were riding for a fall.[21]

The Republicans' dominant position in South Dakota was not secure, for the party was developing a split over the silver issue. During the 1896 campaign, U.S. Senator Richard F. Pettigrew attempted to persuade the state Republican Party to adopt a silver plank at its convention, even though the national convention had already refused to adopt such a statement. When Pettigrew was unsuccessful, he led a group of twenty "silver Republicans" out of the convention and announced he would join the Populists. Senator Pettigrew was present when the Populist State Convention, meeting in Huron on July 14, 1896, decided that a ticket joining all the proponents of free silver could finally topple the Republicans. The Democrats, who decided to back the Populist ticket, soon joined the Populists and silver Republicans. For governor the so-called Fusionists selected Andrew E. Lee, a

20. *Dakota Ruralist*, September 21, November 16, 1893.
21. Platform quoted in Tiffany, "Initiative and Referendum," 348 (see also 349). See also Schell, *History of South Dakota*, 232–33; and Hendrickson, "Some Political Aspects," 88.

successful Vermillion merchant, reform mayor, and free silverite. South Dakota Populists once again included a direct legislation plank in their state platform, whereas the national convention of the Populist Party went beyond its 1892 commendation of the initiative and referendum and formally endorsed the principles, the only national party to do so in 1896.[22]

The results of the national election are well known: McKinley triumphed over Bryan, and the gold standard won over free silver. In South Dakota, though, the Fusionists conducted their campaign "as a struggle of the masses against entrenched privilege, a choice between free institutions of a democratic society and domination by corporate interests" and made direct legislation "the paramount state issue."[23] Nearly 90 percent of qualified voters cast their ballots, and Lee defeated A. O. Ringsrud, his Republican opponent, by a scant 319 votes (41,187 to 40,868). In addition, Fusionists won the attorney general's office, control of the state railroad commission, two congressional seats, and, most important, a majority in the state legislature. Political expediency had triumphed in South Dakota, and voters waited to see how much of the Populist platform—including the initiative and referendum—would be enacted.[24]

The most important reform issues before the new legislature were railroad regulation and the initiative and referendum. This time, in keeping with Populist campaign pledges, the legislature enacted the Palmer-Wheeler Bill, incorporating the provisions of the bill that had been defeated in 1895. The new law placed all railroads under the supervision and rate-setting authority of the state railroad commission and provided for the assessment of railroad property by the State Board of Equalization. These victories were short-lived, however. The Chicago, Milwaukee, and St. Paul Railroad contested the law in court, received injunctive relief from its effects, and ultimately saw the court declare the rate-fixing powers of the state unconstitutional.[25]

Nonetheless, the passage of the Palmer-Wheeler Bill indicated that reformers might have the votes to enact direct legislation as well. On January 15, 1897, Representative Lars M. Benson, a Populist from Brown County, introduced House Joint Resolution 101, an amendment to the state

22. See Schell, *History of South Dakota*, 233–36; Hendrickson, "Some Political Aspects," 88; Kenneth E. Hendrickson Jr., "The Public Career of Richard F. Pettigrew of South Dakota, 1848–1926," 181–213; and Tiffany, "Initiative and Referendum," 349.

23. Quotation is from Schell, *History of South Dakota*, 237. Phrase "the paramount state issue" is from a letter from Henry Loucks to Judson King, February 6, 1915, King Papers, Library of Congress.

24. See Schell, *History of South Dakota*, 236–37; and Hendrickson, "Some Political Aspects," 88.

25. See Schell, *History of South Dakota*, 237; and Hendrickson, "Some Political Aspects," 89.

constitution allowing for the statutory initiative and referendum at both the state and the municipal levels of government and requiring a petition signed by 5 percent of the qualified voters to invoke either procedure. The bill passed the House by a vote of forty-nine to thirty-two. Populists-Fusionists voted unanimously for it, supported by ten Republicans and six Democrats. In the Senate, the vote also ran along party lines, with twenty Populists-Fusionists, four Republicans, and two Democrats in favor and seventeen Republicans opposed. The only hurdle that remained was for voters to accept the amendment at the 1898 general election.[26]

No organized opposition to the amendment materialized as the election neared. The old parties seemed to be willing to let the issue be decided by the voters. Nevertheless, the Initiative and Referendum League and political backers such as Governor Lee campaigned for it, and even a few Republicans offered support. Proratification newspapers such as the *Vermillion Plain Talk* actively discussed the issue and urged voters to grasp the larger significance. In addition to familiar arguments—direct legislation could eliminate legislated special privileges and the autocratic power of the party, the caucus, or the lobby—the editors emphasized the importance of political empowerment and the opportunity that the initiative and referendum presented for voters to gain control of the political agenda:

> The issue of the future is whether or not the people are to rule this country. . . . The socialist, silverite, greenbacker, prohibitionist—in fact every reformer—can unite on a platform which says "give the people a chance to be heard." None of the reforms now contended for can be successful until the people do rule. . . . What then is to be done: Unite the people in an effort to secure the initiative and referendum. . . . We have never had representative government in this country and shall not have it till some improvements are made in our methods.[27]

Populists and Democrats endorsed the amendment at their party conventions, but Republicans appeared reluctant to follow suit. Worried, Henry L.

26. South Dakota did not adopt the initiative procedure for enacting constitutional amendments until 1972. See Virginia Graham, *A Compilation of Statewide Initiative Proposals Appearing on Ballots through 1976*, 203. Party affiliation is difficult to determine for all members of the 1897 South Dakota legislature. I have used the *Biographical Directory of the South Dakota Legislature, 1889–1989*. See also *Journal of the Senate of the South Dakota Legislature, Fifth Session* (1897), 997; *Journal of the House of Representatives of the South Dakota Legislature, Fifth Session* (1897), 421–23; Grant, "Origins of Progressive Reform," 403–4; Tiffany, "Initiative and Referendum," 350; *Direct Legislation Record* 4 (March 1897): 5; 4 (June 1897): 22–23; and 6 (June 1899): 17–19. For an account of the overall failure of the Fusionists to take advantage of their legislative majority during the first Lee administration, see Lindell, "South Dakota Populism," 165–91.

27. *Vermillion Plain Talk*, December 17, 1897, cited in Brian J. Weed, "Populist Thought in North and South Dakota, 1890–1900," 31.

Loucks wrote Republican Party leaders at their August convention announcing his return to the Republican Party and offering his considerable support to the ticket. He asked only that the convention endorse direct legislation. The Republicans refused endorsement but did recommend that voters give the amendment serious consideration. Loucks later stated that his letter "was the culminating factor that secured [the amendment's] adoption."[28]

Prior to the election, Representative William E. Kidd, a Populist from Aberdeen and a member of the South Dakota Initiative and Referendum League who had championed the measure in the legislature, seemed to think that government had become irrelevant: "I care very little who have the offices this year, if we—the people—get the Initiative and Referendum."[29] Representative Kidd seemed to speak for others as well. The failure of the dominant political culture, and even hybrid alternatives to that culture, to improve the effectiveness of representative government in South Dakota convinced voters to secure the tools that would enable them to do the job themselves. In the election that fall, voters rejected all Populist candidates except Governor Lee (who won by only 370 votes), but approved the direct legislation amendment by a vote of 23,816 to 16,483. The amendment carried in all parts of the state—in the corn and wheat belts, and in the mining and ranching areas. Of the fifty-nine counties listed as registering votes, only nine—Aurora, Bon Homme, Campbell, Faulk, Gregory, Hutchinson, Marshall, Turner, and Yankton—had majorities against the amendment. The largest bloc in opposition came from four counties (Bon Homme, Hutchinson, Turner, and Yankton) clustered in the southeastern corner of the state. The "city" vote in South Dakota also seemed to support the amendment. Yankton County (Yankton) voted 58 percent against the amendment, but Brown County (Aberdeen) and Minnehaha County (Sioux Falls) voted 57 percent and 66 percent, respectively, for approval.[30]

The transition from passage of the amendment to its actual implementation proved difficult. To begin with, the amendment included an "emergency" clause that exempted certain laws "necessary for the immediate preservation of the public peace, health, or safety or support of the State Government and its existing public institutions" from the referendum. This provision allowed the legislature wide latitude as to interpretation. The editors of *Equity* estimated in 1913 that 40 percent of all laws passed in South

28. Henry Loucks to Doane Robinson, November 28, 1911, folder 119, Robinson Papers, South Dakota Historical Society.

29. *Direct Legislation Record* 5 (December 1898): 69.

30. See Grant, "Origins of Progressive Reform," 404–5; Tiffany, "Initiative and Referendum," 353–54, 370–71; Smith, *South Dakota*, 679–80; *Equity* 12 (October 1910): 159–60; and 15 (January 1913): 34–35.

Dakota during the previous decade had been designated "emergency" measures. An attempt was made to invoke the referendum in 1901. When the legislature revised a statute pertaining to the Board of Charities and dismissed its Populist members in the process, those outraged by the action attempted to have the bill submitted to a popular vote. The legislature refused, stating that the bill had been passed as an emergency measure and, therefore, was not subject to the referendum. The state supreme court upheld the discretionary power of the legislature. The legislature also exerted its authority over initiated measures. An attempt to invoke the initiative was undertaken in 1904 when more than eight thousand voters signed a petition to enact a primary election law. In this case, the Senate rejected the petition on technical formalities.[31]

Voters in South Dakota successfully used the initiative and referendum for the first time in 1908, and decided nine initiated propositions by popular vote over the next ten years. Statutes proposed by the initiative process included a county-option liquor law, a direct primary law, a law establishing a state banking board, and a law authorizing a verdict by ten members of a jury in civil cases. Only one initiated measure, however—the direct primary law—won popular approval. South Dakota voters also considered fifteen referred measures between 1908 and 1918.[32] Examples of referred measures that met with voter approval included a tougher divorce law, a law prohibiting Sunday theater shows, a law protecting quail, and a law requiring electric lights on locomotives. Referred measures rejected by voters included a "czar law" that empowered the governor to dismiss officials at his discretion, a congressional apportionment law, and a legislative resolution calling for a constitutional convention.

One reason the initiative and referendum might have been used less frequently than some expected was the increased use by the legislature of the constitutional amendment procedure. Between 1908 and 1918 South Dakota voters were asked to make decisions on thirty-eight proposed amendments to the constitution. Voters used the opportunity to vote down woman suffrage in 1910, 1914, and 1916, but approved the proposal in 1918. They approved laws for the taxation of corporation stocks and bonds, road improvements, the irrigation of public lands, the establishment of a state system of rural credits, and prohibition.[33] In the broader context of the di-

---

31. *Equity* 12 (October 1910): 159–60; 15 (January 1913): 34–35.

32. The 1910 ballot upon which five referred statutes were printed was said to be six feet long in fine print. There is no record of how South Dakota voters reacted to this oddity, but opponents hoping to derail ratification of an initiative and referendum amendment in Arkansas that same year used reproductions of the South Dakota ballot in an attempt to frighten wary voters in that state. See *Equity* 13 (January 1911): 35.

33. See *Equity* 15 (January 1913): 35; 17 (January 1915): 57; and 19 (January 1917): 40.

rect legislation movement, however, the real importance of South Dakota's adoption of an amendment for the initiative and referendum was that it was the first of its kind. Ardent direct legislationists in other states could now work toward a similar goal with renewed optimism.

OREGON

Oregonians, like South Dakotans, were also undergoing a crisis in political confidence. Party bosses and political machines controlled the nomination and election process. It was common knowledge that elections were corrupt and that gangs of "repeaters" cast multiple ballots for pay. The quality of elected representatives suffered as a result. According to one observer, "briefless lawyers, farmless farmers, business failures, bar-room loafers, Fourth-of-July orators, [and] political thugs" characterized the legislature.[34] The sensational land-fraud scandals, investigation, and trials that embarrassed state politicians after 1900 were indicative of the corrupt nature of Oregon politics during this period. Corporations, through party influence, controlled the selection of legislative officers and committee assignments and directed legislation in their interest.[35]

Legislative gridlock further compounded problems. The legislature met for only forty days every two years, but partisan factionalism (often triggered by the legislature's efforts to select a U.S. senator) repeatedly disrupted regular legislative business. In speaking of the legislative sessions during this period, former Oregon governor T. T. Geer noted that "out of seven elections for United States Senators, five of them required the entire time of the session—two of those resulting in no election at all, and one of them in no organization of the House, with no legislation on any subject whatever."[36] The inability of the legislature to use its time productively,

34. Burton J. Hendrick, "The Initiative and Referendum and How Oregon Got Them," 240.

35. See Lincoln Steffens, "Taming of the West," *American Magazine* 64 (September–October 1907): 489–505, 585–602; Tony Howard Evans, "Oregon Progressive Reform, 1902–1914," 46–51; Joseph N. Teal, "The Practical Workings of the Initiative and Referendum in Oregon," 310; Hendrick, "Initiative and Referendum," 240; Paul Thomas Culbertson, "A History of the Initiative and Referendum in Oregon," 50–51; and Cecil T. Thompson, "The Origin of Direct Legislation in Oregon: How Oregon Secured the Initiative and Referendum," 60.

36. Quoted in Culbertson, "History in Oregon," 50–51. In 1895 the Oregon legislature required thirty-two days and fifty-eight ballots to choose a senator. The legislature was so deadlocked in 1897 that after fifty-three days it disbanded and failed to elect anyone. In 1901 the selection process required twenty-two days and fifty-three ballots, and in 1903 it took thirty-two days and forty-two ballots. See Evans, "Oregon Progressive Reform," 51–52.

and allegations that large sums of money were being used to influence senatorial nominations in particular, led many to conclude that representative government was a sham. It was in such a political climate that reform-minded individuals first proposed the initiative and referendum as the most effective way of restoring popular control over government.[37]

The origins of the initiative and referendum in Oregon actually date from the state's constitutional convention of 1857. At that time delegates considered a proposal to adopt a form of optional referendum, whereby the legislature could submit laws to the voters for approval. They also considered suggestions that important questions such as slavery and prohibition should be decided by popular referenda. The state constitution as adopted did provide for a mandatory referendum on constitutional amendments and declare that laws locating the state capital and county seats and the submission of town and corporate acts and other "local and special laws" be decided by popular vote. Nevertheless, any discussion of broadening the use of direct democracy did not occur until the early 1880s when A. D. Cridge, writer, editor, Knights of Labor organizer, and single taxer, urged direct legislation in the *Salem Oregon Vidette and Anti-Monopolist*. Cridge, who became associate editor of the *Vidette* in 1884, initially wrote articles in dialect skits under the caption "Uncle Jeff Snow," an aged farmer who discoursed on various topics and included references to and explanations of the initiative and referendum in his folksy summations. Not long after this Max Burgholtzer, a Populist, promoted the merits of direct legislation in a little-known journal called the *Pacific Farmer*.[38]

The actual beginning of the movement to establish the initiative and referendum in Oregon, however, dates from the reading and discussion of a chapter of J. W. Sullivan's *Direct Legislation* at a Farmers' Alliance meeting in Milwaukie, Oregon, in the fall of 1892. The meeting took place in the home of Seth Lewelling, fruit grower, political activist, and one of the leaders in the Farmers' Alliance in Clackamas County. The meetings and discussions at the Lewelling home were regular occurrences, and the topics were those under discussion by farmers everywhere: exorbitant railroad rates, the tight money supply, and control of the legislature by the plutocracy. The Lewelling group had a firm sense of grievance, but had yet to dis-

37. See Evans, "Oregon Progressive Reform," 51–53; and Culbertson, "History in Oregon," 50–51.

38. L. H. McMahan was also reported to have supported direct legislation in the columns of his newspaper, the *Salem Daily Independent*. See Culbertson, "History in Oregon," 48–50, 53–54; A. D. Cridge, "William S. U'Ren, Lawgiver of Oregon and Single Taxer," *Single Tax Review* 10 (March–April 1910): 35; Lute Pease, "The Initiative and Referendum—Oregon's 'Big Stick,'" 565; Evans, "Oregon Progressive Reform," 54; and Samuel Gompers, "The Initiative, Referendum, and Recall," in *American Federationist*, King Papers, Library of Congress.

cover a method for solving the problems plaguing U.S. society. Sullivan's book offered them a means to bring about change. By using the initiative and referendum as tools of democracy, citizens could regain the legislative and fiscal powers they had delegated to legislative bodies that either seemed committed to avoiding controversial issues or were actually determined to abuse the public trust. Adoption of the initiative and referendum would give hope to those who had given up on reform of the political economy.[39]

One young man at the meeting who was especially fascinated by Sullivan's argument was William S. U'Ren. Born in Lancaster, Wisconsin, in 1859, U'Ren was the son of an itinerant blacksmith and had spent most of his early years migrating throughout the West. He held a series of jobs, working at various times as a blacksmith, bookkeeper, lawyer, and editor. While working as an editor for a newspaper in the mining town of Tin Cup, Colorado, in 1882, U'Ren came across a copy of Henry George's *Progress and Poverty* and became a convert to the single tax. Single taxers believed that landownership and opportunity were linked. The way to create opportunity was to make land available. However, speculators prevented this by holding land idle while they waited for community development to increase the value of their holdings. The solution to this problem was to make land too costly to be held idle for speculative purposes. If the government took as a tax the increased value of all unimproved land (the unearned increment), no one could afford to keep land solely for speculation. A few years later, in 1889, while transferring from the train to the ferry in Oakland, California, U'Ren first learned of direct legislation when someone handed him a labor union leaflet on the initiative. There was nothing on the referendum, however, and the pamphlet appears to have stimulated little more than a curious interest in the subject.

U'Ren's general interest in politics took a practical turn after moving to Portland, Oregon, in the early 1890s. He became acquainted with E. W. Bingham, secretary of the Oregon Australian Ballot League, and worked with Bingham in persuading the legislature to pass a secret ballot law in 1891. While working for the adoption of the secret ballot, U'Ren met the Lewelling family, took a job as Seth Lewelling's secretary, and eventually became a partner in the Lewelling nursery business until its collapse during the panic of 1893. He eagerly joined the Lewelling family's political activities and soon became a leading contributor at their frequent discussion groups. He also became an active member of the Farmers' Alliance.[40]

39. See Thomas C. McClintock, "Seth Lewelling, William S. U'Ren, and the Birth of the Oregon Progressive Movement," 200–203, 206; and Pease, "Oregon's 'Big Stick,'" 565.

40. See McClintock, "Seth Lewelling," 203–6; Robert C. Woodward, "William S. U'Ren: A Progressive Era Personality," 4; Hendrick, "Initiative and Referendum," 239; Lincoln Steffens, *Upbuilders*, 287–301; and Evans, "Oregon Progressive Reform," 55–58.

U'Ren reacted enthusiastically to Sullivan's simply stated reform pro-posals. It was as if Sullivan addressed his comments directly to the politi-cally awakening U'Ren. Said Sullivan:

> To radical reformers further encouragement must come with contin-ued reflection on the importance to them of direct legislation. In gener-al, such reformers have failed to recognize that, before any project of social reconstruction can be followed out to the end, there stands a question antecedent to every other. It is the abolition of the lawmaking monopoly. Until that monopoly is ended, no law favorable to the mass-es can be secure. Direct legislation would destroy this parent of mo-nopolies. It gone, then would follow the chief evils of governmental mechanism—class rule, ring rule, extravagance, jobbery, nepotism, the spoils system, every jot of the professional trading politician's influ-ence.[41]

After reading the entire short volume that evening, U'Ren had convinced himself that the initiative and referendum were the solutions to the prob-lems being discussed at the meetings. U'Ren also realized that economic democracy would have to await political democracy. "I forgot, for the time, all about Henry George and the single tax. All these I now saw to be details. The one important thing was to restore the law-making power where it be-longed—into the hands of the people. Once give us that, we could get any-thing we wanted—single tax, anything." The only question remaining was one of how to proceed, and Sullivan had a suggestion there as well. "Unit-ed farmers, wage-workers, and other classes of citizens . . . might natural-ly demand direct legislation. . . . These forces combined in any state, it seems improbable that certain political and economic measures now sup-ported by farmer and wage-worker alike could long fail to become law."[42]

At the next session of the Clackamas County Alliance, U'Ren introduced a resolution asking the executive committee of the State Farmers' Alliance to invite the State Grange, the Portland Chamber of Commerce, the Oregon Knights of Labor, the Portland Federated Trades, and the Central Labor Council of Portland to join in creating a joint committee to direct a cam-paign of education and agitation for the adoption of the initiative and referendum as amendments to the Oregon Constitution. The farmer and la-bor organizations accepted the call, but the Portland Chamber of Com-merce predictably ignored the invitation. The membership of the new com-mittee included W. D. Hare of the Grange and U'Ren of the Farmers' Alliance, while A. I. Mason of the Carpenters' Union, G. G. Kurtz of the Ci-

---

41. Sullivan, *Direct Legislation*, 100. See also McClintock, "Seth Lewelling," 206.
42. Hendrick, "Initiative and Referendum," 239; McClintock, "Seth Lewelling," 207; Sullivan, *Direct Legislation*, 100.

garmakers, and Charles Short of the Typographical Union served successively as representatives of the Federated Trades Assembly. T. E. Kirby, a blacksmith, spoke for the Central Labor Council, and W. S. Vanderburg carried the shield of the Knights of Labor. Hare served as chairman of the new committee, while U'Ren acted as secretary.[43]

Before the Joint Committee on Direct Legislation began its public campaign, W. S. Vanderburg, a state senator representing Coos, Curry, and Josephine Counties and a member of the Joint Committee, introduced a concurrent resolution in the Senate. The resolution requested the governor to place an advisory referendum on the ballot at the next general election. Voters would be asked to vote yes or no on a proposal to establish the initiative (based on a 2 percent petition requirement) and an obligatory referendum on all acts, appropriations, and bills originating in the legislature. Vanderburg's proposal, however, received little support. The Senate referred the matter to the Committee on Federal Regulations where it was buried. The response, or lack thereof, suggested that passage of a direct legislation bill in the legislature prior to an extensive campaign of publicity and education would be a difficult task.[44]

The public campaign for direct legislation got off to an enthusiastic start early in 1893. The Joint Committee raised funds of nearly six hundred dollars and published fifty thousand pamphlets in English and another eighteen thousand in German proclaiming the merits of the "I and R." The printers' unions printed the material, women's groups sewed the covers, and the alliances and labor unions distributed the information. The Joint Committee also furnished material to newspapers in the form of supplements, and circulated fifteen hundred copies of Sullivan's book. Lecturers spoke to the Grange, the alliance, and various teachers' meetings to explain and promote direct legislation. During the political campaign of 1894, advocates of direct legislation convinced the Democratic and Populist Parties to endorse the initiative and referendum in their platforms. The dominant Republican Party, however, refused even to consider the issue.

In the meantime, the Joint Committee had concluded that the quickest way to get the initiative and referendum approved as amendments to the state's constitution was to hold a constitutional convention. To that end, U'Ren and others worked to get candidates to the legislature to pledge themselves to support direct legislation and the calling of a convention to revise the state's constitution. During the election campaign, workers for

43. See Hendrick, "Initiative and Referendum," 239–41; Pease, "Oregon's 'Big Stick,'" 565–66; McClintock, "Seth Lewelling," 207; and Evans, "Oregon Progressive Reform," 58–59.
44. See Homer L. Owen, "Oregon Politics and the Initiative and Referendum," 67–68.

direct legislation secured the signatures of fourteen thousand voters (out of an electorate of eighty thousand) on a petition requesting the legislature to call a constitutional convention. When the legislature assembled in 1895, U'Ren worked the halls as a "legislative agent" employed by the same organizations that had originally formed the Joint Committee. When the legislature took up the question of calling a constitutional convention, U'Ren produced not only the impressive petition but pledges from a majority of the legislators as well. Despite these efforts, the legislature refused (by a single vote in both the House and the Senate) to support the idea. U'Ren blamed Joe Simon, boss of the Republican political machine, for the defeat.[45]

The bitter legislative defeat caused the Joint Committee to rethink its strategy. The leadership now concluded that it was impractical to seek reform by means of a constitutional convention. Even if they succeeded in calling such a convention, there was no assurance that they would be able to influence it. Instead, they opted for the more laborious and time-consuming procedure of working to convince legislators to pass a direct legislation amendment, a process that required the approval of both houses in two consecutive sessions of the legislature. To that end, U'Ren sought and won election to the lower house of the state legislature as a Populist in 1896. During the campaign U'Ren approached Senator John H. Mitchell, perhaps the most influential politician in the state and whose endorsement was essential for passage of an initiative and referendum amendment during the next legislative session, and came away from the meeting convinced that he had Mitchell's support.

When the legislature convened in 1897, U'Ren found himself the leader of thirteen Populists in the House and, oddly enough, a legislative power broker. As in the past, all legislative business awaited the election of a U.S. senator. Senator Mitchell was the Republican candidate for reelection, but his straddling of the monetary question (gold versus silver) caused him to lose the support of several groups. Controlling a small bloc of "silver Republicans" and an even smaller number of Democrats was Jonathan Bourne, a mining investor, candidate for Speaker of the House, and later a leading advocate of direct legislation. Also opposed to Mitchell was Republican "boss" Joe Simon who, as president of the Senate, controlled his own small blocs of "gold Republicans" in both chambers. Potentially, an unlikely coalition of thirteen Populists, five silver Republicans, nine gold Republicans, and three Democrats could deny a quorum and prevent the

45. See McClintock, "Seth Lewelling," 207–9; Claudius O. Johnson, "The Adoption of the Initiative and Referendum in Washington," 292–93; Hendrick, "Initiative and Referendum," 241–43; Pease, "Oregon's 'Big Stick,'" 566; Steffens, *Upbuilders*, 303–5; and *Direct Legislation Record* 5 (March 1898): 19.

House from permanently organizing. When Mitchell refused to support the proposed direct legislation measures, U'Ren and the anti-Mitchell leaders struck a deal. In return for support from U'Ren's Populists, the anti-Mitchell forces promised to work for the initiative and referendum, a voter registration law, and a law regulating the selection of judges in the next session of the legislature, in 1899. As a result, the infamous "hold up" session of the Oregon legislature ended without a single law being passed or a U.S. senator being elected.

Many voters were outraged, viewing the political bargaining, factionalism, and legislative impasse as another example of unscrupulous, irresponsible, unrepresentative government. Populist voters were particularly incensed with their elected representatives for apparently "selling out" to gold Republicans and for participating in the type of corrupt government against which they had so actively campaigned. U'Ren defended himself by stating that he was motivated by principle not by party and, in fact, had no faith in party organization or party governance. "I believe," said U'Ren, "if the Populists had had a two-thirds majority in the legislature for 20 years they would be in the same boat the Republicans are now in." There seemed to be no alternative other than to play the political game by the prevailing rules. Said U'Ren: "I had tried to get the Initiative and Referendum in a responsible way twice—once in 1895 and here again in 1897. Both times our representative legislators had deceived and betrayed us. I now decided to get the reforms by using our enemies' own methods." To U'Ren, the ends justified the means.[46]

After the 1897 legislative session ended, U'Ren and his supporters realized that they needed to revitalize their organization and seek to broaden their base of support. Hard times had severely weakened both farm and labor organizations. The only politically active survivor of the sponsors of the original Joint Committee in 1892 was the Grange, whereas the Populists had all but lost their identity in fusion with the Democrats. It was time to start anew. That September about fifty individuals met in Salem and formed the Non-Partisan Direct Legislation League, with U'Ren once again serving as secretary. The composition of the new organization represented a dramatic departure from the previous Joint Committee. Although labor and agrarian activists remained, the league had broadened at the top. The

46. Robert C. Woodward, "William Simon U'Ren: In an Age of Protest," 45; Hendrick, "Initiative and Referendum," 246. See also McClintock, "Seth Lewelling," 209–15; Steffens, *Upbuilders,* 306–14; Hendrick, "Initiative and Referendum," 243–48; Pease, "Oregon's 'Big Stick,'" 566; Evans, "Oregon Progressive Reform," 61–62; *Direct Legislation Record* 3 (September 1896): 26; 5 (March 1898): 19; Thompson, "Origin in Oregon," 46; and Michael Maben, "The Initiative and Referendum in Oregon: An Historical Perspective," 19–21.

executive committee of the new league now included numerous business-men, several prominent bankers, and the president of the State Bar Association. Having successfully educated the voters on the subject of direct legislation, U'Ren (elected to the executive committee of the National Direct Legislation League in the spring of 1898) now looked to gain the league respectability and legitimacy. With so many prominent individuals willing to endorse the initiative and referendum, critics were increasingly hard-pressed to label direct legislation as either a "Pop" fad or part of some radical ideology.[47]

When the legislature convened in 1899, the outlook for passage of an initiative and referendum amendment to the Oregon Constitution looked promising. The previous election campaign had ended with U'Ren's unsuccessful run for the Oregon Senate against George C. Brownell. U'Ren used that contest to make another political bargain. He pledged to support Brownell in his next political campaign if Brownell would work for the initiative and referendum. Said U'Ren: "I'll trade off parties, offices, bills—anything for that [direct legislation]." And he did. U'Ren again worked the halls of the legislature as a lobbyist, making other "deals" when he could. "We helped through measures we didn't believe in to get help for our measures from members who didn't believe in them. That's corruption, yes; a kind of corruption, but our measures were to make corruption impossible in the end." With added publicity, new recruits, and the single-minded persistence of the pragmatic U'Ren, the Oregon legislature passed a direct legislation bill in 1899. The final vote was forty-four to eight in the House and twenty-two to six in the Senate. The new law set petition requirements at 8 percent of qualified voters for the initiative, and 5 percent for the referendum. Laws necessary for the "immediate preservation of the public peace, health or safety" were exempted from the referendum.[48]

The ease with which legislators voted in favor of direct legislation in 1899 was no guarantee that they would do so for a second time in 1901 as required by Oregon law. Taking no chances, U'Ren and the league continued to work to keep the issue before the public. Proponents wrote articles, de-

---

47. See Pease, "Oregon's 'Big Stick,'" 566–69; Evans, "Oregon Progressive Reform," 62–64; and *Direct Legislation Record* 5 (March 1898): 1. U'Ren attended the organizing convention of the National Direct Legislation League in St. Louis in the summer of 1896 and was elected a vice president representing the state of Oregon. See *Direct Legislation Record* 3 (September 1896): 26. By the late 1890s U'Ren had gained national recognition as a crusader for the "I and R." Much of this notoriety resulted from articles he contributed to the *Direct Legislation Record*: see 1 (July 1894): 43; 2 (June 1895): 15; 3 (March 1896): 16; and 4 (June 1897): 32.

48. U'Ren quoted in Steffens, *Upbuilders*, 316, 318 (see also 315–18). See also *Direct Legislation Record* 6 (March 1899): 1–2; and Evans, "Oregon Progressive Reform," 64–65.

livered speeches, distributed pamphlets, conducted house-to-house can-
vasses, interrogated candidates, and gathered endorsements. U'Ren addressed letters to approximately one thousand individuals he knew, mostly former Populists, pointing out the legislators who had voted "right" in
1899 and encouraging them to support those candidates for reelection
without regard to party. So thorough were their organizing and publicizing efforts that no political "backsliding" occurred when the legislature reconvened in 1901. U'Ren again worked the legislature as a lobbyist. Bourne
and Simon kept their promises, as did state senator George Brownell, who
actively campaigned for the measure. Factionalism over the selection of a
U.S. senator prevented organized opposition to direct legislation from developing. Both senatorial candidates, Henry Corbett and John Mitchell,
feared alienating the supporters of direct legislation and gave the measures
their endorsement. Lorin Kruse, a Republican, reintroduced the bill in the
House where it passed by a margin of forty-three to nine. William Smith, a
Populist, resubmitted the measure in the Senate, which approved it by a
vote of twenty to eight. All that remained was for voters to approve the
amendment at the next general election.[49]

By the time of the election in 1902, the initiative and referendum had
gained strong support throughout the state. George Chamberlain, a successful Democratic reform candidate for governor in 1902, spoke in favor
of the reforms, as did George H. Williams, president of the Non-Partisan
Direct Legislation League and successful candidate for mayor of Portland.
Prominent citizens such as Joseph N. Teal, a corporate attorney and president of the Taxpayer's League of Portland, and Harvey Scott, the conservative editor of the *Portland Oregonian*, published supportive articles and
editorials. Professor Frank Parsons, nationally known proponent of direct
legislation and author of *The City for the People*, conducted a lecturing tour
in Oregon. Eltweed Pomeroy, editor of the *Direct Legislation Record* and
president of the National Direct Legislation League, spoke several times in
the state as well. The Grange, very much a political force in Oregon politics; the Oregon Federation of Labor; and the Portland Federated Trades
Council all passed resolutions in support. Every political party except the
Prohibitionists passed similar platform endorsements. In addition, U'Ren
estimated that two-thirds of the state's newspapers had now lined up behind the reforms. Voters finally settled the issue by deciding overwhelmingly in favor of the initiative and referendum by a vote of 62,024 to 5,668.[50]

49. See Pease, "Oregon's 'Big Stick,'" 570; *Direct Legislation Record* 6 (March 1899): 1;
7 (December 1900): 69–70; 9 (March 1902): 3; Johnson, "Adoption in Washington," 293–
94; and Evans, "Oregon Progressive Reform," 65–66.
50. Scott's initial opposition had softened. He had apparently convinced himself that
direct legislation might serve as a means of preventing unwanted partisan, machine-

The year 1902 marked a turning point in Oregon politics. In addition to adopting direct legislation, voters also elected a Democrat, George Chamberlain, as governor. Sensing that voters demanded political change, Chamberlain, formerly a district attorney of Multnomah County, had promised them a progressive program. In his inaugural address in 1903 Governor Chamberlain warned legislators not to ignore the will of the people as previous legislatures had done and encouraged them to enact a package of progressive reforms.

The Republican-dominated legislature actually went further in enacting a reform program than many had expected. Numerous labor reforms, proposed but denied in previous sessions, gained approval. The centerpiece, an employer-liability law (limited to railway workers), overturned the existing common-law principle of liability and guaranteed workers compensation, regardless of fault. The legislature also created a state labor bureau and an office of labor commissioner, limited the working day for women, and restricted the use of child labor. In addition, the legislature enacted an inheritance tax law, and created a state board of health and a new office of state land agent (to supervise the sale of public lands). Still, there were disappointments. A bill to provide for uniform tax assessments on express, telegraph, telephone, and railroad companies was beaten back by corporate lobbyists. An antitrust law and a bill for tighter regulation of corporations, as well as a measure for local option (on liquor), also failed. What disconcerted reformers most, however, was the legislature's refusal to strike a further blow at machine politics by expanding the existing direct primary law, enacted in 1901, to include towns and cities other than Portland. It was, however, too soon to tell how reformers and voters would react. Would they focus on legislative accomplishments and patiently await legislative fulfillment of the progressive agenda? Or would they demand immediate satisfaction and use the mechanism of direct legislation to that end?[51]

At the 1904 general election, it was evident that reformers and voters favored an aggressive rather than a cautious approach to reform. For the first time two major initiatives appeared on the ballot. The first, a statewide direct primary law, was the work of the Direct Primary Nomination League. Most of the charter members of the new organization had been organizers of the old Direct Legislation League. Members elected A. L. Mills, a Port-

---

dictated legislation and as a method of enacting reforms that were unacceptable to the machine. Scott, who never became an enthusiast, soon changed his mind and resumed the role of leading editorial antagonist. See Evans, "Oregon Progressive Reform," 68. The amendment carried by wide margins in every county in the state. See also Evans, "Oregon Progressive Reform," 67–69, 71–72; *Direct Legislation Record* 9 (March 1902): 3; 9 (September 1902): 41; and Woodward, "William Simon U'Ren," 65.

51. See Evans, "Oregon Progressive Reform," 75–88.

land banker, as president; George Orton, a labor leader, as vice president; and U'Ren as secretary. The membership list included businessmen, politicians, newspapermen, workers, and farmers, and organizers made every effort to emphasize the cross-class nature and respectability of the new body. The proposed direct primary law had the twofold purpose of eliminating the nomination of candidates by party conventions by placing that power directly in the hands of the electorate, and providing for the popular election of U.S. senators by means of Statement no. 1. Candidates for the legislature would be asked to pledge themselves to vote for the senatorial candidate who received a majority of the votes cast in a preference primary. Candidates could opt for Statement no. 2—merely promising to use personal discretion, but not to be bound by popular choice. Again, the intent was to allow the electorate rather than the party to make the choices. Presentation of the statements as "options" preserved the measure's constitutionality. Support for the direct primary bill was strong throughout the state, many seeing the proposal as a solution to one of the state's most embarrassing and persistent political problems. Voters approved the direct primary bill in the general election by a vote of 56,205 to 16,354.[52]

The second initiated measure to appear on the 1904 ballot was a local-option liquor bill. This measure sought to transfer control over the manufacture and sale of intoxicating liquor from the state to the localities. Support for local option came from the Prohibition Party, the Anti-Saloon League, the Women's Christian Temperance Union (WCTU), Protestant church groups, and the Grange. Although many supporters regarded the measure as the first step toward prohibition, others saw it as a move toward popular self-government, or home rule, and a way to clean up local politics by eliminating the corrupting influence of the liquor industry. Those opposed to local option included saloon keepers, brewers, distillers, and hops farmers, as well as many businessmen and organized labor. They charged that the proposal would severely damage the state's economy, create unemployment, and greatly reduce the state's tax revenues. Voters narrowly approved the local-option initiative by a vote of 43,316 to 40,198. With the successful use of the initiative for the first time, Oregon's voters had sent a warning that they were prepared to use direct legislation to implement a program of progressive reform if the legislature continued to act in a conservative or recalcitrant manner.[53]

52. See George H. Shibley, "The Initiative and Referendum in Practical Operation," 142; Pease, "Oregon's 'Big Stick,'" 570–72; Evans, "Oregon Progressive Reform," 88–95; and Jonathan Bourne Jr., "Popular Government in Oregon," 323–28.

53. There was actually a third initiative proposition on the ballot in 1904. This measure authorized the legislature to fix the salary of the state printer and end the practice of lucrative fee collection. See Evans, "Oregon Progressive Reform," 95–101; Shibley, "Initiative and Referendum," 142; John E. Caswell, "The Prohibition Movement in Oregon," 65; and Earl Pomeroy, *The Pacific Slope*, 196.

When the next legislature convened in January 1905, Governor Chamberlain again encouraged legislators to continue their record of accomplishment and noted that the voters "are in a mood to indorse and uphold progressive measures."[54] Regardless, Oregon's elected representatives once again disappointed many voters. The legislature passed legislation creating a tax commission, placed further restrictions on child labor, regulated corporations, and required railroads to extend rail connections to remote, undeveloped regions of the state. However, it rejected proposals for a state railroad commission, the elimination of free railroad passes, a maximum-hour law for railroad employees, a general eight-hour law, a gross-earnings tax on corporations, a comprehensive employer-liability law, and a measure extending the initiative and referendum to municipalities. Raising further ire among reformers and voters was the legislature's attempt to amend the recently approved local-option law. The proposal, backed by liquor interests and some businessmen, sought to raise the petition requirement to call local-option elections from 10 percent to 40 percent and attach an emergency clause that would make the measure immune from any referendum action. U'Ren spoke for many advocates of direct legislation when he warned against allowing the legislature to tamper with a "people's act."

Even more alarming to reformers was a bill proposed by Senator Brownell. This measure called for convening a constitutional convention and stipulated that one-third of the delegates to that convention had to be appointed by the state supreme court. Direct legislationists viewed this measure as a direct attack on the initiative and referendum. Said U'Ren: "The man who votes for the Brownell bill . . . is digging his own political grave and getting into it."[55] The two hostile proposals were defeated, but many Oregonians could only wonder whether the legislature was acting as an agency for change or as a defender of the status quo.

In 1905 U'Ren spearheaded the organization of the People's Power League, a body created to set the progressive political agenda in Oregon. Looking to promote reform measures through the initiative and referendum and protect direct legislation from legislative assault, the new league drew its leadership and membership from the same cross-section of society as the earlier Direct Primary Nominations League. Ben Selling, a Portland clothier, served as president, George Orton as vice president, and U'Ren as secretary. The league sponsored five of the eleven initiated measures that appeared on the ballot in 1906. These included a law to prohibit free railroad passes and amendments that would require a popular referendum to call a constitutional convention, grant home rule for municipal-

54. Evans, "Oregon Progressive Reform," 102.
55. Ibid., 108; see also 102–9.

ities, extend the initiative and referendum to local governments, and regulate compensation for state printers. U'Ren concluded that the increase in the number of initiatives had resulted "principally because the legislature has for many years past . . . held back the political progress of the people." This appeared to be the case, as most of the measures had been previously rejected by the legislature more than once. Other proposals on the ballot included: woman suffrage and two measures seeking to levy a 3 percent gross-earnings tax on sleeping and refrigerator car companies, oil companies, and express, telephone, and telegraph companies. With the exception of woman suffrage, all of the other important proposals passed by large majorities in every county. By popular tally, it seemed as if the legislature was out of touch with popular opinion.[56]

The tension between a cautious legislature and reform enthusiasts continued during 1907 and 1908. Responding to intense pressure from a coalition represented by business boosters, lumbermen, hops growers, trade unionists, and farmers, the legislature passed a railroad commission bill. The new law gave commissioners the power to enforce rules and regulations, prevent carriers from imposing unjust rates, and require railroads to compensate shippers when failing to provide them with an adequate supply of freight cars. The legislature also approved several regulatory measures affecting banking, food, hours of employment, and insurance. Again, though, much additional legislation sought by reformers was rejected: revoking the perpetual franchises enjoyed by Oregon corporations, preventing timber companies from tax dodging, allowing for the recall of public officials, expanding the employer-liability law, regulating public service corporations, and prohibiting corrupt election practices. Adding insult to injury were unsuccessful attempts to weaken both the direct primary and the initiative and referendum laws. To many, and especially to those in the People's Power League, it again appeared as if the legislature was working to limit any further extension of fundamental reform.[57]

The 1908 ballot in Oregon featured eleven initiative and eight referendum measures, and the People's Power League again sponsored what were arguably the four most important proposals. The first allowed for the recall of public officials based on a petition signed by 25 percent of the eligible voters. The second called for the adoption of a corrupt-practices act limiting campaign expenditures. The third sought to remove constitutional restrictions preventing the establishment of a system of proportional representation that would provide for first, second, and third choices at elections

56. U'Ren quoted in ibid., 131–32. See also George A. Thacher, "The Initiative and Referendum in Oregon," *Independent* 64 (May 28, 1908): 1191–95; Shibley, "Initiative and Referendum," 142–43; and Evans, "Oregon Progressive Reform," 112–13, 120, 132–37.
57. See Evans, "Oregon Progressive Reform," 146–51.

so that minority parties could be represented in proportion to their numbers. This measure had the strong personal support of U'Ren. "Real representative government," he said, "is impossible unless all political parties, minorities as well as majorities, are thus fairly represented in the legislature in proportion to the number of supporters that each has among the voters." The fourth called for enacting Statement no. 1 and the popular election of U.S. senators into Oregon law. Also on the ballot was a proposal for woman suffrage.[58]

Adding additional interest to the election was a bill to establish a modified single tax. Many direct legislationists were also vigorous advocates of the single tax, and, like U'Ren, had decided to work to obtain political democracy before attempting to establish the sort of economic democracy envisioned by Henry George. After ratification of the initiative and referendum in 1902 and a direct primary law in 1904, though, many single taxers were restless to begin their campaign. In January 1908 a number of single taxers organized the Oregon Tax Reform Association, and decided to press ahead and initiate a modified single-tax amendment. Joseph Fels, a wealthy Philadelphia soap manufacturer and convert to the teachings of Henry George, donated fourteen hundred dollars to the campaign. The amendment, prepared by H. D. Wagnon and A. D. Cridge, sought to increase taxes on idle landholdings, while exempting homes, manufacturing plants, and machinery. Proponents argued that the tax would target only land speculators and the landholdings of the Southern Pacific Railroad. However, exemptions to manufacturers frightened farmers who thought they would be assessed at a higher level. In the end, the Grange, the *Portland Oregonian,* and the Taxpayer's League of Portland all opposed the amendment that went down to defeat by a vote of 60,871 to 32,066. Surprisingly, single taxers saw hope even in defeat. The measure lost by only 483 votes in Multnomah County (in which is Portland). Single taxers were optimistic that if farmers could be convinced of the soundness of the single-tax idea, an amendment might yet succeed. In the election of 1908, voters approved nine of eleven initiated measures and all four of the proposals put forward by the People's Power League. They rejected woman suffrage, the repeal of local option, and the single tax.[59]

58. U'Ren quoted in ibid., 176. See also George A. Thacher, "The Oregon Election," *Independent* 64 (June 25, 1908): 1444–47; Shibley, "Initiative and Referendum," 144–46; Evans, "Oregon Progressive Reform," 172–81; and Bourne, "Popular Government in Oregon," 328–30.

59. See Robert C. Woodward, "W. S. U'Ren and the Single Tax in Oregon," 49–51; F. C. Young, "The Single Tax Movement in Oregon," 643–45; and Arthur Nichols Young, *The Single Tax Movement in the United States,* 168–70. For a critical overview of the single-tax fight in Oregon, see James H. Gilbert, "Single-Tax Movement in Oregon," 26–34.

The 1909 legislature was less productive than any of its three predecessors. Extending the ten-hour law for women and creating state commissions for insurance and conservation were the sum of its major accomplishments. At the same time, the legislature continued to reject measures put forward by reformers. These included a general employer-liability law, a uniform eight-hour law for workers, and implementation of proportional representation. Even more alarming to reformers was the open hostility that many in the legislature exhibited toward government by popular democracy (now known nationally as the "Oregon System") and the enthusiasm with which they sought either to weaken or to restrict its operation. Despite overwhelming voter support for the direct election of U.S. senators, opponents introduced a bill that would have made it a misdemeanor for a candidate to make any preelection pledge as requested by Statement no. 1. Opponents also proposed measures authorizing political parties once again to hold nominating conventions to "recommend" candidates prior to direct primaries (which reformers regarded as an attempt to resurrect Republican Party control over the nominating process), prohibiting remuneration for initiative and referendum petitioners, and preventing members of one political party from voting in the primary election of another party. All these counterreform measures were defeated.[60]

The debate between the proponents and opponents of direct legislation intensified at the general election in 1910 when voters had to decide on thirty-two initiative and referendum measures. The 1910 "Campaign Book," which included the full text of each ballot proposition and appended arguments for and against each one, totaled 208 pages. Critics derisively referred to the proliferation of ballot measures as the "hit-or-miss scheme of non-deliberative democracy."[61] U'Ren countered by charging that it was the reluctance of the legislature to represent the voters of the state that caused the exceptionally high number of ballot proposals. By U'Ren's tally, eighteen of the thirty-two measures on the ballot were there solely because the legislature had not heeded the wishes of the electorate.

The People's Power League again sponsored several of the more provocative measures, including a presidential preference primary, the establishment of a "Board of People's Inspectors of Government" and the publication of an official gazette (a bimonthly record of governmental operations that would be mailed to all registered voters), and a complicated omnibus bill that included the implementation of proportional representation in the legislature, annual legislative sessions, and restrictions on the legislature's use of the "emergency" clause to exclude measures from ref-

60. See Evans, "Oregon Progressive Reform," 195–96.
61. Ibid., 212.

erendum action. Other propositions on the ballot included statewide prohibition, woman suffrage, and two competing employer-liability laws (one sponsored by the Oregon Federation of Labor, the other by the Oregon Employers' Association). Overall, voters approved only nine of the thirty-two measures presented. Favoring an expanded direct primary system, they adopted the presidential preference primary. They also endorsed the labor-sponsored employer-liability law, protecting workers in cases of job-related injuries. Voters again rejected prohibition and woman suffrage, and turned down both the request for "People's Inspectors" and the league's omnibus bill.

The ballot also included another single-tax proposal. Immediately after the defeat of their measure in 1908, single taxers reorganized as the Oregon Single Tax League. Supported with $16,775 from the Fels Commission, single taxers renewed their campaign in 1910. This time they resorted to subterfuge and submitted their measure in disguised form. Although the Single Tax League prepared the amendment, the Oregon State Federation of Labor and the Central Labor Council of Portland officially "sponsored" it. To further confuse voters, no direct mention of the single tax was made in the amendment. In fact, the amendment was described as a repeal of the poll tax. The principal feature of the bill, however, was to grant counties the flexibility to design their own tax schemes. Even though critics referred to the proposal as the "Trojan horse" tax law, it narrowly passed by a vote of 44,171 to 42,127.[62]

Progressive Republicans gained control of both houses of the Oregon legislature for the first time in 1911. Ben Selling, president of the People's Power League and now state senator, was elected president of the Senate. John P. Rusk, who had established progressive credentials in the previous legislature, was chosen Speaker of the House. The session promised to be intriguing for two reasons: What kind of record could "progressives" establish now that they had gained control of the legislature? Second, would voters relax their use of direct legislation now that the legislature appeared poised to push reform ideas?

62. For a detailed analysis of the measures on the 1910 Oregon ballot, see George H. Haynes, "'People's Rule' in Oregon," *Political Science Quarterly* 26 (March 1911): 32–62. See also George A. Thacher, "The Interesting Election in Oregon," *Independent* 69 (December 29, 1910): 1434–38. The Fels Commission spent $16,775 in the campaign. Legislators attacked the new tax law during the 1911 legislative session and voted to resubmit it to the voters for repeal in 1912. See Woodward, "U'Ren and the Single Tax," 51–55; Evans, "Oregon Progressive Reform," 211–21; F. C. Young, "Single Tax in Oregon," 645–48; Gilbert, "Single-Tax Movement," 34–36; and A. N. Young, *Single Tax in the United States*, 170–74. For a general look at single-tax activities in Oregon and elsewhere to 1912, see Frank Parker Stockbridge, "The Single Taxers: Who They Are and What They Are Doing," 507–22.

The issue that dominated legislative discussion in 1911 was the need for a public utilities commission. Public sentiment in favor of the regulation of public utilities and public discussion of possible public ownership of those corporations had been increasing for years. Politically minded reform groups, such as the Oregon State Grange, were particularly critical of the state's policy of awarding perpetual franchises to corporations as the best method for promoting economic development, and led the call for control of public service monopolies. In 1906, consumers and taxpayers joined the crusade as they became outraged at the actions of the Portland Gas Company. The company had a perpetual franchise to use the streets of Portland to lay its lines and for that privilege paid only two hundred dollars in annual taxes. In January 1907 an ongoing investigation of company policy revealed that the gas company had provided gas of inferior quality, charged consumers exorbitant rates, and dealt with consumer complaints in an arrogant manner. The Portland City Council censured the gas company, but denied a permit to a new company to establish competition. Portland's consumer taxpayers, outraged by the council's action, then used direct legislation to provide the new Economy Gas Company with a twenty-five-year franchise as a gas competitor. The new company agreed to sell gas at a lower rate and pay a 1 percent gross-earnings tax.

Action at the local level prompted progressives in the 1907 legislature to propose measures to repeal perpetual franchises, establish rate controls, demand improved service, and increase the taxes on public utility corporations, but the measures were defeated. That was where the matter stood until Dan Malarkey, a progressive state senator from Portland, introduced a measure to establish a state utilities commission in 1911. The Malarkey Bill created the Oregon Public Service Commission and granted it the power to control both rates and service. The bill, ultimately supported by both progressives and regular Republicans, passed easily in both houses of the legislature.[63]

Surprisingly, a legislature strongly under the influence of progressives and the passage of a long-awaited public utilities act failed to deter either the popularity of direct legislation or the willingness of the People's Power League to expand the boundaries of the Oregon System. The 1912 ballot listed thirty-seven initiative and referendum measures and included a new omnibus amendment sponsored by the People's Power League. The measure, more far-reaching than the 1911 proposals, called for the extensive reorganization of state government. Under the proposed system lawmaking power would be invested in a single legislative body of sixty members

63. See Evans, "Oregon Progressive Reform," 221–26.

elected to four-year terms. The election of legislators would be by proportional representation. The governor would be given primary control over bills for appropriations, whereas similar measures originating in the legislature would have to be approved by the voters. A referendum petition could also be used against legislation on a line-item basis. U'Ren, who drafted the measure, argued that it allowed voters more direct control over lawmaking. Nevertheless, even many in the People's Power League found the proposal too controversial, and voters overwhelmingly rejected it.[64]

Voter reaction to other proposals on the ballot (they approved only eleven of thirty-seven items) was mixed. One proposition sought to require a majority of all votes cast in an election (rather than a majority of those voting on a measure) for passage of constitutional amendments and initiated statutes. Opponents of direct legislation hoped this would severely restrict lawmaking by ballot. They gained support from opponents of prohibition and woman suffrage. Most Oregonians, however, saw the proposal as an attempt to cripple the initiative and rejected it. Gaining popular approval was a statute establishing an eight-hour day on public works projects and, finally, an amendment granting woman suffrage. By 1912 the neighboring states of Washington, Idaho, and California had all granted the vote to women, while the WCTU, the Grange, organized labor, socialists, progressives, and the state press (including the influential *Portland Oregonian*) all actively supported the idea in Oregon. Progressives made a convincing argument that the Oregon System was incomplete without the vote for women. Voters also upheld the law providing for the regulation of public utilities.[65]

Included on the ballot were several other measures regarded by most voters as either too radical or too reactionary. One was a "Graduated Single Tax and Exemption Amendment." The measure offered exemptions to owners of small landholdings, but otherwise applied a graduated single tax to land, franchises, and the rights-of-way of public service corporations. Both sides spent heavily and spoke actively to win voter support, but voters defeated the graduated single tax by an eight-to-three majority. They also repealed the county-option single-tax amendment that had misled many of them in 1910. Voters also showed contempt for measures they deemed too reactionary. Included in this category were two measures, backed by the Employers' Association of Oregon and ostensibly provoked by Industrial Workers of the World activities in Oregon, prohibiting boy-

64. See George H. Haynes, "'People's Rule' on Trial," 24–25; and Evans, "Oregon Progressive Reform," 269–71.
65. See Evans, "Oregon Progressive Reform," 271–74.

cotting and picketing and severely restricting rights of assembly and free speech.[66]

When Oregon voters ratified the Initiative and Referendum Amendment in 1902, they underscored their faith in democratic political institutions and their belief that the will of the people should prevail. By an eleven-to-one popular majority they gave emphasis to the general feeling that government had become captive of the "special interests" and that voters were entitled to more direct control. With the passage of direct legislation, voters seemed primed to follow U'Ren's advice: "[T]he best work that now can be done for Direct Legislation is to make practical work of the system." When the legislature failed to respond to the popular demand for the passage of laws restraining corporate power and machine rule and for other laws affecting the public interest, voters in Oregon assumed those legislative functions themselves. In fact, they proved that once empowered, they hardly needed their state legislature to govern. Between 1902 and 1913 the Oregon electorate voted on 108 ballot measures brought to their attention by either the initiative or the referendum and approved 48, or 44 percent, of them. In enacting the Oregon System, and demonstrating the effectiveness of direct legislation, the citizens of Oregon had made a revolutionary political statement. In doing so, they went beyond South Dakota and placed themselves in the vanguard of progressivism.[67]

66. For a detailed analysis of the thirty-seven measures that appeared on the 1912 Oregon ballot, see G. H. Haynes, "'People's Rule' on Trial," 18–33; Woodward, "U'Ren and the Single Tax," 56–59; Gilbert, "Single-Tax Movement," 36–47; and A. N. Young, *Single Tax in the United States*, 174–80. Single taxers placed two more measures on the 1914 ballot. Both were defeated by votes of more than two to one. See A. N. Young, *Single Tax in the United States*, 180–81.

67. U'Ren quoted in *Direct Legislation Record* 8 (December 1901): 60. Roughly a dozen measures formed the core of the "Oregon System." In addition to the initiative and referendum (1902), other laws that extended the bounds of popular democracy included the direct primary (1904), home rule for cities and towns (1906), an anti–free pass law (1906), the extension of the initiative and referendum to local governments (1906), the recall (1908), the popular election of U.S. senators (1908), a corrupt-practices act (1908), the presidential preference primary (1910), and woman suffrage (1912). See Richard W. Montague, "The Oregon System at Work," *National Municipal Review* 3 (April 1914): 256–83, for a summary of all ballot measures officially submitted between 1902 and 1913. See also *Equity* 15 (January 1913): 36–37; and 16 (April 1914): 73–75.

3

Montana and Oklahoma

MONTANA

Like the Great Plains and the Pacific Northwest, popular interest in direct legislation was widespread in the Intermountain West during the Populist and Progressive Eras. Of the eight states in the region (Arizona, Colorado, Idaho, Montana, Nevada, New Mexico, Utah, and Wyoming), only the voters in Wyoming failed to ratify constitutional provisions allowing for the initiative or referendum or both in some form. Of those eight states, though, only three—Montana (1906), Arizona (1910), and Colorado (1910)—actively utilized those forms of majority rule.[1]

1. Wyoming's voters actually approved an initiative and referendum amendment in 1912 by a six-to-one margin, but it did not gain a supermajority of all those casting ballots at the election as required by state law.

Utah became the second state to adopt the initiative and referendum when voters approved a constitutional amendment on November 6, 1900, by a vote of 19,219 to 7,786. Sherman S. Smith, the lone Populist in the state legislature, is credited with pushing the measure through the legislature in 1899. However, the amendment as passed failed to set the number of petitioners, leaving that important fact to the state legislature at a future date. No action was taken for seventeen years. Finally, in 1917, the Popular Government League of Utah convinced the legislature to enable the original law. In doing so, however, the legislature added encumbrances. Petition percentages (10 percent for the direct initiative and referendum) had to be reached in a majority of the counties in the state, and all signatures had to be signed in an office and in the presence of an officer competent to administer oaths. These two conditions rendered the law all but inoperative. See *Direct Legislation Record* 6 (June 1899): 29; 6 (December 1899): 95–96; 7 (December 1900): 57, 69; 10 (June 1903): 29; *Equity* 14 (April 1912): 95; 19 (January 1917): 40–41; and 19 (April 1917): 94–96.

The Nevada legislature passed a constitutional amendment providing for the referendum (10 percent) on March 19, 1901. The legislature approved the amendment for a second time (Nevada law required constitutional amendments to pass two consecutive sessions of the legislature) on March 6, 1903, and voters ratified it on November 8, 1904, by a vote of 4,404 to 794. However, legislators made use of the referendum difficult by requiring a majority of those voting in the election to revoke a law. Voters invoked the referendum in 1909 to challenge the State Police Bill that organized labor regarded as a strikebreaking militia measure, but the law was sustained in a close vote. An amend-

The first state in the region and the third state overall to adopt the initiative and referendum was Montana. The Treasure State underwent a pe-

---

ment allowing for the indirect initiative (10 percent) on statutes and the direct initiative on constitutional amendments passed the legislature in 1909 and again in 1911. Voters ratified the amendment in November 1912 by a vote of 9,956 to 1,027. They used the statutory initiative for the first time to pass a prohibition law in 1918. See *Direct Legislation Record* 9 (March 1902): 1; 9 (June 1902): 33; *Equity* 11 (January 1909): 18; 11 (July 1909): 91; 13 (April 1911): 78; 14 (April 1912): 98; 15 (January 1913): 39; and Eltweed Pomeroy, "The Nevada Referendum Victory as an Illustration of Democratic Progress," *Arena* 33 (March 1905): 268.

The attempt to establish the initiative and referendum in Idaho proved even more frustrating than in Utah. The Idaho legislature passed an amendment for the statutory initiative and referendum in 1911, but once again left it to a future legislature to determine petition requirements. When voters were asked to record their votes on each reform separately in November 1912, they approved the initiative by a vote of 38,918 to 15,195 and the referendum by a vote of 43,658 to 13,490. In the process of enabling the law in 1915, the Idaho legislature loaded it with numerous restrictions. Statewide initiative petitions had to be signed by 15 percent of the voters in every county of the state, and statewide referenda had to meet a 10 percent requirement, also in every county in the state. All petitions had to be signed (as in Utah) in the office of a law officer. In addition, a favorable decision at the polls required a majority of those voting in the election rather than just those voting on the proposal. Governor Moses Alexander vetoed the enabling act on the grounds that it was unreasonable and left the state without a workable statute. See *Equity* 14 (July 1912): 97; 15 (July 1913): 185; and 17 (April 1915): 114–15.

Voters in New Mexico adopted the referendum (no initiative) when they ratified their original state constitution on January 21, 1911. The Populists started the discussion of direct legislation in New Mexico in 1894 by proposing that a popular referendum be adopted for all laws passed by the territorial legislature. They added both the initiative and the referendum to their platform in 1896, but received no support from either the Democrats or the Republicans. Almost fifteen years later, as the movement for statehood intensified, the topic again came up for serious consideration. In the campaign preceding the election of one hundred delegates to the constitutional convention in 1910, one in which neither the Republican nor the Democratic Party platform had made a definite pledge regarding the initiative and referendum, those questions quickly became the ones that voters wanted to talk about. It was soon apparent that delegate selection and ultimately partisan political advantage depended upon publicly supporting those reforms, and a majority of those elected to the convention (including all twenty-eight Democrats) did so. When the delegates met in October 1910, though, the Republicans, with their seventy-one-member majority, dominated the convention and wrote a conservative constitution that rejected most progressive ideas. Included among that list were a number of direct legislation proposals sponsored by the more liberal Democratic minority. Unable to save the initiative in any form, Democrats settled for a weak referendum provision designed by the conservative Republican majority as better than no provision at all. Petitions had to be signed by not less than 10 percent of the qualified electors in three-fourths of the counties and, in the aggregate, by not less than 10 percent of the qualified electors as determined by the total number of votes cast for governor in the preceding general election. Approval required only a majority of those voting on the measure, but that figure could not be less than 40 percent of the total number of votes cast in the election. Voters used the referendum only once (1912) prior to 1920, and that was to sustain a state highway bond issue. See Robert W. Larson, *New Mexico Populism: A Study of Radical Protest in a Western Territory*, 92, 133–34; Robert W.

riod of rapid economic development during the 1880s. The arrival of the first railroads during that decade opened the way for mining pursuits in the mountainous western part of the state and large open-range cattle ranching across the flat eastern prairie. Soon mining magnates and cattle barons (with mining interests in command) came to dominate state affairs. By the late 1880s Montanans routinely talked of rule by the "Big Four": Butte copper kings Marcus Daly and William A. Clark and Helena capitalists C. A. Broadwater and Samuel T. Hauser. A colorful part of the rising influence of corporate interests in Montana politics was the titanic feud waged between Daly and Clark from 1888 to 1900 for political and economic dominance. Both men bought newspapers and used them to advance their personal interests, and both men spent freely to manipulate state legislators. Histories of the state reveal that Clark most certainly bribed members of the 1893 legislature in his unsuccessful bid to become U.S. senator, whereas his wholesale bribery of the 1899 assembly to gain election to the Senate led to his forced resignation from that body in 1901 following exposure of his actions. In investigating Clark's right to his seat, the Senate Committee on Privileges and Elections noted that Clark's actions were not unique and that "prior to 1895 elections in Montana were accompanied by enormous expenditures of money, unquestionably involving widespread belief that extensive corruption was resorted to in all elections."[2]

The first real challenge to the political status quo in Montana occurred in the early to mid-1890s with the rise of the Populist Party. Dominated by workers rather than farmers (as was the case throughout the mountain states), Montana Populists advanced a political program that centered on the eight-hour day, the free coinage of silver, and the initiative and referendum. As the popularity of the free silver issue intensified in the mining states of the West, Montana's Populist newspapers stepped up their editorial support for the white metal but also for direct legislation as a means of obtaining it. In a novel interpretation of what might be accomplished via the initiative, the *Butte Bystander* argued in 1896 that if enough states adopted that reform and endorsed free silver, they might force the federal government to embrace bimetallism. Fusionist governor-elect Robert B. Smith

---

Larson, "Populism in the Mountain West: A Mainstream Movement," 161; Robert W. Larson, "Statehood for New Mexico, 1888–1912," 193–95; Edward D. Tittmann, "New Mexico Constitutional Convention: Recollections," 181–82; Thomas J. Mabry, "New Mexico's Constitution in the Making: Reminiscences of 1910," 170–72, 174, 177, 179–80; Roy C. Stumph, "The History of the Referendum in New Mexico," 27–50; *Equity* 14 (July 1912): 96; and 15 (January 1913): 45.

2. Merrill G. Burlingame and K. Ross Toole, *A History of Montana,* 201 (see also 191–215). See also Michael P. Malone and Dianne G. Dougherty, "Montana's Political Culture: A Century of Evolution," 46–47.

added weight to the Populist position when he urged the adoption of the initiative and referendum in his state-of-the-state message in January 1897. However, the Democratic majority, allegedly controlled by Marcus Daly and the railroad lobby, in the legislature that same year rejected Governor Smith's recommendation. In describing the legislative situation in the state at that time, newspaperman William Eggleston called it a political "rotten borough." "The people had but little more voice in making the laws under which they had to live than in making laws for Yucatán or Nova Scotia. As compared with what the people got or could get in the way of beneficial legislation, the crumbs gathered by Lazarus were a banquet."[3]

A group of resident intellectuals helped to popularize the initiative and referendum during the Populist period. Will Kennedy, who had migrated to Montana from Maryland in 1881, advocated the ideas throughout the 1890s as editor of the reform-oriented *Boulder Age*. As a representative of the territorial council during the late 1880s, Kennedy introduced the bill to establish the Australian ballot that won council approval in 1889. A convert to Henry George's single-tax theory, like many other direct legislationists, Kennedy ran as a single-tax candidate for the state senate in 1890, organized the Montana Single Tax Association in 1892, and ran as the Populist gubernatorial candidate that same year. Another proponent of direct legislation was transplanted journalist William Greene Eggleston, who had advocated the initiative and referendum in Illinois before moving to Montana to become editor of the *Helena Independent* in 1896. Eggleston acknowledged that discussion of direct legislation had begun prior to his arrival in the state and credited Kennedy, Livingston lawyer E. C. Day, and Judge Theodore Brantly with having generated popular interest.[4]

Montana's labor leaders joined the Populists and the intellectuals in their support for direct legislation. Proclaiming a nonpartisan political stance, the State Trades and Labor Council (STLC) issued a list of labor's priorities at its organizing convention in November 1895. The list included the free coinage of silver, the eight-hour day, government ownership of the railroads and telephone and telegraph lines, and the initiative and referendum. The council organized a committee to lobby for passage of a direct legislation measure in every legislative session between 1897 and 1905. At its annual meeting in 1901 the STLC adopted a resolution that underscored the growing importance of those reforms: "Realizing that if we would gain our

3. *Equity* 15 (January 1913): 47. See also Thomas A. Clinch, *Urban Populism and Free Silver in Montana: A Narrative of Ideology in Political Action*, 113, 128, 154; Larson, "Populism in the Mountain West," 156–57; and Richard B. Roeder, "Montana Progressivism: Sound and Fury and One Small Tax Reform," 21.

4. See Clinch, *Urban Populism*, 53, 83; Roeder, "Montana Progressivism," 21; and *Equity* 15 (January 1913): 47.

industrial freedom we must use our political liberties and that there is only one great avenue through which this can be done, therefore, be it [r]esolved, that we again express our unqualified devotion to the great principle of political emancipation known as the Initiative and Referendum or direct legislation."[5] Late the following year the organization issued a circular to each central and local union in the state requesting they create two special committees. One would call upon candidates for the legislature and request that they publicly pledge themselves to vote to submit a constitutional amendment for the initiative and referendum, and the other would circulate a petition to be signed by voters who would agree to vote only for candidates who had signed the pledge. Despite support from Governor Joseph K. Toole and the reading of from seven to fifteen labor petitions daily during the 1903 session of the legislature, the proposed direct legislation amendment failed to gain Senate approval, even though it passed in the House.[6]

Direct legislation received an added boost and a great deal of popular exposure between 1900 and 1903 as a result of the political battle waged between copper magnate F. Augustus Heinze and the Standard Oil Company for control of Montana's copper deposits. On April 27, 1899, the Standard Oil Company purchased the Anaconda Copper Company from legendary copper king Marcus Daly, who was in declining health, and formed the new Amalgamated Copper Company. To battle the new trust, two unscrupulous copper entrepreneurs, William A. Clark, Daly's old rival, and F. Augustus Heinze, the ambitious owner of Butte's Rarus copper mine, formed an alliance. Clark had money and desperately wanted to become U.S. senator, whereas Heinze had control of the judiciary and a desire to be supremely rich. The initial attack against the trust came from Heinze's loose interpretation of the federal mining law. The so-called apex law held that if a vein of ore apexed, or broke through, the surface on a claim, the owner of that claim had a right to follow the vein any distance underground as long as he remained within the fifteen hundred–foot length of his claim (there were no restrictions as to the lateral variation of the vein underground). Using the apex law as a pretext and his control of the judiciary as a shield, Heinze began to tunnel into Standard Oil (Amalgamated) properties and raid their copper deposits.

As cover for their inevitable legal battles with Amalgamated, Heinze and Clark mounted a political campaign as well. In June 1900 they announced

5. Roeder, "Montana Progressivism," 20.

6. Montana law required a two-thirds majority in each house for the approval of a constitutional amendment. See Clinch, *Urban Populism,* 123; *Direct Legislation Record* 6 (March 1899): 2–3; 9 (December 1902): 67; 10 (March 1903): 5–6; and Ralph Albertson, "Montana Constitution Amended," 199.

that workers in their mines and smelters would be granted the eight-hour day with no reductions in pay, a popular move that Amalgamated refused to follow. During the summer Heinze and Clark stumped the state and used their newly won popularity; attacks against Amalgamated's trust status and company-store practices through Heinze's newspaper, the *Butte Reveille;* and promises of needed labor legislation and the initiative and referendum to all but ensure their Fusionist ticket victory. It seemed so easy and so clever. As Heinze's biographer notes: "So masterfully had Heinze arrayed facts against Standard Oil, that his larceny of Amalgamated ores was forgiven in the belief that he was fighting a battle royal against a coterie of public enemies and judicial bribers, and was therefore justified in the use of any weapons. The public eye was focused on the young, daring, resourceful freebooter. They little cared how selfish his motives might be—his fight was their fight."[7] Heinze and Clark's Fusionist slate won the November election (including three Butte judgeships), and the next legislature, in 1901, passed measures providing for the eight-hour day and making it illegal to pay miners wages in anything but money (no scrip). During that same legislative session, Fred L. Sanden, state representative from Helena, introduced an amendment calling for the initiative and referendum. The bill gained the necessary two-thirds majority in the House by a vote of fifty-one to eight, but fell four votes shy in the Senate. Sanden assigned primary blame for the measure's narrow defeat on the failure of the state's newspapers (many of which had been purchased from a $1.5 million Amalgamated "war chest" during the election campaign of 1900) to print any coverage of the pending legislation.[8]

By October 1903, Heinze's bond with the miners had become so strong, the losses suffered by Amalgamated due to Heinze's apex tactics so great, and Heinze's ability to use the courts to his advantage so frustrating that the directors of Amalgamated felt compelled to take forceful action. On October 22, 1903, the company announced the complete shutdown of its mine and smelter operations in Montana. The abrupt announcement threw approximately twenty thousand wage earners out of work. Amalgamated justified its decision as being necessitated by the actions of Heinze and the corrupt court system he controlled. With the state in the grip of economic paralysis and workers facing severe economic hardship, Heinze's popular support began to erode. Amalgamated made it clear that it would break the impasse if the governor called a special session of the legislature to enact a

7. Sarah McNelis, *Copper King at War: The Biography of F. Augustus Heinze,* 96.

8. After having secured his seat in the United States Senate, Clark ended his alliance with Heinze and joined the Amalgamated camp. See Burlingame and Toole, *A History of Montana,* 206–12; McNelis, *Copper King,* 94–97; and *Direct Legislation Record* 8 (June 1901): 20–21.

"fair trials" bill. Such a measure would allow a change of venue if either party in a civil suit found the presiding judge to be corrupt or prejudiced. Seeing no alternative, Governor Toole called the special session, and the legislature passed the bill.

In one final attempt to stop Amalgamated, a mass convention attended by 650 delegates from every county in the state assembled in Helena as the legislature met. The purpose of the meeting (almost certainly organized and directed by Heinze) was to protest the surrendering of the state to the trust and to form a new Anti-trust Party. The principles upon which the new party would be based included revision of the mine taxation laws, creation of a railroad and public service commission, an employer-liability law, and the initiative and referendum. The convention, however, failed to influence the legislature, and the Anti-trust Party never got off the ground. Three days after the Anti-trust convention issued its platform, the special session passed the Fair Trials Bill. The Anti-trust delegates went home, the miners went back to work, and Heinze contemplated defeat. He remained in the state for a few years, but in 1906 sold his interests to Amalgamated for an estimated $10–$12 million, settled some eighty lawsuits still pending, and moved to New York City.[9]

Lost sight of in the Heinze-Amalgamated feud was the importance the encounter had for the future of reform issues such as direct legislation. Heinze was undoubtedly a rascal, a privateer, and a demagogue who pandered to popular antitrust prejudice for his own ends. Nonetheless, in manipulating the working class to vote in his favor, he had to trumpet the issues they deemed most important: the eight-hour day, elimination of the company store–scrip system, and the initiative and referendum. The hastily formed Anti-trust Party was merely a last-ditch attempt to expand that list to include tax reform, the regulation of railroads, and employer liability.

Confronted with the prospect of an angry electorate during the 1904 elections, the state's politicians decided that it no longer made sense to resist the demand for direct legislation. Governor Toole, who had endorsed the initiative and referendum in a strong message to the legislature in 1903, again took up the cause. With the assistance of the state's major political leaders and the endorsements of the initiative and referendum by both the Democratic and the Republican State Conventions, the next legislature, convened in 1905, approved a constitutional amendment that voters would have an opportunity to ratify at the next general election. The Montana amendment followed the Oregon model: the initiative was based on 8 percent of the total vote for governor in the previous election, and the refer-

9. See Burlingame and Toole, *A History of Montana*, 212–15; and K. Ross Toole, *Twentieth-Century Montana: A State of Extremes*, 99–122.

endum based on 5 percent of the same. However, the Montana law was restricted in two ways. Voters were not allowed to initiate constitutional amendments, and statutory initiatives and referenda had to gain the required percentage of signatures in at least two-fifths of the counties.[10]

The campaign to rally the electorate behind ratification of the direct legislation amendment was one in which proponents seemed to dominate the field. Every political party—Democrat, Republican, Labor, Socialist, and Populist—endorsed the reforms. So, too, did the newly formed Citizen's Independent League. Organized by the citizens of Missoula, the league favored the initiative and referendum as the means by which public control over the power of corporations could be established and the impact of special interests on Montana politics limited. The State Federation of Labor played an active role in the campaign as well. The 1906 state convention instructed its officials to work for direct legislation. To that end, they disseminated fifty thousand circulars in support of the amendment. Further assistance came from the small but vocal Direct Legislation League with less than one thousand dollars to spend on publicity. Apparently, only two newspapers openly opposed the amendment. The *Meagher Republican* of White Sulphur Springs rejected the amendment as "class legislation" advanced by Socialists and trade unionists, whereas the *Helena Montana News*, the state's socialist newspaper, contended that the amendment had been emasculated by "tinhorn lawyers" who excluded appropriation bills and constitutional amendments from its operation. Most of the state's newspapers, however, assisted the overall effort, and many made reference to Oregon's successful experience with the initiative and referendum. In urging voters to follow Oregon's example, the *Helena Montana Daily Record* assured them that the reforms offered "the simple remedy for the evils that have, in one form or another, beset the state for many years."[11]

Voters overwhelmingly approved the amendment, adding the initiative and referendum to their state constitution on November 6, 1906, by a vote of 36,374 to 6,616. At least one individual was quick to claim credit for the result as a labor victory. At the August 1907 meeting of the State Federation of Labor, state president Alexander Fairgrieve assigned almost total credit for the victory to the workers of Montana and accused politicians of having joined the cause only to protect their political careers. In his report to the convention, Fairgrieve asserted that the amendment "will be the means

10. For an excerpt from Governor Toole's 1903 speech to the legislature, see *Equity* 11 (April 1909): 46–47. See also Albertson, "Montana Constitution Amended," 199; and *Equity* 14 (July 1912): 95.

11. Richard B. Roeder, "Montana in the Early Years of the Progressive Period," 178. For a rather complete account of the campaign, see 127–79; and *Equity* 15 (January 1913): 49.

of abolishing the corrupt lobby by making it useless for corporate interests to use money or other considerations to influence legislators in passing laws giving them special privileges."[12]

In addition to passage of the initiative and referendum amendment, the progressive political platforms of the various political parties suggested that Montana was on the verge of entering the Progressive reform era. This was exactly the theme struck by William Jennings Bryan when he made a special address to the legislature on January 11, 1907. After reminding Montana's elected representatives that their role was to carry out the wishes of the voters and that party platforms should be binding, the Great Commoner acknowledged that legislatures were under tremendous pressure from special interests. "Why," asked Bryan, "is there a demand for the initiative and referendum? Because the people have found that there is more virtue in the citizen than there is in his representative . . . because the legislature is subjected to a temptation that does not come to the citizen."[13]

The 1907 legislature responded to the challenge by enacting a list of reforms that included the establishment of a railroad commission, an anti-gambling law, a stricter child labor law, pure-food legislation, and limitations on the hours of continuous employment worked by railroad workers. However, when the legislature failed to enact legislation for the direct election of U.S. senators, an anti-injunction law that would legalize all forms of peaceful striking, and an employer-liability law, supporters of those measures undertook petition drives to initiate those laws. In each instance, however, they failed to meet the petition requirement necessary to get their propositions on the ballot.[14]

In 1912, however, "by dint of tremendous effort and at great expense," the newly formed People's Power League of Montana succeeded in getting enough signatures to qualify four initiative measures for the November ballot. Organized in June 1911 by a group of delegates that included lawyer-politician Thomas J. Walsh, Judge E. K. Cheadle, journalists Miles Romney and W. K. Harber, and labor leaders M. M. Donoghue of the State Federation of Labor and Henry Drennan of the United Mine Workers of America (UMWA), the group proclaimed that its sole purpose was to use the initiative and referendum to obtain "beneficial" legislation. The four initiative propositions sponsored by the league included a direct primary law, a corrupt-practices act, a presidential preference primary, and the di-

12. The vote on the amendment is recorded in Albertson, "Montana Constitution Amended," 199. Fairgrieve's comments are noted in Roeder, "Montana in the Early Years," 176.

13. Roeder, "Montana in the Early Years," 182–83.

14. The 1910 ballot was free of voter-initiated proposals as well. See ibid., 191–222; *Equity* 10 (July 1908): 72–73; and 14 (October 1912): 145.

rect election of U.S. senators. Voters also had to consider a referendum, circulated by the State Federation of Labor, on a law passed by the legislature in 1911 that gave the governor increased power to call out the state militia. Organized labor had argued that the law had been pushed by the corporations so that the militia could be used to crush strikes. Voters approved each of the four initiatives by wide margins and vetoed the legislature's militia bill as well.[15]

The People's Power League continued to press for reform measures after the victories of 1912 and gained support from the new Direct Legislation League of Montana. Organized in March 1913, the new league reflected the changing political climate and included members of the People's Power League and a large number of Bull Moose Republicans. The league worked to raise taxes on mining and other corporations, and pushed two proposals—a workmen's compensation law and a measure that would enable the state to invest money from the common school fund to make mortgage loans to farmers—aimed at broadening the organized reform base in Montana. The progressive-farmer-labor alliance, however, never materialized. Voters, apparently driven more by individual than by common interests, approved an initiative for farm loans in 1914, but rejected a workmen's compensation initiative that same year. Montana voters did, however, approve legislative amendments granting woman suffrage in 1914 and prohibiting the sale of alcoholic beverages in 1916. After a slow beginning, Montanans had become active direct legislationists.[16]

OKLAHOMA

Plagued with economic hardship and burdened by an indifferent and oligarchic territorial government during the late nineteenth and early twentieth centuries, Oklahomans became increasingly critical of an economic and political system over which they had little control. It was not long before various political groups (Populists, Socialists, and Democrats) and organizations (the Farmers' Union and the Twin Territorial Federation of Labor) began to formulate economic and political alternatives that eventually formed the basis of a new progressive reform ideology. Part of that new ideology included expanding the scope of popular democracy by means of the

15. After the election, M. McCusker, secretary of the People's Power League, confided that of the 5,454 signatures required for a ballot initiative, the final 2,050 names had to be secured by paid solicitors at a cost of $165. See *Equity* 14 (October 1912): 145–46; 16 (April 1914): 83; and Michael P. Malone, Richard B. Roeder, and William L. Lang, *Montana: A History of Two Centuries*, 259–60.

16. See Malone, Roeder, and Lang, *Montana*, 260–65.

initiative and referendum. However, unlike other states where advocates sought to establish direct legislation in separate campaigns, in Oklahoma the idea became linked to a larger program of economic and political reform that ultimately found expression as the constitution of the new state of Oklahoma.

As in other areas along the rapidly expanding western frontier, agriculture dominated the economic life of settlers in Indian Territory and Oklahoma Territory (the Twin Territories). Like farmers elsewhere who found themselves inescapably drawn into an ever widening market economy, they too faced a bewildering and frustrating set of economic problems. Lured west by government land acts, railroad promoters, accommodating lenders, and the promises of local boosters and developers, farmers rapidly expanded the amount of land under cultivation. As new technologies enabled them to increase productivity even further, and as marketing machinery favored the production of staple crops, they soon found themselves producing more of those crops than the market could absorb. The results were catastrophic. Between 1889 and 1897 cotton prices fell by 30 percent, wheat prices by 15 percent, and corn prices by 17 percent. Farmers quickly found themselves trapped in a vicious cycle. Using available mortgage money in a futile attempt to expand productivity and recoup economic fortunes served only to generate larger crops that commanded even lower prices. For many, the result was burdensome debt. As territorial farmers continued to clear land, build homes, purchase stock, and acquire tools and machinery, the demand for credit intensified. Federal banks refused to accept land as security for loans, and territorial banks proved woefully inadequate to meet credit demands. Tight credit remained a problem throughout the depressed 1890s and left farmers on the horns of a dilemma. Lack of credit reduced their chances of competing in the market economy, whereas money at exorbitant interest rates further increased their burden of debt. Hard-pressed, farmers easily concluded that railroads, through their high freight charges and discriminatory short-haul rates, victimized them as well.

As the problems of farmers continued to capture the attention of most residents of the Twin Territories, workers, especially those engaged in coal mining operations, also struggled with the forces of a modernizing industrial economy. Working and living in isolated mining communities totally controlled by a single employer, miners found life hard. Workers and their families lived in cramped wooden shacks, built by the companies at a cost of $50 each and rented at a cost of $2 a month. Charges for housing, tools, and medical care were deducted from the workers' pay. Wages were low (about $2.50 a day) and the working season abbreviated (less than two hundred days a year). Pay was usually given in scrip, redeemable only at the company-owned store where prices were usually 20 percent higher than in competitive environments. As the cost of living increased markedly in the late 1890s, wages remained stagnant. The miner, like the farmer, found himself losing ground. The hazardous nature of the work made the exploitative nature of life in the mining camps even more precarious. On average, thirteen miners were killed for every one million tons of coal mined in Indian Territory in the 1890s. In the region's worst disaster, ninety-six men died in an explosion in January 1892 at the Kreb's mine owned by the Osage Coal and Mining Company. Inadequate mine inspection served only to compound the dangers.[17]

Tired of being victimized by impersonal market forces, farmers and workers soon concluded that collective action and organization provided the only means to their empowerment. During the early 1890s, many territorial farmers joined the Farmers' Alliance and hoped to gain independence from the controlling features of the market economy through alliance-sponsored cooperatives. In their search for cures to their economic dilemma, local alliance men embraced the platform of the National Farmers' Alliance and Industrial Union. Commonly known as the Ocala Demands, the program called for, among other things, currency inflation, federal regulation or ownership of railroads, and the subtreasury idea. The latter scheme proposed that the federal government build agricultural storage facilities in the farm region and then loan farmers money against the value of their stored crops. The program would, in theory, allow farmers to choose when to market their products (avoiding the perils of a glutted market) and provide them with working capital (avoiding the interest-related exactions of lenders).

The failure of either of the dominant political parties to embrace the subtreasury idea, or any of the other alliance demands, forced many territorial farmers to consider a national third-party alternative and, finally, membership in the Populist Party. The Omaha Platform of 1892 focused on economic reforms similar to those called for in the Ocala Demands, but added a number of resolutions political in nature. Included in the list were calls for the Australian (secret) ballot, the direct election of senators, term limits for president and vice president, and the favorable consideration of the "legislative system known as the initiative and referendum."[18]

17. See Danney Goble, *Progressive Oklahoma: The Making of a New Kind of State*, 146–49, 153–58.

18. See ibid., 158–60; H. L. Meredith, "The 'Middle Way': The Farmers' Alliance in Indian Territory, 1889–1896," 377–86; and John D. Hicks, *The Populist Revolt: A History of the Farmers' Alliance and the People's Party*, 439–44. As late as 1898 middle-of-the-road Populists in Logan County, Oklahoma, were still demanding the initiative, referendum, and imperative mandate (recall) "for the preservation of republican government to the end that boodlers be headed off from thwarting the will of the people" (*Guthrie Oklahoma State Capital*, August 28, 1898).

The defeat of the Populists failed to deter farmers from seeking collective action, this time in a new organization called the Farmers' Educational and Cooperative Union. Organized at Point, Texas, in 1902, the Farmers' Union, as it was commonly known, entered the Twin Territories the following year. Established to assist farmers in selling and purchasing, promote scientific farming techniques, and "systematize methods of production and distribution," the Farmers' Union again centered itself on the farm cooperative. This time, however, instead of shunning the market system, the new cooperatives embraced it. "Cooperatives" in name only, the new associations quickly fell under the control of wealthy stockholders who just as quickly turned them into privately owned, market-friendly business enterprises. After locals in both territories reorganized as a single, independent body—the Farmers' Educational and Cooperative Union of Indiahoma—in 1905, the power in the organization rested with commercially oriented farmers. With its new orientation, the Farmers' Union looked to establish connections with ambitious farmer-politicians and find common ground with local bankers and merchants who had previously been regarded as adversaries. With talk of statehood in the air, the Farmers' Union, which could boast of having nearly 29,000 members by early 1906, looked to have a say in the organization of the new state as an influential interest group.[19]

Workers also sought to improve their economic condition through collective action and organization. The Knights of Labor had enjoyed some success in organizing workers in the Oklahoma coalfields in the early 1890s, but the organization had already entered upon a period of decline. A more successful effort began in 1898 when the United Mine Workers of America expanded its organizing efforts into the coalfields of Indian Territory. The appearance of the UMWA sparked strikes, walkouts, and labor unrest in the region that continued until 1903. Finally, in August of that year, mine owners, represented by the Southwestern Coal Operators' Association, and the UMWA struck an agreement. In return for labor peace and uninterrupted productivity, the association agreed to accept a list of union demands. Concessions included an eight-hour day, biweekly pay periods, a checkoff system for the payment of union dues, creation of "pit committees" at each mine to settle grievances, and a substantial pay increase. With further union promises to discipline "wildcat" strikers, the association agreed to additional pay raises in 1904 and 1906. Like the Farmers' Union, the UMWA, an affiliate of the American Federation of Labor (AFL), had chosen to seek accommodation with its former adversaries and a mutually beneficial relationship in the modernizing industrial economy.

Although the UMWA remained the largest union in the Twin Territories,

---

19. See Goble, *Progressive Oklahoma,* 160–64; and H. L. Meredith, "The Agrarian Reform Press in Oklahoma, 1889–1922," 89.

with 7,280 members by 1907, there were also some 14,000 additional union-ized workers concentrated in various railroad brotherhoods and in the building trades. Sharing the conservative labor perspective that character-ized the AFL, leaders of the labor movement in the Twin Territories real-ized that labor's voice might be better heard if the various unions consoli-dated into one large labor coalition. With that goal in mind, J. Harvey Lynch, a plasterer and secretary of the Labor Organization Committee in Lawton, issued a call for an organizational meeting in December 1903. The three-day conference that began on December 28 included representatives from fifteen UMWA locals and twelve carpenters' assemblies, as well as delegates from other unions. The result was the formation of the Twin Ter-ritorial Federation of Labor (TTFL). The preamble to the constitution of the TTFL stated that the intent of the new order was to protect its members from "unjust and injurious competition . . . claiming, as we do, that labor is capital."[20] Representatives elected Peter Hanraty, a UMWA leader and strike organizer, as president and Lynch as secretary-treasurer, and en-dorsed a proposal for immediate statehood. The AFL granted the new or-ganization a charter in February 1904. Much like the Farmers' Union, the TTFL stood poised as a powerful interest group looking to assert its influ-ence on the political process as talk of statehood intensified.[21]

Also looking to have an impact on the economic and political develop-ment of Oklahoma was the Socialist Party, which came to the territory in 1899 and ran its first list of candidates the following year. Interestingly, Oklahoma Socialist Oscar Ameringer noted that "nearly all of the local [Socialist] agitators and speakers were ex-middle-of-the-road Populists." Hoping to build a solid grassroots organization in the territory, something neither major party had been willing (Republicans) or able (Democrats) to do, the Socialists immediately proposed a platform that stood in stark con-trast to the vaguely worded appeals of the major parties. Between 1900 and 1906, the Socialists' reform program consistently included calls for woman suffrage, tax reform, an eight-hour day on public works, limited state en-terprise, compulsory education, child labor legislation, and the initiative, referendum, and recall. Although the party's voting strength remained weak for the remainder of the territorial period, the party set the tone of the political debate. The Farmers' Union, the Twin Territorial Federation of La-bor, and the Democratic Party would all be forced to respond to the So-cialists' political challenge.[22]

20. *Proceedings of the Oklahoma State Federation of Labor, 1903–1923*, Oklahoma State Federation of Labor Collection, Western History Manuscripts, University of Oklahoma, Norman.

21. See Goble, *Progressive Oklahoma*, 146, 149–53; and Keith L. Bryant Jr., "Labor in Politics: The Oklahoma State Federation of Labor during the Age of Reform," 260–61.

22. The Oklahoma Constitution of 1907 would include most of the Socialist platform.

Oklahoma Socialists were merely the vanguard of an emerging national reform debate that increasingly focused on the power of corporations to control aspects of American life. Oklahomans were familiar with the rise in the number of "trusts" and, like consumers in other states, associated general price increases with the manipulations of corporate monopolies. When grand jury probes in Ada and Muskogee in 1906 revealed that 30 percent increases in prices on lumber and cement followed the formation of the Southwestern Lumber Manufacturers' Association, Oklahoma consumers received a quick lesson in trust economics. Just as alarming to Oklahoma consumers were reports that suggested that large corporations had little regard for the public's health or safety. When news items in the *Norman Transcript* in January 1907 reported that 90 percent of Muskogee's population was daily being poisoned by adulterated milk that contained bacteria-infested water, chalk, saltpeter, boric acid, and other dangerous ingredients and that commercial butter was found to have been treated with embalming fluid as a preservative, everyone felt threatened. The report of the newly established Oklahoma Pure Food and Drug Commission in 1908 only confirmed what many had thought: that "the two territories [had been used] as a dumping ground for foodstuffs that were not tolerated in the sister states." When Oklahomans read the news in September 1906 that a poorly constructed wooden bridge across the Cimarron River near Dover had collapsed under the weight of a full passenger train and that more than one hundred people had been killed, they learned that corporate arrogance on the part of the Rock Island Railroad could be just as deadly.[23]

Oklahoma's taxpayers felt the influence of corporate power as well. Dependent upon the levy of property taxes for public revenues, Oklahomans discovered that a sizable portion of taxable property in the state was either inadequately taxed or not taxed at all. The most glaring inequity involved railroad property that was commonly taxed at rates well below those in surrounding states. In Kiowa County railroads were taxed at less than 4 percent of their value, whereas other property was assessed at an average rate of 40 percent. Evidence of corporate tax dodging suggested that corporations had used their political influence to "bargain" for special concessions.[24]

To many Oklahomans it would take a variety of reforms—new methods of corporate regulation, remodeled tax codes, and, possibly, limited state-owned enterprises—to check corporate price fixing, restrain corporate arrogance, curb corporate tax dodging, and prevent corporate manipulation of the political process. However, one reform that promised perhaps the

See Goble, *Progressive Oklahoma*, 112–14; Oscar Ameringer, *If You Don't Weaken: The Autobiography of Oscar Ameringer*, 264; and *Oklahoma City Labor Signal*, September 27, 1906.

23. Goble, *Progressive Oklahoma*, 169 (see also 165–70).

24. See ibid., 171–74.

greatest reward, and one that farmers, workers, consumers, taxpayers, and citizens could all support, was the initiative and referendum. As Peter Hanraty of the TTFL put it:

> [W]hy should we vote for rulers when we ourselves can become the sovereign power through the initiative and referendum. It will simpilfy [sic] laws . . . simplify goverment [sic] . . . kill monopoly . . . purify the ballot . . . broaden manhood . . . make people think . . . abolish special privileges . . . wipe out plutocratic dictation . . . reduce taxation . . . prevent the bribery of law makers . . . establish home rule in all municipalities . . . [and] restore to the people their natural rights.[25]

The earliest active proponent of the initiative and referendum in Oklahoma was reportedly S. C. Whitman of Guthrie, who managed to get a bill introduced in the territorial legislature in 1890. Whitman later recounted his early efforts: "The country was new, and we had but a very few people who had ever heard of such a thing. My bill never got out of committee and hence created little interest. . . . Two years ago [1893] I was unable to find a member who would introduce and champion it. This last winter [1895] I again got it introduced by request." According to Whitman, the bill passed the House only to be defeated in the Council. The measure apparently received the support of all four Populists, but one Democrat and eight Republicans voted against it. Whitman claimed that he designed his bill to aid his own efforts when trying to lobby a good measure through the legislature or when attempting to defeat a bad one.[26]

Realizing that unfamiliarity with the idea of direct legislation was his biggest handicap, Whitman tried to link his idea to the program of the Ancient Order of Loyal Americans (AOLA), organized in December 1893. Headquartered in Lansing, Michigan, and supported with its own newspaper, the *Loyal American*, the order favored "giving to every man a direct

25. Letter to the "Officers and Members of Local Unions Affiliated with the Twin Territorial Federation of Labor," October 26, 1905, Peter Hanraty Papers, Oklahoma Historical Society, Oklahoma City. A similar argument in support of the initiative and referendum made by Patrick S. Nagle—a radical agrarian Democrat prior to 1908 and then one of Oklahoma's leading socialists—can be found in the *Poteau Journal*, September 27, 1906.

26. Whitman's account varies from the official record. His original measure, which he actually remembered being introduced in 1891, was probably introduced in 1890 (the territorial legislature did not meet in 1891 and would not meet again until 1893). Populist E. H. Spencer did introduce an initiative and referendum bill (no. 110) in 1895, but the measure originated in the council. The recorded vote on the measure was actually four to eight to defeat it. See Oklahoma, *Journal of the Council, Proceedings of the Third Legislative Assembly of the Territory of Oklahoma, 1895*, and *Journal of the House, Proceedings of the Third Legislative Assembly of the Territory of Oklahoma, 1895*.

vote in local, state and national legislation through the Referendum, without the intervention of political parties." The key element in the order's program was the advisory referendum. Following the formation of a local body, or "brigade," a referendum could be called on any subject. Signatures both for and against a measure would be obtained from as many voters in the locality as possible, and the results of that vote would then be presented to the appropriate legislative body in hopes of legislative action. Whitman claimed to have organized nine county branches of the AOLA in Oklahoma during the summer of 1895, but there is no evidence that any further gains were made.[27]

Four years later, Theodore L. Sturgis of Perry, apparently unaware of Whitman's earlier efforts, called a meeting of friends and organized a direct legislation club, or league. The group drafted a statement of principles and sentiments, collected ten dollars for printing and distributing one thousand copies of that document, and then waited for a groundswell of interest to appear. In writing to the editorial office of the *Direct Legislation Record* soon afterward, Sturgis regretted that he had never heard of the national organization or he would have written asking for advice. In his letter to the *Record*, Sturgis noted that it was his optimistic impression that any future Oklahoma state constitution would include provisions for direct legislation, adding that "every one speaks in favor of it, except those in expectation of office through the dominant [Republican] party." One year later, however, Sturgis admitted that all his efforts had "fallen flat." "The prospects in this Territory are that the Republican Party will force through a bill for Statehood and Constitution without any tincture of D. L. in it—that being their particular abomination."[28]

When Congress passed the Curtis Act in 1898 and declared that all tribal governments in Indian Territory would terminate on March 4, 1906, it signaled that the static political environment in the Twin Territories would soon change. Indian Territory would have to either reorganize administratively in the manner of Oklahoma Territory or become a state (either as a separate entity or in partnership with its neighbor). However, two issues—control of Congress and Indian autonomy—complicated any discussion of statehood. Although both national political parties supported the idea of statehood for the Twin Territories in their platforms in 1900, they disagreed over details. Democrats, confident of popular majorities in the territories and eager to reap the political rewards that would result from four additional Democratic senators, favored the admission of two separate states.

27. AOLA quoted in *Direct Legislation Record* 2 (June 1895): 15. See also *Direct Legislation Record* 2 (June 1895): 13, 15; and 2 (December 1895): 29.
28. *Direct Legislation Record* 6 (June 1899): 25; 7 (December 1900): 67.

Not surprisingly, Republicans favored reducing the number of new states and supported proposals aimed at consolidating Indian and Oklahoma Territories into one state. Further complicating matters was the reluctance of the Indians (Choctaws, Creeks, Cherokees, Chickasaws, and Seminoles), already a numerical minority in their own tribally controlled territory, to accept consolidation and probably further subjugation in a new administrative arrangement dominated by whites.[29]

When President Theodore Roosevelt visited Indian Territory in April 1905 and publicly stated that he favored single statehood for the Twin Territories, he triggered a series of actions that ultimately determined the organization of the new state of Oklahoma. Aware of the upcoming deadline for tribal government and unwilling to passively accept the imposition of single statehood, James A. Norman, a Cherokee, issued a call for a constitutional convention in a last desperate effort to form a separate state for Indian Territory. The meeting, which was held in Muskogee from August 21 to September 8, 1905, included the leaders of the Five Civilized Tribes and delegates selected in local elections in each of the twenty-six recording districts in the territory. The list of delegates, composed primarily of ambitious individuals from Indian Territory looking to advance their own political careers, included Charles N. Haskell, William H. Murray, and Robert L. Owen, soon to become dominant figures in Oklahoma politics. Most delegates accepted the futility of the separate statehood idea, but realized that the publicity, the experience in constitution making, and the political associations formed in that process would prove valuable should a similar convention be called for single statehood. Charles N. Haskell, who would later become Oklahoma's first governor, actually secured a pledge from the leaders of the Five Civilized Tribes to support single statehood should their efforts at separation fail.

Despite the political ambitions of the assembled delegates, the convention gave them the opportunity to articulate specific remedies for the problems plaguing farmers, workers, consumers, and taxpayers. The product of their labors, a thirty-five thousand–word constitution for the proposed state of Sequoyah, outlined, in imperfect terms, the emerging reform agenda that would soon be adopted by the state's Democratic Party. Included in the proposed constitution were features that suggested that the delegates had not abandoned the old Farmers' Alliance–Populist critique of the political economy. Convinced that lawmakers had proved unresponsive to

29. See Keith L. Bryant Jr., *Alfalfa Bill Murray*, 36–37; and Norbert R. Mahnken, "William Jennings Bryan in Oklahoma," 259. For an extended discussion of the debate over statehood, see Charles Wayne Ellinger, "Congressional Viewpoint toward the Admission of Oklahoma as a State, 1902–1906"; and Charles Wayne Ellinger, "The Drive for Statehood in Oklahoma, 1889–1906."

popular demands or needs, that alien landowners and corporations had monopolized land, and that homesteaders had been overburdened with taxes, the designers of the new constitution included provisions for term limits, placed restrictions on landownership, and limited the amount of tax that could be levied on homesteads. Moreover, the drafters of the new constitution showed an awareness of current progressive reforms and expanded their program to include the creation of a state commission with broad powers to regulate corporations, placed restrictions on the sale of impure foods and harmful drugs, and incorporated provisions for agricultural education.[30]

The proposed constitution was not, however, without its "defects." Curiously missing from the document in light of past Populist demands and the current discussion of political reforms were the initiative, referendum, and recall. Although the ideas received a great deal of discussion by the convention, a narrow majority of the delegates successfully argued against their incorporation in the Sequoyah constitution. They feared that inclusion would "militate against immediate statehood." The framers also seemed to ignore entirely the concerns of organized labor. Peter Hanraty commented that he could not "see where the organized wage workers will be benefited by its adoption," and urged TTFL members to boycott the ratification election. There is some indication that many heeded Hanraty's advice. Although an overwhelming majority (47,206) of those who voted in the ratification election on November 7, 1905, favored the constitution, only half of those eligible to vote bothered to do so.[31]

The new state of Sequoyah, however, was not to be. Forced to decide between one state or two for the Twin Territories, the Republican-controlled Fifty-ninth Congress chose the former and passed the Enabling Act of 1906 that provided for the admission of Oklahoma and Indian Territories as a single state. President Roosevelt signed the measure on June 16, 1906. The act called for a new constitutional convention to be composed of 112 delegates (55 from each territory and 2 from the Osage Nation). The convention was to draw up a constitution that met presidential approval, hold a ratification election, and elect the first state officers. With guidelines for the convention in place, and with the date for the election of delegates to the constitutional convention set for November 1906, political parties and interest groups began to mobilize.[32]

30. See Bryant, *Alfalfa Bill Murray*, 37–43; and Goble, *Progressive Oklahoma*, 190–94.

31. C. M. Allen, *The "Sequoyah" Movement*, 44; letter to the "Officers and Members," October 26, 1905, Hanraty Papers, Oklahoma Historical Society. See also Bryant, *Alfalfa Bill Murray*, 42. For a detailed discussion of the separate statehood constitutional convention, see Amos D. Maxwell, *The Sequoyah Constitutional Convention*, 44–121.

32. See Bryant, *Alfalfa Bill Murray*, 47; and Goble, *Progressive Oklahoma*, 194.

In the campaign for the selection of delegates to write the Oklahoma Constitution, Republicans quickly found themselves handicapped by their record as the governing party for most of the territorial period. Territorial legislatures were, as one historian has described them, "usually little more than forums for political haymaking. Charges of waste and maladministration, rumors of bribery and corruption, and bickering over minor appointments comprised the agenda of a growing number of assemblies."[33] By 1906 voters in the Twin Territories had grown tired of Republican-appointed, patronage-driven governance. Labeled the party of corruption, extravagance, and incompetence by their Democratic opponents, and closely associated in the public's mind with policies that favored corporate interests, the GOP found itself with diminishing popular support. Led by federal appointees looking to win presidential favor, territorial Republicans arrogantly ignored local issues. Out of touch with farmers and workers, and out of step with the growing reform sentiment, Republican candidates for the constitutional convention found themselves running for "office" without a political platform.

Denied access to power and cut off from the rewards of federal patronage, territorial Democrats struggled to maintain a cohesive party organization. For most of the territorial period, the party seemed incapable of mounting much of an opposition beyond negative attacks and attempts to label Republican control as "bureaucratic" or "carpetbag" rule. However, as Oklahoma's farmers, workers, consumers, and taxpayers became more politicized, and as the Socialist-led discussion of a new reform ideology gained a public forum, territorial Democrats were forced to pay more attention to reform issues. With the end of Republican preferment at hand, Democrats decided to seize the opportunity and become the party of "positive" ideas.[34]

The formal pronouncement of that decision came on July 10, 1906, when the Democratic Party (which included many veterans of the Sequoyah movement) adopted a list of twenty-one "Suggestions for a Platform." The recommendations, much broader than those incorporated in the Sequoyah constitution, included calls for an eight-hour workday on all public works; a fellow servant law; state mine, factory, and railroad inspection; restrictions on the use of the court injunction against labor; the creation of a bureau of labor and a state board of arbitration; exemptions for farm organizations from antitrust laws; a tax exemption for homesteaders; and the creation of a bureau of agriculture. Seeking to curb the power of corporations, the party favored passage of laws prohibiting trusts, rebates, rate dis-

33. John R. Scales and Danney Goble, *Oklahoma Politics: A History*, 7.
34. See Bryant, *Alfalfa Bill Murray*, 45–48; and Goble, *Progressive Oklahoma*, 194–99.

crimination, and the granting of free railroad passes to public officials. Democrats also supported the creation of state commissions for the supervision of corporations and railroads, municipal ownership of all public utilities, and restrictions that would prevent coal lands from falling into the hands of private monopolies. Underscoring the importance of popular democracy in their reform program, the party also called for the popular election of all state officials, the direct primary and the direct election of U.S. senators, and the "plan of legislation known as the Initiative and Referendum" (item 6 in their list of suggestions).[35]

Realizing the possibilities that participation in the design of a new constitution presented, President Samuel Gompers of the AFL, President John Mitchell of the UMWA, and Peter Hanraty of the TTFL held a series of conferences that led to the calling of a labor convention to be held at Shawnee on August 20, 1906. Looking to broaden their organizational and political base, the TTFL invited the Farmers' Union and numerous railroad brotherhoods to send delegates as well. The 318 delegates in attendance created a joint legislative board and gave it instructions to formulate a program that reflected the wishes of the various groups in attendance. On September 10, the ten-member board, chaired by Hanraty, issued its report in the form of twenty-four demands. The "Shawnee Demands," as they were called, had much in common with the Democratic program, but refined and expanded some of the liberal reform ideas advanced by the Democrats.

Like the "Suggestions for a Platform," the Shawnee Demands advocated fundamental changes to the role of the government in the previously unrestrained market economy. Among the list of demands were new checks on the scope of corporate activity and protections for workers and farmers. Special commissions would regulate rates for all corporations, supervise agriculture and labor, and assess corporate properties for purposes of taxation. Railroads would be prohibited from owning coal land or from leasing any type of mine, and the legislature would be denied the power to grant an irrevocable franchise. As a further defense against corporate domination, and in language that must have sounded like state socialism to many boosters, the labor-farmer coalition demanded that the state be allowed to engage in any industry or enterprise. In addition, the Shawnee Demands proposed that workers receive compensation for injuries even if those injuries were caused by the negligence of a fellow worker and an eight-hour day in mines and on public works, the creation of the office of chief mine inspector, and prohibitions regarding child labor and the con-

35. The list of Democratic suggestions also included a statement favoring laws that provided for separate schools, coaches, and waiting rooms for blacks. For a list of the "Suggestions for a Platform," see Goble, *Progressive Oklahoma*, 230–33. See also Albert H. Ellis, *A History of the Constitutional Convention of the State of Oklahoma*, 41–45.

tracting of convict labor. Farmers would receive a liberal homestead exemption law and a law that would prohibit gambling in farm products.

In an effort to revamp government (and provide safeguards for many of their own administrative creations), the drafters of the Shawnee Demands also looked to extend the scope of popular democracy. All commissioners would be elected by the people rather than appointed by the governor. The nomination of all state officers would be by direct primary instead of party caucus or convention. Furthermore, voters would be given the power to create new laws, veto undesirable legislation, and remove public officials from office via the initiative, referendum, and recall (item 1 in their list of demands).[36]

Taking no chances with the upcoming election, the Democratic State Committee invited several nationally known politicians to the state. The most prominent was William Jennings Bryan, still very much the idol of Oklahoma Democrats. Aware that he might be able to have an impact on the future design of the new state constitution, Bryan agreed to make a speaking tour in support of Democratic candidates. Entering the Twin Territories aboard a special train on September 26, 1906, Bryan made seventeen speeches in three days to crowds that hailed him as a conquering hero. Special trains ran from nearby points to every scheduled stop on the tour. Several thousand people greeted the Great Commoner at each scheduled stop, and throngs estimated at between fifteen thousand and twenty thousand turned out to hear him speak at Enid and Oklahoma City. Schools declared holidays and shops closed in many towns so that everyone could join in the spectacle. At McAlester, coal miners, dressed in their work clothes and carrying their lighted miners' lamps, held a torchlight parade accompanied by marching bands. Bryan repeated the same message at each stop, urging his listeners to vote for Democratic candidates because their sympathies were with the people. He assured them that such delegates would incorporate provisions for the initiative and referendum, the control of corporations, and the protection of workers.[37]

36. Unlike the "Suggestions for a Platform," the Shawnee Demands failed to include a provision calling for segregation. See Bryant, *Alfalfa Bill Murray*, 48–49; Goble, *Progressive Oklahoma*, 164–65, 196–97; Ellis, *Constitutional Convention of Oklahoma*, 45–48; Bryant, "Labor in Politics," 263–66; Keith L. Bryant Jr., "Kate Barnard, Organized Labor, and Social Justice in Oklahoma during the Progressive Era," 150; and *Proceedings of the 4th Annual Convention of the Twin Territorial Federation of Labor*, Oklahoma City, August 13–15, 1907.

37. See Mahnken, "Bryan in Oklahoma," 250–56, 260–64; and *Labor Signal*, September 27, 1906. The leaders of the TTFL and the Farmers' Union actively toured the territories speaking for candidates who had pledged to support the Shawnee Demands, and the Joint Legislative Board created a lecture bureau to campaign for labor-endorsed candidates. See Bryant, "Labor in Politics," 266.

In the end, the Democrats won a stunning victory. Of the 112 delegates elected, voters chose 99 Democrats, 12 Republicans, and 1 independent. The list of convention delegates included 33 farmers, 29 lawyers, 14 merchants, 7 teachers, 6 ministers, 5 stockman, and 3 bankers. Thirty-four of the delegates from Indian Territory had been members of the Sequoyah convention, whereas 30 delegates from Oklahoma Territory were members of the Farmers' Union. That the new constitution would reflect the previously discussed "suggestions" and "demands" seemed all but ensured. As one historian aptly puts it, the "reform agenda that had grown out of common experiences had now taken uncommon political form."[38]

When the delegates assembled in Guthrie on November 20, 1906, to begin the torturous process of writing a constitution, no question demanded more serious consideration than the one involving the power that would be reserved to the people. It was all but certain that some type of measure providing for direct legislation by popular petition and vote would be included in the constitution. Of the 112 delegates elected to the convention, 102 had pledged to support the inclusion of the initiative and referendum. However, the specific wording of such a provision was still up for discussion. President-elect William Murray, who had little enthusiasm for direct legislation, registered his opinions on the topic during his opening address to the convention. Although Murray stated that he favored the adoption of the optional initiative and referendum as currently in use in Oregon, his statements revealed that he had a limited vision of their scope. "The fact that the people have this power," said Murray, "will prevent bribery of the members of the Legislature. The fact that they have this power will make it unnecessary to use it." With even more caution, Murray noted that he did not favor the recall of public officials from office as called for in the Shawnee Demands. Referring to the recall as a "political principle advocated by the Socialist," Murray said he opposed the idea "because it would have a tendency to weaken the courage of our officials rather than encouraging them to do their duty" and because "it would operate to create mob violence."[39]

Far more enthusiastic about the initiative and referendum than Murray, and with a more expansive view of the benefits to be derived from those new political tools, was Democratic icon William Jennings Bryan. Invited by Murray to address the convention in person, Bryan, who was unable to attend, did send a lengthy letter to the convention dated December 11, 1906, in which he offered his advice. In broadly outlining his suggestions, Bryan

38. Goble, *Progressive Oklahoma*, 201. See also Bryant, *Alfalfa Bill Murray*, 49–50.
39. Ellis, *Constitutional Convention of Oklahoma*, 77 (see also 78). See also *Equity* 9 (January 1907): 22.

endorsed the initiative and referendum and argued that those provisions "should be applied as far as circumstances will permit." He also favored providing a method by which voters at the city, county, and state levels of government could initiate legislation "if their representatives refuse to give expression to their wishes," and could "sit in judgment upon the acts of their representatives whenever a considerable number of voters desire to test public sentiment by a popular vote." Unlike Murray, Bryan recommended the recall and saw it as a legitimate method whereby voters might "revoke the commission of an official who has betrayed his trust."[40]

Using the Oregon direct legislation amendment as a model, the Committee on Legislative Department had a final report ready for a vote of the whole convention by the first week of March 1907. As originally designed, the proposed initiative and referendum provisions were the most progressive yet established. The committee set the initiative at 8 percent and the referendum at 5 percent, and allowed 15 percent of qualified voters to propose constitutional amendments (petition requirements based on the total number of votes cast during the last general election for the state office receiving the highest number of votes). Laws falling under the "emergency clause" as necessary for the immediate preservation of the public peace, health, or safety were excluded from the referendum, but a two-thirds vote of the members of each house of the legislature was required to merit such classification. Although the potential for legislative abuse of the emergency clause was worrisome, grants of franchises or licenses that ran longer than one year, any provision for the sale of real estate, and any provision involving the renting or encumbrance of real property for longer than one year were excluded from that classification. The governor could call a special election, but he did not have the power to veto measures approved by the people. Any law rejected by popular vote could be resubmitted, but to do so before a period of three years 25 percent of the eligible voters would have to petition for it. Laws enacted by the initiative could be amended by the legislature, but in such instances the law would have to be referred once again to the people. The committee extended the initiative and referendum for use at the county, district, and municipal levels, but demanded that signature requirements be doubled. Importantly, measures would become law if they received "a majority of the votes cast thereon." The committee did not approve the recall.[41]

40. For the full text of Bryan's letter to the Oklahoma Constitutional Convention, see *Proceedings of the Constitutional Convention of the Proposed State of Oklahoma* held at Guthrie, Oklahoma, November 20, 1906, to November 16, 1907, 389–96. For a discussion of Bryan's overall impact on the formation of the Oklahoma Constitution, see Robert D. Lewallen, "'Let the People Rule': William Jennings Bryan and the Oklahoma Constitution," 278–307.

41. *Oklahoma City Daily Oklahoman*, March 17, 1907.

The full convention overwhelmingly adopted the committee report on March 4 by a vote of eighty-one to five. The *Arena*, which closely followed the proceedings of the Oklahoma Constitutional Convention, gave committee chairman James Buchanan Tosh of Hobart (who was also a leader in the Farmers' Union) credit for the final report. On the motion of delegate Charles N. Haskell, the convention requested that the pen used to sign the article be sent to the State Farmers' Union in "appreciation of the Herculean efforts of the organization in behalf of the principles of the Initiative and Referendum."[42]

The designers of the new constitution added to its radical cast by incorporating detailed proscriptions governing the scope of corporate activity, popular checks on gubernatorial power and popular control over political nominations, and special protections for consumers, taxpayers, workers, shippers, small businessmen, farmers, and homesteaders. A corporation was prohibited from purchasing, selling, or speculating in land as its primary endeavor, from receiving tax exemptions on any of its property, from owning stock in a competing firm, and from forming a monopoly. Restrictions were also placed on the amount of land a corporation (such as a railroad) might own. A new three-member state corporation commission would have power to monitor railroad rates, utility charges, the issuing of stocks and bonds, and corporate pricing policies, and could impose fines for violations. All state officials (including judges) were to be elected by popular vote, and all party nominees were to be selected by the voters at direct primaries. Cities were allowed to operate municipally owned utilities, and the state was authorized to engage in enterprises for public purposes (agriculture excepted). Workers gained the eight-hour day in mines and on public works, and there were prohibitions against child labor and the use of the court injunction during a strike. A special labor commission would have power to enforce the new laws, and there would be a new board of arbitration to resolve labor disputes. Farmers gained provisions prohibiting alien landownership and won exemptions from foreclosure for 160-acre homesteads.[43]

By stamping the spirit of the Sequoyah convention, the "Suggestions for a Platform," and the Shawnee Demands on the new constitution, however, Oklahoma's framers flirted with federal censure from President Roosevelt. Aware that the Enabling Act required that the proposed state of Oklahoma have a constitution and government that were "republican" in form, a committee of the convention's Democratic leadership traveled to Washington after the first long session to gauge the temper of the Republi-

42. *Arena* 37 (March 1907): 312–13; *Proceedings of the Constitutional Convention,* 255–56; *Oklahoma City Daily Oklahoman,* March 5, 1907.
43. See Bryant, *Alfalfa Bill Murray,* 58–59, 61–63; and Goble, *Progressive Oklahoma,* 215–17.

can administration. Once there, they met with Attorney General Charles J. Bonaparte who asked for time to study the document before making any recommendations.

When the convention reconvened on July 10 to consider revisions to the constitution, Bonaparte mailed them a list of sixteen reservations. Although most of the administration's criticisms were ignored, the convention did make one fundamental revision to Article V of the constitution detailing the provisions for the initiative and referendum. Instead of requiring only a majority of all votes cast on the measure to ensure passage of a statute or amendment proposed by the initiative, the wording was changed to require that such measures receive a supermajority of all votes cast in the election (amendments passed by the legislature were required to have a similar "constitutional" majority for passage). The original referendum provisions were left intact. Although few delegates probably understood the potential impact of the change (or, like Murray, might not have cared), other observers were more perceptive. George H. Shibley, chairman of the national Initiative and Referendum League and author of the statute placing the Oklahoma system in operation, labeled it a "bad provision" that was "forced in" by the federal administration. Years later, Patrick S. Nagle, an ardent direct legislationist and a severe critic of the revised amendment, could still refer to the action of the convention as the "assassination" of the initiative and referendum and how the farmer and labor unions were "flim-flammed," "cold-decked," and "goldbricked."[44]

The campaign for ratification of the constitution actually began before the final revisions had been made. The honor of keynoting the Democratic campaign went once again to William Jennings Bryan. Bryan indicated what he thought of the Oklahoma Constitution even before coming to the state to campaign. On May 1, 1907, in a speech to the People's Lobby in Newark, New Jersey, titled "Let the People Rule," Bryan remarked that Oklahoma's "cornfield lawyers" (a phrase applied to the drafters by the *New York Times*) had "corrected the things that had been found weak in the constitutions of other states, and the best thing in that constitution is the provision for the initiative and referendum." Speaking before the Democratic State Convention in Oklahoma City on June 18, the Nebraskan told the delegates that they had "the best constitution today of any State in this Union, and a better constitution than the constitution of the United States."[45]

44. Goble, *Progressive Oklahoma*, 219. See also *Oklahoma City Daily Oklahoman*, May 16, 25, 30, July 12, 13, 1907; *New York Times*, July 20, 1907; *Arena* 40 (July 1908): 96; *Proceedings of the Constitutional Convention*, 352; *Oklahoma City Oklahoma Pioneer*, August 20, 1910; and W. B. Richards, *The Oklahoma Red Book*, 1:46–48.

45. Lewallen, "'Let the People Rule,'" 289. See also *Oklahoma City Daily Oklahoman*, June 19, 1907.

The highlight of the Republican campaign came on August 24, when Secretary of War William Howard Taft censured the work of the Democratically controlled constitutional convention before an enthusiastic GOP gathering in Oklahoma City. Taft, assumed to be President Roosevelt's spokesperson on the matter, stated that he feared placing the initiative and referendum in the hands of a voting population "largely unused to governmental practices." He also accused the convention of excessive partisanship in redrawing the state's election districts, and charged the framers of the constitution with hypocrisy for purporting to have produced a document by which the will of the people would be sustained and then, by sheer political chicanery, adopting a plan to gerrymander voting districts. To Taft, such action made a mockery of the principle behind the initiative and referendum and showed the emptiness of the declaration, "Let the people rule." Taft also criticized the statutory nature of the document (contemptuously describing it as a "code of by-law"), and objected to its extreme corporate regulations that he thought would discourage business from entering the state. For these reasons, and a good many more, Taft recommended that voters reject the constitution and wait for Congress to pass a new enabling act and call for a new convention.[46]

Taft's attack gave the Democrats an opportunity to offer Bryan a curtain call. During the first week of September, and less than two weeks before election day, Bryan returned to give speeches at Vinita, Tulsa, Sapulpa, Bristow, Chandler, Oklahoma City, Woodward, and Alva, and, in effect, provided the Democrats with the last word in the debate. On election day, September 17, voters overwhelmingly approved the constitution by a vote of 180,333 to 73,059. With President Roosevelt's signature on November 16, Oklahoma became the nation's forty-sixth state and the first to adopt the initiative and referendum as part of its original constitution.[47]

Oklahomans used the initiative and referendum for the first time at the general election in 1908. On the ballot that year were a measure proposed by initiative petition and a special advisory referendum submitted by the legislature. The lone initiated measure, reportedly sponsored by William Murray, the recently elected Speaker of the lower house of the legislature, allowed for the state to sell its school lands to homesteaders. The special advisory referendum, called the "New Jerusalem plan," was simply a ques-

46. *Oklahoma City Daily Oklahoman*, August 25, 1907; *New York Times*, August 25, 1907; *Outlook* 87 (October 5, 1907): 229–31. Years later Taft could still refer to the framers as a "zoological garden of cranks" (Bryant, *Alfalfa Bill Murray*, 70).

47. See Mahnken, "Bryan in Oklahoma," 266, 268–69; Goble, *Progressive Oklahoma*, 223, 225–26; and Bryant, *Alfalfa Bill Murray*, 70–71. The Oklahoma legislature passed legislation (H.B. 174) to give the law effect on April 16, 1908. See Oklahoma, *Session Laws of 1907–1908*, 440–52.

tion of whether the state should select a site for a model capital city to be located near the geographic center of the state. The city would be owned and controlled by the state, which would benefit financially from the sale of lots. Voters rejected the school land measure, which failed to receive even a simple majority. The special New Jerusalem referendum won by a wide margin, but was nonbinding.[48]

Voters utilized the initiative and referendum at three different elections in 1910. At a special election held on June 11, they considered one initiated amendment and one initiated statute. The amendment would have allowed railroads to consolidate. Promoters of several independent railroads sought the amendment in order that they might sell their properties to larger trunk-line operators. The statute proposed to move the state capital and asked voters to vote upon its location at Guthrie, Shawnee, or Oklahoma City. As this was a special election (no candidates), amendments required only a simple majority for passage (a point not lost on governors with pet projects and the power to call for such elections). Voters rejected the railroad consolidation amendment by a large majority, but approved the capital removal proposal and selected Oklahoma City as the site. At the August primary voters considered a Democratic-sponsored amendment proposed via the initiative that would have imposed a "grandfather clause" and a literacy qualification for voters. To vote against the amendment, voters had to scratch out the words "For the Amendment," which were confusingly placed at the bottom of the ballot. As a result, unmarked ballots were counted as favoring the proposal. The Jim Crow amendment received a constitutional majority and was upheld by the state supreme court.

Two additional initiated amendments (for woman suffrage and repeal of the prohibition law), one initiated statute (the New Jerusalem plan), and one referred statute (an election law) appeared on the ballot at the general election in November 1910. The Woman Suffrage Association led the petition drive for the suffrage amendment, but even with the support of the Socialist Party (both the Democrats and the Republicans had ignored the question in their party platforms) and the State Federation of Labor the proposal failed to win voter approval. Looking to replace prohibition with local option, Oklahoma's wets, led by the Sons of Washington (an Oklahoma lodge dedicated to repeal) and the Oklahoma Business Men's Protective League, argued that the prohibition law threatened personal freedom, had proved unenforceable, and denied the state considerable revenue. Various church groups and the Women's Christian Temperance Union, however,

48. See John H. Bass, "The Initiative and Referendum in Oklahoma," 136–37; *Equity* 10 (October 1908): 101–2; 11 (April 1909): 56–58; Bryant, *Alfalfa Bill Murray,* 54, 59–61, 78–79; *Independent* 66 (February 25, 1909): 421–23; and Jimmie Lewis Franklin, *Born Sober: Prohibition in Oklahoma, 1907–1959,* 25–35.

waged an effective campaign against repeal and convinced a majority of the voters to reject local option. Also on the ballot was a measure submitted by the voters calling for the aforementioned New Jerusalem plan and a Republican-sponsored referendum against another Jim Crow election law. The ongoing contest between Guthrie and Oklahoma City for the new state capital killed New Jerusalem, but voters upheld the racially discriminatory election law. In what many direct legislationists and political minorities perceived as a partisan political maneuver on the part of the Democratic majority, the 1910 Oklahoma legislature reduced the time period for the circulation of referendum petitions from ninety to sixty days. Such action provoked the Socialist Party of Oklahoma to demand that new laws be passed that would "effectively give into the hands of the people the use" of those tools.[49]

From 1911 to 1913 voters considered one referendum, two initiated amendments, and one initiated statute. At the primary election in 1912, voters approved an initiated measure (sponsored by the People's Power League) allowing for the direct election of U.S. senators following the Oregon plan then in operation. The general election in 1912 offered voters two more initiated amendments. The first, filed by the citizens of Guthrie, asked for the capital question to be resubmitted, and the second proposed the creation of an eleven-member board of agriculture to be composed entirely of farmers. The state capital amendment was soundly defeated, but the board of agriculture proposal received the required supermajority. At a special election in August 1913, voters petitioned for a referendum on a mining bill. The campaign had the united support of mine workers and was successful. This was the only instance during the 1908–1918 period in which Oklahoma voters vetoed an act of the legislature. Critics argued that the Oklahoma legislature abused the emergency clause of the initiative and referendum amendment and precluded frequent use of the referendum as a result.[50]

The primary election in 1914 found four more voter-initiated proposals before the voters. Two of them were referenda: one against the Antigambling and Race Horse Bill, the other against a law abolishing slot machines. Voters, however, sustained the legislature in each case. Another statute, initiated by the people, called for the establishment of a system of direct tax-

49. Bass, "Initiative and Referendum," 137–39. For a discussion of the election law, see *Equity* 11 (July 1909): 96–97; 12 (January 1910): 34–35; and Irvin Hurst, *The 46th Star: A History of Oklahoma's Constitutional Convention and Early Statehood*, 155–62. For a discussion of the attempt to repeal the prohibition law, see Franklin, *Born Sober*, 45–49. See also Oklahoma, *Session Laws of 1910*, 121–24; and *Oklahoma City Oklahoma Pioneer*, June 8, August 20, 1910.

50. See Bass, "Initiative and Referendum," 139–41; and *Equity* 16 (April 1914): 83.

ation. The proposal found popular approval, but failed to obtain a super-majority. The final ballot proposition, an initiated amendment sponsored by church groups, made excessive drunkenness grounds for removal from public office and won overwhelming voter approval.[51]

An odd twist to the initiative process occurred at the general election in 1914. Oklahoma attorney general Charles West, a candidate for governor, prepared initiative petitions calling for four amendments to the state constitution. The so-called West Amendments, in reality his political platform, sought reform of the appellate court system to expedite cases, a reduction of the state tax rate, the imposition of a 2 percent tax on oil and gas production (revenues to be used for schools, roads, and bridges), and the creation of a unicameral legislature. Each proposal received a majority of the votes cast, but none received a supermajority.[52]

In 1915 the United States Supreme Court invalidated Oklahoma's discriminatory "grandfather clause" that had been enacted in 1910. While the Democrats looked to find a new means of continuing black exclusion, the Socialists jumped at the opportunity to challenge Democratic control of the state's election machinery via the initiative. Endorsed by the Republicans, the Socialist-sponsored initiative amendment sought to abolish all existing election boards and replace them with ones that would allow for equal, tripartite representation. The proposed amendment would be voted on at the general election in 1916.

In the meantime, the Democrats rushed to head off the revolt. In a special legislative session, called for January 1916, the Democratic legislative majority pushed forward two "corrective" pieces of legislation. One, a legislative measure, altered the state's election law by requiring all Oklahoma voters to register under the supervision of Democratically appointed precinct officials. All those eligible to vote in 1914 (when the grandfather clause was still in effect) were automatically registered, whereas those ineligible, that is, blacks, had to register during a brief two-week period or be forever barred from casting a ballot. The law also required registrants to state their place of residence and their party affiliation. Socialists and Republicans, who found the registration period too short and the disclosure information too intrusive (Socialists feared that landlords and creditors could intimidate tenants with radical sympathies), unsuccessfully sought to challenge the law via a referendum petition. The other Democratic-sponsored measure was a proposed constitutional amendment to replace the recently invalidated grandfather clause with a literacy test. Socialists especially ob-

---

51. See Bass, "Initiative and Referendum," 141–42; and Bertil L. Hanson, "Oklahoma's Experience with Direct Legislation," 266.

52. See Bass, "Initiative and Referendum," 142; and *Equity* 17 (January 1915): 53–54.

jected to this plan as it would disfranchise not only blacks but also illiterate whites who the Socialists presumed would primarily be the working poor. The combined opposition of the Republicans and the Socialists was sufficient to defeat the literacy test by a vote of 133,140 to 90,605.[53]

Two initiated amendments—the Socialist-sponsored election law and a proposal to replace legislative control over voter registration with a requirement that all further changes to election laws be subjected to popular control via the initiative process—appeared on the ballot at the general election in 1916. Democratic governor Robert L. Williams used his prerogative to place the two amendments on the general election ballot where adoption required approval by a majority of all votes cast rather than merely a majority of those voting on the questions. Although both measures received solid majorities of those who voted on them, they failed, by narrow margins, to gain constitutional majorities. Embittered by the defeat, Socialists and Republicans charged the Democrats with manipulating the vote by deliberately creating a ballot shortage and fraudulently tearing off the stubs of unused ballots to inflate the actual number of ballots cast to ensure defeat of the propositions.[54]

Oklahoma's experience with the initiative and referendum proved frustrating for many direct legislationists. Hampered by the revision to the original amendment requiring a supermajority to pass a statute or amendment proposed via the initiative, proponents quickly realized that making effective use of the new tools would be extremely difficult. During the 1908–1918 period voters considered fourteen initiated amendments and four initiated statutes at various primary, special, and general elections. Although twelve of these measures (67 percent) received simple majorities, only four of the eighteen voter-initiated propositions (22 percent) gained the necessary supermajority or constitutional majority required to become law. Oklahoma's initiative and referendum amendment also suffered from problems resulting from the partisan and often ideological nature of Oklahoma politics. Speaker Murray and Attorney General West used their political influence to further pet projects via the initiative process, and governors frequently called special elections to facilitate personal or party agendas. Partisanship also worked to subvert the intent of the law. The Democratically controlled legislature reduced the time period for securing referendum petitions from ninety to sixty days in an obvious move to restrict their use, and Governor Williams forced propositions that threatened

53. See Scales and Goble, *Oklahoma Politics: A History,* 83–84.
54. See Bass, "Initiative and Referendum," 142–44; *Equity* 19 (January 1917): 37; Scales and Goble, *Oklahoma Politics: A History,* 86; and Garin Burbank, *When Farmers Voted Red: The Gospel of Socialism in the Oklahoma Countryside, 1910–1924,* 86.

4

Missouri and Maine

MISSOURI

As in the other states previously mentioned, it was especially easy for Missourians to conclude that representative lawmaking had failed, and that political power seemed to have become more responsive to the needs of the special rather than the public interest. Reformers frequently charged that a small group of unscrupulous businessmen and politicians—the "Big Cinch" and "Combine" in St. Louis, and the "Lobby" in Jefferson City—had joined to enrich themselves at public expense, and the famous St. Louis boodle and bribery prosecutions of 1902 and similar indictments of state legislators in 1903 proved that bribery and malfeasance had, in fact, become the norm. In 1906 Thomas Sheridan, president of the Missouri Federation of Labor, expressed the sentiments of many when he stated: "We have permitted the political parties, which were intended to be agencies through which people would express their will through legislation, to pass under the control of special interests that dictate the laws of the state and prevent the legislature from enacting laws in the interests of the people."[1] Before events in Missouri deteriorated to such a degree, a few reformers in that state had concluded that the answer to their predicament lay in restoring popular control of government. For that to happen, though, reforms would have to be adopted that would allow voters to have a more direct influence on the political process. The solution that seemed to offer the most promise as an effective method of gaining that result was direct legislation, or the initiative and referendum.

Discussion of the topic of direct legislation in Missouri dates at least to the early 1890s. The platforms of the Socialist Labor and People's Parties of

1. Gary M. Fink, *Labor's Search for Political Order*, 34. For accounts of the boodle and bribery investigations, see Lincoln Steffens and Claude Wetmore, "Tweed Days in St. Louis," *McClure's* 19 (October 1902): 577–86; Lincoln Steffens, "The Shamelessness of St. Louis," *McClure's* 20 (March 1903): 545–60; and Lincoln Steffens, "Enemies of the Republic," *McClure's* 22 (April 1904): 587–99.

Missouri both favored the adoption of direct legislation as early as 1894. The following year the state Populist Committee passed a resolution recommending that the People's Party include a demand for the initiative and referendum in its next national platform. Missouri was also represented at the organizing conference of the National Direct Legislation League held in St. Louis on July 21, 1896. Listed as vice president in charge of organizing for the state of Missouri at that time was J. A. Wayland, editor of the soon-to-be-famous socialist newspaper *Appeal to Reason,* then published in Kansas City. Wayland's title, however, appears to have been primarily ceremonial, as Missouri was still three years away from any sign of an active organizing drive.[2]

The first sustained effort to establish the initiative and referendum in Missouri began in January 1899 when a group of St. Louisans organized the Direct Legislation League of Missouri. The executive committee of the league, inspired by the adoption of the first direct legislation amendment in South Dakota in 1898, hoped to obtain passage of a similar amendment to the Missouri Constitution and to have that amendment placed before the voters at the general election of 1900. To that end, the committee held frequent organizational meetings, drafted a proposed constitutional amendment to establish direct legislation in Missouri, and sent out circulars to publicize the issue. Members also chose Silas L. Moser, an ardent single taxer, as president of the new league.[3]

Moser, born in Pike County, Ohio, in 1850, moved to Monroe County, Iowa, when he was sixteen and took up farmwork and attended school. Graduating from the State University of Iowa in 1877, he worked for a while as a school principal before moving to St. Louis to accept a position as a business manager. Attracted to political reform, Moser managed the Live Question Bureau of the American Press Association, a service that provided reports to newspapers in forty-two states. He also worked to establish the equal taxation of property in Missouri and became chair of the Equal Taxation Committee, a single-tax body, in 1896. His efforts soon gained him membership on the National Committee of the Single Tax League.[4]

Moser was a compelling personality. One of his longtime associates, William Preston Hill, described him as a "magnetic man" of "great force

2. *Official Manual of the State of Missouri, 1895–1896,* 258, 269. See also *Direct Legislation Record* 2 (December 1895): 28; 3 (September 1896): 25–30; and Elliott Shore, *Talkin' Socialism: J. A. Wayland and the Role of the Press in American Radicalism, 1890–1912,* 75–76.

3. The members of the executive committee included Lee Meriwether, George Bullock, N. O. Nelson, F. M. Crunden, Mrs. F. H. Ingalls, Joseph T. Tatum, Leon Greenbaum, and George M. Jackson (*Direct Legislation Record* 6 [June 1899]: 24).

4. See *Direct Legislation Record* 10 (September 1903): 60.

and character." A large man, with a look that exuded honesty and sinceri-
ty, he had a knack for convincing even the most indifferent individuals that
they should contribute time or money to his political causes (the single tax
and the initiative and referendum). "He got the prohibition party," said
Hill, "to aid our movement and they helped considerably for motives of
their own perhaps. He also got the socialists lined up actively. They were
of course in favor of our measure on general principles but they were not
so sure that they cared to get behind it actively, but Moser persuaded
them." He used his background and his continuing interest in agriculture
(with his full beard he even looked the part of a prosperous farmer) to convince farm organizations to support the initiative and referendum as well.
"All these [groups]," Hill stated, "helped to circulate petitions and alto-
gether we had many channels all over the state concentrating on our movement." Moser was also a faithful church member. Occasionally asked to
preach from the pulpit on Sunday evenings, he would use those opportunities to extol the virtues of direct democracy. Indefatigable and persistent,
he never stopped working for a cause to which he had committed himself.
It was this part of his character that most impressed associates. Again according to William Preston Hill,

> He was always on the job everywhere and at all times. . . . This is what
> contributed to our success largely. Without Moser we would likely have
> failed. . . . [S]uccess is for those who are willing to stand by their ideas
> . . . [and] persist in spite of every obstacle regardless of disappointment.
> When such a man appears, make way for him because he carries the fu-
> ture with him. Such a man was Moser. In an earlier period . . . he would
> have made a prophet or crusader.[5]

Under Moser's direction the Direct Legislation League of Missouri managed to get its direct legislation amendment introduced into the 1899 session of the Missouri legislature. The measure allowed for the initiative and
referendum if 5 percent of the qualified voters petitioned for its use; it exempted from the process laws deemed necessary for preserving the "public peace, health or safety" or for supporting state government and existing
public institutions. Nonetheless, the amendment failed to pass in the House,
and it never came to a vote in the Senate, in spite of a petition drive and
modest lobbying effort conducted by the league.[6]

Unsuccessful in their first foray into state politics, the leaders of the Direct Legislation League of Missouri hoped that improved organization and

5. Letter from Hill to N. D. Houghton, October 31, 1922, N. D. Houghton Papers, University of Missouri, Western Historical Manuscript Collection, Columbia.
6. See *Direct Legislation Record* 6 (June 1899): 24; and 7 (December 1900): 67.

further educational efforts would bring victory when the next Missouri legislature convened in 1901. With that goal in mind, league officials decided
to target political candidates, editors of small county newspapers, elected
officials, and known campaign speakers. They found that winning adherents through the dissemination of information was a slow process. The major newspapers, almost always linked to one of the two dominant political
parties, gave direct legislation little attention. Debate over other state issues
often seemed to eclipse any vibrant discussion of the initiative and referendum as well. In addition, local organizations, created specifically to promote direct legislation, did little.[7]

Direct legislationists also discovered that it cost a lot more to print and
distribute information than they had anticipated. They received some unexpected financial assistance, however, from J. Eads How. The eccentric
How, grandson of the famous engineer James Eads and known to many as
the "millionaire tramp," had inherited approximately three hundred thousand dollars. However, because How believed that no man should own
anything he had not earned, he felt he was not morally entitled to his inheritance. To divest himself of the "unearned increment" of his estate, How
decided to establish in 1900 a "People's Fund and Welfare Association,"
with offices located in a building at 312 North Twelfth Street in St. Louis.
Part of How's bequest was set aside to provide rooms in the building in
which reform literature could be made available to the public and where
various reform groups could hold their meetings. A variety of reform organizations—the Union Reform Party, the Single Tax League, the Franchise
Repeal Association, the Social Democratic Party (Socialists), the Labor Exchange, and the Social Problems Club—soon set up offices in the building.
The address became known locally as "Reform Headquarters." The one
common thread uniting nearly all the groups housed at the headquarters
was the belief that direct legislation was a "national necessity."[8]

How instructed St. Louis reformers to call a meeting to elect a board to
manage the fund, with the simple stipulation that the money be distributed
in a manner that would be beneficial to the public good. At the organizational meeting, Silas Moser and Dr. William Preston Hill, a fellow single
taxer and avid direct legislationist, rounded up enough like-minded individuals to control the proceedings and succeeded in electing Hill as president of the new association. Hill was born in St. Louis in 1855. Educated at
Phillips Exeter and Phillips Andover Academies, Washington University in
St. Louis, and the University of Pennsylvania, he also studied for two years
at Heidelberg University in Germany and for four years at the Medical

7. See *Direct Legislation Record* 7 (December 1900): 67; and 8 (December 1901): 63.
8. *St. Louis Post-Dispatch,* August 12, 1900.

School of Paris before returning to practice medicine in Missouri. Dr. Hill became a socialist while in Germany, and a single taxer and direct legislationist after returning to the United States.[9]

Once established, the board then decided that the money should be spent in an effort to establish the single tax in Missouri, and that the quickest way to do that was to gain approval of a constitutional amendment establishing the initiative and referendum. The small but aggressive Single Tax League, perhaps the best-known reform organization in St. Louis, and one that had been promoting the initiative and referendum since 1899, again formally endorsed direct legislation in its platform. The league also promised to send printed material on the initiative and referendum to political candidates and legislators and proposed the organization of a direct legislation caucus during the next session of the Missouri legislature. As a result, the single tax and direct legislation became inextricably linked in Missouri.[10]

When the legislature assembled in 1901, direct legislationists saw indications that their campaign had made progress. Every member of the legislature appeared to be informed on the topic, and most appeared to be favorably disposed to it. The Direct Legislation League of Missouri dispatched Moser to Jefferson City as a lobbyist. While there Moser won the support of Henry F. Sarman, a member of the Central Labor Union and a fellow single taxer, and together they persuaded the Missouri State Federation of Labor to support the idea. A direct legislation measure passed the House by a vote of seventy-nine to thirty-five. In the Senate, however, the bill met the forceful opposition of Democratic senators John F. Morton, James Orchard, John C. Whaley, and Frank H. Farris. Hill, who had come to Jefferson City to assist Moser, labeled these senators the "Big Four" and charged that they were controlled by the "Railroad lobby." According to Hill, the Big Four managed to defeat the measure, despite pledges from a majority of senators that they would support it.[11]

Disappointed by the defeat of their amendment in the legislature in 1901, but hopeful of success in the next legislative session in 1903, the Direct Legislation League of Missouri resumed its educational campaign. The league sent Moser on a statewide canvass. Moser gave speeches, wrote articles,

9. See *Direct Legislation Record* 10 (March 1903): 20.

10. Direct legislationists also received at least tacit support at this stage from the Municipal Ownership League and the Workingmen's Bryan Club. See *Direct Legislation Record* 6 (December 1899): 87; 7 (December 1900): 67; Frank Parker Stockbridge, "The Single Taxers: Who They Are and What They Are Doing," 520; and *St. Louis Post-Dispatch*, August 12, 1900.

11. See *Direct Legislation Record* 8 (December 1901): 63–64; and letters from Hill to N. D. Houghton, October 25, 1922, and from Sarman to N. D. Houghton, March 8, 1923, Houghton Papers, University of Missouri.

held personal conferences, and solicited pledges from prospective candidates. The plan was to focus on districts with upcoming senatorial elections and seek support regardless of party affiliation. The league solicited the services of prominent speakers to debate and discuss the initiative and referendum in various public forums. The league's nonpartisan approach also carried over to the organization of local direct legislation bodies, which it actively encouraged.[12]

As Moser traveled the state as an organizer, he found labor unions especially receptive to direct legislation as a means of securing improved conditions for wage earners. Many workers regarded the initiative as a means by which they might win the eight-hour day, antistrikebreaking ordinances, child labor laws, and workmen's compensation. Workers underscored their support for the initiative and referendum in response to a questionnaire sent out by William Anderson, commissioner of labor statistics in Missouri, to all state labor organizations. The Missouri State Federation of Labor formally endorsed the reforms in the fall of 1901. Additional assistance came from outside the state. The Non-Partisan Federation for Majority Rule, a national organization centered in Washington, D.C., printed two pamphlets for organized labor in Missouri touting the merits of direct legislation. The Missouri Joint Committee on Direct Legislation, headquartered in Jefferson City and composed of the legislative committee of the State Federation of Labor and a committee of the Central Labor Union, directed the mailing of both pamphlets to each legislative candidate.[13]

In looking back on the period 1899 to 1901, William Preston Hill remembered a shared sentiment "among all classes of people" that corruption in the legislature had to be stopped. "The Baking powder scandal and the United Railway of St. Louis scandal," said Hill, "in which . . . notorious bribery was used, had created a general idea among the people that something must be done. Our measure presented itself as the most logical method to put an end to corruption and it was easy to get people to sign petitions to have [a direct legislation amendment] adopted."[14] Moser and Hill either addressed civic bodies personally or sent petitions to organization leaders to be circulated and signed by their members.

During the political campaign of 1902 their efforts seemed to be paying off. The league won support of the Prohibition, Socialist, and Public Ownership Parties of Missouri; the Missouri Single Tax League; and, most important, the state Democratic Party, which added an initiative and referen-

12. See *Direct Legislation Record* 8 (December 1901): 64; and 10 (September 1903): 60.
13. See *Direct Legislation Record* 8 (December 1901): 64; 9 (September 1902): 45; and N. D. Houghton, "The Initiative and Referendum in Missouri" (master's thesis), 13.
14. Letter from Hill to N. D. Houghton, October 31, 1922, Houghton Papers, University of Missouri.

dum plank to its platform for the first time. Henry F. Sarman later recalled that he and Dr. Hill were the ones responsible for getting the initiative and referendum written into the Democratic platform. According to Sarman, Perry Alexander, editor of the *St. Charles Banner* and a convention delegate, managed to get him before the platform committee to read a statement written by himself and Dr. Hill. It was, he said, "so foreign to them, they could not, or did not attact [sic] it. When no one objected, Alexander moved its adoption and it was done."[15]

Realizing that passage of an amendment would be extremely difficult without first breaking the influence of the Big Four, William Preston Hill, newly elected president of the Direct Legislation League of Missouri, carried the political fight directly into their districts, attacking the legislative records of Senators Morton, Orchard, Whaley, and Farris and opposing their reelection. His most damaging weapon was a pamphlet he published titled "Political Corruption in Missouri." In it he linked the Big Four to recent scandals at the state capitol and contributed to the defeat of Orchard and the retirement of Whaley. Hill claimed that his "victory against the Big Four crooks" gave direct legislationists "great prestige" in the next legislature, in 1903.[16]

When the legislature convened in January 1903, Hill and other direct legislationists hoped that the Democratic Party, which controlled both houses, would honor its platform pledge and pass a direct legislation amendment. Moser, as secretary of the Direct Legislation League of Missouri, was again on hand to lobby for the measure. He was assisted by Sarman, now chairman of the legislative committee of the State Federation of Labor, and by Hill. Senator John L. Bradley introduced a direct legislation amendment on January 8. The proposal called for the referendum based on a petition of 5 percent of the eligible voters and the initiative based on an 8 percent figure. The measure was referred to the Committee on Constitutional Amendments, which suggested revisions. The final draft, passed by the legislature on March 11, was much different from the original proposal and revealed the rather conservative means by which the Democratic Party chose to accommodate the new political demands.

The final bill called for the referendum based on 10 percent of the eligible voters and an initiative based on a 15 percent figure *in each congressional district*. The figure necessary to propose constitutional amendments by initiative petition was set at 20 percent of the voters *in each congressional district*. There were sixteen congressional districts in Missouri at the time. In

15. Letter from Sarman to N. D. Houghton, March 8, 1923, ibid.

16. *Direct Legislation Record* 8 (December 1901): 64; 9 (September 1902): 44; letter from Hill to N. D. Houghton, October 25, 1922, Houghton Papers, University of Missouri; *Official Manual of the State of Missouri, 1903–1904*, 310, 381, 390, 395, 403.

addition to the exception of laws pertaining to the "preservation of the public peace, health and safety," drafters expanded exemptions to include appropriation bills and all laws passed by a two-thirds vote of the legislature.
It appeared as if party leaders wanted the favorable image of having voted for the bill but were willing to support only a weak and ineffective measure. Many proponents accused lawmakers of "cowardice," "shuffling,"
"evasion of party platforms and individual pledges," and "subservience to
corporation influence." Even though the percentages were high and the ex-
clusions broad, though, most proponents accepted the amendment as written as better than nothing. Voters would be given an opportunity to approve the amendment at the general election of 1904.[17]

When the political campaign of 1904 finally got under way, both major
political parties in Missouri found it politically expedient to take positions
on the upcoming initiative and referendum amendment. The Democrats
rather disingenuously congratulated themselves on fulfillment of the party's pledge. The party urged voters to approve the amendment as a means
of securing the power to veto bad legislation and create new laws, while
"rendering ineffective the results of corrupt methods in legislation and less-
ening the inducements to the same." The Republicans seized the opportunity to criticize Democratic hypocrisy, but they did so in a manner that
made them sound equally duplicitous. Although they approved of the initiative and referendum in principle, the Republicans disapproved of the
current amendment and stated: "We condemn the insincerity of the Democratic party in proposing a plan . . . so cumbrous as to make its application impracticable, and we are in favor of a just and honest measure that
shall give to the people of this State the largest control of and participation
in legislation and government."[18] Looking to win votes from an electorate
that harbored widespread and deep misgivings about government, the Republicans worded their position to take advantage of that mistrust.

William Preston Hill, convinced that the proposed initiative and referendum amendment was worth fighting for and optimistic that it could be
improved in the future, led the league's campaign to get voters to ratify it.
Hill first attempted to interest voters by mailing more than 150,000 publicity circulars that stressed the merits and importance of the initiative and
referendum. Then, faced with the dilemma of finding other cost-effective
ways of reaching and acquainting voters with an issue that most newspapers in the state either slighted or ignored, Hill displayed a bit of clever-

17. Quotations are from *Direct Legislation Record* 10 (June 1903): 28. See also *Direct Legislation Record* 10 (March 1903): 4; and 10 (June 1903): 28, 30–31.
18. Democratic and Republican comments are quoted in *Official Manual of the State of
Missouri, 1905–1906*, 255, 229, respectively. See also *St. Louis Wetmore's Weekly*, March 3,
1905.

ness. He submitted a short article titled "The Initiative and Referendum [and] What These Legislative Reforms Might Accomplish for Missouri," which the *St. Louis Post-Dispatch* published on its editorial page on June 8, 1904. Hill then purchased 1,000 copies of the newspaper, marked "Copy This" in red ink above the article, and sent a copy to every newspaper in Missouri. He claimed that 545 newspapers reprinted the article during the next five weeks. Hill also claimed to have scored a hit with voters when he issued a political cartoon that depicted the "Honest Citizen" standing atop the capitol steps at Jefferson City and using the initiative and referendum whip to drive boodlers and franchise grafters from the capitol. The caption read, "Will You Vote to Put This Whip in the Hands of Honest Citizens?" With the St. Louis and Jefferson City bribery scandals fresh in voters' minds, the cartoon must certainly have attracted the attention of many. The league also received valuable assistance from the legislative committee of the State Federation of Labor, which sent out thousands of direct legislation leaflets to every union in the state. Hill estimated that with the guaranteed support of organized labor, Prohibitionists, Socialists, and old Populists, the amendment would easily receive more than 300,000 votes in its favor.[19]

The election, however, did not turn out as Hill had expected. Four other amendments appeared on the 1904 ballot along with direct legislation, and voters rejected them all by majorities ranging from 53,000 to 123,000. Of the 643,969 who voted for governor (the popular, crusading St. Louis circuit attorney Joseph W. Folk, a Democrat, was elected), only 285,022 voted on the initiative and referendum question, which lost by 53,540 votes. It was the first time in which voters in any state had failed to approve a direct legislation amendment after the question had been put before them. Supporters groped for explanations. The editors of the *St. Louis Wetmore's Weekly* argued that voters were in a mood to reject anything their "rotten" legislature submitted to them. Hill, who took the defeat bitterly, found a different explanation—he caustically lashed out at rural Missourians for not being well enough informed. Said Hill: "We carried or came near carrying every center of enlightenment and civilization where there was no active campaign against us. If we add the returns from all the large cities we have a

19. Hill published a similar but expanded version of his article under the heading "Voters of Missouri—Attention! The True Remedy for Corruption in Our Politics Is Now in Your Hands." The article appeared in the *St. Louis Wetmore's Weekly*, October 19, 1904. Hill estimated the membership of the State Federation of Labor to be at more than one hundred thousand. See letter from Hill to Dr. John R. Haynes, July 15, 1904, and a photocopy of "Copy This" dated June 8, 1904, in box 44, John Randolph Haynes Papers, University of California at Los Angeles Research Library, Special Collections; *St. Louis Wetmore's Weekly*, November 2, 1904; and letter from Hill to N. D. Houghton, October 13, 1922, Houghton Papers, University of Missouri.

substantial majority, nearly 5,000. It was the ignorant backwoods counties, where the people probably never heard of the referendum, that snowed us under." Voting statistics appeared to support Hill's claim. The initiative and referendum amendment received a 53 percent majority from the five most urbanized counties in the state, but only a 33 percent vote from the remaining counties.[20]

The defeat in 1904 devastated the leaders of the direct legislation movement in Missouri, and it was not until reform-minded governor Joseph W. Folk focused attention on the issue during his message to the Missouri legislature in January 1907 that their interest revived. Folk had gotten elected primarily as a result of his efforts as prosecuting attorney during the famous St. Louis boodle trials of Boss Edward Butler and members of the Combine in the municipal assembly in 1902. By 1907 he was nationally known as the champion of the "Missouri Idea"—the conviction that Missouri could set an example in civic righteousness by reclaiming popular control of the law and enforcing it. In his address, Folk lent support to direct legislation and linked the reforms to his ongoing crusade against corruption. Said the governor: "Government by the people is best where government is nearest to the people. I hope you will adopt a resolution for a constitutional amendment providing for the Initiative and Referendum in legislation. . . . I regard this as of much importance in the final elimination of corruption, and the establishment of true representative government."[21]

Seizing the moment, Representative Nathaniel C. Whaley and Senator Frank W. McAllister introduced joint resolutions in their respective houses of the legislature calling for the initiative and referendum. The proposal was a liberal revision of the amendment that legislators had approved in 1903. The new proposal asked for the initiative and referendum based on petitions of 8 percent and 5 percent, respectively. There were no county restrictions in the amendment as initially proposed. With the governor's endorsement and Democratic majorities in both houses, the chances of getting the measure passed looked favorable.[22]

The Direct Legislation League of Missouri wasted no time in reinvigorating its campaign in support of the measure. The league again sent Moser to Jefferson City to lobby for it and began to distribute educational pam-

20. Hill quoted in *St. Louis Wetmore's Weekly*, March 3, 1905. See also N. D. Houghton, "The Initiative and Referendum in Missouri" (*Missouri Historical Review*), 275; and letter from Hill to N. D. Houghton, October 13, 1922, Houghton Papers, University of Missouri. Voting statistics cited in David P. Thelen, *Paths of Resistance: Tradition and Dignity in Industrializing Missouri*, 231.

21. *Equity* 9 (January 1907): 18.

22. See ibid. and Houghton, "Initiative and Referendum in Missouri" (master's thesis), 30. For information on Folk and his bribery investigations, see Steven L. Piott, *Holy Joe: Joseph W. Folk and the Missouri Idea*.

phlets and broadsides throughout the state. Organized labor again lent its full support. The Joint Labor Legislative Board, composed of twenty members representing nine labor organizations in the state, directed labor's political campaign in Jefferson City. Assisting the efforts of proponents was the near absence of any open opposition in the legislature. As a result, both the Senate (by a vote of nineteen to six) and the House (by a vote of ninety to seven) approved the amendment.[23]

The final version, however, was not without its encumbrances, the result of political compromise. Petition requirements were set at 5 percent for the referendum and at 8 percent for the initiative (as originally requested), but these percentages had to be obtained *in at least two-thirds of the state's congressional districts.* Nevertheless, these were liberal adjustments from the 1903 measure. The new amendment once again exempted laws necessary for the preservation of the public health, peace, or safety from the referendum. It also excepted acts pertaining to appropriations, but only those relating to the maintenance of the public schools, the support of state institutions, and the payment of current expenses of state government. The task now before the league was to inform as many voters as possible of the merits of the initiative and referendum so that they would not only vote but vote in favor of the amendment when given the opportunity at the general election of November 1908 as well.[24]

With some money remaining from the People's Fund and Welfare Association, small contributions raised in the state, and at least one sizable contribution from Hill himself, the league revived its educational campaign. Realizing that they were most vulnerable in the rural districts of the state, league officials sent plates of editorial material and plates of political cartoons to rural editors. They found that the political cartoons were especially effective in gaining voter attention and interest, and with that in mind Hill issued a slightly modified version of his famous cartoon from the previous campaign. The revised cartoon depicted the "Honest Voter" as a hardworking *farmer* using the same whip to the same ends.

During the first six months of 1908, the league claimed to have mailed material to seventy-five thousand addresses taken from telephone directories throughout the state. The league also generated nearly one million one-page leaflets, each containing a brief statement explaining the initiative and referendum as well as an argument that such reforms were necessary to

23. John F. Morton lost his Senate seat in the election of 1906. Frank Farris, the only remaining active member of the "Big Four," left the Senate for a seat in the House that same year. See *Official Manual of the State of Missouri, 1907–1908,* 627, 634.

24. Houghton, "Initiative and Referendum in Missouri" (master's thesis), 30–33; *Equity* 9 (April 1907): 11. See also copy of "Official Ballot on Amendments" (1908) in Houghton Papers, University of Missouri.

combat political corruption, corporate-influenced legislation, and legislative inefficiency. Volunteers across the state distributed the leaflets shipped
to them. In addition, President Hill authored a twenty-four-page pamphlet
titled "National Decay Caused by Political Corruption and the Remedy."
The pamphlet provided a more detailed argument than could be developed
in the briefer broadsides, and it was sent to the more "serious" voters who
requested additional information on the topic. League officials claimed to
have circulated several ten thousand–copy editions of the pamphlet. Hill
personally financed the publication and mailing of the pamphlet and
claimed to have spent seventy-five hundred dollars on the campaign.[25]

The Direct Legislation League of Missouri assumed a cautious approach
in its campaign. Proponents assured potentially wary voters that the initiative and referendum did not seek to abolish the representative form of
government, but, instead, sought to guard it "from abuse and from being
misrepresentative." The plan would, they argued, "perform the same function as the safety valve in an engine; silent and unnoticed when not needed, but useful in time of danger."[26] Hill made speeches in support of the
amendment in most of the major cities in the state. He also claimed to have
presented approximately fifty addresses to trade unions and labor gatherings. To carry the message directly to other voters around the state, and to
explain any misconceptions about the proposed amendment, the league
engaged the services of John Z. White. League officials regarded White, a
veteran in the single-tax movement and a national lecturer for that cause,
as "the best man that can be secured [for the job]." The participation of White
in the campaign underscored the strong connection that the single tax continued to have to the direct legislation movement in Missouri. In fact, all the
officers of the Direct Legislation League of Missouri at this time—President
Dr. William Preston Hill; Vice Presidents William H. Priesmeyer, Joseph For-
shaw, and Frank K. Ryan; and Secretaries S. L. Moser and Stephen Ryan—
were also leaders in the single-tax movement in Missouri.[27]

During the 1908 political campaign the initiative and referendum amendment received formal endorsements from most of the political organiza-

25. Moser was away from the 1908 campaign much of the time working on a "land
deal" in Arkansas. As a result, Hill fought the campaign largely through the literature
he sent out. A copy of the 1908 "Honest Voter" cartoon can be found in the Houghton
Papers, University of Missouri. See also *Equity* 9 (October 1907): 2; 10 (January 1908):
19; 10 (July 1908): 73; Stockbridge, "Single Taxers," 520; and letters from Hill to N. D.
Houghton, January 7 and October 13, 1922, Houghton Papers, University of Missouri.

26. *Equity* 10 (July 1908): 73.

27. *Equity* 9 (October 1907): 2. See also Stockbridge, "Single Taxers," 519; 10 (July
1908): 65–67; Houghton, "Initiative and Referendum in Missouri" (*Missouri Historical
Review*), 279–80; and letter from Hill to N. D. Houghton, October 13, 1922, Houghton
Papers, University of Missouri.

tions in the state. The Socialist Party, the Prohibition Party, and the Single Tax League actively worked for its adoption. The initiative and referendum again appeared as a plank in the state Democratic platform. The Republicans, on the other hand, omitted any direct reference to it and merely advised voters to consider carefully all the proposed amendments on the ballot and to adopt or reject them on their merits. Most of the state's newspapers once again gave the amendment little publicity and almost no support. Hill described the overall newspaper coverage as a "conspiracy of silence." Nevertheless, in spite of the rebuff from the press, Hill predicted victory, and he was correct: on November 3, 1908, voters surprised many by adopting the initiative and referendum by a majority of 30,325. The five most urbanized counties in the state again favored the amendment most strongly, giving it a 67 percent majority, while 45 percent of the electorate in the remaining counties supported it. For many in the direct legislation movement, the passage of an amendment was a major triumph, but it remained to be seen whether Missourians would embrace the new reforms.[28]

In 1910 Missouri voters had the opportunity to use the initiative and referendum for the first time. On the ballot for voter approval in that year's general election were the first two amendments proposed by initiative petition. One of the initiatives called for statewide prohibition, whereas the other sought to provide financial support for the state university by enacting a direct tax levy. Voters, however, rejected both of these proposals by large majorities. Hill blamed the negative vote on a flaw in the enacting clause of the original direct legislation amendment, which required that proposals be published only in newspapers. Because the state had not assumed the cost of printing and mailing copies of the proposals to each voter via a pamphlet system, Hill estimated that only one-third of the voters were actually informed on the matter. He concluded that an uninformed voter generally voted no.[29]

A similar result occurred at the general election of 1912. This time the ballot included four amendments proposed by initiative petition. Each of the initiated propositions—to abolish the State Board of Equalization and replace it with a state tax commission, to give grand juries the right to investigate election frauds, to levy a tax to support state-funded educational in-

28. Houghton, "Initiative and Referendum in Missouri" (master's thesis), 37; *Equity* 11 (January 1909): 3; letters from Hill to N. D. Houghton, October 13 and October 25, 1922, Houghton Papers, University of Missouri. See also *Official Manual of the State of Missouri, 1909–1910*, 373, 464, 470, 810. Voting statistics cited in Thelen, *Paths of Resistance*, 231. The legislature amended the direct legislation provisions in 1909 and reduced the petition requirements for the initiative from 8 to 5 percent (Floyd C. Shoemaker, *Missouri and Missourians*, 2:230).

29. *Equity* 13 (January 1911): 29; 15 (January 1913): 42–43. See also *Official Manual of the State of Missouri, 1911–1912*, 784–89.

stitutions, and to establish a graduated tax on land values (a version of the single tax)—was again defeated by a large majority. The editors of *Equity*, the pro–direct legislation publication, blamed negative voter reaction to the single-tax amendment for carrying everything else down.[30]

The single-tax forces, organized in Missouri in 1912 as the Equitable Taxation League and led by Hill and Moser, had always regarded direct legislation as the means by which they might someday obtain at least a modified version of the single tax in Missouri. Single taxers believed that landownership and opportunity were linked. The way to create opportunity was to make land available. However, speculators prevented this by holding land idle while they waited for community development to increase the value of their holdings. The solution to this problem was to make land too costly to be held for speculative purposes. If the state took as a tax the increased value of all monopolized, unimproved land (the "unearned increment"), no one could afford to keep land solely for speculation. After voters ratified the initiative and referendum amendment in 1908, the question to single taxers became merely one of timing—deciding when to push for a major revision in the tax structure. Seeking to give voters the opportunity to test the new, unfamiliar initiative device, and needing time to perfect their organization, raise campaign funds, and begin a statewide educational campaign, single taxers set their sights on the general election of 1912. To support their efforts, the Joseph Fels Fund Commission provided them with a grant of fifteen hundred dollars. Joseph Fels, a wealthy Philadelphia soap manufacturer and convert to the teachings of Henry George, established the Joseph Fels Fund Commission in 1909. The purpose of the organization was to see the single tax enacted somewhere in the United States within five years. With such support, proponents were optimistic that Missourians would be receptive to the single-tax idea.[31]

Public reaction to a proposed single-tax amendment in 1912, however, was overwhelmingly negative. The measure would have increased tax values on unimproved land while granting tax exemptions for personal property and most landed improvements. Single taxers had grossly misjudged the amount of educational work required to explain a complicated tax revision. As a result, farmers feared that the amendment really amounted to increased taxes on land rather than the reverse. The editors of *Equity*, worried as much about possible backlash to the initiative, chastised the single

---

30. *Equity* 15 (January 1913): 42. See also *Official Manual of the State of Missouri, 1913–1914*, 1107–10.

31. Stockbridge, "Single Taxers," 514, 520. Fels conducted a two-week speaking tour in Missouri in support of the single-tax amendment during the closing weeks of the 1912 campaign. See Arthur P. Dudden, *Joseph Fels and the Single Tax Movement*, 199–02, 230; and Arthur Nichols Young, *The Single Tax Movement in the United States*, 164–67.

taxers for their "ill-judged impulsiveness" and for mistakenly thinking that they could push their ideas into law in an agricultural state like Missouri. Moser, serving as secretary of the Equitable Taxation League, agreed: "Public sentiment against the Single Tax became very intense. . . . Inflammatory misstatements as to the effect of the amendment were circulated very extensively in all the agricultural districts, in nearly all of which a veritable panic prevailed." As a result, voters overwhelmingly rejected the amendment by a vote of 86,647 to 508,137.[32]

Many direct legislationists feared that the negative public reaction to the single-tax proposal might endanger the entire system of direct legislation in Missouri, as thousands of voters had come to link the initiative and the single tax. Their fears soon intensified. When the Missouri legislature convened in January 1913, many of the new members, who had ridden into office by promising their frightened constituents that they would provide them with protection from the single tax, pushed for an anti-single-tax amendment to the constitution. Responding to their efforts, the legislature approved an amendment that would prohibit the use of the initiative to propose any law or constitutional amendment affecting taxation. The intent was to deny voters the power to reclassify property for purposes of levying different rates of taxation, or to authorize the levying of any single tax on land or land values at a higher rate than that applied to improvements on land.[33]

To Hill and other direct legislationists, the proposed anti-single-tax amendment was the opening wedge in an effort to curb direct legislation by convincing voters that they could not trust themselves. Said Hill:

> Why should the Initiative and Referendum be destroyed because an amendment was submitted under it that the people did not like? Our legislatures have made . . . serious mistakes which the people have had no chance to correct and yet nobody has urged that as a reason for abolishing the legislature. At least, if a mistake was made under the Initiative, the people immediately had the chance to rectify the mistake by a record breaking majority at the polls.

Former governor Folk agreed: "If we tie our hands from voting on something we do not want now, we will find ourselves powerless someday to secure something we do want."[34] Voters would have to decide if these

32. Moser quoted in *Equity* 15 (April 1913): 125. A copy of the proposed single-tax amendment for 1912 can be found in Houghton Papers, University of Missouri. See also *Equity* 15 (January 1913): 42; 15 (April 1913): 125; 16 (October 1914): 183; *Official Manual, 1913–1914*, 1107–10; Norman L. Crockett, "The 1912 Single Tax Campaign In Missouri," 40–52; and A. N. Young, *Single Tax in the United States*, 191–96.

33. See *Equity* 15 (April 1913): 125; 16 (July 1914): 139; and 16 (October 1914): 182–83.

34. Hill and Folk quoted in *Equity* 16 (July 1914): 140.

warnings were valid when the amendment came up for popular approval at the next general election.

In November 1914 Missouri voters were handed a ballot that included the anti-single-tax amendment, four referred statutes, and three initiated amendments. The four acts brought to a vote by referendum petition—the first use of the referendum in Missouri—were a minimum crew bill for passenger, mail, express, and freight trains; an amended local option law giving jurisdictional control to counties rather than municipalities; and two laws abolishing the governor-appointed office of excise commissioner and the governor-appointed boards of police commissioners in cities of three hundred thousand or more and the transfer of that authority to the mayors. The initiated amendments were woman suffrage, a highway bond issue, and a special tax levy for road improvements. As they had done in each election since 1910, Missourians rejected all the ballot propositions and did so by wide majorities. The only bright spot for those who had crusaded for direct legislation was the defeat of the anti-single-tax amendment proposed by the legislature by a vote of 138,039 to 334,310.[35]

The conservative tendency registered by Missourians toward ballot propositions continued in 1916 and 1918. In 1916 voters considered two initiated amendments, one to create a state land bank with power to make loans to farmers and one for statewide prohibition. Voters defeated both measures. The 1918 ballot contained three amendments proposed by initiative petition: a law creating a homestead loan fund, a law establishing a version of the single tax for the collection of public revenues, and a law authorizing cities with more than one hundred thousand inhabitants to design their own special charters. Voters rejected all three proposals. All told, from 1910 to 1918, Missourians considered eighteen measures proposed under the initiative and referendum on a wide range of issues, but approved none of them.[36]

---

35. See *Equity* 17 (January 1915): 50; Houghton, "Initiative and Referendum in Missouri" (*Missouri Historical Review*), 283–84; A. N. Young, *Single Tax in the United States,* 196–97; and *Official Manual of the State of Missouri, 1915–1916,* 570–76. In February 1915, Edwin S. Potter reported that an effort had been undertaken in Missouri to improve the wording of ballot propositions. The intention was to eliminate the practice of printing in fine type the full text of every measure on the ballot "with all the legal circumlocution." "To the utterly impossible character of this blanket ballot (the 1914 ballot in Missouri was said to fill a sheet as large as two daily newspaper pages)," said Potter, "is attributed in large measure the long succession of negative decisions on measures submitted . . . since . . . 1908" ("Reforming the Initiative and Referendum," *Review of Reviews* 51 [February 1915]: 214–15).

36. Voters also considered twenty-nine constitutional amendments proposed by the Missouri legislature between 1910 and 1918 and approved only one. See Houghton, "Initiative and Referendum in Missouri" (*Missouri Historical Review*), 284–85; *Official Manual of the State of Missouri, 1917–1918,* 484–85; *Official Manual of the State of Missouri, 1919–1920,* 424–29; and *Official Manual of the State of Missouri, 1921–1922,* 468–77.

Students of Missouri history might argue that Missouri voters' cautious consideration of ballot propositions was predictable—the result of their reluctance to embrace change and their antigovernment and low-tax attitudes. Further, they might argue, as others have, that Missourians have traditionally found it difficult to transcend local attachments to region and place and concerns for local problems to embrace a statewide vision.[37] However, Missouri's record on ballot propositions should not totally diminish the achievement of the advocates of direct legislation in the state. The consideration of eighteen measures proposed by the initiative and referendum between 1910 and 1918 underscored a significant change in the way the political system operated. Partisan politicians could no longer cavalierly ignore issues or arrogantly dictate policy. The adoption of the initiative and referendum in Missouri stimulated the discussion of issues—such as woman suffrage, prohibition, and the single tax—and expanded the boundaries of political debate. Though supporters undoubtedly found the legislative results disheartening, they could take solace in the fact that voters could now participate in determining the political agenda. And that in itself was no small accomplishment.

MAINE

Joining Missouri in adopting the initiative and referendum in 1908 was Maine. The origins of the movement to enact direct legislation in the Pine Tree State can be found in the growing concern that voters had over several economic and political questions. The most important of these was taxation. The state possessed millions of acres of unsettled lands owned by a relatively small number of individuals and a few corporations. These "wild lands" with their valuable timber resources had traditionally been assessed at a low tax valuation. In fact, a history of large land grants to railroads and cheap land sales to individuals had created a situation in which private concerns owned roughly one-half of the state's total land area, but contributed less than one-ninth of the state's direct tax revenues. As the people living in the "organized" townships began to feel the pinch of municipal, county, and state taxes, they began to complain of an inequitable tax burden and argued that owners of "unorganized" lands should contribute more to maintain schools and highways in the state. The state had also been generous in granting valuable franchises worth millions of dollars for which it had received little in return—rebating taxes that should have been

37. For studies that help to understand the Missouri temperament, see Christopher C. Gibbs, *The Great Silent Majority: Missouri's Resistance to World War I*; Thelen, *Paths of Resistance*; and Lawrence O. Christensen, "Missouri: The Heart of the Nation," 86–105.

paid by railroads and granting other corporate exemptions that denied the state revenue.[38]

The economics of taxation had a political dimension as well. Kingsbury Piper, a leading Maine progressive, summed up the attitude of many: "For years the public had become more and more cognizant of the power of wild-land owners who were responsible for the existence of a powerful lobby at the State House and there seemed to be some relationship between that lobby and the fact that wild-land owners paid a smaller per cent of taxation than equity demanded." The result, according to Piper, was civic demoralization: "The public had found out that year after year desired legislation of merit suffered defeat after defeat, sacrificed to the successes of legislation asked for by private and corporate interests and accomplished by well-paid lobbies."[39] Abner W. Nichols, a close observer of the direct legislation movement in Maine, agreed:

> The common people of Maine were already alive to the futility of appealing to a legislature selected and controlled by those who through such control were securing for themselves special privileges and immunity from taxes. They were convinced that it did not lay in the power of the people, by any method at present available, to secure the passage of laws to make taxes even a little more fair and equal, to protect the people from being robbed of their wild-lands and valuable franchises, or to prevent monopoly in both the necessaries of life and the means of acquiring them.[40]

Under existing circumstances, there seemed to be only two options open to reformers: elect a number of legislators sufficient to challenge the wild-land, railroad, and corporate lobbies or alter the existing representative plan of government to give voters a voice.[41]

The first individual to suggest that the state should modify its form of government to include provisions for direct legislation was Roland T. Patten. Patten first heard something of direct legislation around 1894 as an idea that had been put to practical use in Switzerland. At the time an ardent believer in the idea of municipal ownership, he initially thought that if the people could initiate laws, they might actually obtain the public ownership of public utilities. He quickly realized, though, that direct leg-

38. See J. William Black, "Maine's Experience with the Initiative and Referendum," 161.

39. Piper, "The Victorious Campaign for Direct-Legislation in Maine," 547.

40. Nichols, "Present Status of the Referendum Movement in Maine," *Arena* 36 (November 1906): 517.

41. See Black, "Maine's Experience," 162–63.

islation promised even greater rewards. According to Patten, and in words that echoed the "conversion" of William S. U'Ren in Oregon, "I . . . discovered that Direct Legislation was much broader than the idea that led me to it." He soon found that others were traveling the same road that he was, "but at the time I knew nothing of them."[42] Using his position as editor of the *Somerset Reporter* printed in Skowhegan to propagandize for direct legislation, Patten attempted to get the two major parties to adopt resolutions favoring the initiative and referendum in 1902, but managed to convince only the minority Democratic Party to do so. During the 1903 session of the legislature, Representative Cyrus W. Davis of Waterville introduced a measure that had been written by Patten calling for the initiative and referendum. The bill was referred to the judiciary committee, which held hearings at which both Patten and Davis presented supportive statements. Intrigued by the logic of their arguments but plagued by indecision, the committee decided to refer the measure to the next legislature.[43]

The nomination of Davis as the Democratic candidate for governor in 1904 established the initiative and referendum as a major campaign issue and generated a great deal of discussion of the topic. An early proponent of the idea again proved to be the State Federation of Labor, which began an active campaign to win approval for a direct legislation amendment in the next legislature. Hoping to widen the support base and demonstrate that the idea had broad geographic appeal in the state, the State Federation of Labor enlisted the cooperation of the State Grange, a strong political force in the state and influential with rural legislators. After a petition drive that netted sixteen thousand signatures, the two organizations formally memorialized the 1905 legislature to enact a constitutional amendment embodying the initiative and referendum.

The combined actions of the two organizations caught the attention of the state's political parties. Senator E. S. Clark of Bar Harbor introduced a new bill, and the judiciary committee again held rather extensive hearings. Representatives of the State Federation of Labor, the State Grange, and the Maine Civic League and several prominent spokesmen for direct legislation from outside the state offered supportive arguments. The final vote on the measure (thirteen to thirteen in the Senate and sixty-two to forty-eight in the House), however, was well short of the two-thirds majority required for constitutional amendments. Opponents argued that the proposal was a radical departure from well-established methods of legislation, labeled the measure a union-labor idea, and created enough misgivings in the minds

42. *Equity* 11 (April 1909): 44.
43. See Black, "Maine's Experience," 163–64; Rod Farmer, "The Maine Campaign for Direct Democracy, 1902–1908," 15; and *Equity* 11 (April 1909): 43–44.

of some legislators to defeat it. Embittered supporters charged that the amendment had been defeated by the influence of the corporation lobby.[44]

The leaders of the campaign in Maine realized that they would have to make a more systematic effort in order to be successful. With that in mind, they organized the Referendum League of Maine in the early summer of 1905. The Referendum League, much like the People's Power League in Oregon, described itself as "inter-partisan" in membership and "strictly non-partisan" in methods, and stated that its goal was to secure "the people's right to a direct vote on questions of public policy." Using the tactic of candidate accountability that had worked well in other states, the Referendum League wrote letters to every individual who had been mentioned as a possible candidate for the legislature asking for their views on the initiative and referendum. The league regarded failure or refusal to comply with their request as a formal "No" and made it clear that any individual who did so would become a target in the next political campaign. The Referendum League won the formal support of the State Grange, comprising 450 locals and 50,000 members, which adopted a strong resolution favoring the initiative and referendum at its annual convention in December 1905.[45]

During the summer of 1906 both the Republican and the Democratic Parties adopted favorable planks in their party platforms, and both gubernatorial candidates—Republican William T. Cobb and Democrat Cyrus W. Davis—favored the idea. Davis assumed the more forceful position and argued that the initiative and referendum offered "the only means of escape from the terrible weight with which the institutions of the state were loaded," and cited the "glaring inequalities of taxation" and the "wicked contracts made with the railroads" as examples. Even though the Republican Party again won the September election, it did so with a much smaller majority than before. In addition, most of those who had pledged to support a bill for direct legislation won election to the legislature, whereas many candidates who opposed those reforms did not.[46]

With the members of both parties pledged to the concept of direct legislation, with the legislative committee of the Referendum League working in conjunction with similar committees from the State Grange and the State Federation of Labor, and with Governor Cobb lending his support, it seemed that passage of an initiative and referendum amendment in some form was all but a certainty. The proposal did meet with some resistance from banks, timberland owners, railroads, and other corporate interests.

44. See Black, "Maine's Experience," 164; and Piper, "Victorious Campaign," 548.
45. Referendum League quoted in Piper, "Victorious Campaign," 548 (see also 548–49). See also Black, "Maine's Experience," 164–65; and *Equity* 9 (January 1907): 15–16.
46. Davis quoted in R. Farmer, "Maine Campaign," 17. See also Piper, "Victorious Campaign," 548–49; and Black, "Maine's Experience," 165.

Before the opposition lobby could mount its strongest attack, though, the legislature became embroiled in a fight over a proposal to move the state capital from Augusta to Portland. According to Roland Patten, press secretary of the Referendum League, this was a lucky break for the direct legislationists. "We soon found that we could force a vote on our measure before the capitol [*sic*] removal bill came to a vote, one side being so greedy to get, and the other to retain, the seat of government, that neither dared be found opposing a measure that they knew was so universally demanded as the Initiative and Referendum."[47] Nonetheless, the legislature still had to decide on the type of amendment it would accept.

This time two competing measures appeared before the legislature—one backed by each of the major political parties. Representative George G. Weeks of Fairfield introduced the Republican measure that authorized the initiative and referendum for statutes only. Representative Charles F. Johnson of Waterville offered a broader Democratic bill that favored the inclusion of constitutional amendments in the proposed law. As a reassurance that the latter provision would not be abused, Johnson proposed that signature requirements be doubled for proposing constitutional amendments under the initiative process. Members of the Referendum League, however, feared that the provision allowing for the amendment procedure might imperil the measure's chances of gaining a two-thirds majority in the legislature and a popular majority at the polls. Compounding their anxiety was a real fear that many voters would reject the amendment out of concern that it would lead to the resubmission of the state's long-standing prohibition law. When it became evident that a two-thirds majority would not favor the Johnson proposal, the Democrats agreed to support the Weeks Bill as better than no bill at all. The measure eventually passed both houses without a dissenting vote. Voters would be given the opportunity to accept or reject the proposed amendment at the next election in September 1908.[48]

The initiative and referendum amendment included a standard emergency clause that exempted measures deemed necessary for the public peace, health, or safety from the law. In an attempt to circumscribe the emergency designation, which was open to interpretation and could be used to narrow the scope of direct legislation, the law specifically stated that the emergency clause could not infringe upon home rule for municipalities, allow franchises or licenses to be granted for longer than one year, or provide for the sale, purchase, or long-term rental of real estate. The amendment also included a provision allowing cities to establish the initiative and referendum for municipal affairs.

47. *Equity* 11 (April 1909): 44–45. See also *Equity* 9 (January 1907): 16.
48. See Black, "Maine's Experience," 165–66; and Piper, "Victorious Campaign," 550.

The final measure did, however, include several restrictive features that would work against its frequent use. In addition to the exclusion of constitutional amendments from the scope of the initiative, the amendment also altered the usual signature requirement for petitions. Instead of designating a specific percentage of the voting population, the law set the statewide initiative at simply twelve thousand voters and the statewide referendum at ten thousand. The amendment also prohibited the direct initiative whereby measures are submitted directly to the voters without prior legislative consideration. Instead, the law required that popular initiatives be presented to the legislature for consideration prior to a popular vote being taken. If the legislature decided to enact the law as presented, the initiative election would be canceled. Should the legislature, however, decide to offer an amendment to the initiated proposal or should it decide to design its own alternative bill, both measures would be presented to the voters. The one gaining the higher majority vote would become law. Proponents of the direct approach argued that the possible delay caused by legislative deliberation served to undermine the momentum generated by the petition campaign. As a further hedge against hasty or irrational popular action, the legislature retained the right to amend or repeal any initiated legislation.[49]

Having been unable to make an all-out assault on the direct legislation during the legislative session, opponents made a concerted effort to convince voters to reject the proposed amendment during the eighteen-month interval before the election. Portraying the initiative and referendum as radical ideas that threatened representative government, opponents gained a hearing in most of the state's Republican newspapers. The leading corporation lawyers in Bangor even published a public letter in the two leading newspapers in the eastern part of the state urging readers to vote no. Corporation money also funded the publication of a publicity pamphlet that contained negative letters from opponents of the initiative and referendum in Oregon and California as well as one from one of Maine's most prominent judges. Joining the opposition was Senator Eugene Hale, who used his federal franking privilege to circulate to his constituents in Maine a reprint of a speech made by Senator Henry Cabot Lodge of Massachusetts. In the speech, an attack on a proposed advisory Public Opinion Bill for Massachusetts, Lodge denounced the idea of legislation by petition and direct vote as "nothing less than a complete revolution in the fabric of our Government." To Senator Lodge, direct legislation would "weaken" or

49. For a discussion of the details of the proposed law, see Ralph Albertson, "Victory in Maine," 512–14; Black, "Maine's Experience," 166–67; R. Farmer, "Maine Campaign," 19; William Bennett Munro, *The Initiative, Referendum, and Recall*, 10; and *Equity* 9 (April 1907): 11–12, 21–23.

"impair" the principle of representation by depriving the people of the opportunity for "consideration, debate, deliberation, and . . . amendment." The result could mean only a tyranny of the majority by "small and active minorities" seeking to obtain legislation that they could not secure by "legitimate methods."[50]

Working both to counter the anti–direct legislation argument and to help voters understand the proposal about to be put before them were the State Grange, the State Federation of Labor, and the Referendum League. The league asked members from both major political parties to explain the amendment, and at least one newspaper, the *Waterville Morning Sentinel* (owned by Cyrus Davis), aided that effort. Kingsbury Piper, secretary of the Maine Referendum League, presented a memorial to the United States Senate in which he answered the arguments of Senator Lodge. Whereas Lodge regarded direct democracy as a "revolutionary" threat to representative government, Piper saw it as "reformatory"—the way to improve upon a system of government plagued by special interest lobbies and machine politics. Senator Robert L. Owen of Oklahoma (an ardent direct legislationist) first asked that the memorial be printed as a Senate document, and then requested that twenty thousand copies be made available for distribution to the public. The Referendum League eventually disseminated those copies throughout the state under Senator Owen's frank. Seconding Piper's argument, the Reverend Henry Dunnock, a leading Maine Progressive, remarked: "This measure . . . certainly makes for a larger commonwealth, a stronger government, a more efficient citizenship." Most voters agreed, approving the amendment establishing the initiative and referendum by a two-to-one majority in September 1908. The amendment carried in each of the state's sixteen counties. However, the final tally (53,785 to 24,543) represented only 54 percent of those who voted for governor. Kingsbury Piper blamed "the shameful duplicity of election officers in withholding referendum ballots" for having "contributed towards keeping down the 'Yes' vote."[51]

Maine's conservative electorate proceeded to utilize the amendment cautiously. The first opportunity to use direct legislation came at the 1910 election in which voters invoked the referendum on three measures passed by the legislature. Two of the three measures involved purely local issues— the division of the old town of York and the reconstruction of the Portland

50. Albertson, "Victory in Maine," 511; Piper, "Victorious Campaign," 551; R. Farmer, "Maine Campaign," 20; U.S. Congress, Senate, "The Public Opinion Bill."

51. Dunnock quoted in R. Farmer, "Maine Campaign," 20; Piper, "Victorious Campaign," 551. See also Albertson, "Victory in Maine," 511; *Congressional Record,* 60th Cong., 1st sess., 6954, 7155; and U.S. Congress, Senate, "Memorial of State Referendum League of Maine Concerning Initiative and Referendum."

Bridge—and voters rejected both of them. The third measure was an attempt on the part of the prohibition element to expand the existing prohibition law to prevent the sale of light beers (less than 3 percent alcohol). Because defense attorneys had frequently overturned convictions by arguing that the liquor in question was "not an intoxicating beverage within the meaning of the law, or according to the interpretation of the courts," proponents hoped that broadening the scope of the law would increase its effectiveness. Voters vetoed this measure as well.[52]

Voters considered three constitutional amendments passed by the legislature and gave the initiative its first test in a special election held in 1911. The principal issue in the 1910 election campaign had been the question of resubmitting the state's prohibition law and repealing the unpopular "Sturgis law" of 1905 that gave state liquor commissioners the power to supersede the authority of local officials in the enforcement of the "Maine law." As a result of the ensuing debate over the prohibition issue as well as charges of "extravagance" and "inefficiency" on the part of the preceding Republican administration, the Democratic Party captured the governor's office and majorities of both houses of the state legislature. Fulfilling their party's campaign pledges, Democratic legislators proceeded to repeal the obnoxious Sturgis law and to pass a resubmission act in the form of an amendment invalidating the existing prohibition law that had been part of Maine's constitution since 1884. A heated campaign involving the Anti-Saloon League and the Women's Christian Temperance Union followed during the summer of 1911. Finally, in an extremely close vote (60,853 to 60,095), voters decided to overrule the legislature and retain the "Maine law." On other amendments, voters rejected moving the state capital from Augusta to Portland and approved raising the debt limit of cities of more than forty thousand inhabitants, that is, Portland, to allow for the borrowing of funds needed for various municipal improvements.[53]

The use of the initiative in 1911 resulted from a debate over the design of a direct primary law. Agitation for such a law began with the organization of the Direct Primary League of Maine in 1908. Proponents argued that political bosses and corporate interests, especially the Maine Central Railroad, dominated the nominating conventions of the major political parties. Both the Republican and the Democratic Parties included planks favoring such a statute in their platforms in 1910. Governor Frederick W. Plaisted recom-

52. Some argued that the real intent behind the proposed amendment to the liquor law was to make prohibition in Maine so ridiculous that voters would demand its repeal. See *Equity* 12 (October 1910): 151–52; Black, "Maine's Experience," 168–69; and Lawrence Lee Pelletier, "The Initiative and Referendum in Maine," 26.

53. See Black, "Maine's Experience," 171–74; *Equity* 13 (October 1911): 176; and Pelletier, "Initiative and Referendum," 28.

mended passage of a direct primary law in his inaugural address as well. Formal proposals quickly appeared in the legislature. One, proposed by Representative William M. Pennell, called for the adoption of a direct primary, but limited its use to the governorship and congressional representatives and allowed for only a preference primary for U.S. senators. Representative Howard Davies introduced a competing bill that would have applied the primary to all candidates for state and county offices in addition to those included in the Pennell measure. The legislature, however, chose to approve Pennell's more modest proposal. Davies refused to admit defeat and started an initiative petition on behalf of his plan. Assisted by the Direct Primary League, his petition gained the 12,000 necessary signatures and won a place on the ballot in the September election. Deciding they preferred the "Davies law" over the "Pennell law," voters approved the initiative by a vote of 65,810 to 21,774.[54]

The use of the initiative by Maine's voters in 1911 was the only time they invoked that provision prior to 1918. They did, however, decide the fate of four laws referred by popular petition between 1912 and 1918 and, even though they lacked the constitutional initiative, voted on eight constitutional amendments proposed by the legislature during that same period. In 1912 voters upheld a uniform ballot box statute. Supporters defended the law as being necessary to counteract ballot box "stuffing" and irregularities in the printing of ballots. In 1914 voters sustained a law creating the Public Utilities Commission, and in 1916 upheld a statute establishing a fifty-four-hour workweek for women and for children under the age of sixteen. William Pennell, acting as agent of the Hill Manufacturing Company (a textile concern), led the petition drive against the maximum-hours law by hiring petition circulators who were paid 5 cents for every signature they collected. Supporting Pennell with a publicity campaign and the mass mailing of thousands of circular letters and pamphlets was the Maine Industrial Expansion Commission. The State Federation of Labor led the campaign in favor of the fifty-four-hour law and persuasively argued that working a longer week (especially in overheated textile factories) was detrimental to the health and well-being of women and minors.[55]

54. See Black, "Maine's Experience," 174–75; *Equity* 13 (October 1911): 150; Pelletier, "Initiative and Referendum," 26; and George Judson King Papers, Library of Congress, Manuscripts Division, Washington, D.C.

55. In 1916 the legislature voluntarily attached a referendum provision to a measure calling for state and county aid in the construction of highways. Voters approved the measure. See Pelletier, "Initiative and Referendum," 15 n. 25. For an overview of the history of the initiative and referendum in Maine prior to 1952 (as well as a record of all measures considered and all vote totals), see ibid. See also King Papers, Library of Congress.

Explanations for the infrequent use of the initiative and referendum in Maine are not easy to come by, but Lawrence Pelletier, an authority on direct legislation in Maine writing in 1951, has at least offered a few. One reason cited was that most pressure groups in the state were not as well organized or financed as those elsewhere, and that the more significant interest groups such as the Associated Industries of Maine, the State Grange, and the State Federation of Labor could "expect to get about as much from the legislature as from the people—and with less effort and expense." Another factor offered was the "decidedly middle of the road" political climate of opinion in Maine that may have made legislators more receptive to new ideas than the voters. Last, Pelletier found the state legislature to be "reasonably representative" and that the potential split between urban and rural interests (notable in this study in Missouri, North Dakota, Ohio, and Maryland, for example) had not asserted itself to the extent that groups in the more populated urban centers might have been provoked into making direct appeals to the people.[56]

56. Pelletier, "Initiative and Referendum," 23.

5

Colorado and Arkansas

COLORADO

The campaign to obtain direct legislation in Colorado involved the coming together of disparate elements—urban consumers and taxpayers, organized labor, progressive-minded reformers, and liberal Democrats—driven to seek common ground by the refusal of the dominant political culture to respond to their demands. To understand how that process began, it is necessary to look to the early 1890s and the rise of the Populist Party in the Centennial State. Although the silver crisis precipitated the political revolt in Colorado, a deeper, more fundamental cause for the upheaval can be found in the negative effects of a boom-and-bust capitalist economy that exploited the mineral wealth of the West. Developed to a great extent by outside capital, Colorado had become a state characterized by absentee ownership and control. Mining, railroad, and irrigation development generated an economic boom that was largely underwritten by eastern and foreign investors. State legislators encouraged such investments, and investors operated in an environment largely unencumbered by state regulation. In such a laissez-faire economy, the entrepreneurial spirit ran unchecked. Greedy owners stripped their mining properties, while reckless speculators wildly promoted mining stocks, pyramided farm mortgages, and inflated real estate values.

As unregulated capitalism reigned supreme, the government of Colorado quickly became subordinate to its vested economic interests. The influence of private monopolies, coupled with the indifference of an electorate swept up in the acquisitive spirit of the time, engendered a level of political corruption that made a mockery of popular government. A "lobby" dictated legislation at the state capitol and bribed accommodating legislators to protect the interests of railroads and corporations. Governance in the state's dominant municipality was no different. Tax laws favored Denver's large property holders and corporations and reflected the legislative influence of that city's powerful public utility interests.

Corporate interests held sway as long as the state's economic boom, fueled by the production of silver, continued. However, a downward swing in the business cycle in the late 1880s caused many eastern creditors to liquidate their holdings in the West. As the state's economy began to suffer, an increasing number of Coloradans blamed the "money power." Deflationary pressures reached a climax in the summer of 1893 when Congress repealed the Silver Purchase Act, causing the price of silver to plummet. The result was a severe economic crisis that shook the foundation of the existing corporate-dominated political economy in Colorado. Mines and smelters closed, railroads fell into receivership, and banks failed. As business became paralyzed, unemployment soared, farm debts deepened, and discontent intensified.

The political expression of that discontent was the People's Party of Colorado, organized in 1891. Headed by Davis H. Waite, a relatively unknown editor of a radical labor newspaper in Aspen, Colorado, the new party won at the polls in 1892. Although the popularity of the silver issue enabled the Populists to triumph, Governor Waite had campaigned on a program that demanded fundamental reform of the political-economic order. Included in his platform were calls for the end of private monopoly in land and state regulation of railroads (nationalization if that proved ineffective), while he declared himself opposed to any proposals that might increase the powers of corporations or reduce their liabilities. Governor Waite's strong antimonopoly position and strident anticorporate remarks reflected a rising popular apprehension over the growing power of organized capital.[1]

Convinced that existing laws favored the interests of the privileged elite, Governor Waite actively sought to revise those laws to protect the interests of the masses. During his brief tenure in office, he attempted to expand the role of state government by proposing a series of laws aimed at protecting the equity of debtors, safeguarding the rights of labor, and guaranteeing employment. To curb the influence of privilege and to make government more responsive to the popular will, he advocated changes in the state's election laws to discourage election fraud and the adoption of an amendment to the state constitution to provide for the initiative and referendum. However, the Waite-led Populists failed to realize their legislative goals. Lacking the votes to force their will on the Republicans and Democrats (or the finesse to build an accommodating political coalition), often divided among themselves, and helpless against the ever present influence of the lobby, they saw their legislative program stymied. In the end, militant Populism actually worked to revive the elements of conservative opposition under Republican Party leadership.[2]

1. See Leon W. Fuller, "Colorado's Revolt against Capitalism," 344–55.
2. See ibid., 355–60; and James Edward Wright, *The Politics of Populism: Dissent in Colorado,* 171–77.

It was during the term of Davis Waite that Denverites in particular realized the extent to which political control in their city had been usurped from them. In 1891, as the Republican Party sought to increase its direct control over municipal politics in Denver, the Republican-dominated state legislature created the Denver Fire and Police Board and gave the governor power to appoint all board members. The power was significant, as the board had control over the granting of saloon licenses and the operation of the Department of Public Safety. The legislature extended similar executive control over appointments to the existing Board of Public Works two years later. The latter department authorized all contracts for public improvements in the city, and greatly enhanced the governor's power at the expense of the city council.[3]

Shortly after taking office in 1893, Governor Waite, looking to undermine Republican control and eliminate organized vice that had allied itself with the local political machine in Denver, appointed Populists to the Police Board. Several months later, however, the governor removed two of his appointees for failing to investigate reports of police corruption and for refusing to enforce existing statutes governing dance halls, dram shops, gambling dens, opium houses, and brothels. Less than six months later Governor Waite took action to remove two members of the new board for similar failings. This time, however, the appointees refused to surrender their positions and obtained a court injunction to prevent their dismissal prior to judicial review. Impatient, Waite ordered a regiment of the state guard to surround City Hall where the Police Board members had barricaded themselves in their offices. Opposing the militia were loyal city policemen and sheriff's deputies. Finally, as twenty thousand bystanders watched with amazement, a group of Denver's leading citizens convinced the governor to withdraw his troops to prevent bloodshed and almost certain harm to the city's image. The governor then agreed to submit the dispute to the Colorado Supreme Court, which ultimately decided in his favor. The affair, known as the "City Hall War," caused Waite considerable political damage in the metropolitan area and convinced many Denverites that state control over municipal politics was unacceptable. That same year, 1894, concerned citizens organized the Municipal League of Denver and began what would be a long and tortuous campaign to obtain "home rule" for the capital city.[4]

The defeat of Governor Waite in 1894 brought peace to Denver but not

3. See Carl Abbott, *Colorado: A History of the Centennial State,* 198–200; Clyde Lyndon King, *The History of the Government of Denver with Special Reference to Its Relations with Public Service Corporations,* 184–88; and Marjorie Hornbein, "Denver's Struggle for Home Rule," 338–41.

4. See Abbott, *Colorado,* 200–201; C. L. King, *Government of Denver,* 193, 211–16; and Hornbein, "Denver's Struggle," 341–45.

an end to the feeling of political powerlessness experienced by many of its taxpaying citizens. Central to this dissatisfaction was the growing popular sense that certain public utility corporations exerted too much power over municipal government. During the 1895 mayoral election, the Taxpayers' Reform Association charged both the Union Water Company and the Denver Tramway Company with tax dodging, using bribery to prevent the city council from allowing a popular referendum on public ownership of the waterworks, and having sufficient influence in the state legislature to block legislation that might provide relief to taxpayers. The association promised to secure for the people a "larger share in their own government by Direct Legislation."[5]

Outraged taxpayers succeeded in electing Thomas S. McMurray as mayor in 1895. McMurray, a Republican not allied with corporate interests, headed a nonpartisan Taxpayers' ticket that promised reform and economy. Although popular enough to win reelection in 1897, McMurray was handcuffed by the city's existing charter that allowed the legislature to veto any extension of mayoral power. As a result, McMurray was unable to make any fundamental changes during his two terms in office. McMurray suffered defeat in the corrupt election of 1899 when the city's Democratic political machine, allegedly financed by Denver's public service corporations, organized an army of ballot-box stuffers known as the "Big Mitt." Amid allegations of election fraud and collusion, Denver's reformers charged that a "cabal" composed of the directors of the telephone, water, gas and electric, and tramway monopolies had conspired to protect their exclusive franchise privileges and render the electorate politically powerless. An official of the water company aptly summed up the situation: "The people have nothing to do with nominations and elections. We rule and we are going to continue to rule." To a growing number of reformers, government in the public interest in Denver could be obtained only by a revision of the city's charter that would allow for home rule and the inclusion of the initiative and referendum.[6]

Understanding the importance of education and organization in mobilizing the public behind direct legislation were two capable individuals: Persifor M. Cooke and J. Warner Mills of Denver. Cooke ran a column on direct legislation in the Sunday edition of the *Rocky Mountain News* during the spring of 1896 in which he acquainted readers with the merits of direct legislation as practiced in Switzerland. He also served as the state's correspondent to the *Direct Legislation Record* and as an outspoken advocate

5. *Direct Legislation Record* 2 (December 1895): 29.
6. Official quoted in Abbott, *Colorado*, 202 (see also 201–2). See also Hornbein, "Denver's Struggle," 345–48; and C. L. King, *Government of Denver*, 217–18.

of the initiative and referendum while serving as a member of the state legislature. Joining Cooke was the indefatigable Mills. Trained as a lawyer at the University of Wisconsin, Mills migrated to Colorado in 1877 and opened a law office in Lake City. Moving his practice to Denver in 1886, he quickly made a name for himself in the legal profession as the author of *Mills' Annotated Statutes of Colorado*. During the 1890s Mills became increasingly active in politics. He prepared the measure authorizing woman suffrage that passed the legislature in 1893, and served as both president of the State Board of Charities and chairman of the State Board of Pardons under Governor Waite. He also began to develop an active interest in various reform causes that included the public ownership of municipal utilities, prohibition, the single tax, and, most important, direct legislation. Mills served as Colorado's delegate to the St. Louis convention that organized the National Direct Legislation League in 1896 and won election to the executive committee of that body. He also served as president of the Direct Legislation League of Colorado until 1906, when a critical illness forced him to step aside.[7]

Also working to advance the cause of direct legislation was organized labor. Founded in 1896 and led by Otto F. Thum, a member of the Typographical Union, a Socialist, and a leader in the fight to establish the initiative, referendum, and recall in Colorado, the Colorado State Federation of Labor (CSFL) followed an active but independent course in politics. In doing so, the organization developed a broad-ranging program that included the eight-hour day, employer liability, the abolition of company scrip, municipal ownership of utilities, and the adoption of the initiative and referendum. However, the CSFL found that amending the state constitution to allow for protective labor legislation was all but impossible. The stumbling block was a provision that prohibited the legislature from proposing amendments to more than one article of the constitution during any one legislative session. Practical experience over the previous fifteen years had shown that questions of revenue, finances, or public debt always took priority (the woman suffrage amendment of 1894 being the lone exception). In an attempt to break that impasse, organized labor joined with members of the Direct Legislation League of Arapahoe County and other reform groups looking to capitalize on the revision to assist their own reform efforts and secured passage of an amendment in the 1899 legislature. The measure specifically allowed the legislature to propose amendments on up

---

7. See *Direct Legislation Record* 3 (January 1896): 2; 3 (March 1896): 10; 3 (September 1896): 25–27; 10 (December 1903): 81–82; *Rocky Mountain News*, March 4–8, 10, 12, 15, 17, 20, 1896, May 18, 1907; *Arena* 38 (July 1907): 90–91; and Wilbur Fiske Stone, ed., *History of Colorado*, 631, 634.

to six articles of the state constitution during any legislative session. Voters approved the amendment at the general election in 1900.[8]

As noted, the scandalous Denver municipal election of 1899 had renewed the agitation for home rule. Leading the fight, which had become easier with the expansion of the amendment process, were local business leaders represented by the Chamber of Commerce, reformers such as lawyer-politician John A. Rush, former mayor Thomas S. McMurray, attorney J. Warner Mills, and newspaper owner–politician Thomas M. Patterson. Unexpected support came from Democratic governor James B. Orman and other Democrats in the state legislature who perceived home rule as a means by which Democratic control of the city under the strong arm of Robert W. Speer, the emerging leader of a disciplined Democratic political machine, could be secured.

Drafted by J. Warner Mills and John A. Rush, and introduced in the legislature by Rush who was also chairman of the Senate Judiciary Committee, a home rule amendment passed the legislature in 1901. Known as Article XX, or the "Rush Bill," the amendment consolidated an area of nearly sixty square miles into a new entity known as the City and County of Denver. Article XX placed political control of the new corporation in the local council rather than the state legislature, granted the council full power over municipally owned utilities, and placed the Departments of Fire and Police and Public Works under civil service. Article XX also greatly expanded popular democracy by mandating that new franchises be submitted to a vote of the city's taxpayers, that exclusive power to make charter amendments be reserved to the citizens of Denver, and that every charter provide for the initiative and referendum. Extending home rule privileges to all cities of the first and second class (populations greater than two thousand) further enhanced the amendment's appeal, and it was approved by the voters by a majority of nearly thirty-five thousand at the general election in November 1902.[9]

The election of twenty-one delegates to the charter convention took place on June 2, 1903, and voters returned a "civic" ticket composed primarily of

8. Although acknowledging that several organizations (CSFL?) cooperated to achieve that triumph, Henry H. Roser, secretary of the Direct Legislation League of Arapahoe County (Denver), claimed that his group "took the initiative in the matter" (*Direct Legislation Record* 6 [June 1899]: 23). See also *Direct Legislation Record* 5 (September 1898): 59; 6 (June 1899): 22–23; Wright, *Politics of Populism*, 226–27, 234; Abbott, *Colorado*, 129; and David Brundage, *The Making of Western Labor Radicalism: Denver's Organized Workers, 1878–1905*, 126.

9. See Hornbein, "Denver's Struggle," 348–50; *Direct Legislation Record* 10 (December 1903): 82; C. L. King, *Government of Denver*, 221–22, 225–33; Rush, *The City-County Consolidated*, 331–43; Frank H. H. Roberts, "The Denver Situation and the Rush Amendment," 126; Mills, "The Economic Struggle in Colorado," *Arena* 34 (September 1905): 262–63; and Paul J. Mitchell, "Progressivism in Denver: The Municipal Reform Movement, 1904–1916," 62–65.

reformers. Among the delegates elected were John A. Rush, Edward Keating (managing editor of the influential *Rocky Mountain News,* a forum for antimachine Democrats), J. Warner Mills, and John H. Gabriel (an attorney who would succeed Mills as president of the Direct Legislation League from 1906 to 1914). The convention proceeded to frame a liberal charter that vested legislative power in a small unicameral council elected at large and constrained by the mayor's veto and popular control through the initiative and referendum (a petition signed by 5 percent of the electorate could place a question on the ballot at the next general election, whereas a petition signed by 10 percent of the voters could trigger a special election). The proposed charter also provided for the short ballot, the recall, a simple procedure for municipal ownership of public utilities, and a provision allowing for municipal inspection of the records of public service corporations. Because the proposed charter reduced party patronage and threatened public utility corporations, though, both the party political machines and the public utility trust strenuously opposed it. Their opposition proved crucial, as the charter was ultimately defeated at the polls on September 22, 1903, by what John A. Rush described as "brazen election frauds." In that election, the reform press charged that the various utilities, working through the Speer machine and its election managers (dubbed the "savages"), intimidated voters, harassed poll watchers, and stuffed ballot boxes with more than ten thousand illegal votes.[10]

On December 8, voters elected delegates to a second charter convention to repeat the process. This time the interests that had worked to defeat the first charter succeeded in electing a list of delegates primed to protect those very interests. As the *Rocky Mountain News* accurately predicted the day after the election, "The Corporations Will Write the Next Charter for Denver." When it completed its work the following spring, the convention had replaced the model of a unicameral council with a larger bicameral one elected by district, multiplied the number of elective and appointive offices, limited the application of civil service, rendered public ownership difficult and costly, eliminated the recall, and emasculated the initiative and referendum (no right to initiate ordinances and a referendum on ordinances only on a petition signed by 25 percent of the electorate). In an election marred by voter turnout that was down nearly 25 percent from the first charter vote and charges of vote fraud, the second charter easily won ratification on March 29, 1904.[11]

10. See C. L. King, *Government of Denver,* 233–35, 311–17; Hornbein, "Denver's Struggle," 350–51; Rush, *The City-County Consolidated,* 343; Roberts, "Denver Situation," 127–28; *Direct Legislation Record* 10 (December 1903): 71; Richard Snyder, "The Election of 1904: An Attempt at Reform," 18; and James Baker and Leroy Hafen, *History of Colorado: Biographical,* 4:220–21.

11. *Rocky Mountain News* quoted in Mitchell, "Progressivism in Denver," 71. See also

The frustration felt by reformers over seeing their hopes for genuine home rule denied in the charter fight intensified during the electoral campaign of 1904. In order to maintain its dominant political influence, the Republican Party needed Governor James Peabody to win reelection over his Democratic opponent, Alva Adams, and to hold on to its majority in the Senate. Having accomplished that goal, the party could continue to control appointees to the state supreme court, where a proposed constitutional amendment promised to expand the existing three-member body by adding four new justices.[12] With the power to oversee the state canvassing board (established to review election returns), appoint poll watchers, void elections, strike down popular amendments, and issue injunctions, the supreme court had proved itself to be a staunch defender of the status quo.

The two gubernatorial candidates were a study in contrasts. Governor Peabody represented corporate interests, and his declaration of martial law and his use of the state militia to break the recent Cripple Creek strike made him an anathema to organized labor. Alva Adams had the support of reformers and campaigned on a platform that included the initiative and referendum, antiusury laws, and an eight-hour day for miners. With their slogan "citizens must vote if they are to win over the money interests," the Democrats rolled to a smashing victory. Adams won by ten thousand votes, and Democrats gained a four-seat majority in the Senate. The amendment expanding the state supreme court also carried and seemingly opened the way to Democratic appointees.

The Republicans, however, refused to yield power without a fight. Charging election fraud, the party used its influence with the state supreme court to eliminate votes in ten Denver precincts and two outlying counties, thereby cutting Adams's margin of victory and reducing Democratic majorities. Then, three days prior to leaving office, Governor Peabody sent the names of two Republican supreme court nominees to the lame-duck Senate, which confirmed them one day before Adams was sworn in as governor. The Republicans then used the recent decisions of the court regarding election fraud to charge that Adams himself had been fraudulently elected and that Peabody should be maintained instead. In the end, the two parties struck a "compromise." Adams would be denied election due to voting irregularities, while Peabody would be declared governor but with the provision that he immediately resign the office in favor of conservative Re-

---

C. L. King, *Government of Denver*, 235–36, 252, 269; Hornbein, "Denver's Struggle," 351; Abbott, *Colorado*, 204; and Roberts, "Denver Situation," 128.

12. Two of the new members would come from the circuit court of appeals that was being abolished. The other two appointees, however, would be nominated by the governor and approved by the Senate.

publican Jesse McDonald, the lieutenant governor–elect. Reformers were left to wonder how long the will of the people would be thwarted.[13]

Those hoping for political reform in Colorado got a second chance in 1908. Taking advantage of divisions within the Speer-led "City Hall Machine," the reform element within the Democratic Party managed to secure the nomination of John F. Shafroth. Shafroth, a former silver Republican turned Democrat, possessed a commitment to reform, and his years in Colorado politics had earned him a reputation for honesty and integrity. Speaking for many who had come to regard political corruption and special interest politics as intolerable, the party convention authored a platform that called for a number of remedies aimed at restoring popular democracy and enhancing the regulatory powers of the state. The most striking feature of the platform was its emphasis on a number of fundamental political reforms that were gaining popularity nationwide. Included in the list of political demands were a direct primary law, the direct election of U.S. senators, a "headless" ballot, an antipass law, a campaign expense law, and the adoption of the initiative and referendum. Supplementing the political reforms were economic ones: new state railway and tax commissions, a bank guarantee law, prohibition of holding companies, and an endorsement of municipal ownership of public utilities. All in all, the Democrats had set a highly progressive agenda.[14]

Supported by the *Rocky Mountain News*, reform-minded Democrats and Republicans (many of the latter split their tickets in the contest), and the endorsement of William Jennings Bryan and his network of Colorado Bryan Democratic Clubs, Shafroth appeared to have the edge over former Republican governor Jesse McDonald (a poor choice in light of lingering memories of 1904), running on a conservative platform that paled in comparison to what the Democrats had promised. Casting the Republicans as servants of the corporations, Shafroth conducted a whistle-stop campaign that carried him to a sweeping victory and his party to majorities in both houses of the state legislature. The *Denver Times* presumptuously proclaimed the election to be "a glorious victory for the people against the bosses."[15]

Legislative implementation of the Democratic Party's progressive plat-

13. See Snyder, "Election of 1904," 19–25.

14. See Mitchell, "Progressivism in Denver," 155–56; Lloyd Musselman, "Governor John F. Shafroth and the Colorado Progressives: Their Fight for Direct Legislation, 1909–1910," 22–23; E. K. MacColl, "John Franklin Shafroth, Reform Governor of Colorado, 1909–1913," 37–39; and Frances A. Huber, "The Progressive Career of Ben B. Lindsey, 1900–1920," 150.

15. *Denver Times* quoted in Huber, "Progressive Career of Lindsey," 150. See also Musselman, "Governor Shafroth," 23–26; and Mitchell, "Progressivism in Denver," 156–57.

form in 1909 became a contest between the so-called platform Democrats on one side and the Speer, or machine, Democrats allied with conservative Republicans on the other. An early indication of how the session would go occurred when the machine Democrats elected loyal Speerite H. L. Lubers as Speaker of the House over H. A. Hicks, the nominee of the reform-minded platform Democrats. This victory severely handicapped the reformers, as the Speaker appointed the chairs of the various committees who, in effect, could prevent the timely consideration of reform legislation. Even a special appearance by the popular William Jennings Bryan, who spoke before a joint session of the legislature in support of the entire Democratic platform, failed to move the obstructionists. In the end, the delaying tactics of the machine proved too strong to overcome. When the legislature adjourned in April only one platform pledge—the enactment of a campaign expense law—had been redeemed. To reform groups such as the Direct Primary League and the Direct Legislation League, the failure to achieve those reforms only underscored the need for them.[16]

While Governor Shafroth mulled over the timing of a call for an extra session of the legislature to reconsider his legislative priorities, the reform campaign received some unexpected assistance from Judge Ben Lindsey. Lindsey had won national attention for his work in establishing Denver's juvenile court system and special praise as "the Just Judge" from muckraking journalist Lincoln Steffens in three articles written for *McClure's* in 1906.[17] In October 1908, Lindsey showed a rough draft of a manuscript he had been working on—a personal account of Denver politics from 1898 to 1908—to Upton Sinclair, the author of *The Jungle*. The manuscript had evolved from a minor 1908 campaign booklet privately published by Lindsey titled *The Rise of the Plutocracy in Colorado*, a sixty-eight-page account detailing the pernicious influence that public utility corporations exerted over the state's political system.

Sinclair, excited by what he read, sent the manuscript to John O'Hara Cosgrave. Cosgrave was the editor of *Everybody's*, one of the premier muck-

16. The new campaign expense law, a state-funded scheme designed to equalize campaign spending between the major parties, divide campaign money equally between the state and county committees of those parties, and set limits on the amount of money a candidate could contribute, proved to be short-lived. In a decision handed down in October 1910, the state supreme court deemed the law "class legislation" and declared it unconstitutional. See E. K. MacColl, "Progressive Legislation in Colorado, 1907–1917," 111–13. See also Huber, "Progressive Career of Lindsey," 151–58; *Equity* 11 (July 1909): 83; and Richard D. Lamm and Duane A. Smith, *Pioneers and Politicians: 10 Colorado Governors in Profile*, 92–94.

17. For Steffens's articles on Lindsey, see "Ben B. Lindsey: The Just Judge," parts 1–3, *McClure's* 27 (October 1906): 563–82; 28 (November 1906): 74–88; (December 1906): 162–76. The articles also constituted one of the chapters in Steffens's *Upbuilders*, published in 1909.

raking magazines in the country, with a circulation of more than a half million. Cosgrave agreed to publish Lindsey's story and arranged to have staff writer Harvey J. O'Higgins go to Denver to work with Lindsey as his stylistic collaborator. Lindsey and O'Higgins had the revised manuscript ready by the late summer, and *Everybody's* began serialization of "The Beast and the Jungle" in October 1909. Lindsey's saga of his battle with "the System," which ran in monthly installments between October 1909 and May 1910, created a national sensation. Newspaper publisher E. W. Scripps even went so far as to predict that "The Beast and the Jungle" "might possibly be as effective as . . . *Uncle Tom's Cabin.*" Its local impact was equally significant, as the entire muckraking exposé appeared just before the Denver municipal election on May 17. In advocating that power be returned to the people, Lindsey emphatically underscored the importance of measures such as the initiative and referendum.[18]

The most important issue in Denver politics during the year leading up to the Denver municipal election involved the so-called water question. The twenty-year franchise of the Denver Union Water Company (DUWC) was due to expire in 1910. The city had the option of either renewing the franchise or purchasing the property at its "fair cash value" as stipulated in the original franchise agreement and operating the concern as a municipally owned utility. Commonly considered to be part of the city's powerful public utility trust, citizen groups had assailed the DUWC for years for tax dodging, failing to comply with its contracts, refusing to lower rates, supplying impure and polluted water, and providing inadequate water supply and pressure. When a five-member commission (chosen by the city and the company) appraised the buyout value of the company's property at $14.4 million when it paid taxes on a valuation of only $2.5 million, Denverites, with a history of animosity toward the DUWC, were angered as consumers and outraged as taxpayers who might be required to redeem an enormous overcapitalization. The time had come for a serious discussion of municipal ownership.[19]

Leading the fight against renewal of the DUWC franchise and what they perceived as corporate arrogance was the Water Consumers' League, an organization formed from the Denver Trades and Labor Assembly. Led by George Eisler and Sidney Eastwood of the Typographers' Union and James

---

18. Scripps quoted in Huber, "Progressive Career of Lindsey," 174 (see also 163–78). The interest shown for the magazine series convinced Doubleday, Page, and Company to publish it in book form in 1910 as *The Beast*. See also Mitchell, "Progressivism in Denver," 163–67; Louis Filler, *Crusaders for American Liberalism*, 262–67; and Lindsey and O'Higgins, *The Beast*, xvii–xxiii.

19. See C. L. King, *Government of Denver*, 201–6, 280–84; and Huber, "Progressive Career of Lindsey," 179.

E. Faulkner of the Cigarmakers' Union, the new body began to publicize the merits of public ownership. It was not long, however, before the discussion of public ownership assumed a broader context. Speaking for the league, Eisler charged Mayor Speer with malfeasance in office for disregarding the public interest and exhibiting a corporate bias on the water question. To Eisler, the problem was political as much as economic. As a result, the solution would require charter amendments that would expand the democratic aspects of home rule by reenacting the initiative; strengthening the referendum; allowing for the removal of public officials from office, that is, the recall; as well as allowing for municipal ownership. In expanding the parameters of the consumer-taxpayer debate to include outraged citizens, Eisler pushed the water fight in a new direction under labor's leadership.[20]

Sensing that Eisler had generated a challenge that had both popular support and the potential to bring about fundamental reform of the municipal power structure, veteran reformers took interest and activated numerous unallied reform organizations such as the Municipal Ownership League, the Christian Citizenship Union, the Denver City Club, the Direct Legislation League, and others behind the effort. In doing so, the names of many familiar Denver reformers—John Rush, Edward P. Costigan, Ben Lindsey, James Causey, John Gabriel, George Kindel, Albert Mauff, J. S. Temple, Otto Thum, and C. S. Thomas—appeared. Concerned Denverites soon began forming neighborhood discussion groups called Water Users' Clubs. This was followed by the formation of a United Water Users' Club, with lawyer–small businessman–politician Edwin W. Hurlbut as president, to coordinate their activities. It began to look as if the reform drive had both the grassroots support and the united leadership necessary to be successful.[21]

As the campaign progressed, veteran reformers began to assert greater leadership in the reform drive and soon reorganized the original Water Consumers' League as the Citizens' Water League. As the municipal election approached, it became evident that the political issues had taken precedence over the economic. Reorganized again as the Citizens' Party, the reform coalition nominated a full ticket of candidates and successfully petitioned to have amendments to the Denver charter calling for municipal ownership of the water company, the initiative and referendum of city ordinances (by petition of 5 percent of the preceding vote for mayor), and the recall of all elected city officials (by petition of 25 percent of the votes

20. The State Federation of Labor had supported the idea of direct legislation for years and worked to build support for the initiative and referendum through the efforts of its legislative lobbying committee and attempts to obtain campaign pledges from political candidates. See, for example, *Direct Legislation Record* 9 (December 1902): 66.

21. See Mitchell, "Progressivism in Denver," 184.

cast for the office of the official being recalled) placed on the ballot. The last few weeks of the campaign were energized with activities that ranged from small discussion groups to mass rallies and street gatherings sponsored by various organizations. Rival newspapers kept the discussion lively, with the *Denver Post* attempting to discredit the Citizens' program by linking it with Ben Lindsey's "Beast and the Jungle" series (a tactic that probably did their cause more harm than good). The election was a victory for the Citizens' ticket and a triumph for voters who had adopted municipal ownership of the waterworks (financial arrangements left to the courts to decide) as well as the initiative, referendum, and recall. The *Denver Express* called the election the "greatest victory ever achieved by the reform forces in Denver." The real significance of the election, however, was the encouragement it gave to those calling for reform of state government.[22]

In the summer of 1910, Governor Shafroth exercised his gubernatorial prerogative and called the legislature into special session to reconsider the legislative proposals that had been blocked in the previous session. Encouraged by the results of the recent Denver municipal election and aware that the various county conventions would soon be meeting and exerting pressure on legislators in anticipation of the upcoming state elections, Shafroth was optimistic that some of his party's original reform pledges could still be salvaged. In his message to the legislature opening the special session on August 9, Governor Shafroth reiterated his legislative priorities, referred to the initiative and referendum as "one of the most important" items on his agenda, and warned the Democratic majority that voters would not forgive them if they ignored their campaign promises. "A shock to the moral sense, followed by a feeling of resentment, occurs," said Shafroth, "when electors find they have been duped and deceived."[23]

At the start of the special session, which convened only thirty-five days before the state nominating convention, Representative Onias C. Skinner introduced a bill designed by the Direct Legislation League of Colorado and modeled on the Oregon law proposing a constitutional amendment al-

22. *Denver Express* quoted in Huber, "Progressive Career of Lindsey," 185–86 (see also 179–86). See also Mitchell, "Progressivism in Denver," 175–203; and C. L. King, *Government of Denver,* 252–54, 284–87. John H. Gabriel, president of the Direct Legislation League of Colorado, gave credit for leading the campaign to "Major E.W. Hurlbut . . . [and] ably supported by such able captains as Governor John Shafroth, ex-Governor Charles S. Thomas, ex-United States Senators Thomas M. Patterson and Frank J. Cannon, and Judge Ben Lindsey, with a number of lieutenants of great power, among whom were Miss Ellis Meredith, . . . Mrs. A.B. Conine, one of the mothers of direct legislation in Colorado, Miss Gale Laughlin, and Mrs. Dora Phelps Buell, with hundreds of equally able workers in the ranks, supported by . . . the *Rocky Mountain News,* the *Denver Times,* the *Evening Express,* and the *Denver Post*" (*Equity* 12 [July 1910]: 103).

23. *Rocky Mountain News,* August 10, 1910. See also *Equity* 12 (October 1910): 139.

lowing for the initiative and referendum. The measure provided for an 8 percent petition to initiate laws and a 5 percent petition to refer any law passed by the General Assembly (petition percentages were based on the votes cast for secretary of state in the previous general election) and, with minor adjustments, quickly won approval in the House by a vote of fifty-one to eleven.

In the Senate, however, where divisions between the platform and machine Democrats persisted, the debate was more heated and the outcome far less certain. The platform Democrats, led by state senator Mark A. Skinner, began the process by submitting a measure similar to the one introduced in the House. The machine Democrats quickly burdened the bill with restrictive amendments. Initiative petitions would have to be signed by 15 percent of the electorate in at least two-thirds of the counties, and approval would require a vote equal to 51 percent of those cast for governor in the preceding general election (a figure for constitutional amendments that had been reached only once in the previous twenty-seven years!). Under the machine-backed alternative, voters would finally get a direct legislation law but one that would be all but useless. Finally, after nearly three weeks of debate, arm-twisting from Governor Shafroth, newspaper exposure of attempts by corporate lobbyists to defeat any initiative and referendum law, and what the *Rocky Mountain News* referred to as "an aroused public sentiment," eleven Republicans joined nineteen Democrats and accepted the original Skinner Bill that had been sent to the Senate by the House by a vote of thirty to two.[24]

The final measure, although liberal in its state petition requirements, did include some restrictions. The law extended the initiative and referendum to every city, town, and municipality in the state, but raised the petition requirements at the local level to 15 and 10 percent, respectively. Legislators also attached a "safety clause" that exempted appropriation bills and measures necessary for the immediate preservation of the public peace, health, and safety from challenges under the referendum. They also allowed initiated and referred acts, when approved, to be amended or repealed by the legislature, and limited consideration of such acts to the regular biennial general elections. As was the case with all proposed constitutional amendments in Colorado, all ballot propositions were subject to the costly requirement that they be published in two newspapers of opposite political preference in each county of the state for four consecutive weeks.[25]

24. See *Equity* 12 (October 1910): 139–41; 13 (January 1911): 21; and *Rocky Mountain News*, August 14, 16–31, September 1–2, 1910.
25. See Charles H. Queary, *The Initiative and Referendum in Colorado*, 1–8; and *Laws Passed at the Extraordinary Session of the Seventeenth General Assembly of the State of Colorado*, 11–14.

Leading the campaign in support of the amendment were Governor Shafroth (campaigning for reelection) and the state Democratic Party, the Direct Legislation League, the Trades and Labor Assembly of Denver, the Colorado State Federation of Labor, several women's organizations, and the Christian Citizenship Union, assisted by the *Denver Post*, the *Rocky Mountain News*, and the *Denver Catholic Register*. Heading the opposition were the Representative Government League (formed for the purpose) and a large segment of the Republican Party, assisted by the *Denver Republican*, the *Denver Times*, the *Colorado Springs Gazette*, and the *Pueblo Chieftain*. Joining the opposition was the Colorado State Medical Society that urged its membership to oppose the amendment because it would permit laws harmful to the state's financial and social welfare and adversely affect the scientific control and supervision of public hygiene, sanitation, and preventive medicine. After listening to both sides, voters overwhelmingly approved the amendment at the general election in November 1910 by a vote of 89,141 to 28,698.[26]

At the general election in 1912 voters were asked to consider twenty-six voter-initiated ballot measures—nine initiated amendments, eleven initiated statutes, and six referred laws—in addition to five legislative amendments and one measure referred by the legislature. The large number of ballot propositions surprised many, but John H. Gabriel, president of the Direct Legislation League of Colorado, attributed the number to the fact that many of the proposals had previously been before the legislature and ignored. Said Gabriel: "This move on the part of the voters is but an expression of their freedom from the domination of the political machine in the legislature." Gabriel's organization sponsored ten initiative measures that included implementation of an election pamphlet to replace the expensive requirement of newspaper advertising (defeated), the recall of any elective state official (judges included) based on a 25 percent petition (approved), a headless ballot to reduce straight-ticket voting (approved), the right of voters to overrule decisions of the state supreme court declaring laws unconstitutional (approved, but declared unconstitutional by the Colorado Supreme Court in 1921 as denying due process of law), a mother's compensation act providing state-funded child support to widowed and indigent mothers (approved), the creation of a public utilities court (defeated), and an eight-hour law for women (approved). George E. Hosmer, chairman of the finance committee of the Colorado Direct Legislation League, acknowledged that his organization spent hundreds of dollars in

26. See Paul Dean Starr, "The Initiative and Referendum in Colorado," 16–20; and *Direct Legislation in Colorado: A Report by the Special Committee on Direct Legislation of the City Club,* 9–10.

correspondence to obtain volunteers to circulate petitions and finally had to pay two thousand dollars to hire circulators to secure the required number of signatures. Other intriguing proposals introduced by other groups included a new civil service law (approved), statewide prohibition (defeated), and an eight-hour law for mine and smelter workers (approved). Of the twenty-six initiated and referred measures, voters approved nine.[27]

Over the next three general elections the popularity of direct legislation diminished. Thirteen voter-initiated ballot propositions appeared on the ballot in 1914, seven in 1916, and only three in 1918, but voters still used the reforms to consider fundamental issues. In 1914 the Colorado Social Service League, led by Judge Ben Lindsey as president and George Eisler as secretary, initiated four measures—an amendment to allow 25 percent of the electorate to demand a special election to consider initiated and referred items, a statute to establish a child welfare commission to codify laws relating to the employment of women and children, an amendment to allow a three-fourths vote of a jury to decide verdicts in civil cases and permitting women to serve on juries, and a statute to permit probation for minors and first offenders—but saw all of them defeated. Voters also passed on a second opportunity to change the method of advertising ballot proposals (finally approved in 1918), and declined to increase the powers of the Public Utilities Commission. Nonetheless, voters defeated an attempt to cripple the initiative by requiring a six-year waiting period before an initiated proposition could be resubmitted, and approved measures relieving workmen of industrial risk, extending the powers of the State Board of Equalization in levying taxes, and enacting statewide prohibition (toughened by a "bone-dry" initiative statute in 1918). Voters also defeated an attempt to abolish the State Tax Commission in 1916 and approved a proposal to give the state civil service system constitutional protection in 1918. All told, Coloradans considered sixty-one ballot measures between 1912 and 1918. Forty-nine of them were voter initiated, and the electorate approved twenty-one.[28]

27. Gabriel quoted in *Equity* 14 (October 1912): 141. There were actually two eight-hour measures affecting mine, mill, and smelter workers on the ballot in 1912. A true eight-hour law (the Hurd Bill) had passed the legislature in 1911, but corporate interests circulated petitions and gained enough signatures to call for a referendum. As a result, the statute remained suspended until voters could decide the issue in 1912. In the meantime, the same corporate interests initiated an eight-hour law more acceptable to them. In the confusion, voters actually approved both of the conflicting bills in 1912. Finally, after a ruling from the Colorado Supreme Court, the 1913 legislature repealed both laws and passed a new one similar to the Hurd Bill. See David L. Lonsdale, "The Fight for an Eight-Hour Day," 352–53; *Equity* 14 (October 1912): 140–41; 16 (April 1914): 83; Queary, *Initiative and Referendum,* 12–15; MacColl, "Progressive Legislation," 125–31; and Huber, "Progressive Career of Lindsey," 331–43.

28. See *Equity* 16 (July 1914): 131–32; 16 (October 1914): 176–77; 17 (January 1915): 43–44; 19 (January 1917): 29; Queary, *Initiative and Referendum,* 15–17; and Huber, "Progressive Career of Lindsey," 345–47.

ARKANSAS

The popularity of the idea of direct legislation in Arkansas arose from a growing popular frustration with the failure of the Arkansas General Assembly to function in a responsible manner during the first decade of the twentieth century. The legislature's apparent inability to control the length of its sessions, the number of bills regularly under consideration, and spending angered many. Overwhelmed by drastic increases in the number of measures submitted to the legislature (and the voluminous amount of printed matter that accompanied them), the Arkansas legislature routinely extended its standard sixty-day session to meet its increased workload.[29] Over a ten-year period from 1901 to 1911 the average legislative session lasted 116 days and cost taxpayers from $115,000 to $125,000 per session (nearly $200,000 in 1911). The money was not insignificant, as for years state expenditures exceeded revenues. By 1911, as a result of natural increases in expenditures, inadequate tax levies, and a hopelessly inefficient system of assessment and collection, the state deficit had ballooned to nearly $500,000. The general feeling was that legislators stayed too long at the state capitol and spent too much of taxpayers' money.

Compounding the growing sense of disillusionment with the legislative process was the feeling that the standards of those in public office had declined markedly in recent years. Near the close of the 1905 session of the legislature, four members of the Senate and two members of the House came under indictment for accepting bribes in connection with legislation affecting the construction of the new state capitol. Also connected in the public mind with boodle was the St. Francis Levee Board. Originally created in 1893 to supervise the construction of levees and the reclamation of flood lands in northeastern Arkansas, the board had evolved into a powerful political tool for the governor (who appointed members to the board) and a centerpiece of the state's Democratic political machine. The governor, in effect, used the board to support his programs, while the board itself controlled millions of dollars earmarked for levee construction and flood control projects. Legislative scandal and the suggestion of corruption at the highest level of state government, added to the popular perception that the railroad lobby exerted too much influence in Little Rock, caused many Arkansans to conclude that representative government had fallen into the grasp of special interests and was no longer responsive to the will of the people.

Another factor adding to the intensifying popular dissatisfaction with

29. The increase in the number of measures was even more problematic, as most fell into the less important category of local, special and private acts, resolutions, and memorials. See David Y. Thomas, "Direct Legislation in Arkansas," 86.

the legislature, and at the same time generating interest in the idea of direct legislation, was the legislature's refusal to consider issues of special importance to certain interest groups in the state. One such group was the prohibitionists. Encouraged by increases in the antiliquor licensing vote in county elections, prohibitionists had tried several times to get the legislature to enact a state law or to submit a prohibition amendment. However, they had been defeated by the liquor interests each time. In a state in which the number of "dry" counties had increased from twenty-nine out of a total of seventy-five in 1900 to forty-four in 1903, the refusal of the legislature to put the question of statewide prohibition to a popular vote left many prohibitionists frustrated. Equally upset was the leadership of the Arkansas State Federation of Labor, who felt slighted that only a portion of their legislative agenda had been favorably received by Arkansas's lawmakers. As angry taxpayers, outraged citizens, disappointed moral purists, or neglected wage earners, many Arkansas voters had come to the conclusion that the existing system of representative government could be improved if voters had more direct influence in the legislative process.[30]

Public discussion of direct legislation in Arkansas dates from 1896, when the state Populist Party endorsed the initiative and referendum. No organizational effort, however, developed to push the idea until December 1905, when the Arkansas State Federation of Labor, an American Federation of Labor (AFL) affiliate, endorsed those reforms at its state convention. The leaders of organized labor regarded the referendum as a means of preventing the enactment of "bad and oppressive laws" that the people did not want, whereas the initiative could allow them to obtain "some very important laws" that they had been unable to get. That year, in a state not usually known for its active, well-organized labor movement, the State Federation of Labor entered into a potentially advantageous agreement with the Arkansas Farmers' Union. The compact, a more formal labor-farmer agreement than existed in any other state, allowed organized labor to link itself with "the controlling power legislatively in this State." The two organizations agreed to cooperate on matters of mutual interest and to work for adoption of the initiative and referendum. As a step in that direction, the two bodies adopted a resolution by which they agreed to question all political candidates to determine their views on the topic.[31]

30. See ibid., 85–87, 90; Calvin R. Ledbetter Jr., "Adoption of Initiative and Referendum in Arkansas: The Roles of George W. Donaghey and William Jennings Bryan," 204; Richard L. Niswonger, *Arkansas Democratic Politics, 1896–1920*, 111, 230–31; *Direct Legislation Record* 10 (September 1903): 48; David Michael Moyers, "Arkansas Progressivism: The Legislative Record," 59, 344–50; and *Proceedings of the Third Annual Convention of the Arkansas State Federation of Labor*, Little Rock, December 11–15, 1905, 42.

31. See Ledbetter, "Adoption of Initiative and Referendum," 202–3; Rod Farmer, "Di-

Formal consideration of direct legislation actually began with the 1905 session of the Arkansas legislature when Representative William A. Anderson of Benton County introduced an amendment providing for the initiative, referendum, and the recall of judicial decisions. His proposal received little attention, though. Rising popular dissatisfaction with the legislature and increased pressure for direct legislation from the State Federation of Labor and the Arkansas Farmers' Union suggested that there might be an opportunity for some progress during the 1907 session of the legislature. Senator Edgar R. Arnold, a Clark County Democrat and former Populist, took the lead and submitted an initiative and referendum resolution without the recall. The Arnold proposal allowed voters to initiate laws and amendments to the constitution when 8 percent of the legal voters "in each of the majority of the congressional districts in the State" should so petition, and to call for the referendum on petitions signed by 5 percent of the voters on the same basis. Any measure referred to the people would become law when approved by a "majority of the votes cast thereon." When the measure came to a vote in the Senate, however, it was defeated by a vote of nine to twelve, with fourteen senators not voting. The legislative committee of the State Federation of Labor chose to look at the defeat positively and optimistically predicted that now that the proposal had been given a public hearing, "it will not be many years until it is passed."[32]

The campaign to win approval of the initiative and referendum in the legislature received a boost in 1907 when George W. Donaghey, a Conway businessman and contractor, entered the Democratic primary as a candidate for governor and made the reforms part of his progressive political platform. Donaghey had been encouraged to seek office by L. H. Moore, secretary-treasurer of the State Federation of Labor, and Ben Griffin, secretary-treasurer of the Farmers' Union. Though neither organization could officially endorse any candidate, the active involvement of Moore and Griffin in the Donaghey campaign sent a strong message to their respective memberships as to which candidate they should support. As Donaghey stumped the state he denounced legislative corruption and heralded the initiative and referendum as the cure for legislative ills. In a speech at Morrilton in October 1907, he referred to direct legislation as "another step in the direction of the rule by the people . . . [that] will enable them even when the men they have elected to office can no longer be trusted, to recall their measures and pass upon them for themselves." Although the

rect Democracy in Arkansas, 1910–1918," 101; and *Proceedings of the Third Annual Convention, 27,* 41–42.

32. *Proceedings of the Fifth Annual Convention of the Arkansas State Federation of Labor,* Pine Bluff, December 9–13, 1907, 33–34. See also Thomas, "Direct Legislation," 87–88; and Ledbetter, "Adoption of Initiative and Referendum," 203–4.

initiative and referendum were not the only issues discussed in the campaign, Donaghey's victory in the Democratic primary (he carried forty-eight of seventy-five counties and 42 percent of the vote in a three-way race), which was tantamount to election in a one-party state like Arkansas, gave the reforms legitimacy. The endorsement of the initiative and referendum by the Democratic State Convention in 1908 merely underscored their respectability as Democratic issues.[33]

As part of his inaugural address on January 14, 1909, Governor Donaghey recommended passage of a constitutional amendment incorporating the initiative and referendum in some form. Senator Arnold introduced a resolution similar to his 1907 proposal. Modeled after the 1902 Oregon law, it allowed for both the statute and constitutional initiative based on petitions signed by 8 percent of the state's registered voters (based on the number of votes cast for the office of governor in the previous general election) and the referendum based on a 5 percent figure. "Any measure" referred to the people would become a law when approved by a "majority of the votes cast thereon." An emergency clause excluded all laws deemed necessary "for the immediate preservation of the public peace, health, or safety" from the referendum.

Arnold's measure easily passed in the Senate by a vote of twenty-eight to one, but ran into some opposition in the House, where the committee on constitutional amendments attempted to make two changes. The first, which seemed harmless at the time, extended the initiative and referendum to municipalities and counties by adding the phrase "the people of each municipality, each county and of the state, reserve to themselves power to propose laws and amendments to the constitution." The second significantly raised the minimum signature requirements for petitions. Once on the House floor, however, members approved the first amendment but rejected the second. Although one disgruntled House member described the final bill as "socialistic, anarchistic, and Populist," the full House approved the revised measure by a vote of seventy-eight to four. The Senate concurred with the House bill by a vote of twenty-six to one. Voters would decide the issue at the general election in September 1910.[34]

Opposition to ratification of the proposed initiative and referendum amendment (known as Amendment 10) came primarily from the state's le-

33. Donaghey quoted in Ledbetter, "Adoption of Initiative and Referendum," 206 (see also 205–8). See also Thomas, "Direct Legislation," 88; Timothy P. Donovan, Willard B. Gatewood Jr., and Jeannie M. Whayne, eds., *The Governors of Arkansas: Essays in Political Biography*, 134–38; and Calvin R. Ledbetter Jr., *Carpenter from Conway: George Washington Donaghey as Governor of Arkansas, 1909–1913*.

34. See Ledbetter, "Adoption of Initiative and Referendum," 208–10; Thomas, "Direct Legislation," 88–89; *Equity* 11 (April 1909): 47; and Arkansas, *Biennial Report of the Secretary of State for the Years 1909–10–11–12*, 67–68.

gal establishment, led by the conservative Arkansas Bar Association, certain prominent Democratic state officials, and the influential *Little Rock Arkansas Gazette*. Years later Governor Donaghey remembered the bitter opposition to direct legislation in the state and that "most of the lawyers were against it, and many of the state officials." An especially vocal critic was Uriah M. Rose, one of the state's most influential jurists and a former president of the American Bar Association. According to Judge Rose, there was "only one way to deal with this spurious and bastard amendment. Vote it down!" Joining Rose as opponents of the initiative and referendum were a number of well-known Democrats that included former governor Dan Jones, former attorney general George Murphy, Secretary of State O. C. Ludwig, Attorney General Hal L. Underwood, and Commissioner of Mines, Manufacturers, and Agriculture Guy B. Tucker.[35]

Opponents criticized Amendment 10 from a variety of angles. The editors of the *Little Rock Arkansas Gazette* questioned whether the average voter should be allowed to make decisions on complicated questions of public policy and argued that the ignorant "hillbilly" in the "back districts" did not even know what the initiative and referendum meant. They warned that the ballot would become cluttered with needless propositions and even displayed copies of the six foot–long 1910 South Dakota ballot in the window of the Gazette Building to frighten timid voters. They also complained about the amount of money being spent by the proamendment forces as well as their use of an out-of-state press bureau to supply country newspapers with information on the initiative and referendum. Lawyers, one hundred of whom actually signed a public letter condemning Amendment 10, and judges vigorously joined the attack. In their minds the initiative and referendum would undermine the system of representative government, enable the majority to tyrannize the minority, make it too easy to amend the constitution, and encumber the ballot with unreasonable proposals. Direct legislation would also require the average citizen to pay more attention to lawmaking than his basic nature or level of intelligence allowed. The arguments presented by the conservative opponents of Amendment 10 prompted one official of the Arkansas Farmers' Union to remark that they "must think we farmers and common people are a set of fools and anarchists."[36]

Most of Arkansas's barristers, however, centered their attack on legal technicalities rather than philosophical differences. The portion of the law they found especially suspect from a legal point of view was that which ex-

---

35. Donaghey, *Autobiography*, 229; Rose quoted in Ledbetter, *Carpenter from Conway*, 101. See also Ledbetter, "Adoption of Initiative and Referendum," 214.

36. R. Farmer, "Direct Democracy," 105.

tended direct legislation to cities and counties for use on local laws. They asserted that because the clause was so clumsily drawn, it would allow counties and municipalities to propose or repeal state laws and constitutional amendments. Conservative opponents even circulated a statement from former Georgia Populist Tom Watson—who by 1910 was better known for his racist and reactionary demagoguery—that although he favored the initiative and referendum in principle, he feared that because of the local initiative "the Socialists could capture a town or county, confiscate private property and help themselves to everything in sight." Although most of the state press favored the amendment, many criticized the local initiative portion that came, in time, to be known as the "joker."[37]

Despite the "joker," passage of Amendment 10 looked promising. Supporters argued that the authors of the amendment did not intend the local initiative option to be in conflict with state law or the constitution and that basic common sense would prevail when voters initiated local statutes. However, Donaghey and others realized that the amendment had to win the approval of a majority of all votes cast in the election (a constitutional majority) as required by the Arkansas Constitution. A simple majority of those voting on the measure would not suffice. With fears real or imagined, supporters of Amendment 10 took the challenge seriously. The state's Democratic, Republican, and Socialist Parties all endorsed the amendment. Governor Donaghey lent his enthusiastic support as well. Renominated in the March 1910 primary, Donaghey used his popularity to try to convince voters that the "joker" was merely a legal technicality that could be corrected in the courts. He also wrote a public letter, "Final Message about Amendment 10," that he made available to newspapers for publication. Supporters also distributed some thirty-five thousand pro–Amendment 10 pamphlets during the campaign.

Exerting an especially strong influence in the campaign was the State Federation of Labor, assisted by the Arkansas Farmers' Union. George H. Shibley, president of the People's Rule League of America, credited L. H. Moore with having "pulled the stroke oar" in the Arkansas campaign. The State Federation of Labor held a series of meetings with various labor unions to encourage support and arranged for George Judson King, a nationally known field lecturer for the People's Rule League of America, to come to the state. During his three-month stay in Arkansas, King gave speeches, organized local direct legislation chapters, and directed the strategy that brought all the various groups together. Complementing orga-

37. Watson quoted in *Little Rock Arkansas Democrat,* September 6, 1910. The arguments against Amendment 10 are discussed in R. Farmer, "Direct Democracy," 102–8; Thomas, "Direct Legislation," 89–90; and Ledbetter, "Adoption of Initiative and Referendum," 210–11, 214–15.

nized labor was the Arkansas Farmers' Union. With its hundreds of local chapters, the organization provided an important means of educating rural voters on the question. Moreover, by every indication farmers appeared to be united behind Amendment 10. When Judson King spoke before three thousand members at the opening session of their state meeting in August 1910, the *Little Rock Arkansas Democrat* reported that he was "cheered to the echo, and nowhere was a dissenting voice heard."[38]

Prominent religious publications also actively discussed the measure, but often took different positions on the question. The editors of the *Western Methodist* argued that the initiative and referendum would bring an end to bribery and machine politics, and suggested that those who opposed the bill either did not understand it or were representatives of corporate interests. The editors charged that liquor distillers, fearful of statewide prohibition, were particularly active in opposition to the amendment. The *Baptist Advance,* in contrast, expressed reservations about the initiative, referring to it as the "paradise of cranks" and a "sugar-coated pill, with poison instead of purgative on the inside." The editors did, however, endorse the referendum.[39]

Worried that the combined opposition of distinguished members of the state bar and prominent Democrats might prevent Amendment 10 from obtaining a constitutional majority, Governor Donaghey employed one additional line of defense. Using his own personal finances, the governor chartered a special train and convinced William Jennings Bryan, the idol of popular democracy, to come to Arkansas and assist in the campaign by making a whistle-stop speaking tour of the state. Donaghey had met Bryan at the Democratic National Convention in 1908 as head of the pro-Bryan Arkansas delegation, and the two had become friends. Bryan spent five days in Arkansas, traveled 1,750 miles aboard the Bryan Special, and gave fifty-five speeches before an estimated 75,000 to 125,000 people. Accompanying Bryan on his blitz of the state were Donaghey; George A. Cole, president of the Arkansas Farmers' Union; E. W. Hogan, president of the State Federation of Labor; and Judson King.

The Bryan tour, which began in Fort Smith on September 6 and ended in Eureka Springs just two days before the election, was great theater. Large crowds and brass bands met the train at every stop. Speaking in intense summer heat Bryan carried a large palm-leaf fan that he employed frequently as he spoke. Stores in small towns closed for hours in Bryan's honor, and people rode "wagons, buggies, hacks, and saddle animals" to see

38. Shibley and *Little Rock Arkansas Democrat* quoted in R. Farmer, "Direct Democracy," 102–3. See also Ledbetter, "Adoption of Initiative and Referendum," 211–13; and David D. Schmidt, *Citizen Lawmakers: The Ballot Initiative Revolution,* 221.

39. Moyers, "Arkansas Progressivism," 356–57.

and hear him. In Little Rock 15,000 people turned out to hear Bryan speak at the City Park. Opponents of Amendment 10 were simply no match for the Great Commoner's personal magnetism. Bryan and Donaghey shook hands with as many people as possible at each stop, while supporters distributed pamphlets (the text of the amendment and Donaghey's "Final Message about Amendment 10") and handed out Amendment 10 buttons to the crowds.

Wherever he spoke, Bryan kept his message simple, repeatedly telling listeners that the people could be trusted. In a humorous reference to his famous free-silver campaign of 1896, Bryan predicted that the odds were about sixteen to one that "the people [as opposed to legislators] will come nearer to deciding what is right when they have to stand there with lobbyists on one side and the people at home on the other side."[40] He assured voters that the "joker" would be corrected, and obtained a public pledge from Governor Donaghey to that effect. He reminded voters that the initiative and referendum were working well in other states, and that the reforms were gaining momentum nationwide and had already been adopted in the neighboring states of Missouri and Oklahoma. He also insisted that the majority of those in opposition to Amendment 10 ostensibly because of the "joker" were, in reality, opposed to the principle of the initiative and referendum. In implying that opponents of the amendment did not trust the people, Bryan reminded voters that the state motto was Let the People Rule. On election day, September 12, 1910, Arkansas became the first truly southern state to adopt the initiative and referendum. Amendment 10 carried sixty-six of the state's seventy-five counties and won by a vote of 92,781 to 38,648, more than enough to meet the constitutional majority required for ratification. As one historian has noted, the vote reflected "the deep popular contempt for the Arkansas legislature and a strong desire for some alternative."[41]

Arkansans proceeded to make immediate use of the new reforms. Voters used the referendum in 1912 to overturn the so-called Turner-Jacobson tax law designed to raise additional revenue to counterbalance a growing state deficit by increasing the general property tax. As much as they abhorred legislative waste and inefficiency, voters did not regard a tax increase as the

40. *Little Rock Arkansas Gazette,* September 7, 1910.
41. See Ledbetter, "Adoption of Initiative and Referendum," 215–20; Donaghey, *Autobiography,* 229–31; R. Farmer, "Direct Democracy," 109; and Ledbetter, *Carpenter from Conway,* 102. The secretary of state's office reported two different vote totals for Amendment 10. See Arkansas, *Biennial Report, 1909–1912,* 68, 399. For a detailed account of the Bryan tour, see *Little Rock Arkansas Democrat,* September 7–10, 1910; and *Little Rock Arkansas Gazette,* September 7–9, 1910.

best way to solve what they undoubtedly perceived as a spending problem. In addition, voters initiated three ballot propositions: to establish
statewide prohibition (defeated), to create new bipartisan boards of election commissioners and judges (defeated), and to have the state supply free
textbooks (defeated). They also considered three initiated amendments:
limiting the length of legislative sessions (to sixty days) and the amount of
pay for legislators (six dollars a day for the first sixty days only), allowing
for the recall of all elective officials and judges, and granting municipalities
authority to issue bonds for public improvements. Also decided were two
amendments proposed by the legislature: woman suffrage (with a grandfather clause to disfranchise blacks) and a tax exemption for cotton manufacturers. Although only the suffrage amendment failed to win majority approval, the only amendment to receive a constitutional majority was the
one limiting the length of legislative sessions and pay for legislators.[42]

An indication of the role played by the Arkansas State Federation of Labor in preparing and submitting proposed constitutional amendments and
in securing those propositions for the 1912 ballot can be found in the proceedings of that organization's state convention held in December 1912. In
submitting its report to the convention, the Initiative and Referendum
Committee described the procedure it had followed in meeting its instructions "to initiate a number of proposed laws in the interest of the wage earners and farmers of the state." Working in conjunction with representatives
of the Arkansas Farmers' Union, the committee prepared constitutional
amendments calling for the recall, the creation of a uniform textbook commission, and the establishment of a state printing plant. The committee acknowledged that it had been successful only in securing a sufficient number of signatures to guarantee submission of the first two measures. In an
interesting aside, the committee reported that it had been necessary to employ solicitors and to pay them at a rate of two to three cents per name in
order to secure enough signatures to qualify the two proposals (12,500 signatures were required in 1912). The committee noted that it had resorted to
that course of action during the final weeks of the canvass only when it
looked like their proposals might fail to qualify. In summarizing the difficulties encountered in obtaining signatures, the committee criticized both
the membership and many convention delegates for failing to secure
names to the petitions and, in some instances, for having "actually worked
against the measures at the polls on election day." The committee reported

42. See Thomas, "Direct Legislation," 90–91, 98–100; R. Farmer, "Direct Democracy,"
111–14; David Y. Thomas, "The Initiative and Referendum in Arkansas Come of Age,"
70–71; and Ledbetter, "Adoption of Initiative and Referendum," 204. For the votes on
each ballot proposition, see Arkansas, *Biennial Report, 1909–1912*, 411, 415.

that had it not been for the support of the Arkansas Farmers' Union, "the entire matter would have been a complete failure."[43]

Between 1912 and 1918 Arkansas voters considered one referendum, seven initiatives, six constitutional amendments initiated by petition, and eight constitutional amendments passed by the Arkansas legislature. Among the initiated measures that gained popular approval in 1914 were a child labor law prohibiting the employment of children under the age of fourteen and a "publicity" law requiring that all measures to be voted on by the people be published in newspapers. In 1916 voters approved a new primary election law. The only initiated measure to be rejected by voters was a local option liquor law in 1916. In addition to the initiated amendments considered in 1912, voters also rejected two amendments in 1914 and 1918 that would have allowed municipalities to issue bonds. Constitutional amendments passed by the legislature but either meeting outright defeat or failing to win constitutional majorities were proposals in 1914 to provide for a lieutenant governor and to fix salaries of members of the legislature, in 1916 to invoke a good-roads tax, and in 1918 to increase the number of supreme court justices and to authorize the state to issue farm loans. The only successful legislative amendment was one in 1916 calling for an increase in the school district tax.[44]

While Arkansas voters tried the new initiative and referendum law, the Arkansas Supreme Court tested it. The spirited criticism of Amendment 10 by lawyers and judges in 1910 all but guaranteed that the law would encounter legal challenges. In the 1912 case of *Hodges v. Dawdy*, the court struck down the infamous "joker." The court ruled that the words *each municipality* and *each county* had been "inaptly thrust into the amendment, as originally framed." Without placing limitations on the original phrase, the words meant that the people of any municipality or county could enact any law and thereby destroy the sovereignty of the state. Because the wording led arguably to an absurdity, it had to be rejected by the court for that reason. However, instead of clarifying the language and preserving for towns and counties the authority to decide local questions, the court ruled that Amendment 10 had no local applicability and voided that section of the law.

The court shocked proponents of Amendment 10 for a second time in 1912 in the case of *State ex rel Little Rock v. Donaghey* when it ruled that the passage of Amendment 10 did not alter the number of constitutional amendments that could be submitted in any two-year period. The consti-

43. *Proceedings of the Tenth Annual Convention of the Arkansas State Federation of Labor*, Pine Bluff, December 2–7, 1912, 41–42.

44. See Arkansas, *Biennial Report of the Secretary of State for the Years 1913–1920*, 340, 352, 364; Arkansas, *Biennial Report of the Secretary of State for the Years 1924–1926*, 229–231; *Equity* 15 (January 1913): 43; 17 (January 1915): 39; and 19 (January 1917): 27.

tution of 1874 had limited that number to three. In discerning no difference
between amendments passed by the legislature or initiated by petition, the
court concluded that the last two amendments placed on the ballot in 1912
(the recall and local bond authority) were in conflict with the constitution
and had, therefore, been improperly submitted. Three years later, in the
case of *Hildreth v. Taylor*, the court further weakened Amendment 10 when
it decided that even though the official wording of the law had stated that
"any measure" referred to the people would become law when approved
by "a majority of the votes cast thereon," it now interpreted the words *any
measure* to mean nothing more than bills referred to the people by the legislature. Initiated statutes and amendments to the constitution proposed either by the legislature or by petition would have to receive a majority of the
total votes cast in the election![45]

The decisions of the Arkansas Supreme Court, as well as the legislature's
generous application of the emergency clause to prevent use of the referendum, had so crippled Amendment 10 that direct legislationists concluded that a new law was needed. Led once again by the State Federation of
Labor and the Arkansas Farmers' Union, voters petitioned for a new initiative and referendum amendment in 1916. Working from a model
amendment prepared by the National Popular Government League and
adapted to Arkansas requirements by attorney Ben D. Brickhouse of Little
Rock, the new proposal was more carefully drawn than the earlier law. The
amendment allowed for 8 percent of the voters (based on the votes cast for
governor in the previous election) to propose any law, 10 percent to propose any constitutional amendment, and 6 percent to refer any act of the
legislature. The proposal restored the initiative and referendum to municipalities and counties for use on local laws if 15 percent of the voters (based
on the votes cast for mayor and circuit clerk, respectively, in the previous
election) should so petition. To guard against abuse of the emergency
clause such legislation had to be approved by two-thirds of the legislature
in a roll-call vote. As an added protection, franchises were not subject to inclusion under the emergency clause. Moreover, in an attempt to remove the
most onerous feature of the law, any measure, including a proposed constitutional amendment, initiated by petition would become law if approved by a majority of those voting on it. Finally, the amendment eliminated the restriction ("the rule of three") on the number of constitutional
amendments that could be submitted by petition at any election. In an

45. See Ledbetter, "Adoption of Initiative and Referendum," 220–22; Thomas, "Direct Legislation," 93–96, 100–104; Thomas, "Initiative and Referendum," 66–67; and
Moyers, "Arkansas Progressivism," 360. For formal discussion of the specific cases, see
Hodges v. Dawdy (104 Ark. 583, 149 S.W. 656), *State ex rel Little Rock v. Donaghey* (106 Ark.
56, 152 S.W. 746), and *Hildreth v. Taylor* (117 Ark. 465, 175 S.W. 40).

attempt to appease their conservative critics, supporters of the revised amendment made two major concessions. They agreed to allow the Arkansas Supreme Court (by unanimous vote) to set aside any initiated measure and to allow the legislature (by a three-fourths majority vote) to amend or repeal any act approved by the voters.[46]

In an effort to duplicate the successful organizing campaign of 1910, Judson King, now executive secretary of the National Popular Government League headquartered in Washington, D.C., returned to Arkansas to lead the drive for the new law (known as Amendment 13). Assisted by Minnie U. Rutherford-Fuller, a leader of the Arkansas Federation of Women's Clubs and a prominent Arkansas suffragist; David Y. Thomas, a professor of political science at the University of Arkansas; and Thomas Mehaffy, an attorney and later president of the Arkansas Constitutional Convention of 1918, the proponents of Amendment 13 seemed to be well organized. They also had the support of T. A. Wilson, J. E. Rogers, and L. H. Moore, presidents of the State Federation of Labor, the State Farmers' Union, and the Initiative and Referendum League of Arkansas, respectively; seven Arkansas congressmen; and popular Arkansas senator Joseph T. Robinson. Joining in the fight was Senator Robert M. La Follette of Wisconsin, the idol of many progressives, who sent a message of support. Also helping their cause at least indirectly was the Arkansas Bar Association, which, unlike in 1910, did not adopt an official position on Amendment 13. Even though the influential *Little Rock Arkansas Gazette* again lined up in opposition, pro-amendment leaders counted ninety-six state newspapers that favored the revised initiative and referendum amendment.

Even with the safeguards built into the revised amendment, conservative critics again referred to the proposal as a "radical" and "dangerous" departure from the existing system of government. They strongly objected to the inclusion of the local initiative provision, and alarmed many moral purists by suggesting that the amendment would encourage horse racing and gambling and undermine the statewide prohibition law (enacted by the legislature in 1915) by allowing local option elections. Frightened by what he considered to be the circulation of false information, King secured a letter from William S. U'Ren of Oregon, now nationally known as a leader in the movement for direct legislation, and a telegram from William Jennings Bryan that assured voters that they had nothing to fear. In October, King wrote to Senator Robert L. Owen of Oklahoma, president of the Na-

46. See Ledbetter, "Adoption of Initiative and Referendum," 221; R. Farmer, "Direct Democracy," 114–15; Thomas, "Initiative and Referendum," 67–68; Moyers, "Arkansas Progressivism," 361, 363; and circular, "The Truth about Amendment No. 13," n.d., David Yancey Thomas Papers, University of Arkansas Libraries, Special Collections, Fayetteville.

tional Popular Government League and a vigorous advocate of the initiative and referendum, asking for a statement on the prohibition issue. "It is going to be hard work to run this lie down and nail it," he told Owen, but "your emphatic denial as a constitutional lawyer" would put an end to the rumor that direct legislation would open the door for local gambling and liquor. Senator Owen's response, which the Direct Legislation League of Arkansas released as a public statement, denied that local use of the initiative would reopen saloons and even cited George A. Thornburgh, president of the Anti-Saloon League of Arkansas, as one who supported his position. Despite protestations to the contrary, however, the arguments of the opposition had taken their effect. Voters rejected Amendment 13 by a vote of 69,817 to 73,782.[47]

During the 1916 political campaign, Governor-elect Charles H. Brough, a supporter of direct legislation, called attention to the Arkansas Supreme Court's ruling that upheld the "rule of three" restricting the number of constitutional amendments that could appear on the ballot at any one time. Brough argued that the rule nullified the intent of the initiative. It was not just the court's ruling on the "rule of three" and the way in which that ruling handcuffed the initiative that angered Brough, though. The real problem rested with an antiquated state constitution. "Instead of being a great protector of the rights and liberties of the people," said Brough, "some times the ponderous provisions of the present constitution are the greatest menace to their protection."[48] At the crux of the problem was the constitutional restriction on the state's power to intervene in economic affairs. Especially frustrating was the way in which the constitution placed severe limitations on the power to tax and denied cities and counties the freedom to contract interest-bearing debts. As a way to expand the power to the government, facilitate local public improvement projects, and add more flexibility to the initiative process, Brough recommended calling a convention to revise the constitution of 1874.

When Governor Brough convinced the Arkansas legislature to make such a call in 1918, Judson King and a reorganized Initiative and Referendum League of Arkansas worked to get pro–direct legislation advocates elected to the constitutional convention. Delegates eventually adopted a revised initiative and referendum proposal, but retained the objectionable "rule of three" restriction. As a result, supporters of direct legislation joined with many rural Arkansas voters who distrusted increased governmental

47. King quoted in Niswonger, *Arkansas Politics,* 245 (see also 244–46). See also Thomas, "Initiative and Referendum," 67; Arkansas, *Biennial Report, 1913–1920,* 352; and letter from King to "The Fighting Editors, Who Won Amendment No. 10," October 25, 1916, Thomas Papers, University of Arkansas Libraries.

48. Niswonger, *Arkansas Politics,* 246.

power to defeat ratification of the new constitution in a special election held in December 1918. Proponents of direct legislation successfully petitioned to have the original 1916 proposal placed on the ballot again in 1920. Although the amendment received almost a two-thirds majority in its favor (86,360 to 43,662), it once again failed to gain a constitutional majority and was defeated.[49]

Ironically, the problem of the deficit that had helped trigger the call for the initiative and referendum in the first place served to rescue the amendment in the end. Proposed amendments that would have allowed municipalities to issue bonds (increasing their indebtedness) for public improvements had failed to receive constitutional majorities on several occasions. As a result, the financial condition of many Arkansas cities had reached a stage of crisis. Municipalities could not issue bonds, and taxation was limited to five mills. Attempting to break the revenue impasse, the legislature submitted yet another amendment to allow cities to issue bonds to assume the floating debt in 1923. This time they sought to enhance the attractiveness of the proposal to wary taxpayers by adding a clause that would have forbidden cities to incur any new debt (known as "pay as you go"). The amendment (known as Amendment 11) again won a majority of those voting on it but not a majority of the total votes cast in the election.

After the election, Ben D. Brickhouse, the mayor of Little Rock, pushed an ordinance through the city council empowering the city to issue bonds as if Amendment 11 had been approved. The mayor took the action to trigger a legal challenge and a ruling from the Arkansas Supreme Court. Complicating the court's decision, however, was another measure that appeared on the same ballot authorizing the legislature to fix the salaries of supreme court judges and providing for the addition of two judges to the court. As this amendment also received a majority of the votes cast on it but not a constitutional majority, the two amendments became legally intertwined. Because the second amendment directly affected the current judges, they were forced to disqualify themselves from making a decision. As a result, the governor appointed a special supreme court to decide the case.

Under tremendous pressure to modify the amendment process, the special court declared in 1925, in the case of *Brickhouse v. Hill*, that the court's earlier decision in *Hildreth v. Taylor* was in error and overturned it. In effect, the special court decided that any measure (statute or constitutional amendment) submitted to the people by the initiative process did not require a constitutional majority. The decision had the effect of validating all previous initiated propositions (since 1912) that had received a majority of

49. See ibid., 246–50; Thomas, "Initiative and Referendum," 67; and Arkansas, *Biennial Report, 1913–1920,* 376.

the votes cast on them. With the new legal interpretation, the revised initiative and referendum amendment of 1920 became law. It is unclear whether the new amendment owed its existence to accident or to ingenuity. Although the special court rested its decision upon legal precedent, practical considerations certainly influenced their thinking. As one justice remarked: "The credit, honor, prosperity, and growth of the counties, cities, and towns that are in debt, and the saving from debt of those that are not so involved, depend largely upon amendment No. 11."[50]

Despite its limited success in Arkansas, direct legislation never became popular in the South during the Progressive Era. David D. Schmidt, in his book *Citizen Lawmakers*, has offered at least a partial explanation. According to Schmidt, from its organizational beginnings in 1896, the national direct legislation movement had always sought to unite the reform impulses of the urban labor movement with those of rural farmers. Both groups thought that the adoption of direct legislation would result in government becoming more responsive to their needs. The popularity of the initiative and referendum in the Midwest and West indicated that they also appealed to a general frontier spirit of optimism, independence, and self-sufficiency. In contrast to the self-reliance and egalitarianism of the West, however, the South seemed bound by a conservative, elitist, racist tradition that precluded any serious consideration of those reforms. Historian Dewey W. Grantham has acknowledged that southern progressives "talked about the virtues of 'the people,' identified morality with majority rule, and urged the desirability of preserving and expanding traditional democratic principles." He also notes, though, that the southern concept of democracy was limited to whites only and that did not include all whites. Beneath the rhetoric, Grantham found that "well-to-do and middle class Southerners . . . often revealed a deep distrust of the masses, whether black or white." Such distrust generated a "need to cleanse the political process and limit participation to those who were prepared for responsible citizenship."[51] With no active, assertive labor movement to lead it (as in Arkansas) and with traditional fears of "black domination" (noticeably muted in Arkansas) programmed to reject it, direct legislation made little progress south of the Mason-Dixon line.[52]

---

50. For the full text of the 1920 amendment, see Arkansas, *Biennial Report, 1924–1926,* 213–18. See also Ledbetter, "Adoption of Initiative and Referendum," 222; R. Farmer, "Direct Democracy," 115; Thomas, "Initiative and Referendum," 68; and David Y. Thomas, *Arkansas and Its People: A History, 1541–1930,* 325–26. For a formal discussion of the special court's reasoning, see *Brickhouse v. Hill* (167 Ark. 513, 268 S.W. 865).

51. Grantham, "The Contours of Southern Progressivism," 1044–45.

52. Voters in Mississippi came close to duplicating Arkansas's feat, but a legal tech-

In Arkansas, the only southern state to ratify an amendment to its constitution establishing direct legislation, the citizenry was not as conservative as the southern elitist-racist stereotype might suggest. The fight to win adoption of Amendment 10, led by organized workers and farmers and Governor George Donaghey, was a triumph over the conservative establishment, led by lawyers, judges, politicians, and the *Little Rock Arkansas Gazette*. Despite charges from extremists that direct legislation was the evil scheme of socialists, anarchists, and Populists to subvert representative government and establish "mob rule," the electorate overwhelmingly endorsed the initiative and referendum in 1912.

Handicapped throughout the 1912–1918 period by the restrictive decisions of the conservative Arkansas Supreme Court, Amendment 10 proved ineffective. Voters did, however, use the initiative to approve several "progressive" measures: limiting legislative sessions, establishing a child labor law, and enacting a new primary election bill (the initiated amendment establishing the recall of public officials failed as a result of the "rule of three"). The decision of the special court in the Brickhouse case liberalized the use of the initiative and referendum and validated two previously defeated measures: municipal bond authority and the revised initiative and referendum amendment. Nonetheless, by 1925 the progressive reform spirit that had motivated Arkansas voters to accept the idea in 1910 had passed. As the national electorate became more conservative so too did the voters in Arkansas who used the initiative to prohibit the teaching of evolution in 1928 and to require compulsory Bible reading in schools in 1930.[53]

---

nicality eventually negated their efforts. Mississippians approved an initiative and referendum amendment by nearly a two-to-one margin in 1912, but the measure failed to receive a "supermajority" of all votes cast in the election and was defeated. Supporters of the initiative and referendum, led by state representatives N. A. Mott of Yazoo City and Frank Burkitt of Okalona, succeeded in getting an amendment placed on the ballot again in 1914 that actually met the supermajority requirement. Two years later voters used the referendum to reject a law passed by the legislature appointing Z. A. Brantley to the office of fish and game commissioner. A disgruntled Brantley then challenged the validity of the referendum in court. The state supreme court upheld the law in 1917 (*State v. Brantley*, 113 Miss. 786, 74 South 662). Five years later a citizen group collected petition signatures sufficient to initiate an amendment seeking to change the salary of the state revenue agent. Stokes V. Robertson, the affected agent, again contested the validity of the initiative and referendum amendment in court. Reversing its 1917 decision, the state supreme court ruled (*Power v. Robertson*, 130 Miss. 188, 93 South 769) that initiated statutes and referenda were different from initiated constitutional amendments and that the two categories should have been approved in separate amendments in 1914. Because they were not, the court declared the law to be unconstitutional. See also Schmidt, *Citizen Lawmakers*, 7, 13–14, 245–46.

53. See Diane D. Blaire, *Arkansas Politics and Government: Do the People Rule?* 126.

6

Arizona and California

ARIZONA

The history of Arizona's territorial period is similar to that of Montana in that railroad and mining companies controlled the territorial legislature and that it was common practice for their lobbyists to bribe legislators to influence legislative decisions. One of the most notable lobbyists was Henry J. Allen, who worked for the United Verde Copper Company owned by William Clark, one of Montana's infamous copper kings. George W. P. Hunt of Globe, the most dynamic politician of the era and a central figure in the debate over direct legislation, reportedly stated that a mere two thousand dollars could buy a veto from the governor and that copper companies hired administrators to act as lobbyists to manipulate territorial legislatures. Judson King, national organizer for the Direct Legislation League, charged that Arizonans had been living "at the mercy of Federal judges, governors and office holders, appointed from Washington at the dictation of railroads and mining interests," for a generation. "The people," said King, "were helpless and knew it. They were mercilessly exploited by Big Business—literally 'robbed'—(there is no other word), political corruption was an accepted thing; the corporations ruled."[1]

Corporate directors primarily wanted to maintain their tax privileges and thwart costly and intrusive labor legislation. Issues of taxation were significant. Mines worth $100 million were officially assessed at only $2 million. Much of the land granted to the powerful Santa Fe Railroad was either untaxed or undervalued. Furthermore, new railroads were commonly granted tax exemptions that ran for ten years or more. Many Arizonans found the situation increasingly intolerable. Small businessmen and property holders felt they were being asked to shoulder the territorial tax burden, whereas organized labor felt stymied in their attempts to gain protections and regulations for their working environment. During the 1899

1. King, "The Arizona Story in a Nut Shell," *Equity* 14 (January 1912): 7.

141

legislative session, bills to reinstate a bullion tax on minerals, to regulate hours for underground miners, to prohibit the issuing of scrip, and to create the office of mine inspector were all thwarted by the corporate lobby. Taxpayers and laborers felt powerless.[2]

One possible remedy for the situation was direct legislation. The idea of empowering the voters through the initiative and referendum first gained circulation in Arizona in the mid-1890s when W. O. "Bucky" O'Neill, an unsuccessful Populist candidate for territorial delegate to Congress in 1894 and 1896, advocated it. O'Neill had formerly been the editor of the *Prescott Hoof and Horn,* the weekly newspaper of the Territorial Livestock Association, and was known for his opposition to corporate control of territorial politics. Joining O'Neill was Harry W. Nash of Globe who became a vice president of the National Direct Legislation League and organizer for Arizona Territory in 1897. Like O'Neill, Nash used an obscure publication from which to promote direct legislation, contributing a column on the topic in the weekly *Prescott Pick and Drill.* The efforts of both men were cut short by war, however. O'Neill and Nash both enlisted in the First U.S. Volunteer Cavalry, known as Teddy Roosevelt's Rough Riders, during the Spanish-American War. O'Neill died fighting in Cuba, and Nash died in the Philippines working as a civilian in 1902.[3]

Democrat George W. P. Hunt introduced the first direct legislation bill to come from a representative of one of the major political parties during the legislative session of 1899. The measure provided for the initiative and referendum based on petitions signed by 7 percent of the voters in the territory or 15 percent of the voters in a locality. Supporting Hunt's measure was the Globe Miner's Union of the Western Federation of Miners, which wrote to Hunt: "We want to see if it is possible for one bill for the benefit of labor to become a law at the hands of the Arizona legislature." The bill passed the legislature, but Governor Nathan O. Murphy, a political appointee of the McKinley administration and said to be closely associated with mining and railroad interests, pocket vetoed it. The topic of direct legislation did not gain a hearing in the legislature again until 1909 when Hunt introduced basically the same measure he had proposed ten years before (after amendment the petition requirements for local use of the initiative and referendum were raised to 25 percent). The Globe Miner's Union again backed Hunt's bill and stated: "The bill introduced by Mr. Hunt making di-

2. See Thomas Sheridan, *Arizona: A History,* 173–74; N. D. Houghton, "Arizona's Experience with the Initiative and Referendum," 183; H. A. Hubbard, "The Arizona Enabling Act and President Taft's Veto," 308; and John Braeman, "Albert J. Beveridge and Statehood for the Southwest, 1902–1912," 327.

3. See Charles Foster Todd, "The Initiative and Referendum in Arizona," 7–8; *Direct Legislation Record* 4 (June 1897): 22; 4 (December 1897): 62; and 9 (December 1902): 76.

rect legislation the law of the land . . . we recommend as a great step in the march of progress."[4] This time the bill passed the upper house, but failed when the lower house voted on the last day of the session to postpone consideration of the measure so that it could consider essential appropriation bills.

The proponents of direct legislation got another chance to push their cause in 1910 when the quest for statehood became a reality for both Arizona and New Mexico. President Taft signed the Enabling Act giving Arizona and New Mexico permission to form constitutions for statehood on June 20, 1910. Immediately thereafter, Governor Richard E. Sloan set the date for the special election for the fifty-two delegates to the Arizona Constitutional Convention for September 20, 1910. Interest groups excluded from territorial politics envisioned a golden opportunity.

Realizing that delegate selection would be critical to the final outcome of the convention and desperate to have its voice heard in those proceedings, organized labor decided to press its case more forcefully. Prior to 1906 labor organization in the territory was confined to local unions (there was as yet no State Federation of Labor), and its political cohesion and effectiveness suffered as a result. A strike against the Phelps-Dodge Corporation for alleged use of the blacklist in 1906 changed that. Although the strike failed, labor emerged more unified than ever before and more willing to follow a concerted program of direct political action. With the date for the election of delegates to the constitutional convention set, organized labor, with large, disciplined concentrations of voters in Bisbee-Douglas, Globe-Miami, and the mining towns of Yavapai County, decided that the best way to gain a hearing was to organize their own Labor Party. Taking the lead in this endeavor was the Bisbee Miner's Union, which sent out a call for representatives from the various territorial labor unions to meet in Phoenix on July 11, 1910. The meeting produced a platform of principles that labor wanted to see written into the new state constitution, and included the initiative, referendum, and recall. J. C. Provost, who chaired the meeting, closed it by stating: "I see in the gathering of the representatives of labor the grasping of one of the greatest opportunities which has ever been offered to the working class to conduct the government of their own commonwealth in their own interests."[5]

The formation of the Labor Party was a blow to the Democrats who had counted on working-class support in the upcoming election. As a result, the leaders of the Democratic Party, who included George W. P. Hunt, offered

4. Todd, "Initiative and Referendum," 10, 13 (see also 9, 11).
5. Ibid., 16 (see also 12–16). Both the Socialist Party and the Democratic Party in Gila County, the center of labor strength, had included provisions for the initiative and referendum in their platforms in 1908 (12). See also Sheridan, *Arizona: A History*, 175.

a compromise by which the Democrats would agree to adopt Labor's platform if the party would dissolve itself and agree to support the Democratic ticket. With Labor's agreement, the Democrats incorporated the initiative, referendum, and recall planks into their platform adopted at their convention in August. Joining the progressive Labor-Democrat alliance (referred to by one historian as the labor-bourgeois coalition) were woman suffragists and prohibitionists who found the initiative and referendum appealing options should the convention decide not to include their demands in the new constitution.[6]

As the campaign for delegate selection heated up, the initiative and referendum not only became the major topics of discussion, but had, in the words of one historian, also "achieved shibboleth status on par with statehood and, in an earlier era, free silver."[7] Looking to enlighten the voters on the merits of direct legislation, proponents circulated a pamphlet, "Code of the People's Rule," written by Senator Jonathan Bourne of Oregon, a nationally known authority on the topic. Further publicity came from the territory's newspapers that picked up the issue and discussed how the initiative and referendum had worked in other states. Hoping to help coordinate the overall effort, Judson King, organizer, strategist, and point man for the National Direct Legislation League, traveled to Arizona to lend his support. The result was an overwhelming victory for the Labor-Democrat alliance that claimed to control forty-one of the fifty-two delegates at the constitutional convention that was set to convene in Phoenix on October 10.[8]

That the initiative and referendum (along with the recall) would be written into Arizona's constitution was a foregone conclusion. According to one historian, Arizonans "were 'bursting out all over' with progressive ideas."[9] Any lingering doubts certainly disappeared with the election of George Hunt as president of the convention. As the acknowledged leader of Arizona's progressive and labor Democrats, and as the leading political advocate of direct legislation in the territory, Hunt had traveled to Oregon and California to study their liberal constitutions and talk to politicians there. Between October 10 and December 9, 1910, when delegates finally approved the constitution, the Committee on Legislative Department considered five direct legislation proposals. The plan finally agreed upon was slightly more demanding than the Oregon model favored by organized la-

6. Todd, "Initiative and Referendum," 16–18. The "labor-bourgeois coalition" is referred to in Sheridan, *Arizona: A History,* 182.

7. David R. Berman, *Reformers, Corporations, and the Electorate: An Analysis of Arizona's Age of Reform,* 169.

8. Five of the eleven Republican delegates came from Pima County, a center of Republican strength and Southern Pacific influence. See Todd, "Initiative and Referendum," 18, 22; and *Equity* 12 (October 1910): 136.

9. Howard R. Lamar, *The Far Southwest, 1846–1912: A Territorial History,* 501.

bor. Constitutional amendments could be initiated on petitions of 15 percent of the electorate (based on the total votes for governor in the preceding election). Similarly, 10 percent of the voters could initiate state laws, and 5 percent could refer statutes passed by the legislature. The convention also extended direct legislation to localities where 15 percent of the voters could initiate a ballot proposition and 10 percent could call a vote on a local ordinance. The convention also granted the legislature the option of referring measures directly to the voters for approval or rejection.[10]

Included in the constitution were numerous provisions advocated by organized labor: the eight-hour day, a compulsory employer-liability law, prohibition of child labor, creation of the office of state mine inspector, and the recall (by 25 percent of the votes cast for the office of the official being recalled) of all elected officials, including judges. This last provision was important to organized labor, as they believed that judges routinely sided with corporations in labor-management disputes. The constitution also established a corporation commission with power to regulate railroad passenger fares and freight rates, a tax equalization commission, antilobbying and corrupt-practices clauses, and the direct primary system. Overall, the new Arizona Constitution was an extremely progressive document, and there was a feeling among many that it might be too radical for the conservative Republican administration in Washington. Those fears soon proved to be accurate. Although Arizonans overwhelmingly approved the constitution at a special election on February 9, 1911, with 77 percent voting for it, it failed to meet the approval of President William Howard Taft, ostensibly because of the provision allowing for the recall of judges. As a result, he vetoed the congressional resolution providing for the admission of Arizona as a state on August 15, 1911. Seeing little choice, voters agreed to delete the provision allowing for the recall of judges from the constitution in December 1911, and Arizona formally became a state on February 14, 1912. Ironically, Arizonans would get even with Taft just nine months later by approving (by a vote of 16,272 to 3,705) a legislative amendment reinserting the recall of judges into their state constitution.[11]

The election of George Hunt as the new governor and prolabor majorities to both houses of the new state legislature enabled labor advocates to secure a series of laws for the benefit of the working class. Included on the list were laws that outlawed the injunction and gave workers the right to assemble and picket, and others that eliminated the exemption of "productive" mines from property taxation and tripled the assessment of min-

10. See Todd, "Initiative and Referendum," 26, 31; *Equity* 13 (January 1911): 14–19; and Lamar, *Far Southwest*, 502.

11. See Sheridan, *Arizona: A History*, 176; *Equity* 13 (January 1911): 14–19; and Lamar, *Far Southwest*, 503.

ing properties. Seven other prolabor bills relating to railroads and mining operations also received approval. However, labor quickly found itself on the defensive, as each of these laws was challenged in successful referendum petitions directed by the Southern Pacific Railroad and other affected corporations in 1912. Although all seven referenda failed, corporate interests proved they could generate petitions to defend their interests as well. In addition to the recall amendment previously referred to, voters also approved an initiated amendment backed by the Arizona State Suffrage Association that allowed for woman suffrage.[12]

In 1914 Arizonans initiated fifteen ballot propositions, seven of which were sponsored by the Arizona Federation of Labor. This time labor successfully initiated laws that prohibited blacklisting, established old-age and mothers' pensions, and required that 80 percent of the workers on a job be U.S. citizens. This last measure was a nativistic response to a perceived economic threat posed by Mexican workers. Railroads, some small employers, and mine owners vigorously opposed the proposition on economic grounds. The United States Supreme Court declared the law unconstitutional in 1915. Perhaps their biggest success, however, was an initiated amendment that protected their recent gains under the initiative and referendum by depriving the governor and the legislature of the right to repeal or amend measures approved by popular vote. The Arizona State Federation of Labor led the petition campaign for the amendment, arguing that the protections were necessary to guard against abuses of power by the governor or the legislature. Voters also approved an initiated amendment sponsored by the Temperance Federation of Arizona establishing statewide prohibition and rejected an initiated statute that would have abolished the death penalty.[13]

Corporate interests undoubtedly regarded much of the legislation either enacted or initiated in 1912 and 1914 as class legislation and significantly threatening to warrant a counteroffensive. To reverse the trend, the corporations decided to mount a concerted assault on organized labor and its

12. The list of prolabor laws included those that regulated headlights on engines, required three years of experience for engineers, limited the number of cars on a train, reduced railroad passenger rates, and established a semimonthly pay date. Rounding out the list was a train crew law and a miners' lien law. See Todd, "Initiative and Referendum," 55–57; Sheridan, *Arizona: A History*, 179, 182; and George Judson King Papers, Library of Congress, Manuscripts Division, Washington, D.C.

13. The anti–death penalty statute that voters narrowly defeated in 1914 was narrowly approved in 1916. Voters, however, elected to restore capital punishment in 1918. All three actions were by initiative petition. See Todd, "Initiative and Referendum," 52–53; Sheridan, *Arizona: A History*, 179; *Equity* 16 (October 1914): 173–74; and King Papers, Library of Congress.

liberal-progressive-Democratic allies. As World War I drove up the price of copper and generated an atmosphere of extreme patriotism, the directors of the largest copper companies undertook a major campaign to get sympathetic politicians elected to the upper house of the Arizona legislature. To shift public opinion in their direction, they purchased newspapers and bribed editors to support their views. The Phelps-Dodge Corporation alone controlled the *Clifton Copper Era*, the *Bisbee Daily Review*, the *Douglas International Gazette*, the *Phoenix Arizona Gazette*, and the *Tucson Arizona Daily Star*. They also attempted to influence public school curricula, intervened in church affairs to eliminate liberal ministers, and organized an unsuccessful recall campaign against Governor Hunt. After America's entry into the war, the same companies took advantage of the patriotic fervor to cripple the union labor movement in Arizona.[14]

Indications that the antilabor offensive was having its effect began to appear in 1916. In the election that year labor failed to secure two measures—an amendment designed to abolish the state senate and establish a unicameral legislature and a measure to create a department of labor—that it sponsored via the initiative. In campaigning unsuccessfully for the unicameral idea, organized labor conceded that a second legislative body was a check on bad legislation, but argued that it also served, in practice, to block good legislation. To the State Federation of Labor, the special interests had too much power under the bicameral system and legislation was often the result of "trading" in conference committee. Organized labor also failed to convince voters that the gathering of statistical information (and its importance in enacting protective labor legislation) was worth the cost of adding to the state bureaucracy. It also had to fight against two amendments allegedly backed by corporate interests: one designed to undercut the existing workmen's compensation system and another that would have emasculated the direct legislation amendment itself. The latter amendment, approved by the legislature, would have prevented any initiated measure from taking effect unless it gained a majority of all those voting in the election rather than a majority of those voting on the measure. Only 605 votes prevented the amendment from being approved. No prolabor or anticorporate measures appeared among the ten propositions on the ballot in 1918, a final indication that the antilabor campaign had succeeded.[15]

As Arizona's contentious reform era came to an end, voters could take stock of the fact that they had established the state as one of the leaders in

---

14. See Sheridan, *Arizona: A History,* 182–86.
15. See Houghton, "Arizona's Experience," 192; and King Papers, Library of Congress.

the use of direct legislation. Between 1912 and 1918 Arizonans considered forty-seven voter-initiated ballot propositions: fifteen initiated amendments, eighteen initiated statutes, and fourteen referenda.[16]

CALIFORNIA

The effort to establish direct legislation in California grew out of ever increasing public dissatisfaction with machine-controlled politics at the state and local levels. Representative government seemed unresponsive to the popular will, and legislative decisions seemed biased in favor of special interests. Criticism of the control that the Southern Pacific machine exerted over the political economy in California triggered a search for a means by which voters could regain control of "popular" government.

The informal origins of direct legislation in California date from the early 1890s. During the political campaign of 1892, California Populists introduced the initiative and referendum as a unifying plank in their agrarian-oriented platform. Realizing that many within the labor movement desired a broader expression of the reform spirit than allowed by a growing craft union structure that shied away from political partisanship, and sensing that many urban consumers and taxpayers felt distanced from mainstream Populist demands, the People's Party tried to win broader support for its reform program by including measures that appealed directly to those groups. The Los Angeles County platform of the People's Party, for example, endorsed measures for public ownership of utilities, an improved mechanics lien law, and both direct legislation and proportional representation in legislative assemblies. The city convention of the People's Party followed similar lines when it approved a shorter platform that stressed municipal ownership of public utilities and the initiative and referendum in city government. Nonetheless, the Populist appeal met with little success in 1892, and no straight Populist candidate was elected in southern California.[17]

As the Populists prepared for the next national political contest, they continued to lure potential allies (especially workers) with the idea of direct legislation. One natural constituency was the Knights of Labor. The Knights of Labor made its first appearance in California in the late 1870s. By 1882 it had organized eight local assemblies in the San Francisco–Oakland–San Jose area and claimed to have influenced the state legislature when that body created the California Bureau of Labor Statistics in 1883.

16. For a complete list of all measures that appeared on the Arizona ballot and the votes cast thereon between 1912 and 1918, see Russell Roush, "The Initiative and Referendum in Arizona, 1912–1978," app. A–C.
17. See Grace Heilman Stimson, *Rise of the Labor Movement in Los Angeles,* 145–48.

Soon after, local assemblies of the Knights organized in the southern California cities of Los Angeles, Anaheim, Santa Ana, and Azusa. By 1886 the order had expanded to six assemblies, with more than three hundred members in the Los Angeles area. The platform of the Knights emphasized the formation of cooperative enterprises, but also strongly condemned the Republican and Democratic Parties for their hostility to organized labor, their corruption, and their subservience to monopolies. It was this political dimension that led the Knights to cooperate with the Union Labor Party in 1888 and demand a political system responsive to workingmen and women. The organization's attraction to direct legislation was only natural, but by the early 1890s its strength was waning.

Shortly after their defeat in 1892, representatives of the People's Party organized a national subsidiary known as the Industrial Legion. In 1893, under the pressure of hard times, local branches of the legion in the Los Angeles area held a major conference with a program that featured a discussion of direct legislation. Labor undoubtedly saw in these devices a means to obtain legislation (such as the eight-hour day, police neutrality during strikes, and antistrikebreaking ordinances) denied them by the dominant political culture. Looking to test the popularity of direct legislation within its own organization, the Los Angeles Council of Labor polled thirteen of its member unions and found all but one in favor of the initiative and referendum. In 1894 the Los Angeles Council of Labor, with the assistance of Assembly no. 2405 of the Knights of Labor, campaigned to amend the city charter by including provisions for an enforceable eight-hour workday, a minimum daily wage of two dollars for public works and the employment only of citizens on such projects, the appointment of a superintendent of labor statistics, the initiative and referendum, and the reduction of salaries for civic officials. The charter committee, however, took action on only the salary issue. Interest in direct legislation seemed to be broadening as the statewide Labor Congress (which included both workers and farmers) also endorsed the reforms at a convention held in San Francisco in February 1894.[18]

The appeal of direct legislation spread rapidly during the mid-1890s, spurred by the circulation of J. W. Sullivan's book *Direct Legislation*. Sulli-

18. The Los Angeles Council of Labor was formed during a prolonged printers' strike against the *Los Angeles Times*, a newspaper owned by the rabidly antiunion Harrison Gray Otis. The council sought the organization and affiliation of new unions and championed such economic issues as a minimum daily wage, enforcement of the eight-hour day, the appointment of a superintendent of labor statistics for Los Angeles, and the establishment of an employment office to be maintained by the city and county. The council also had a limited political agenda that coalesced around the idea of direct legislation. The council formally affiliated with the American Federation of Labor in September 1894. See Stimson, *Labor Movement*, 55–56, 77, 92, 127–28, 148–50, 178.

van personally added to the growing interest in the idea by presenting speeches in California in 1895. That same year interested citizens organized the first Direct Legislation League of California, and joined what was quickly becoming a national reform movement. Modeled after the initial organization in New Jersey, the league focused its attention on seeking to restore the machinery of government to the people by means of the initiative and referendum. When Eltweed Pomeroy, the corresponding secretary of the Direct Legislation League of New Jersey and editor of the nationally subscribed *Direct Legislation Record*, called the first national Direct Legislation Conference, several Californians took active roles. Henry C. Dillon of Los Angeles and Thomas V. Cator of San Francisco represented California, and Dillon was elected to the executive committee of the new National Direct Legislation League.[19]

The first significant attempts to secure direct legislation in California at any level occurred in the cities of San Francisco and Los Angeles. Under the California Constitution of 1879 home rule cities had been granted the privilege of drafting their own charters for submission to the legislature. Mayor James D. Phelan appointed the Committee of One Hundred to frame a charter for the city of San Francisco in 1897. Having been granted only advisory powers, the Committee of One Hundred elected fifteen freeholders to assume the task of composition. The majority of the members of the general committee were conservative commercial and professional men, but there were a few labor and "progressive" members. Significant in this latter category was Alfred Cridge. Cridge, the father of Oregon's direct legislation advocate by the same name, migrated to San Francisco in 1877 and began a career as a journalist. Over the next two decades he pursued interests in publishing, writing, and lecturing that soon made him a well-known advocate of the single tax, direct legislation, and proportional representation. Cridge actually viewed direct legislation more as a means to an end: "I have advocated the Initiative and Referendum . . . because they will lead to proportional representation, under which they would be rarely used, because a real representative board would greatly supersede their use. But the knowledge on the part of boards, legislatures, etc., that they could be used would be a great safety valve to keep them straight."[20] Elected to the Board of Freeholders and subsequently appointed to the legislative, public utilities, and revision committees, Cridge was largely responsible for the inclusion of the initiative and referendum sections in the charter.

Under the proposed charter voters could petition for a popular vote on

19. See *Direct Legislation Record* 3 (September 1896): 25–28; and "Government Directly by the People," box 34, John Randolph Haynes Papers, University of California at Los Angeles Research Library, Special Collections.
20. Cridge, "The San Francisco Charter," *Direct Legislation Record* 5 (March 1898): 8.

either proposed or legislated city ordinances and future charter amendments. A compulsory referendum provision also gave voters the right to veto all light and water franchises, the sale or lease of any public utility, and the purchase of land property valued at more than fifty thousand dollars. Various organizations and clubs involved in the cause of municipal reform actively supported the charter. One such group, the Citizens Charter Association, urged voters to approve the charter "to save San Francisco from the rule of the bosses, the water, lighting and railroad corporations . . . which have in the past and will in the future, unless they are restrained, debauch our politics, rob the people and paralyze the orderly operation of the law." Critics, however, charged that the Board of Freeholders was not representative of the various social classes and organizations in the city, that the referendum was limited in that it did not apply to all municipal franchises, and that the 15 percent initiative requirement was too high. They also suggested that the addition of the direct legislation provisions in 1898 was merely a deception to get the charter adopted (it had been rejected by the voters on four previous occasions). Voters only narrowly approved the charter by a vote of 14,386 to 12,025 at a special election on May 28, 1898, but most supporters of direct legislation were elated. It was ratified by the state legislature in 1899 and went into effect on January 1, 1900.[21]

Close behind San Francisco, and soon to supersede it in the movement for direct legislation, was Los Angeles. Spearheaded by groups such as the Municipal Reform Association and the League for Better City Government, urban reformers made periodic attempts during the 1890s to revise the city's 1889 charter. These largely nonpartisan efforts focused their attention on limiting the power of the political machine. The Southern Pacific Railroad's "Political Bureau" centered in San Francisco in reality controlled the political machine in Los Angeles. Walter Francis Xavier Parker, land agent for the Southern Pacific Corporation and its chief lobbyist in Sacramento, ran the machine in southern California. Joining with local public utility corporations, public works contractors, and liquor dealers, Parker controlled ward politics in Los Angeles, managed the election of his men to the powerful city council, and usually exerted considerable influence with the current mayor. Businessmen who were dependent upon the Southern Pacific for transportation or who wished to see the Republican Party continue in control usually found it in their interest to cooperate. Known in the political culture as "the Octopus," the Southern Pacific had a reputation for ruthless manipulation of the political economy.

21. Citizens Charter Association quoted in Ellis Paxson Oberholtzer, *The Referendum in America*, 352 (see also 308, 351–52, 386). The city of Vallejo also adopted initiative and referendum provisions for its charter in 1898. See also *Direct Legislation Record* 5 (March 1898): 7–9; 5 (May 1898): 23–24; 5 (June 1898): 42–43, 52; and 9 (March 1902): 17–18.

To restrict the influence of machine-controlled political parties, reform-ers hoped to increase the number of nonpartisan officials and departments and to strengthen the power of the mayor. They also looked to eliminate the ward as a political division and replace it with an at-large system and fewer elected officials, and to inaugurate a system of civil service. In 1898 it looked as if they would finally succeed. That year Mayor Meredith P. Sny-der invited representatives of the major political parties, the Merchants' and Manufacturers' Association, the Board of Trade, the Chamber of Com-merce, the Teachers' Alliance, the Council of Labor, the Socialist-Labor Party, and the Christian Socialists to make nominations for a board of free-holders to write a new charter for the city. When the fifteen elected free-holders finally got down to business, they included a provision for the ini-tiative and referendum in the proposed charter. Then, just before the charter was submitted to a popular vote, labor publicly criticized the doc-ument for not setting a minimum daily wage on public works and not re-stricting the use of labor contracts on those same projects. As a result, the charter was decisively defeated in December 1898, even though business and the League for Better City Government supported it.[22]

One organization that worked enthusiastically for the addition of direct legislation to the proposed charter in 1898 was the Union Reform League. The league was a Christian-socialist body led by William Dwight Porter Bliss, an Episcopal minister from Boston. Bliss, familiar with the poverty of New England mill towns and influenced by the writings of Henry George and the British Fabian Socialists, dedicated his life to applying Christ's Gospels to society's social and economic problems. His deep concern for social justice drew him into the trade union movement, membership in the Knights of Labor, and even nomination for political office by the Massachu-setts Labor Party in 1887. Two years later Bliss organized the first Christian Socialist Society in the United States, and began publication of a monthly magazine called the *Dawn*. Bliss used his new forum to criticize both the in-dividualistic and competitive nature of industrial capitalism that worked to widen the gap between rich and poor and the Protestant Church that supported such a system. In its place he envisioned a cooperative com-monwealth that benefited everyone and a Protestant Church that preached a true social gospel. Yet, as an advocate of the gradual transformation of the social order, Bliss favored expediency and allied himself with a variety of reform causes.

22. See Stimson, *Labor Movement*, 221; and Kevin Starr, *Inventing the Dream: California through the Progressive Era*, 201, 248. Information on Parker and the Los Angeles machine can be found in Samuel G. Blythe, "Putting the Rollers under the S. P.," 6–7; and George E. Mowry, *The California Progressives*, 15, 38–39. See also Robert M. Fogelson, *The Frag-mented Metropolis: Los Angeles, 1850–1930*, 205–28.

While lecturing in San Francisco in 1897, Bliss launched the Union Reform League, an attempt to unite all social reformers under one banner (the symbol for the league was a red flag with a white cross). Organized as a national society, the league showed its most enthusiastic growth in California and soon claimed branches in San Francisco, Oakland, Alameda, Ventura, and Los Angeles. The platform for the new organization favored full employment, public ownership, increases in the taxation on land and income, inheritance taxes, limitation of the use of the injunction in labor disputes, woman suffrage, prohibition of child labor and restrictions on the hours and regulations on the conditions affecting women workers, compulsory accident insurance, unemployment compensation, social security, and direct legislation and proportional representation. The league's involvement in the charter revision fight in Los Angeles in 1898 provided Bliss with an opportunity to help purify government, humanize society, and generate converts to his beliefs.[23]

One individual that listened to what Bliss had to say with careful attention was Dr. John Randolph Haynes. Graduating from the University of Pennsylvania with both a Ph.D. and a medical degree in 1874, Haynes had ample opportunity to witness urban poverty and political corruption before moving from Philadelphia to Los Angeles in 1887. Haynes established a medical partnership and soon built up a thriving medical practice in Los Angeles that made him personal physician to many civic leaders. Haynes invested in real estate and used his financial independence to endow his later reform efforts. In 1897 he joined the League for Better City Government, a bipartisan organization concerned with municipal reforms such as civil service and charter revision. Haynes, already to the "left" of his colleagues for better government, became fascinated with the idea of the initiative and referendum and worked to get those provisions included in the 1898 charter. As he later recalled: "Many years observation of misgovernment in American cities ... convinced me that the cure for the evils of democracy was more democracy—the bringing of the control over their affairs the nearest possible to the people." As he became acquainted with the social reform philosophy of W. D. P. Bliss, he soon added public ownership to his personal reform platform. When Bliss visited Los Angeles early in 1898 to establish a chapter of his new Union Reform League, Haynes arranged a banquet so that Bliss and his ideas could be introduced to civic

23. See Howard H. Quint, *The Forging of American Socialism,* 109–26, 256–60; Christopher L. Webber, "William Dwight Porter Bliss: Priest and Socialist"; Richard B. Dressner, "William Dwight Porter Bliss's Christian Socialism," 66–82; Tom Sitton, "California's Practical Idealist: John Randolph Haynes," 4–5; Stimson, *Labor Movement,* 223; *Dictionary of American Biography,* s.v. "Bliss, William Dwight Porter"; and *The National Cyclopedia of American Biography,* s.v. "Bliss, William Dwight Porter."

and church leaders. Bliss found the reform atmosphere in Los Angeles so receptive that he spent a year as rector at the Church of Our Savior in San Gabriel. Supporters soon established a branch of the league, and Haynes became chairman of the Committee of One Hundred to guide the work of the organization. The following year the league reorganized as the Social Reform Union and chose Haynes to head its California branch. Haynes was also elected president of the first Christian Socialist Club of Los Angeles in 1900. With wealth, influence, zeal, a political agenda, and a social philosophy, J. R. Haynes was ready to crusade for reform.[24]

In 1900 Dr. Haynes led a group of citizens who again took up the issue of charter revision and sought to have the initiative and referendum become a reality in Los Angeles. Once again the major political parties, leading commercial groups, and socialist and labor organizations were invited to nominate candidates for a new board of freeholders to revise the charter. Among those elected to the fifteen-member board on July 27, 1900, were Haynes; Harry Chandler, the conservative managing editor of the *Los Angeles Times;* and H. Gaylord Wilshire, a wealthy Los Angeles socialist. Haynes, supported by both the major political parties and organized labor, was appointed to the committee on legislation along with attorney Nathaniel P. Conrey and businessman Richard J. Colyear. Haynes submitted the draft of the initiative and referendum measure and added a provision for the recall, although no municipal government in the United States had as yet adopted the idea. Looking back on the charter fight from the vantage point of 1912, Haynes confessed that neither he nor anyone else involved at the time knew that the recall had been used in Switzerland or that it had been advocated in various platform statements of the Populist Party as the "imperative mandate." Haynes claimed that the idea came to him after reading *The City for the People,* by Frank Parsons. According to Haynes, "we could find no precedent anywhere to aid us, so we were forced to evolve the scheme out of our inner consciousness." Haynes, for his efforts, became nationally known as "Father of the Recall."[25]

With a favorable vote from the committee, and with some active lobbying with other members of the Board of Freeholders (Haynes presented copies of Frank Parsons's book, which contained a convincing argument for direct legislation, to each freeholder), the initiative and referendum passed

24. Haynes quoted in letter to William E. Rappard, May 6, 1912, box 45, Haynes Papers, University of California at Los Angeles Research Library. See also Sitton, "Practical Idealist," 4–5; and Stimson, *Labor Movement,* 223–24. For a more detailed discussion of Bliss's influence on Haynes and the depth of Haynes's commitment to Christian socialism, see Tom Sitton, *John Randolph Haynes: California Progressive,* 26–33.

25. Letter from Haynes to Dr. William E. Rappard, May 6, 1912, box 45, Haynes Papers, University of California at Los Angeles Research Library.

unanimously and the recall by a vote of thirteen to two. However, during a discussion of the charter revisions a question arose concerning the legality of the actions of the new Board of Freeholders in superseding the work of the original board in 1888. The California Supreme Court ultimately decided the question, ruling that a city could adopt only one charter by a vote of freeholders and that changes to that charter could be secured only as amendments. Simply put, the entire process had to be repeated.[26]

In March 1902 a new charter revision committee, appointed by the city council, again undertook the task of amending the charter. Even though Haynes was not a member of the new committee, several of its members were his close personal friends. The new committee worked from a draft prepared by the previous board, but Haynes refused to concede that this guaranteed passage of the initiative and referendum. He continued to champion direct legislation in speeches before civic groups and in newspaper articles. As a member of the executive committee of the recently formed Municipal League of Los Angeles, Haynes used his influence (and the active cooperation of well-known civic leader Charles Dwight Willard) to have the Municipal League formally recommend both direct legislation and civil service reform to the charter revision committee. Haynes then hosted a formal dinner for members of the charter committee and invited Eltweed Pomeroy, president of the National Direct Legislation League, to be the guest speaker. At the conclusion of the dinner, the charter committee held an impromptu business session and adopted a motion in favor of including direct legislation provisions (including the recall) in the new charter. The charter committee unanimously approved these measures in early July as well as a provision to establish civil service reform for the city.

The Direct Legislation League of Los Angeles (organized in 1900 and now with Haynes as president) directed the political campaign for ratification. With additional support from nearly all the city's newspapers (the *Los Angeles Herald* was especially active, conducting a popular cartoon campaign in addition to its strong editorial support), the Council of Labor, the Southern California Convention of Farmers' Clubs, and the Republican, Democratic, and Union Labor Parties, passage of the amendments for popular and responsible government seemed almost ensured. Then, just prior to the special election on December 1, 1902, it appeared as if the *Los Angeles Times* and the Municipal League had decided upon a last-minute cam-

26. See Janice Jaques, "The Political Reform Movement in Los Angeles, 1900–1909," 12–17; Frederick L. Bird and Frances M. Ryan, *The Recall of Public Officers: A Study of the Operation of the Recall in California*, 23–28; *Los Angeles Record*, July 17, 1929; letter from Haynes to the Referendum League of Philadelphia, 1906, box 41, Haynes Papers, University of California at Los Angeles Research Library; and Sitton, *John Randolph Haynes*, 37–39.

paign to defeat the recall. The Municipal League objected that the recall was too "experimental" and that it might discourage "good citizens" from running for office, whereas the *Times* questioned its constitutionality. In response, Haynes quickly authorized the printing of thirty thousand small yellow cards requesting voters to approve all the direct legislation amendments. Members of the Union Labor Party distributed the cards to every voter coming to the polls. When the votes were counted, the initiative and referendum amendment won by a majority of more than six to one (12,846 to 1,942), the civil service amendment by a majority of five to one (11,180 to 2,306), and the recall by a majority of four to one (9,751 to 2,470). The California legislature approved the amendments in January 1903.

The initiative provision allowed voters to propose laws at a special election if they obtained the signatures of 15 percent of the electorate. Signatures of only 5 percent of the voters would allow them to propose a law at a regular election. The referendum provision required a petition signed by 7 percent of the voters to challenge a law passed by the city council. The recall provision required signatures of 25 percent of the voters to call a special election to consider the removal of elective officials from office. The city of Los Angeles amended its charter again in 1911 and extended the recall to all appointive officials.[27]

In June 1902, in the midst of the drive to get direct legislation included in the Los Angeles charter, Haynes led the effort to reorganize the Direct Legislation League of California. The purpose of the league was twofold: to create an organization that might more efficiently direct the local direct legislation forces in Los Angeles and to lay the groundwork for an effective organization that would campaign for the same reforms at the state level. In doing so, Dr. Haynes, as president of the "new" league, adopted the tools of the practical, pragmatic, even "Machiavellian" politician. One of the most effective devices used by Haynes and the league was an impressive letterhead that included (in addition to three officers and a five-member executive committee) no fewer than twenty-two vice presidents. The latter group included judges, bank presidents, military officers, high churchmen, prominent civic leaders, and even a former governor. Representatives of organized labor, temperance societies, socialists, and other "militant minorities" were actively recruited, but their names were conspicuously missing

27. See Jaques, "Political Reform," 17–27; *Direct Legislation Record* 9 (September 1902): 46–47; 10 (March 1903): 7–9; Bird and Ryan, *Recall of Public Officers,* 28–33; Donald R. Culton, "Charles Dwight Willard: Los Angeles' 'Citizen Fixit,'" 158–71; *Los Angeles Record,* July 17, 1929; J. W. Park, "The Adoption of the Recall in Los Angeles," scrapbook, Haynes Papers, University of California at Los Angeles Research Library; letter from Morton B. Curtis to Haynes, n.d., box 35, ibid.; letter from Haynes to the Referendum League of Philadelphia, 1906, box 41, ibid.; and Sitton, *John Randolph Haynes,* 40–42.

from inclusion in the letterhead. The league hoped to gain the support of any group interested in direct legislation, but chose to appear "respectable."

In California such respectability required correct partisanship as well, as Assemblyman Edgar W. Camp advised Haynes in January 1903: "[B]ear in mind that this legislature is very strongly Republican and that measures advocated by [the] Union Labor Organization are viewed with suspicion. Therefore, have as many letters as possible and as many resolutions as possible come here from men prominently identified with the Republican Party."[28] Haynes obviously learned his lesson well, as he described his "method" in a letter to the Referendum League of Philadelphia a few years later:

> Get inlisted [sic] upon your side as many wealthy, conservative men as possible. . . .
>
> Go to the bishops of the different churches; the presidents of your banks; your college professors; your prominent lawyers and doctors; your prominent labor men; your prominent prohibitionists, and explain to the latter that it is through the initiative that they can get local option, and through the referendum they can prevent wide open towns. . . .
>
> Now if there are some prominent men you do not know, convert your friends who know them and get them to go and see them.
>
> It will be fatal to your cause if you get the idea abroad in the land that this is a prohibition, socialistic, or labor movement, so when you have any of these men sandwich their names in among those who have the reputation of being the most eminently respectable. . . .
>
> Above all influence the editors of your newspapers and get them interested.
>
> Be sure and consult a first class attorney (who believes as we do) about the legal methods to be pursued.[29]

Excited by the successful campaign in Los Angeles, and by the recent approval of an initiative and referendum amendment by the voters in the neighboring state of Oregon, Haynes hoped to tap and direct the growing public support for direct legislation that he felt certain existed statewide in California. Utilizing personal appeal, a circular letter–direct mail cam-

28. Letter from Camp to Haynes, January 20, 1903, box 41, Haynes Papers, University of California at Los Angeles Research Library. See also *Direct Legislation Record* 9 (September 1902): 42; and Winston W. Crouch, "John Randolph Haynes and His Work for Direct Government," 436.

29. Letter from Haynes to the Referendum League of Philadelphia, 1906, box 41, Haynes Papers, University of California at Los Angeles Research Library.

paign, and a petition drive, Haynes quickly began to marshal his forces. When a delegation of state senators and assemblymen from southern California held a conference at the Chamber of Commerce to solicit proposals for legislation at the upcoming session of the legislature, Haynes was present to urge the adoption of a statewide initiative and referendum amendment. Haynes also successfully recruited thirteen religious leaders to sign an open letter to the "Ministers and Christian People of California" as an endorsement of direct legislation that read, in part: "[C]ivic reform and a revival of practical righteousness cannot be secured by individual or religious efforts alone, without regard to environment and practical means of working. Our duty and responsibility as voters require us also to secure a simple method by which Christian influences can be made most effective in promoting the public welfare. The best method yet proposed for nonpartisan political action is Direct Legislation."[30]

Haynes followed this coup with letters to prominent individuals throughout the state, asking each for the names of fifty additional businessmen and professionals in their city so that he could send them a personal letter soliciting their cooperation in the work for direct legislation. The Direct Legislation League also mailed letters and leaflets to every state assemblyman encouraging them to support direct legislation in the upcoming 1903 session of the state legislature. The league succeeded in obtaining the endorsement of both major party conventions in Los Angeles County as well as the state Democratic Party for this idea, but failed to get formal support from the state Republican Party.[31]

Supporting the work of the Direct Legislation League was the California State Federation of Labor and, to a lesser extent, various Farmers' Clubs.[32] Both groups sought to obtain pledges from candidates for state office that they would support the initiative and referendum. Shortly after the legislature convened in January 1903, the State Federation of Labor appointed a special committee to work in conjunction with a similar committee from the Direct Legislation League in arousing support among trade unionists. This joint committee mailed letters to each of the five hundred trade unions in the state requesting them to sign a statement endorsing the two constitutional amendments for direct legislation that had been proposed by the

30. Letter from Haynes to the "Ministers and Christian People of California," December 20, 1902, box 35, ibid.

31. See *Direct Legislation Record* 10 (March 1903): 6–7; *Los Angeles Herald*, December 5, 1902; and Sitton, *John Randolph Haynes*, 43.

32. The first convention of the California State Federation of Labor held in San Francisco in June 1901 passed a resolution instructing its executive committee to prepare a bill providing for the initiative and referendum and to have such measures submitted to the legislature for enactment into law. See Samuel Gompers, "The Initiative, Referendum, and Recall," in *American Federationist*, King Papers, Library of Congress.

Direct Legislation League and introduced by Assemblyman Edgar Camp of Los Angeles. The culmination of the entire statewide campaign came when Haynes personally presented a petition with twenty-two thousand names to the legislature, which, when taken together with the resolutions from the various labor and farm organizations, was said to represent about one hundred thousand California voters.

Haynes and his allies, however, still lacked the political strength to en-sure passage of the direct legislation amendments. On March 13, 1903, af-ter passing by a vote of sixty-five to one in the House, the constitutional amendment for the initiative and referendum in city and county affairs was rejected by a thirteen-to-fourteen vote in the Senate. The Senate refused even to consider the question of allowing the initiative and referendum in state government, a measure that had previously been approved by the House by a vote of fifty-five to four. P. B. Preble, secretary-treasurer of the Alameda County Federated Trades Council and unofficial lobbyist for the Direct Legislation League, offered the following explanation in a letter to Haynes shortly after the stunning defeat: "[Y]ou were doubtless misled by reports from interested parties, for it is a noticeable fact that the corpo-ration attorneys to a man voted in the negative."[33]

However frustrated by their defeat in 1903, the supporters of direct leg-islation still hoped that a more effective campaign could get the initiative and referendum passed at the next session of the California legislature in 1905. Over the next eighteen months, the Direct Legislation League missed no opportunity to press its case. The league mailed two thousand blank forms to three hundred labor unions urging union members to petition the assemblymen and senators from their districts. Letters were also mailed to ten thousand voters statewide urging them to do the same. The league sent postcards to four hundred newspapers in California asking if they would lend support to the cause, and mailed letters to five hundred ministers re-questing they provide the names of ten to twenty "good men" in their com-munities who might be in favor of the initiative and referendum and who might be able to have some influence with their elected representatives in Sacramento. Haynes personally wrote the National American Woman's Suffrage Association asking its support and urging its membership to con-

33. Letter from Preble to Haynes, April 12, 1903, box 35, Haynes Papers, University of California at Los Angeles Research Library. Walter Parker, the political manager of the Southern Pacific Railroad in the legislature, agreed to support the initiative and ref-erendum in the House but not in the Senate (see Sitton, *John Randolph Haynes,* 43, 87). See also *Direct Legislation Record* 10 (March 1903): 6–7; *Los Angeles Times,* February 19, 1903; "Referendum and Initiative Amendments in the Legislatures," box 35, Haynes Pa-pers, University of California at Los Angeles Research Library; "How Monopolists De-feat Majority Rule," ibid.; and Haynes, "The Birth of Democracy in California," box 34, ibid.

sider the relevance of direct legislation to their cause. He also entertained socially members of the legislature from southern California, made personal visits to the state capitol, and hired paid lobbyists to work for him. The league sent letters to all legislative candidates in 1904 asking them to state publicly their views on the subject of direct legislation, and urged senators who had voted for the measures in the previous session to hold the line. By this process, a majority of those chosen to the legislature in 1904 had pledged to support direct legislation.

Despite their exhaustive efforts, the league's campaign again met defeat. William F. Herrin, head of the Southern Pacific Railroad's "Political Bureau," prevented legislators from making good on their pledges by effectively delaying any vote on measures for the initiative and referendum at the state level. Herrin, in charge of the railroad's legal department in San Francisco, coordinated the activities of a statewide political machine. Through the lavish use of retainer fees, free railroad passes, special shipping rates, and political campaign contributions, the machine was able to control both Democratic and Republican Party organizations at the state and local levels, party nominating conventions, and, ultimately, legislative actions at the state capitol. The editors of the *Los Angeles Express* suggested that little had changed since 1903: "W. F. Herrin and he alone can simplify the situation for Dr. Haynes, and unless [he] . . . becomes interested, the initiative and referendum will not be [favorably] considered."[34]

The movement for direct legislation in California had reached an impasse at the state level, but continued to gain momentum at the local level. The city of Sacramento in 1903 and the cities of San Bernardino, San Diego, Pasadena, and Eureka in 1905 all adopted either amendments or new charters that provided for direct legislation. These cities were joined by Santa Monica and Alameda in 1906; Santa Cruz, Long Beach, Riverside, and Santa Barbara in 1907; Palo Alto, Richmond, Berkeley, and Salinas (referendum only) in 1909; and Petaluma, Modesto, Monterey, and San Luis Obispo in 1910. In November 1907 the voters of San Francisco amended their charter to provide for the recall.[35]

34. *Los Angeles Express*, January 23, 1905. For information relating to the 1905 campaign, see letter from Haynes to the National American Woman's Suffrage Association, June 13, 1905, box 50, Haynes Papers, University of California at Los Angeles Research Library; "Government Directly by the People," box 34, ibid.; Sitton, "Practical Idealist," 7; and Sitton, *John Randolph Haynes*, 60. For information on Herrin and Southern Pacific control, see K. Starr, *Inventing the Dream*, 200–201; Blythe, "Under the S. P.," 6–7; Mowry, *The California Progressives*, 12–16; Franklin Hitchborn, "Sources of the Opposition to Direct Legislation in California," Haynes Papers, University of California at Los Angeles Research Library; and Haynes, "Birth of Democracy," box 34, ibid.

35. See *Equity* 10 (January 1908): 9–10; 12 (January 1910): 12–13; and V. O. Key Jr. and Winston W. Crouch, *The Initiative and Referendum in California*, 428.

Enthusiasm for direct legislation received a further boost when Los Angeles became the first municipality to recall a public official. In May 1904 the city council voted to award the city printing contract to the *Los Angeles Times*, a paper known for its antagonistic position toward organized labor. To make matters worse, the *Times* had submitted a bid ten thousand to twenty thousand dollars higher than any other daily newspaper. The competing presses quickly charged the council with wasting taxpayers' money and with attempting to please the organ of the dominant political machine. The *Times*, in turn, argued that because its circulation was greater, its advertising costs were justifiably higher. Mayor Snyder refused to sign the contract, but six members of the council stood together and overrode the mayor's veto. One of the councilmen, James P. Davenport of the Sixth Ward, was singled out as the target of a recall campaign. Davenport appeared especially vulnerable for several reasons. As chairman of the supply committee that had recommended the awarding of the printing contract, he seemed, in a special sense, responsible for the scandal. His record was further marred by the fact that he had previously voted to abolish a streetcar-transfer privilege (popular among workers), and was widely regarded as being a "tool" of the public utility corporations. The constituents of Davenport's Sixth Ward were largely working-class people who generally felt betrayed by his irresponsibility and by his apparent subservience to the antiunion *Times* and its hated owner, Harrison Gray Otis. After a successful petition drive (requiring the signatures of 25 percent of the registered voters of the Sixth Ward), an unsuccessful legal challenge by Davenport, and a bitter political campaign, voters decided to discharge him from office. As the first use of the recall in the United States, the incident captured national attention.[36]

36. See Charles Dwight Willard, "A Political Experiment," *Outlook* 78 (October 1904): 472–75; *Equity* 9 (July 1907): 4–6; Eltweed Pomeroy, "The First Discharge of a Public Servant," *Independent* 58 (January 12, 1905): 69–71; Eltweed Pomeroy, "Really Masters," *Arena* 33 (January 1905): 51–52; Haynes, "The Recall of Councilman Davenport," box 48, Haynes Papers, University of California at Los Angeles Research Library; Bird and Ryan, *Recall of Public Officers*, 227–31; Stimson, *Labor Movement*, 282–86; and Sitton, *John Randolph Haynes*, 48–50. For a revisionist interpretation of the Davenport recall, see Fred W. Viehe, "The First Recall: Los Angeles Urban Reform or Machine Politics?" 1–23. The recall process would be repeated in 1909 when Los Angeles voters conducted a campaign to recall Mayor Arthur Harper. Harper, allegedly connected to the Southern Pacific machine, was charged with protecting organized vice in the city. When the *Los Angeles Herald* published evidence that linked Harper directly to the corruption and graft in his administration, his political fate was sealed. On March 26, 1909, Los Angeles again set historical precedent by becoming the first municipality in the nation to remove its mayor from office. See Charles Dwight Willard, "The Recall in Los Angeles," *La Follette's Magazine* 1 (August 7, 1909): 7–9, 15; Reynold E. Blight, "The Recall of the Mayor of Los Angeles," *Independent* 66 (April 22, 1909): 861–63; *Equity* 11 (July 1909): 81–82; Stimson, *Labor Movement*, 323–25; K. Starr, *Inventing the Dream*, 249–51; Bird and Ryan, *Recall of*

There were other indications that voters were becoming increasingly disgusted with the unrepresentative character of local politics and increasingly resentful of the political control exerted by various corporations. When the city council of Los Angeles hurriedly granted, to an unnamed individual, a franchise for a railroad right-of-way over the only unoccupied riverbed access to the city in 1906, voters were curious. Pressed for further information, the councilmen asserted that the franchise was for a new transcontinental railroad carrier for the city. However, when reporters revealed that such application had not been made and that the local Huntington street-railway interests were actually behind the initial application, curiosity turned to indignation. The press quickly joined with civic leaders to assail the legislation as "indefensible" and "the most outrageous thing ever seen or heard done in Los Angeles by a public body." As the editor of the *Los Angeles Record* summed it up: "The Boss did it. No better example of machine politics ever was exhibited to this city than the control of the city council in the river-bed franchise grab. . . . Walter F. Parker, political boss, agent for the Southern Pacific, owns the city council." Leaders of the major civic and commercial bodies then notified the council that unless the franchise was withdrawn, they would call for a referendum on the franchise and initiate a recall campaign against the members of the council. This forced the council to admit that it had acted irresponsibly and to revoke the original grant.[37]

The attempted franchise grab in Los Angeles in 1906 triggered a political protest movement in that city that successfully undermined machine control of local politics for the first time. Led by Russ Avery, Marshall Stimson, and Meyer Lissner (all Los Angeles attorneys), as well as Edward Dickson (associate editor of the *Los Angeles Express*)—all leaders in the crusade for good government in Los Angeles—an independent political organization was set in motion. As the idea gathered momentum the Committee of One Hundred selected the Non-Partisan City Central Committee, which, in turn, nominated an independent municipal ticket to oppose candidates with alleged machine, that is, Southern Pacific, backing. If successful, the new administration would reflect government by the "best" men (largely businessmen and professionals) who would then work to curb the influence of large corporations, ethnic groups, and unions. The focal point of

Public Officers, 234–40; and Jaques, "Political Reform," 92–110. See also "Recall of Mayor Harper," scrapbook, Haynes Papers, University of California at Los Angeles Research Library.

37. Quotations are from Bird and Ryan, *Recall of Public Officers*, 233–34. See also Hichborn, "Sources of Opposition," Haynes Papers, University of California at Los Angeles Research Library; "Government Directly by the People," box 34, ibid.; and "The Movement for Guarded Representative Government," *Arena* 35 (June 1906): 641–42.

their campaign, however, was "Boss Parker" and the "S. P. Machine." In the surprising election that followed, the Non-Partisans carried seventeen out of twenty-three offices contested and claimed a major victory.[38]

The election also had a relevant side note. Totally ignored by the good-government Non-Partisans with their narrow antimachine focus was organized labor. Feeling excluded from the operation of city government, workers organized their own Public Ownership Party and used the *Union Labor News* to assert that the desire of the working people of Los Angeles to rid the city of graft and corruption was "more genuine than any self-appointed committee of one hundred which does not contain the name of a single working man or even one small business man." With that thought in mind, the platform of the Public Ownership Party denounced private ownership of public utilities as the source of political corruption, advocated municipal ownership of public utilities instead, and called for "a rigid adherence to the principles of direct legislation." The Non-Partisans seemed to think that the political system could be improved by electing the "best men" to office, whereas workers seemed to suggest that the initiative, referendum, and recall already in place could be used by the community to effect the same result.[39]

The success of the Non-Partisan movement in Los Angeles in 1906 served as a catalyst for a broader statewide reform campaign. On May 21, 1907, at the urging of Chester H. Rowell, the legislative representative of the *Fresno Republican,* and Edward A. Dickson, legislative writer for the *Los Angeles Express,* fifteen reform-minded individuals from northern and southern California held a preliminary meeting in Los Angeles to discuss the feasibility of organizing an expanded reform league. Most of the fifteen were reform-oriented journalists and lawyers, and most had strong attachments to the Republican Party. Encouraged by the ongoing graft prosecutions of Boss Abe Ruef and Mayor Eugene Schmitz in San Francisco, and by the recent electoral victory over the Democratic and Republican machines in Los Angeles, the participants hoped to create an organization that would ultimately be strong enough to overturn the Southern Pacific–dominated party machines that controlled state politics. Reform issues discussed at the meeting included the need for public utility regulation, child labor legislation, penal reform, and woman suffrage. Because their highest priority was the destruction of the Southern Pacific machine, though, political reforms—the direct primary, the direct election of U.S. senators, and the initiative, referendum, and recall—received most of their attention. Dr.

38. See Sitton, *John Randolph Haynes,* 66–71.
39. *Union Labor News* quoted in Jaques, "Political Reform," 60 (see also 58–69). See also Bird and Ryan, *Recall of Public Officers,* 39–40.

Haynes, who attended the initial meeting, proposed that the group formally declare its support for direct legislation, but his suggestion was rejected as premature. Instead, the group decided to focus its attention on organizing a statewide league to oppose machine control of the state Republican Party.

When those in sympathy with these early reform soundings gathered in Oakland on August 1, 1907, for their first statewide meeting, their numbers had grown to approximately fifty. There they formally adopted the name League of Lincoln-Roosevelt Republican Clubs (known popularly as the Lincoln-Roosevelt League) to symbolize the political heritage they sought to reclaim. These "California Progressives" were, for the most part, high-minded, cautious, and conservative, regarding organized labor as an enemy of reform and tending to favor purified republicanism over expanded popular democracy. As a result, they again agreed to push direct legislation aside (at least for the time being) and concentrate their efforts on obtaining a direct primary law. With such legislation they hoped to wrest control over the nomination of political candidates from the Southern Pacific–manipulated party conventions and place honest, efficient, independent, reform-oriented men in state and local offices. In July 1908 leaders of the Lincoln-Roosevelt League claimed that one hundred state newspapers were behind them. In the elections in the fall of 1908, the league managed to elect a near majority of candidates pledged to support its program in the next legislative session.[40]

Sensing that the reform climate in California was improving, the Direct Legislation League reinvigorated and reorganized its own independent campaign and looked forward once again to having an initiative and referendum amendment introduced in the 1909 session of the state legislature. With a northern branch in San Francisco directed by Isidor Jacobs and Milton T. U'Ren, and a southern branch in Los Angeles directed by Dr. Haynes, the league inaugurated an energetic organizing campaign across the state. Thousands of copies of a statement explaining the objectives of the Direct Legislation League were mailed to sympathizers in every township in California asking for assistance in obtaining funds and enrolling new members. Organizers hoped that direct legislation committees would be established in every township as well. Senator Jonathan Bourne of Oregon sent

40. A number of the leaders in the Lincoln-Roosevelt League had "reservations" about direct legislation. Chester Rowell, in particular, felt that the initiative and referendum had been misused in local politics and promised to be even more problematic at the state level. According to Rowell, it was "the worst possible way" to deal with complex issues. See John M. Allswang, *The Initiative and Referendum in California, 1898–1998*, 14. See also K. Starr, *Inventing the Dream*, 235–42; Jaques, "Political Reform," 71–85; Key and Crouch, *Initiative and Referendum*, 432–33; and Sitton, *John Randolph Haynes*, 89–90.

the league seventy-five thousand copies of an address made by him on the workings of direct legislation in his state that were distributed throughout California. Correspondence was carried on with the state Socialist Party, the state Prohibition Committee, and the Building Trades Council asking each organization to appoint a representative to the executive committee of the Direct Legislation League. A publicity committee met with the managing editors of the leading newspapers to ask for cooperation and publicity, and letters were sent to hundreds of smaller newspapers in the state seeking support. Using a mailing list of citizens known to be favorable to direct legislation, the league solicited donations and cultivated personal contacts.

Plans were made to maintain a headquarters in Sacramento while the legislature was in session. The league also formed a "People's Lobby" at the state capitol under the direction of George Baker Anderson, editor of the *Pacific Outlook;* Edward Dickson; and Isidor Jacobs. The lobby served primarily as a center for information on activities within the legislature. Haynes himself continued to be a tireless correspondent, constantly supplying information to various interested groups.[41] When the legislature convened, the Direct Legislation League sought only the initiative. Yet when the league-sponsored 8 percent (a figure later compromised to 12 percent) initiative amendment was introduced in the Senate, it was defeated by a vote of fifteen to twenty. The measure was never reported out of committee in the assembly. In spite of a tremendous organizing campaign and the endorsement of the California State Grange, organized labor, the state Democratic Party, numerous municipal and county Republican conventions, and well-known reformers such as Rudolph Spreckels, Francis J. Heney, and James D. Phelan, the machine still had the votes to block passage. The only reform proposals that met with any success were two bills sponsored by the Lincoln-Roosevelt League—a direct primary law and a railroad regulation law—but even these measures managed to pass only after being diluted in committee.[42]

41. These groups included the Anti-Saloon League (San Diego), the Federated Trades and Labor Council (Eureka), the Good Government Club (Vallejo), the *Union Label* trade union newspaper (San Jose), the Independence League (San Francisco), the Advancement Association (Alameda), the Board of Freeholders (Santa Cruz), and the Civic League (Napa) (box 41, Haynes Papers, University of California at Los Angeles Research Library).

42. See letter from Jacobs to Haynes, December 9, 1908, box 42, ibid.; newspaper clipping, December 31, 1908, box 35, ibid.; *Los Angeles Herald,* March 9, 1909; correspondence, box 41, ibid.; letter from Anderson to Haynes, January 14, 1909, box 50, ibid.; Franklin Hichborn, *Story of the Session of the California Legislature of 1909,* 192–201; Franklin Hichborn, *Story of the Session of the California Legislature of 1911,* 94–95; "Report of the Secretary of the Direct Legislation League of California," February 1910, box 50, Haynes Papers, University of California at Los Angeles Research Library; *Equity* 11 (April 1909): 53; 12 (October 1910): 149; and Sitton, *John Randolph Haynes,* 90.

Even though the direct primary law was not exactly what the leaders of the Lincoln-Roosevelt League had wanted, they felt sufficiently encouraged by their organizational success statewide to place a full slate of candidates in the field for the 1910 election. The league's candidate for governor was Hiram Johnson, who had risen to prominence as the prosecuting attorney in the San Francisco graft trials in late 1908. Johnson conducted a well-focused and well-orchestrated campaign, and used his considerable oratorical skills to maximum effect. Promising to kick the Southern Pacific machine out of politics in California, Johnson canvassed the state in populist fashion, speaking to ever increasing crowds with dramatic effect. Taking advantage of the new primary law, Johnson won nomination in August along with almost the entire Lincoln-Roosevelt ticket. The Lincoln-Roosevelt League soon seized control of the regular state Republican Party organization. The newly reconstituted Republicans, running on a broadly based reform platform that included a direct legislation plank, were then swept into office in the fall elections. In just three and one-half years, dating back to the Non-Partisan victory in Los Angeles, the Progressive movement had managed to unseat the seemingly invincible Southern Pacific machine.[43]

As soon as the election was over the Republican State Central Committee, looking to honor its campaign pledges, called a planning session to set the upcoming legislative agenda. Senator-elect Lee C. Gates of Los Angeles chaired the committee on direct legislation, which included Dr. John R. Haynes and Milton T. U'Ren of the Direct Legislation League. The result of that meeting was significant, for it confirmed the Progressive commitment to direct legislation in California. That the Progressives were now prepared to expand their reform program was made evident in Governor Johnson's inaugural address in 1911:

> If we can give to The People the means by which they may accomplish such other reforms as they desire, the means as well by which they may prevent the misuse of the power temporarily centralized in the Legislature and an admonitory and precautionary measure which will ever be present before weak officials, and the existence of which will prevent the necessity for its use, then all that lies in our power will have been done in the direction of safeguarding the future and for the perpetuation of the theory upon which we ourselves shall conduct this government. . . . I most strongly urge, that the first step in our design to preserve and perpetuate popular government shall be the adoption of the Initiative, the Referendum, and the Recall.[44]

43. See Key and Crouch, *Initiative and Referendum*, 433–34; K. Starr, *Inventing the Dream*, 252–54; and Blythe, "Under the S. P.," 6–7.
44. Key and Crouch, *Initiative and Referendum*, 435.

Senator Gates of Los Angeles and Assemblyman William C. Clark of Oakland introduced amendments calling for the initiative, referendum, and recall in the 1911 legislative session. The amendments extended direct legislation to voters in all cities and counties as well as to voters at the state level. The initiative was based on a petition of 8 percent of all the votes cast for all candidates for governor in the last general election, whereas the referendum was based on a similar petition of 5 percent. The limited amount of debate over the measures related to raising these numerical percentages, but all proposed adjustments were easily defeated. The initiative and referendum amendment was finally adopted by votes of thirty-five to one in the Senate and seventy-one to zero in the assembly. There was, however, a great deal of debate over the accompanying recall amendment. On this question there was disagreement even among Progressives. Opponents generally favored the principle of the recall, but wished to exclude from its use all members of the judiciary. After lengthy argument and counterargument, the recall amendment (based on a 20 percent petition figure for elective state officers) passed the Senate by a vote of thirty-six to four, and the assembly by a margin of seventy to ten. All that remained was for the amendments to be ratified by the voters.[45]

Both the friends and the foes of direct legislation refused to be complacent while waiting for voters to decide the fate of the initiative and referendum and recall amendments in addition to twenty-one other amendments at a special election to be held on October 10, 1911. Newspaper editors, lawyers, civic leaders, and legislators all enthusiastically stated their points of view in an attempt to influence public opinion. Opponents argued that direct legislation would mean the destruction of representative government, the establishment of an absolute tyranny of the majority, and the triumph of radicalism and incompetence. Proponents countered with the argument that only "misrepresentative" government was being threatened, that the people could be trusted, and that direct legislation would protect the people from corporate greed and political domination.

By late August the campaign had intensified. Both sides debated the issues (especially the recall) before civic groups and in newspapers, and speakers from both inside and outside the state were recruited to address numerous mass meetings. The leaders of the Direct Legislation League took a most active part, putting into practice the campaign techniques they had been honing for almost a decade. They mass-mailed postcards to all registered voters in the state reminding them to vote yes on the amendments. They hired Judson King, the noted initiative and referendum advocate and campaign organizer, to run a publicity bureau as a conduit to

45. See Hichborn, *Story of 1911*, 93–138; Bird and Ryan, *Recall of Public Officers*, 44–51; and *Equity* 13 (April 1911): 68–72.

newspapers in the state. They also coordinated train and automobile speaking tours by Governor Johnson in the larger cities and other speakers in the smaller towns. In the end it almost looked too easy, as the results of the special election showed an overwhelming triumph for Progressive reform. The initiative-referendum amendment won by a vote of 168,744 to 52,093, while the recall amendment (to the surprise even of supporters) passed by a vote of 178,115 to 53,755.[46]

The early movement for direct legislation in California was sparked largely by "radical" elements: by the Populist Party that "commended" the initiative and referendum to its followers in 1892, formally endorsed the principles in 1896, and first suggested the "imperative mandate" (that is, the recall); by the Los Angeles Council of Labor and the Knights of Labor who saw direct legislation as a means of focusing attention on economic and labor-related issues, as well as a way to include labor in the political debate; by J. W. Sullivan and the Direct Legislation League who sought to provide legitimacy and an organizational structure to the movement; and by individuals such as Alfred Cridge and John Randolph Haynes who took advantage of opportunities made available by the reform-minded mayors in their respective cities to champion the initiative and referendum as the first stage of a larger reform crusade.

By the late 1890s, however, the direct legislation movement in California had begun to assume a unique "good government" dimension. Led by local groups such as the Citizens Charter Association in San Francisco and the Municipal Reform Association, the League for Better City Government, and the Municipal League in Los Angeles, nonpartisan civic reformers sought to "modernize" city charters. With input from groups such as the Council of Labor and the Union Reform League and from socially conscious advocates such as Alfred Cridge, W. D. P. Bliss, and J. R. Haynes, provisions for the initiative, referendum, and recall were eventually included

---

46. In addition to the two direct legislation amendments, twenty-one other constitutional amendments were submitted to the voters of California at the special election on October 10, 1911. Of the twenty-one submitted, twenty were approved. Some of the more significant amendments included granting woman suffrage, authorizing a compulsory workmen's compensation law, giving the railroad commission the power to fix the rates of public service corporations, and authorizing cities to own and operate public utilities. See John R. Haynes, "The Actual Workings of the Initiative, Referendum, and Recall," 600–601. Voters ratified twenty-two of the twenty-three proposed amendments. See also Bird and Ryan, *Recall of Public Officers*, 51–52; Key and Crouch, *Initiative and Referendum*, 437–40; letter from Milton U'Ren to Haynes, September 11, 1911, box 42, Haynes Papers, University of California at Los Angeles Research Library; and Sitton, *John Randolph Haynes*, 92–93. For a brief discussion of the various propositions that appeared on the California ballot between 1912 and 1918, see Allswang, *Initiative and Referendum*, 18–26.

in those revised city charters. Dr. Haynes reorganized the dormant Direct Legislation League in California and gave the movement its state-level focus. Blessed with a seemingly inexhaustible commitment to the principle of direct legislation and an astute organizational mind, Haynes incorporated farmers, workers, prohibitionists, socialists, doctors, lawyers, churchmen, prominent business and civic leaders, and newspaper support into a workable reform coalition. Aided by the insurgent political campaigns of the Non-Partisan and Public Ownership Parties against the political machine in Los Angeles in 1906, Haynes was soon able to place the issue of direct legislation before the newly organized Lincoln-Roosevelt League. Rebuffed in 1907 Haynes improved his statewide organization, gained the attention of well-known reformers such as Francis Heney and Hiram Johnson, and waited for his next political opportunity. When the anti–Southern Pacific good-government California Progressives triumphed in 1910, Haynes was finally able to convince them that direct legislation was indeed a popularly supported idea whose time had come.

7

Ohio and Washington

OHIO

As in every state that developed an active interest in direct legislation, frustrated reformers in Ohio looked for ways to make government more representative of the public interest and more responsive to public need. This proved to be especially difficult in the Buckeye State during the 1890s, as the Republican Party held the scepter of political power and governed with the interests of business in mind. When insurgents undertook antitrust action, struck at tax inequities, or spoke out against the corruption and inefficiency of "boss" or machine-controlled municipal governments in the state, they were stymied by those in government who saw their interest as that of defending the established order.[1]

Credit for starting Ohio on the path to eventual adoption of the initiative and referendum in 1912 should go to R. S. Thompson and the Union Reform Party.[2] Starting out as a newspaperman, Thompson worked as a temperance advocate, developed an expertise in scientific agriculture, and

1. For information on Ohio politics during the 1890s, see Hoyt Landon Warner, *Progressivism in Ohio, 1897–1917*, 3–18.
2. There is evidence that the Ohio State Federation of Labor raised the topic of direct legislation with legislators in the early 1890s. In a report to the organization's state convention held in early January 1894, the federation's legislative committee reported that it had distributed several dozen books on the general subject of direct legislation (titles not given) to members of the Ohio legislature, which resulted in the consideration of a joint resolution. The action was apparently taken toward the close of the session and too late to offer time for reconsideration. See Samuel Gompers, "The Initiative, Referendum, and Recall," in *American Federationist,* George Judson King Papers, Library of Congress, Manuscripts Division, Washington, D.C. Ohio was well represented at the organizing convention of the National Direct Legislation League held in St. Louis in July 1896. Jacob Coxey (Massillon), R. S. Thompson (Springfield), Charles R. Martin (Tiflin), and Professor W. J. Seeley (Wooster) all gained nomination as vice presidents for the conference, while E. M. Davis (Cincinnati) won election to the new organization's seven-member executive committee. However, a willingness to participate in the organizational activities of that body seemed to belie any broader intellectual or organizational base in that state in 1896. See *Direct Legislation Record* 3 (September 1896): 25–26.

joined the Populist Party before embracing direct legislation as his political panacea. After the failure of the Populist challenge in 1896, Thompson
faced a dilemma. He believed that reform was necessary at both the state
and the national levels, but was convinced that such change could not come
about as long as the power to create laws remained vested in legislatures
controlled by special interests. He also believed that meaningful change
could not come about outside organized politics, but regarded both the
Democratic and the Republican Parties as politically bankrupt. The only solution seemed to be to find a way to circumvent both the special interest–
controlled legislatures and the established political parties.

Using his position as editor of the *Springfield New Era* as his forum,
Thompson led the call for delegates from the Populist, Silver Republican,
Liberty, Socialist-Labor, and Negro Protective Parties to assemble in convention at Columbus, Ohio, on May 25, 1898, to create a new independent
party. Known as the Union Reform Party of Ohio, the new organization
rested on the simple precept that the people should have the right to make
their own laws. Building on that basic principle, the new party constructed a platform comprising three simple planks: "Direct Legislation under
the system known as the Initiative and Referendum"; "the honest and effective enforcement of all laws, so that the will of the people . . . shall not
be nullified by indifference or opposition on the part of public servants";
and "the honest and economical administration of the Government, to the
end that the people be not burdened with unnecessary taxes."[3]

Meeting the following year in Cincinnati, delegates, again led by Thompson, reorganized their party on a national basis. With representatives from
sixteen states in attendance, the new party pledged to expand its organizing efforts into every state and adopted a preamble that stated, in part:

> Representatives cannot always know certainly the will of their con-
> stituents, and even where that will has been clearly manifested it has
> been continually disregarded.
>
> Legislative bodies from municipal councils to the national congress
> have been controlled by corrupt influences. Legislation has conse-
> quently been in the interest of the corrupt few and against the interest
> of the voiceless masses.
>
> Under this system the people are disfranchised on all matters of leg-
> islation. They are allowed to vote for men, but are denied the right to
> vote for measures. The people are governed by laws which they did not
> enact and cannot repeal.

3. *Direct Legislation Record* 5 (September 1898): 68; 5 (June 1898): 38; 6 (March 1899):
12–13.

Reducing their previous platform to the single issue of direct legislation, the delegates invited all those who believed in the principles of liberty and the Declaration of Independence to join.[4]

Although the Union Reform Party never made the political advances it had envisioned, it certainly helped to popularize the issue of direct legislation in Ohio and attracted the attention of the Reverend Herbert S. Bigelow. Bigelow, the fiery minister of the Vine Street Congregational Church in Cincinnati, had become a convert to Henry George's single-tax idea after rereading *Progress and Poverty* in 1897. The book, which "gripped" him "as no other book ever has," convinced him that the single tax provided a remedy for social injustice. "The world," said Bigelow, "is suffering more from the lack of a social conscience and a sound political economy than from the lack of agencies to give aid and comfort to the victims of social wrongs; . . . freedom of opportunity is the brand of charity that is needed." George's book caused Bigelow to reexamine his religiosity and led him to conclude:

> Religion has vastly more to do with the question of wages than with the question of the Trinity. I saw more religion in the Declaration of Independence than in all the creeds. I began to realize that unless the church substituted for lifeless doctrines the doctrine of the sovereignty of the people and made it her business to guard popular liberties against the encroachments of subsidized politics, her name would become the synonym for treason and her doors the gates of hell.

The desire for economic betterment and political regeneration prompted Bigelow to reorganize his church to make it more accurately reflect the mission of a "crusading church" in a democracy. Sunday and Wednesday prayer meetings gave way to economic and political discussion clubs. These clubs invited speakers and held open discussions on a variety of topics including the initiative and referendum.[5]

Following his growing interest in questions of the political economy, Bigelow entered politics for the first time and joined the Union Reform Party in 1899. Convinced that the power to initiate laws by petition and veto unfavorable legislation by referendum would be valuable tools in the fight for social justice as well as a way to bring single-tax measures to a popular vote, Bigelow began to speak in favor of direct legislation from his pulpit.

4. *Direct Legislation Record* 6 (June 1899): 19–20.
5. Bigelow quoted in Frank Parker Stockbridge, "Ohio Wide Awake," 703–4. See also Daniel R. Beaver, *A Buckeye Crusader*, 9, 11; Warner, *Progressivism in Ohio*, 123–24; and autobiography dated 1943, Herbert Bigelow Papers, Historical and Philosophical Society of Ohio, Cincinnati.

As a further indication of both his increasing national profile as a reformer and his growing interest in direct legislation, Bigelow served as secretary at the national meeting of the Direct Legislation League held in Detroit on June 27, 1901.[6]

It was at the Democratic National Convention in Kansas City in July 1900, however, that Bigelow began to find his political footing. There he met Cleveland reformer Tom L. Johnson, another ardent single taxer and soon to be his political mentor. As the two William Jennings Bryan supporters grew closer during the ensuing presidential campaign, Johnson told Bigelow of his plan to capture control of the state Democratic Party and encouraged the idealistic minister to join him in that effort by broadening his political involvement and seriously considering a run for elective office. Also aiding Bigelow's political maturation was Daniel Kiefer, a successful clothing manufacturer turned reformer, savvy political tactician, and yet another recent convert to the single tax, who joined the Vine Street congregation and soon became Bigelow's intimate friend and political adviser.[7]

In the spring of 1902, with Johnson's encouragement, Bigelow decided to run for office as secretary of state on a reform ticket.[8] Converting the basement of his church into campaign headquarters, Bigelow toured the state with Johnson, the newly elected mayor of Cleveland, in a high-speed red automobile known as the "Red Devil." Employing Johnson's famous traveling circus tent as an auditorium, Bigelow spoke as often as six times a day to gatherings in rural Ohio. However, the Bigelow-Johnson populist campaign that centered on issues of tax reform (which many rural Ohioans feared would mean the radical single tax) and municipal home rule failed to win broad popular support. A similar fate befell Johnson the following year when his reputation as a single taxer and political radical again alienated voters and caused him to be soundly defeated in his bid for governor. During the campaign, Bigelow toured the state stumping for Johnson, worked to popularize the initiative and referendum (a plank in the Democratic platform had called for its use for all municipal legislation), and tried to convince voters that the followers of Henry George were primarily mo-

6. See Beaver, *A Buckeye Crusader,* 14; and *Direct Legislation Record* 8 (September 1901): 41.

7. See Beaver, *A Buckeye Crusader,* 14–15; Stockbridge, "Ohio Wide Awake," 705; and Warner, *Progressivism in Ohio,* 122, 124.

8. Historian Hoyt Landon Warner has told the story that Johnson first asked Bigelow to find an attorney in Cincinnati who would be willing to run for secretary of state as a reform candidate. Johnson wanted to broaden the geographic base of support for his program and wanted someone from the Queen City who might provide leadership to those eager to challenge the Republican political machine there headed by Boss George B. Cox. When Bigelow could find no one else, he agreed to enter the race himself. See Warner, *Progressivism in Ohio,* 122.

tivated by political reform rather than immediate enactment of the single tax. According to Bigelow's later recollection, it was after this second defeat that he became "discouraged with that kind of politics" and concluded that "more progress might be made if the people had a way of voting directly on measures." In a real sense, it marked the beginning of Bigelow's formal campaign to get the state legislature to submit to the people a constitutional amendment providing for the initiative and referendum.[9]

Others in the state were becoming interested in direct legislation as well. A group that included some of the most prominent men in Cleveland met in February 1903 and formed a direct legislation league for that city. During the spring political campaign, the new league printed and circulated "voter's pledge" cards asking candidates for municipal office to endorse the use of the initiative and referendum in city affairs. Following the election, the league shifted its focus to the state level and made plans to use its "pledge" system to encourage candidates for the General Assembly to submit to a popular vote a practicable direct legislation amendment to the Ohio Constitution.

The actions of the Cleveland reformers seemed to inspire others. In Medina, Ohio, for example, proponents of the initiative and referendum launched their own local direct legislation league in December 1904. By July of the following year the membership stood at fifty, a gain of 50 percent within that time. Members included manufacturers, merchants, ministers, teachers, professional men, farmers, and workers. To arouse interest and generate publicity, the Medina league routinely invited outside speakers to address their group. They also had several hundred seven-by-nine-inch cards printed summarizing the nature, results, and possibilities of direct legislation and had them widely posted. The league also made available copies of Frank Parsons's book on direct legislation and began to persuade some editors to give space to their cause in the local newspapers. The league was successful in obtaining a pledge from F. W. Woods, a successful candidate for the state assembly, to work for a direct legislation amendment. A state organization (the Ohio Direct Legislation League) was finally created in 1906, but by that time the center of activity had shifted to Cincinnati. Directing operations at the state level were Bigelow, who served as secretary, and George W. Harris, a Cincinnati businessman and single taxer who had retired at the age of forty-five to devote his life to the cause of reform, who became chairman of the organization's executive committee.[10]

9. Bigelow quoted in autobiography dated 1943, Bigelow Papers, Historical and Philosophical Society of Ohio. See also Beaver, *A Buckeye Crusader*, 16–17; Stockbridge, "Ohio Wide Awake," 705; and Warner, *Progressivism in Ohio*, 122, 124–29.

10. See *Direct Legislation Record* 10 (March 1903): 2; 10 (June 1903): 2; 10 (December

The effort to establish direct legislation in Ohio was closely linked to the larger reform impulse that was building nationally as well as within the state. In 1905 *McClure's* published a chapter in Lincoln Steffens's ongoing series on municipal corruption titled "Ohio: A Tale of Two Cities." In his account, Steffens praised the Tom Johnson administration in Cleveland, but condemned governance in Cincinnati under the rule of Boss George B. Cox. There were signs that Bigelow's and Johnson's reform campaigns and the spread of muckraking journalism were triggering a crusading spirit among some of Ohio's newspapers as well. The *Cleveland Plain Dealer* regularly featured articles on crusading politicians such as Joseph W. Folk of Missouri or the campaigns against bossism then being waged in cities such as New York, Philadelphia, Baltimore, Indianapolis, and San Francisco that underscored the growing preoccupation with reform issues. During the summer of 1905 the *Plain Dealer* began its own daily series of muckraking articles by reporter William S. Crouch that exposed machine-controlled politics in each Ohio city where it existed. Adding breadth and emphasis to this moral revival in Ohio politics was the Scripps-McRae newspaper chain. Catering to the lower middle class and the workingman, and including such in-state dailies as the *Cincinnati Post,* the *Toledo News-Bee,* and the *Columbus Citizen,* the chain reached a previously uninformed audience for the first time.[11]

Despite indications of a changing political climate in Ohio, results were slow in coming. Planks endorsing the initiative and referendum were included in the state Democratic platforms of 1903, 1905, and 1908 (a constitutional amendment adopted in 1905 shifted state elections to even-numbered years), and constitutional amendments were introduced in the General Assembly in 1906, 1908, 1909, and 1910. Despite the ardent support of in-state reformers such as Bigelow, Washington Gladden of Columbus, and Frederic C. Howe of Cleveland, and organizational support from the Ohio Direct Legislation League, the Ohio State Federation of Labor, the Ohio Mine Workers, and the Ohio State Grange, bills either died in committee or became so burdened with encumbrances and unrealistic petition requirements that even enthusiastic supporters ultimately preferred to see no bill passed rather than a bad one.[12] The lone exception came in 1911 when the legislature passed the Crosser Bill allowing for use of the initiative and referendum in municipal affairs. The "victory," however, was a costly one, as reformers had to make crippling concessions to ensure pas-

---

1903): 75–76; *Equity* 8 (July 1906): 28–29; Stockbridge, "Ohio Wide Awake," 705; and Beaver, *A Buckeye Crusader,* 17.

11. See Warner, *Progressivism in Ohio,* 150–51.

12. Both the House and the Senate passed initiative and referendum measures in 1908. However, when a specially appointed conference committee failed to reconcile differences in the two measures, no law was enacted. See *Equity* 10 (July 1908): 71–72.

sage of the measure. As a result, conservatives were able to set the percentage of voters required to sign petitions at 30 percent to propose a local ordinance and 15 percent to call for a referendum on either a franchise grant or large appropriation bills approved by city councils. Reformers had established the principle of the initiative and referendum in Ohio, but the high number of petition signatures rendered the law itself almost useless.[13]

A unique feature of the Ohio Constitution at the time was that it required the mandatory submission to the voters of a call for a constitutional convention every twenty years. Anticipating that requirement (due in 1911), and prodded by three well-organized interest groups, the Ohio legislature approved such a ballot measure in the spring of 1910. The three groups seeking constitutional revision were the Ohio Board of Commerce, which desired a tax amendment that would eliminate the rule of taxing all property—tangible and intangible—at a uniform rate and allow for classification of property for tax purposes; the liquor industry, which wanted to license saloons in the hope that regulation would head off the growing sentiment in favor of statewide prohibition; and reformers, led by the Ohio Direct Legislation League, who looked to end more than a decade of legislative frustration and obtain a list of badly needed reforms highlighted by the initiative and referendum. Under the legislature's call, delegates would be nominated by petition, listed on a separate ballot without party labels, and elected at the municipal elections in November 1911. The constitutional convention itself would convene in January 1912, and a new constitution would be submitted to the voters later that year. Voters overwhelmingly approved the call for a constitutional convention at the general election in 1910.[14]

In an effort to ensure that the new document included direct legislation among its reform-oriented revisions, 155 initiative and referendum enthusiasts led by Bigelow gathered in Columbus on June 4, 1911, and formed the Progressive Constitution League (PCL). The delegates, who embraced all political parties, committed themselves to an organized campaign to elect men to the convention who favored municipal home rule and the initiative and referendum. They elected Brand Whitlock, the mayor of Tole-

13. See Warner, *Progressivism in Ohio,* 129, 162, 181, 193–96, 204 n. 21, 215, 236, 270; Stockbridge, "Ohio Wide Awake," 706; *Equity* 10 (January 1908): 9; 11 (April 1909): 56; 11 (July 1909): 94–95; 12 (April 1910): 64; and 13 (July 1911): 127.

14. The division at the convention would be between conservatives and progressives rather than between Republicans and Democrats following party alignments. See Warner, *Progressivism in Ohio,* 295–96; Stockbridge, "Ohio Wide Awake," 707; Hoyt Landon Warner, "Ohio's Constitutional Convention of 1912," 13; Robert E. Cushman, "Voting Organic Laws," *Political Science Quarterly* 28 (June 1913): 207–8; and Lloyd Sponholtz, "The 1912 Constitutional Convention in Ohio: The Call-up and Nonpartisan Selection of Delegates," 209–12.

do, as president; a professor, an editor of a labor journal, and an officer of the Ohio State Grange as vice presidents; another Grange official as treasurer; and Herbert Bigelow as secretary and principal field-worker charged with speaking and fund-raising. The PCL called for the formation of "constitution committees" in each county and sent Bigelow and other field-workers in search of endorsements from organizations and pledges from candidates to the convention. The PCL established a press bureau to handle publicity but also had the support of the Scripps-McRae newspaper syndicate, which highlighted the drive for self-government on a daily basis. Especially active was the *Cincinnati Post*, which ran statements endorsing the initiative and referendum from such notables as James Bryce, Woodrow Wilson, Theodore Roosevelt, and Robert La Follette.[15]

The strongest support for the initiative and referendum came from voters in the major cities of Cleveland, Columbus, and Cincinnati. A branch of the PCL in Cuyahoga County surrounding Cleveland, which included 150 civic and labor organizations, nominated a slate of ten candidates who pledged themselves exclusively to that issue. Although the Socialists and Democrats prepared separate tickets, all their nominees were also pledged to the initiative and referendum. In Columbus, representatives from more than 100 civic, professional, farm, and labor organizations joined to form the United Constitution Committee of Franklin County. The committee regularly held open discussions of the major issues, nominated candidates from each of the major economic groups (labor, agriculture, and business), and required that candidates commit themselves to a platform that featured municipal home rule, reorganization of the state's court structure, and direct legislation.

Bigelow assumed leadership of the effort in Cincinnati and organized the Hamilton County Progressive Constitution Committee. Controlled by a small group of single taxers at the outset, the committee quickly expanded to encompass more than 50 groups that included the Central Labor Council and the Federated Civic Clubs and soon changed its name to the United Constitution Committee to reflect its broad base of support. All prospective candidates were expected to support a common platform that embraced municipal home rule, tax reform, and the initiative and referendum. Primary funding for the campaign to elect delegates to the constitutional convention came from the Joseph Fels Foundation. Heading the commission chosen to administer the money was Bigelow's friend and adviser Daniel Kiefer. Cleveland mayor Tom Johnson served as the first treasurer.

15. See Stockbridge, "Ohio Wide Awake," 707; *Equity* 12 (July 1910): 108–9; 13 (July 1911): 127–28; Beaver, *A Buckeye Crusader*, 20; Warner, *Progressivism in Ohio*, 296–98, 308 nn. 5–6; and Sponholtz, "Constitutional Convention," 213.

Viewing the adoption of the initiative and referendum as a means to achieve the single tax, the Fels Commission financially supported direct legislation campaigns in New Mexico, Arizona, Colorado, Arkansas, and Ohio.[16]

As the constitutional reform forces consolidated their efforts, Bigelow launched his own personal campaign for nomination to the convention. To win over leery conservatives, he assumed the posture of a moderate—adopting the committee platform, downplaying the single tax, and favoring the indirect initiative. Under this form, a voter-initiated measure would have to be submitted to the legislature for action before any popular vote could be taken. Bigelow also refused to sponsor amendments for either woman suffrage or the recall out of fear that they were too provocative and might hinder chances for the revised constitution to be adopted. To make his moderate position known to the voters, Bigelow authored a series of articles for statewide distribution and conducted an active speaking campaign. When the Cincinnati Board of Education refused to allow use of public school buildings for public meetings to discuss the issues in the campaign, Bigelow turned his own church into a public meetinghouse. With solid support from loyal groups such as the Central Labor Council and the Ohio German Alliance, and backed editorially by the *Cincinnati Post*, Bigelow made a strong candidate.[17]

Opposing the constitutional reform forces in general and the outspoken Bigelow in particular was an extremely vocal conservative opposition. Included in that group were the editors of the *Ohio State Journal*, who underscored Bigelow's identification with the single tax and attempted to link that contentious issue with the initiative and referendum. Arguing that single taxers could make use of direct legislation at any time to advance their cause, the *Journal* editorially urged its readers to stop this "tremendous conspiracy against representative government." Other attacks came from the Ohio State Board of Commerce (OSBC), which levied an assessment on its members to fund the distribution of printed matter to small-town and rural newspapers. The formulaic material implied that the proposal to revise the constitution was communistic and cautioned unwary readers that the initiative and referendum would be used to enact the dreaded single tax. Aside from its bombasts in the press, the OSBC organized support for candidates who favored tax classification and opposed direct legislation. Nevertheless, the conservative challenge never gathered momentum and was,

16. See Warner, *Progressivism in Ohio*, 298–99; Beaver, *A Buckeye Crusader*, 21. Sponholtz, "Constitutional Convention," 214–15; Warner, "Ohio's Convention," 14–17; Arthur P. Dudden, *Joseph Fels and the Single Tax Movement*, 199–202; and Arthur Nichols Young, *The Single Tax Movement in the United States*, 164–67.

17. See Beaver, *A Buckeye Crusader*, 21–23.

in effect, marginalized by the design of the original call. Once delegate selection was removed from party control and placed on a nonpartisan basis,
the clout of established partisan interest groups like the OSBC was greatly
diminished. On election day, November 7, 1911, Cincinnati's United Constitution Committee captured all but 2 delegate slots. Bigelow, despite being the target of conservatives, ran third out of 9 elected. Statewide, a clear
majority of the 119 delegates elected to the constitutional convention had
pledged themselves to support the initiative and referendum.[18]

Once the delegates had been elected, battle lines quickly shifted to the
selection of a chairman for the convention. The position was important, as
the presiding officer would have the power to make all committee assignments. After some deliberation, the progressive bloc agreed to support
Bigelow for that position and Edward Doty, a leader of Cleveland's single
taxers and an expert parliamentarian, as floor leader. The opposition, looking to elect its own man, rallied behind conservative judge Caleb H. Nor-
ris of Marion. They then immediately began a propaganda campaign to discredit Bigelow and head off the most disturbing items on the progressive
agenda. Leading the attack was Warren G. Harding, who used his *Marion
Star* to charge that Bigelow was "the paid agent of the Socialist propaganda [single tax] founded by Henry George and financed by Joseph Fels."
Bigelow responded by claiming that he was the paid agent of no one, and
accused Harding and his conservative allies of merely using the single tax
"bugaboo" to frighten voters into opposing the initiative and referendum.
Although the public attacks on Bigelow in the press did not prevent his
election as presiding chair of the constitutional convention, they did undermine his support. On January 9, 1912, the opening day of the convention, it took the beleaguered Bigelow eleven agonizing ballots to secure his
majority.[19]

The next consideration for the progressives was that of tactics. With their
superior numbers and Bigelow's power of appointment, the progressive
bloc controlled the membership on the various committees and had almost
dictatorial power. They realized, however, that they would have to compromise with the conservatives, and some of their own more moderate
members, on the more volatile issues if they hoped to get all the progressive features they wanted in the new constitution. After agreeing on the
adoption of amendments dealing with funding for road improvements,
woman suffrage, direct primaries, judicial reform, home rule for cities, civ-

18. *Ohio State Journal* quoted in ibid., 22. For a discussion of the impact of the nonpartisan process on the selection of delegates to the constitutional convention, see Sponholtz, "Constitutional Convention," 209–18. See also Beaver, *A Buckeye Crusader,* 22–24;
and Stockbridge, "Ohio Wide Awake," 707.

19. Harding quoted in Beaver, *A Buckeye Crusader,* 25 (see also 24–26).

il service, workmen's compensation, and an eight-hour workday on all state building projects, delegates were left with the contentious issues of liquor, taxation, and direct legislation.

The liquor question pitted "wets," who favored a licensing system that amounted to a form of liquor control, against the "drys," who wanted to maintain hard-won local option laws and limit the number of saloons according to population. In the end, delegates accepted the licensing idea but limited the number of saloons to one for every five hundred people. They also outlawed the brewery-owned saloon (believed to be a contributing factor to machine government and boss rule). The struggle over taxation and its assumed burden was largely between farmers–property holders and businessmen. The first group favored adoption of a uniform rule taxing all property—real estate and intangible property such as stocks and bonds— at the same rate, whereas the second group favored the classification of property and presumably lower tax rates for the holders of stocks and bonds. After lengthy argument, delegates adopted the uniform rule but allowed for exemptions on all outstanding municipal bonds. The convention also provided for both an inheritance and an income tax and accepted the idea of progressive taxation.[20]

The most provocative issue debated at the constitutional convention, however, was the initiative and referendum. Discussion of the topic, which progressives favored as a means to fight the corruption, irresponsibility, and unresponsiveness of the legislature, quickly revealed that the progressives themselves held differing points of view as to how the principles should be implemented. Bigelow, who had campaigned as a proponent of the indirect initiative based on a petition signed by a certain percentage of the voters, found himself in disagreement with Robert Crosser, the chair of the committee on the initiative and referendum. Crosser, who had written and pushed the successful municipal initiative and referendum bill through the legislature in 1911, favored the direct initiative based on a petition signed by a fixed number of electors with no requirement for geographical distribution of petition signatures around the state. His original proposal called for eighty thousand signatures to initiate a constitutional amendment, sixty thousand to initiate a law, and fifty thousand to call for a referendum on any law ("emergency" measures included) passed by the legislature. Initiative and referendum powers would be made available to voters in each political subdivision of the state.

In an effort to obtain some sort of compromise that could be presented

20. See ibid., 19–20, 27–28, 32; Warner, *Progressivism in Ohio,* 319; Warner, "Ohio's Convention," 25–27; Ernest I. Antrim, "The Ohio Constitutional Convention," *Independent* 72 (June 27, 1912): 1423–26; and Henry W. Elson, "Making a New Constitution for Ohio," *Review of Reviews* 46 (July 1912): 83–86.

to the full convention with solid progressive backing, Bigelow appointed a special sixty-member caucus committee friendly to the principle to work out the details. The committee ultimately agreed to a hybrid proposal: a direct initiative based on an 8 percent petition requirement and an indirect initiative set at 4 percent. Twelve percent of the voters could propose an amendment to the constitution, and 6 percent could call for a referendum on an act passed by the legislature. The committee also added a geographic distribution provision that required petitioners to obtain the signatures of not less than one-half of the required percentage of electors from half of the counties in the state on all initiative and referendum petitions. Petition requirements would be based on the total number of votes cast for governor in the preceding election. Agreed to by the progressives, the proposal still had to be discussed and approved by the full convention. Just as the progressive proposal was about to be presented to the larger body, however, Bigelow made an error in judgment that severely hurt the reform cause. Compounding his ill-advised use of Fels money in the delegate campaign, he now invited Joseph Fels himself to address a public gathering at the Grand Opera House in Cincinnati. In doing so, he allowed the single-tax issue to once again intrude on the current deliberations.[21]

When the progressive initiative and referendum resolution with its direct initiative feature and low-percentage petition requirements was finally introduced in Columbus, conservatives were ready to assail it. Many of those opposed to the amendment regarded the initiative as nothing more than an insidious device to impose the single tax on Ohioans. Delegate E. L. Lampson, who opposed both the statutory and the constitutional initiative, angrily stated that he would defend the home owners and farmers of Ohio against this "monstrous single tax" until "my tongue is palsied and clings to the roof of my mouth." Also worried about the tax implications of the initiative and referendum was at least one Roman Catholic organization in Ohio that issued a pamphlet describing direct legislation as the "advance guard of Socialism" and cautioned that "[i]n this is hidden the taxation of churches and charitable institutions." Other delegates feared that the initiative and referendum would undermine rural control of the legislature and allow the center of power in that body to shift to the state's populated urban centers. Another rural delegate echoed the same sentiment, as he imagined bills being drafted in secret and then placed in the hands of the "great Cleveland and Cincinnati Initiative and Referendum Trust Company, Limited." Adding a final cataclysmic note to the debate, delegate

---

21. See Beaver, *A Buckeye Crusader*, 29–30; Warner, *Progressivism in Ohio*, 320–21; Robert Crosser, "The Initiative and Referendum Amendments in the Proposed Ohio Constitution," 192–93, 198; and Warner, "Ohio's Convention," 21.

James Halfhill, a wealthy corporate attorney from Lima, warned that "if this disgrace to the history of representative government is enacted, . . . the Huns and Vandals" would overrun the state.[22]

The severity of the conservative attack and the ensuing debate convinced the progressive leadership that the proposed resolution in its current form was unacceptable to the majority of the delegates. As a result, Bigelow appointed a committee of ten to arrive at some sort of compromise. The committee recommended that petition requirements for the indirect initiative be increased from 4 to 6 percent. Although the committee retained the direct initiative for constitutional amendments, it dropped it for laws and prohibited the use of the initiative to propose any law authorizing a single tax on land. The only political subdivision other than the state specifically granted powers of direct legislation were municipalities where a 10 percent petition requirement governed use of the initiative or referendum on local ordinances. Interestingly, voters at the municipal level were allowed to directly initiate ordinances (instead of indirectly through the city council) and to submit ballot propositions at special elections. As a result, the local features of direct legislation were more liberal than those governing its use at the state level.[23]

After further debate, however, Crosser managed to get the direct initiative reinstated in modified form (he was unsuccessful in removing the single-tax exclusion). Under his proposal, 3 percent of the voters (reduced from 6 percent) could invoke the indirect initiative. If the legislature then failed to act on a proposed measure, a supplemental petition signed by not less than 3 percent of the electors in addition to and other than those signing the original petition could call for the measure to be placed directly on the ballot. One final compromise reduced the petition requirement to initiate constitutional amendments from 12 to 10 percent. Only a majority of those voting on a question rather than a majority voting in the election was required for ratification. The revised resolution was adopted by the entire convention on March 27, 1912. Fearing that a combination of antagonistic interest groups might try to defeat the new constitution if it was submitted as a whole, the delegates decided that each amendment would be voted on

22. Lampson quoted in Warner, *Progressivism in Ohio*, 321; Roman Catholic Church quoted (along with other examples of conservative reaction) in Lloyd Sponholtz, "The Initiative and Referendum: Direct Democracy in Perspective, 1898–1920," 57; Halfhill quoted in Beaver, *A Buckeye Crusader*, 30.

23. To the angry single taxers who had led the effort to gain direct legislation in Ohio, Bigelow defended this concession as minor. When public opinion became ready to accept the single tax, he argued, it could still be obtained, as the prohibition applied only to initiated statutes and not to initiated constitutional amendments. In fact, the procedure to amend the constitution via the initiative could be used to remove the existing restriction against the single tax itself. See Warner, *Progressivism in Ohio*, 322–23, 392.

separately. They then designated September 3, 1912, as the date for the special ratification election and adjourned on June 7, 1912, to prepare for the summer ratification campaign.[24]

Leading the effort to convince voters to support the work of the convention was the New Constitution League of Ohio. Representatives from the state's five major cities formed the league's executive committee, whereas progressives from each of the twenty-one congressional districts made up its advisory board. The purpose of the new organization was to educate the public on the merits of the initiative and referendum and urge voters to support all the proposed amendments. Assisted by Democratic congressman James M. Cox's and Democratic senator Atlee Pomerene's franking privileges and donations from supporters, Bigelow mailed copies of his speeches and took to stumping the state with Brand Whitlock and Newton D. Baker, the popular progressive mayors of Toledo and Cleveland, respectively. In Cincinnati, Bigelow used the city's public park system and Tom Johnson's traveling-circus-tent idea to talk up the constitution and especially the proposed initiative and referendum amendment. The state's newspapers, again led by the *Toledo News-Bee*, other Scripps-McRae dailies, and the *Cleveland Plain Dealer*, supported the efforts of the revisionists.[25]

Conservative opponents of the revised constitution waited until late July to begin their antiratification campaign. Led by Allen Ripley Foote, president of the Ohio State Board of Commerce, and supported by the state's public utility corporations, the antirevisionists strongly opposed the direct legislation and labor reform amendments and were still embittered that the convention had not supported the principle of tax classification. Repeating their earlier efforts to thwart the election of progressive delegates to the constitutional convention, they released a barrage of boilerplate to the rural press attacking the work of the convention. One publication opined that "owing to the influence of the Socialists, the whole scheme [constitution] is red." The *Cincinnati Commercial Tribune*, the voice of the local Cox machine, echoed the same sentiment and claimed that the proposed constitution was "the great work of a small group of radical schemers." When editors refused to publish some of the hyperbolic mailings, the antirevisionists resorted to mass-circulated pamphlets and dodgers. As the campaign came to a close, opponents advised voters, "When in doubt, vote No."[26]

Voting day, September 3 (the day after Labor Day), had been selected to give labor speakers one last opportunity to urge workingmen to go to the

24. See Beaver, *A Buckeye Crusader*, 29–31; Warner, *Progressivism in Ohio*, 322–23; and Crosser, "Initiative and Referendum," 193–94, 200.

25. See Beaver, *A Buckeye Crusader*, 32–33; and Warner, *Progressivism in Ohio*, 339.

26. Quotations are from Beaver, *A Buckeye Crusader*, 33. See also Warner, *Progressivism in Ohio*, 339–40.

polls and vote. Most voters, however, seemed more absorbed in the 1912 presidential campaign than in changes to their state constitution, and turnout at the special election was relatively light (voter response to the various amendments ranged from 50 to 63.4 percent of the votes cast for governor in 1910). Despite the disappointing turnout, those who did vote approved all but eight of the forty-two proposed amendments. The initiative and referendum amendment passed by a vote of 312,592 to 231,312.[27]

In 1913 the Ohio legislature passed legislation designed to protect the initiative and referendum process from abuse. The resulting legislation made it a corrupt practice to offer or accept money for signing a petition and required organizations that circulated petitions to list their expenses and the names of their solicitors. It was not, however, against the law to pay petitioners to collect signatures. In the summer of 1913, the Equity Association, a front for a group of liability insurance companies that were strongly opposed to the state's new workmen's compensation law on grounds that it would cost them business, circulated referendum petitions on three acts (the aforementioned workmen's compensation law and two tax reform measures) passed by the legislature. Friends of the initiative and referendum, including Governor James M. Cox, believed that the Equity group intended not only to defeat the three laws but to discredit the new system of direct legislation as well.

After Ohio attorney general Timothy Hogan uncovered evidence of widespread fraud in the collection of signatures, Governor Cox ordered a hearing to expose the abuses. The revelations that followed were shocking. Paid solicitors confessed to forging hundreds of signatures and to having purposely smeared petitions to give them a well-handled look. In summing up their testimony, Attorney General Hogan issued the following statement: "Dead men, livery stables, vacant lots, empty houses, children, public parks, churches, stores, convicts, brick yards, public playgrounds, factories, flop houses, houses of ill-repute, and non-residents all have attempted to exercise the right of suffrage in Ohio." Ohio secretary of state Charles S. Graves responded to the evidence by throwing out the petitions (an action later sustained by the Ohio Supreme Court). At the special session of the legislature in 1914, legislators rewrote the protective features of the law to guard against further abuse.[28]

In 1916 the Varsity Debate Association of Ohio contacted more than 190 legislators, former members of the constitutional convention, and other

27. See Beaver, *A Buckeye Crusader*, 32–33; Warner, *Progressivism in Ohio*, 340–43; Warner, "Ohio's Convention," 28; and Ohio, *Annual Statistical Report of the Secretary of State for the Year Ending November 15, 1912*, 669.

28. Warner, *Progressivism in Ohio*, 393–94, 415. For a discussion of the new protections, see *Equity* 16 (April 1914): 98.

prominent Ohioans to ask their opinion on the operation of the initiative and referendum since its adoption in 1912. The general consensus was that although voters had decided to use direct legislation sparingly, the new system of popular government had influenced the legislature in a positive manner. In their collective opinion, direct legislation had proved valuable as the "gun behind the door," frightening off corrupt legislative agents and causing legislators to become more responsive to the popular will.[29]

The respondents, however, missed the point. The numbers of ballot propositions were relatively few (sixteen voter-initiated or -referred ballot propositions between 1913 and 1918), but this was primarily the result of the progressive-oriented constitutional convention that had incorporated the core of the reform agenda into the new state constitution. When well-organized interests, such as those advocating tax classification, woman suffrage, and prohibition, failed to benefit from either the constitutional revision process or the actions of a more "responsive" legislature, they vigorously employed the initiative process in an attempt to obtain what they had been denied.

Supporters of both tax classification and woman suffrage used the initiative to get their propositions on the ballot on two different occasions. Although delegates to the constitutional convention had rejected the idea of allowing property to be classified for purposes of taxation and farmers were known to be opposed to the idea, proponents used the initiative to get their proposal on the ballot in 1914. However, even the support of Governor Cox and the inclusion of a limit of fifteen mills on general property to allay the fears of the state's agrarians could not convince voters, who overwhelmingly rejected the proposal. Nevertheless, the idea was not dead, and when proponents again placed an initiated proposition on the ballot in 1918, voters narrowly approved it. Also lending itself to the initiative was the question of the vote for women. Despite the fact that voters had rejected the idea of woman suffrage when it was presented to them as a constitutional amendment in 1912, proponents secured enough signatures to get an amendment on the ballot in 1914, only to see it soundly defeated. In 1917 opponents of woman suffrage called for a referendum on a statute passed by the legislature that would have allowed women to vote for presidential electors. Voters again said no to woman suffrage by vetoing the law.

"Drys" wasted no time in initiating a statute in 1913 seeking to prohibit the shipment of liquor into "dry" territory. Voters rejected it. At the same election, "wets" initiated a constitutional amendment that sought to reduce the size of the General Assembly by consolidating rural counties into single-representative districts. Seen as an obvious attempt by liquor inter-

29. *Equity* 18 (April 1916): 76–77.

ests to reduce the voting strength of prohibitionists in the legislature, voters rejected this measure by an even wider margin. "Drys" put forward another initiative calling for statewide prohibition in 1914, but saw it too go down to defeat. "Wets," however, fared better in 1914, winning voter approval for an initiative allowing for home rule on the subject of intoxicating liquors. The two forces again faced off in the election of 1915. "Drys" resubmitted statewide prohibition, and voters again rejected it (although by a narrower margin). Tired of dealing with annual demands for prohibition, "wets" also initiated an amendment in 1915 that would have prohibited the resubmission of twice-defeated ballot initiatives. Ardent direct legislationists, alarmed by this infringement on principle, joined with antisaloon forces to defeat this insidious scheme obviously directed at prohibitionists. "Drys" again initiated an amendment for statewide prohibition in 1917 only to see it narrowly defeated. The gap disappeared in 1918 when voters finally approved an initiative calling for statewide prohibition.[30]

WASHINGTON

Voters in Washington faced many of the same problems that confronted Ohioans. Machine politics characterized state government, and railroads and other corporations had a controlling influence on decisions made at the state capitol in Olympia. According to one historian, "[L]egislative arrangements continued to be made between legislators and lobbyists over private bars in downtown hotel rooms and United States Senators were chosen in similar fashion." Likewise, political machinations masked economic ones. Farmers complained that railroads deliberately delayed the process of securing patents on federally granted lands as a way of avoiding their share of the tax burden. Shippers in eastern Washington complained that discriminatory "terminal rates" forced them to ship and receive goods at twice the rate required of coastal shippers. Adding the common practice of issuing free railroad passes to government officials to their list of grievances, it was easy for farmers and shippers to conclude that the railroads had manipulated government to their disadvantage.[31]

Articulating the concerns of farmers in the state of Washington during the Populist-Progressive Era was the Washington State Grange. Washing-

30. See Warner, *Progressivism in Ohio*, 395, 437–38 n. 13. For a comment on the role of the liquor interests in vetoing the law allowing women to vote for presidential electors in 1917, see *Equity* 20 (January 1918): 68–69. For summaries of the ballot propositions submitted to voters in 1913, 1914, 1915, and 1917, see *Equity* 16 (January 1914): 38–39; 17 (January 1915): 53; 18 (January 1916): 32–34; and 20 (January 1918): 67–69.

31. Quotation is from Claudius O. Johnson, "The Adoption of the Initiative and Referendum in Washington," 294–95. See also Gordon B. Ridgeway, "Populism in Washington," 284–311.

ton farmers had hurriedly formed the organization in 1889 when delegates to the state's constitutional convention that year began to incorporate provisions into the new constitution that they opposed. In their minds, delegates appeared poised to create wasteful expenditures in the form of redundant public offices and high public salaries. Such policies, they argued, would generate a perpetual office-seeking class, promote the growth of corrupt machine politicians, and encourage legislative extravagance that would result in burdensome taxation. They also objected to provisions that would allow for secret legislative sessions and require a two-thirds vote of both houses of the legislature to propose an amendment to the state constitution. Even though voters eventually ratified the new document by overwhelming numbers (40,153 to 11,879), the Grange steadfastly opposed adoption. In the process, even as a small but vocal minority, the Grange established itself as an outspoken critic of state-level policy makers and would continue to voice its opinions on questions important to its membership.[32]

Among the numerous issues favored by the Grange during the 1890s— a state railway commission to oversee fare and freight charges, the taxation of railway property on par with all other property, an antiusury law, woman suffrage, and prohibition—was direct legislation. The Grange first endorsed the idea at its annual convention in 1893, even though farmers were not yet familiar with the term. In a resolution adopted by the convention, delegates proposed that the legislature should "pass any or all laws demanded by the people when said demand is made by the people by petition signed by a sufficient number of people" and that "all acts or laws shall be submitted to a vote of the people for ratification before they become laws." The organization continued to endorse the idea at each annual meeting thereafter.[33]

The actions of fellow Grangers in neighboring Oregon worked to intensify interest in direct legislation within the Washington State Grange. The active role that the Oregon State Grange had played in the successful effort to obtain the initiative and referendum in that state was well known to Grangers in Washington. The two organizations periodically supported a joint publication that recorded the activities of each order and provided a forum for the discussion of important topics through editorial comment and letters from individual members. Watching Oregonians battle to obtain a constitutional amendment and, later, struggle to defend it against hostile interests certainly offered valuable lessons for their own campaign.[34]

32. See Harriet Ann Crawford, *The Washington State Grange, 1889–1924: A Romance of Democracy,* 12–17, 55.
33. Resolution quoted in ibid., 160–61. See also Ridgeway, "Populism in Washington," 292.
34. See H. A. Crawford, *Washington State Grange,* 161–62.

Beginning in 1900, one year after the Oregon legislature passed a direct legislation amendment for the first time, leaders of the Washington State Grange announced that the way to improve the unrepresentative machine-controlled political system in their state was by adopting a similar measure. To follow up their new demand, the Grange requested that candidates to the state legislature pledge themselves, if elected, to support a constitutional amendment for the initiative and referendum. As expected, they made little headway in the ensuing legislative session. As one Grange official put it: "We have no hopes whatever of securing its passage at this session. The railroads have this legislature sold." However, they did succeed in having Senator L. C. Craw and Representative T. C. Miles, both farmers and Democrats from Whitman County, introduce amendments in their respective chambers and took at least the first steps in a formalized political campaign.[35]

Over the next eight or nine years, the State Grange labored to push the issue of direct legislation forward through political action. In 1902 the organization appointed a committee in each county to interview legislative candidates and persuade them to support direct legislation. The technique had worked well in Oregon and was strongly endorsed by George Shibley, chairman of the Non-Partisan Federation for Majority Rule in Washington, D.C. The Grange continued to endorse the initiative and referendum as its highest legislative priority at its convention in 1903, and retiring state master J. O. Wing encouraged cooperation with other agricultural groups to secure direct legislation in 1905. As Wing's replacement, the Grange elected C. B. Kegley. A former Populist and socialist, Kegley would provide dynamic leadership for the organization until his death in 1918. Kegley immediately expanded the organization's political program to include demands for the direct primary, the direct election of U.S. senators, and the recall of elected officials, and urged that cooperative efforts be broadened to include *all organizations* working for direct legislation. When the legislature enacted a direct primary bill in 1907, it looked as if an amendment for direct legislation might pass as well. Although the House approved such a measure by a wide margin, the Senate failed to follow suit. Kegley blamed the "bosses" representing the railroad and lumber interests for the defeat. The Grange lobbied unsuccessfully for another amendment in 1909, this time apparently blocked by what Kegley referred to as the "saloon power."[36]

Legislative defeats convinced Kegley that a broader political campaign to obtain direct legislation was needed. Realizing that direct legislation pro-

35. Johnson, "Adoption in Washington," 295.
36. See ibid., 295–97; *Equity* 12 (January 1910): 22; Robert D. Saltvig, "The Progressive Movement in Washington," 118–19; and Carlos A. Schwantes, *Radical Heritage: Labor, Socialism, and Reform in Washington and British Columbia, 1885–1917*, 107, 160–61.

vided a basis for cooperation between farm and labor groups, Kegley decided to seek closer political cooperation with the State Federation of Labor. He began the process of courting organized labor in earnest in 1906. That year the State Grange appointed a special committee to attend sessions of the legislature at Olympia to monitor the actions of various representatives and work with the existing committee on legislation of the State Federation of Labor. The idea of a farmer-labor lobby was appealing to organized labor as well. Stymied in its attempts to secure labor legislation by the growing power of employers' associations, the State Federation of Labor was eager to obtain support from other reform-minded organizations. Kegley next suggested that both organizations examine the corrupting influence that the awarding of valuable urban franchises by the legislature had on state politics and begin to discuss plans by which corporate influence over that process might be curtailed. The State Federation of Labor quickly signaled that it was willing to cooperate. At its 1906 convention the federation proposed not only to push for specific labor reforms such as the eight-hour day for miners, but also to support a direct primary law and to work with the Grange to secure direct legislation. Such political bonding continued in 1908 when the State Grange approved a resolution that endorsed labor's demands for an employer-liability law and eight-hour laws for women and miners, and urged farmers to buy only union-made farm implements.[37]

Liberal urban reformers also played a significant role in the coalition that would form behind direct legislation. Finding political expression as urban Populists in the city of Seattle during the 1890s, and aided by a small but vocal group of single taxers, these urban reformers looked to reclaim local government for the people by eliminating special privileges and democratizing government. To that end they hoped to obtain charter amendments that would allow for the municipal ownership of public utilities and the initiative and referendum in city affairs (first-class cities would gain the right to amend their charters by initiative as a result of state legislation passed in 1903). Although they failed to achieve success during the 1890s constituted as Populists, Fusionists (with the Democrats), or Non-Partisans, they succeeded in keeping the issues at the forefront of the political debate in Seattle.[38]

When the Seattle City Council refused to grant a franchise for the construction of a competing street-railway line in 1905, the advocates of municipal ownership rallied together on a nonpartisan basis and ultimately

37. See H. A. Crawford, *Washington State Grange,* 162–63; Johnson, "Adoption in Washington," 297; Saltvig, "Progressive Movement," 119, 121; and Schwantes, *Radical Heritage,* 160.
38. See Saltvig, "Progressive Movement," 32–45.

forced the council to rescind its approval of "exclusive" franchise rights. This limited victory triggered the creation of first the Municipal Ownership League and then the Municipal Ownership Party, and inaugurated a campaign to obtain a municipally owned transit system for Seattle. Voters narrowly defeated a bond issue that would have financed construction of a public system in 1906. As a result of that setback, the Municipal Ownership Party changed its name to the City Party in 1907 and repositioned itself accordingly. Although the party continued to favor municipal ownership, it sought to broaden its base of support by more strongly emphasizing nonpartisanship and greater democracy in government.

In the process of reorganizing, the City Party also created a special direct legislation committee under the direction of reformer-journalist Joe Smith. Smith, the son of a successful farmer in eastern Washington, attended the University of Missouri and Washington State College and developed an interest in journalism and politics. He was an active Bryan Democrat in 1896 and worked as a war correspondent for the *Seattle Post-Intelligencer* during the Philippine insurrection of 1898–1902. Returning to Seattle, Smith worked for a number of Washington newspapers and soon developed a reputation as a muckraking journalist. A genuine activist, Smith became involved in several state political campaigns, helped organize the Municipal Ownership Party in Seattle, and began to garner prominence as an advocate for direct democracy. In 1907 and again in 1909, Smith covered the state legislature as a reporter and became sympathetic with and lent his support to a rising group of reform-oriented politicians known as "insurgents" who had begun to advocate progressive reforms at the state level.

When Smith activated his special direct legislation committee in 1907, he did so with the benefit of previous experience. Two years after the state legislature passed a measure that granted first-class cities the authority to amend their charters by initiative, Adella M. Parker, a high school teacher with a law degree from the University of Washington, formulated the idea of using this new power to obtain an amendment to the Seattle charter allowing for the recall of public officials. She drew up an amendment and, using her father's name, tried to mobilize popular support. When her efforts failed to produce immediate results, energetic Joe Smith took up the cause and managed to get enough petition signatures to qualify the recall amendment for the ballot in 1906. Voters approved the charter revision at the city election that same year.

Two years later Smith, with the help of the City Party, decided to undertake a similar campaign to secure charter amendments allowing for the initiative and referendum in city affairs and requiring that streetcar franchises be submitted to popular vote for approval. To rally voters behind the idea Smith, in a manner that resembled the approach of Dr. John Randolph

Haynes in California, convinced the presidents of the Civic Union, Central Labor Council, Workingmen's League, Manufacturers' Association, and YMCA to allow themselves to be listed as officers of the new Direct Legislation League of Seattle. Appearing, somewhat disingenuously, as a broadly based reform organization, the league conducted a successful petition drive and secured a place for the proposed charter amendments on the ballot. Voters approved the amendments in 1908. With a significant local victory for direct legislation in hand, Seattle's liberal reformers, now organized on a bipartisan basis, were ready to channel their efforts toward securing a direct legislation amendment to the state constitution.[39]

The campaign for direct legislation broadened its organizational base in 1910 with the creation of the Direct Legislation League of Washington. The league came about as a result of a call from Ernest M. Smith, a state lecturer for the Grange, for a meeting of all the "progressive elements" in the state to explore the possibility of a united plan for political action. Delegates from the State Grange, the State Federation of Labor, various civic reform groups, and reform-minded "insurgents" from both the Republican and the Democratic Parties formally met in Seattle on February 12, 1910.[40] The meeting eventually divided into two groups. One group, favoring a broad-based reform program, formed the Progressive Political Alliance, whereas the other, choosing to devote full attention to a single issue, established the Direct Legislation League. Under the leadership of Christopher W. Horr of the Seattle Civic Union as executive secretary and Charles R. Case of the State Federation of Labor as treasurer, the new league immediately mounted a publicity campaign to stir up interest and educate voters. Senator Jonathan Bourne of Oregon, a nationally known spokesman for direct legislation, assisted their efforts with fifty thousand copies of an address he had delivered to the United States Senate titled "Popular Government" and traveled to Washington State in the fall of 1910 to aid the campaign. Also involved was William S. U'Ren, now nationally famous as Oregon's "Lawmaker," who contributed articles and advice. The Grange continued its work of pledging legislative candidates, and the Farmers' Educational and Cooperative Union, primarily a business organization for more prosperous

39. See ibid., 88–106, 140–43. The Civic Union was organized in 1904 to promote honesty and efficiency in local government. Its three hundred members included business, professional, and working-class men. See ibid., 117 n.

40. A large number of candidates elected to the state legislature in 1906 had pledged themselves to work for passage of a direct primary law. A group of more than twenty senators soon began calling themselves "insurgents" and promised to work for other reforms aimed at restoring popular democracy and favoring efficiency and economy in government. They succeeded in enacting a direct primary law in 1907 and a local option prohibition law in 1909, but made no progress on direct legislation. See ibid., 126–39; and Schwantes, *Radical Heritage*, 193–94.

farmers with a good deal of political influence, lent its support. Adding its voice was the State Federation of Labor, which decided to hold its annual convention in Olympia in January 1911, just as the legislature began its session.[41]

To encourage the legislature in its deliberations, representatives of the Grange, the Farmers' Union, the State Federation of Labor, and the Direct Legislation League formed a reform coalition known as the Temporary Joint Legislative Committee to coordinate lobbying efforts. Judson King, a national organizer for direct legislation, commented that it was the first time in the state's history that organized groups of farmers, workers, and middle-class progressives had united for common action. In a state like Washington where party lines were weak, pressure-group politics had a chance to be successful in Olympia. Charles Case, with membership in three of the four organizations and experience as a legislative lobbyist for organized labor, assumed leadership of the joint committee, which met each evening in the offices of the State Federation of Labor to share progress reports and formulate plans of action. The joint committee favored a reform program that included public ownership, good roads, employers' liability, and an eight-hour law, but focused its primary attention on obtaining direct legislation. The joint committee eventually persuaded a majority of the members in the House to sign a petition pledging them to support the direct legislation measure drawn up by the league, known as House Bill 153, "without any amendment except those agreeable to its authors."[42]

The original proposal allowed bills to be initiated either to the voters for consideration at the next general election or to the legislature for approval or rejection before the end of the next legislative session. Petitions for either option required signatures of 8 percent of the qualified voters (based on the votes cast for governor in the last election). Measures passed by the legislature could be referred to the voters based on petition of 5 percent of the same (unless deemed necessary for the preservation of the public peace, health, or safety, or for the support of the state government and its existing public institutions). If the legislature either failed to act on or rejected an initiated proposal, it would then automatically go to the voters. Under this procedure, the legislature could submit a competing proposal dealing with the same subject. The legislature could also refer measures to the voters. A simple majority of those voting on any ballot proposition could pass it. The

41. See Saltvig, "Progressive Movement," 151–52, 170; Johnson, "Adoption in Washington," 297–99; and Schwantes, *Radical Heritage*, 161.
42. See Johnson, "Adoption in Washington," 299–300; H. A. Crawford, *Washington State Grange,* 166–67; Saltvig, "Progressive Movement," 175–76; "Washington—Seven Sisters Campaign of 1914," King Papers, Library of Congress; and Schwantes, *Radical Heritage,* 162.

legislature could amend or repeal any measure approved by the voters, but would have to wait four years before doing so. The proposed amendment, however, did not include the constitutional initiative that had been proposed as a separate measure (known as House Bill 60). This latter bill easily passed the House but met resistance in the Senate. Opponents refused to support the bill unless it was amended to require that no vote on any initiated constitutional amendment would be effective unless 60 percent of the voters participating in the general election voted on the question. Rather than accept what they considered to be an unworkable amendment, the Temporary Joint Legislative Committee decided to drop the idea and wait for a more favorable opportunity later.[43]

Although the House approved House Bill 153 without revision, the Senate modified the original proposal in three areas: it raised petition requirements for the initiative from 8 to 10 percent (but in no case more than fifty thousand qualified voters) and for the referendum from 5 to 6 percent (but in no case more than thirty thousand qualified voters); it shortened the period during which the legislature was prohibited from amending or repealing an initiated law from four years to two; and it stipulated that no initiative or referendum would take effect unless at least one-third of the voters participating in the election voted on the measure. The Senate narrowly rejected (by one vote) a proposal that would have severely impeded the initiative process by requiring voters to sign petitions in the office of the county auditor. Agreeing that the Senate's revisions did not significantly impair the measure, the joint committee advised its supporters in the House to accept the Senate version. That being done, the amendment was slated to go before the voters at the next general election.[44]

During the lengthy interval between the passage of the amendment in the spring of 1911 and the election in November 1912, the joint committee worked to further its campaign of publicity and education. The State Grange was especially active, using the columns of the *Pacific Grange Bulletin* to underscore the importance of voting in favor of the amendment and urging voters to support only those candidates who had signed cards distributed by the Temporary Joint Legislative Committee that pledged them to work for the extension of direct legislation (to include constitutional amendments). The editors of the *Tacoma Times* complimented both the Grange (representing seventeen thousand farmers) and the State Federation of Labor for "going down the line . . . to put a legislature at Olympia

43. See Claudius O. Johnson, "The Initiative and Referendum in Washington," 29–30; and Johnson, "Adoption in Washington," 302.

44. See Johnson, "Adoption in Washington," 300–301; Lester Burrell Shippee, "Washington's First Experiment in Direct Legislation," 235–37; and Saltvig, "Progressive Movement," 176–77.

that will be responsive to the real will of the people instead of the manipulation of corporate lobbyists and political bosses with axes to grind." Although the rural weekly newspapers and the agricultural and labor publications actively supported direct legislation, the urban dailies tended to adopt a noncommittal stance on the issue. Also working to diminish awareness, and crowd even important state questions into the background, was the national political campaign, with the candidates and platforms of four national parties vying for the voters' attention. In the final vote, Washingtonians decisively approved the initiative and referendum amendment by a vote of 110,110 to 43,905, even though only 46 percent of those who voted for a presidential candidate bothered to register an opinion on direct legislation.[45]

The Temporary Joint Legislative Committee remained politically active after voters adopted the direct legislation amendment. Having agreed to establish itself on a permanent basis at a direct legislation conference held in Yakima in September 1911, the joint committee broadened its political agenda to include prohibition of employment-agency fees (collected by private employment agencies from unemployed workers to find them jobs) and a "Blue Sky" law (to protect investors from unscrupulous promoters), in addition to its demand for a constitutional initiative. A majority of the legislators elected in 1912 had pledged to support these reforms during the campaign, but the joint committee quickly discovered that some of them were willing to go back on their promises when offered special considerations. E. P. Marsh, president of the State Federation of Labor, blamed such backsliding on the system rather than the individual. To Marsh, as long as pork-barrel appropriations controlled politics, commitments would be abandoned and reform legislation deserted because legislators were expected to further the interests of their constituents and districts. As a result, the joint committee failed to find the support necessary to pass any of its reforms. A measure calling for the constitutional initiative did come up in the 1913 legislature but fell five votes shy, with a vote of sixty to thirty-three, of the necessary two-thirds majority.[46]

Blocked in the legislature, the Temporary Joint Legislative Committee

45. William H. Kaufman, editor of the *Pacific Grange Bulletin* and a resident of Washington since 1904, had been active in the direct legislation campaign in South Dakota during the 1890s. See Saltvig, "Progressive Movement," 117–18. *Tacoma Times* quoted in H. A. Crawford, *Washington State Grange*, 172 (see also 171–72). See also Johnson, "Adoption in Washington," 302–3.

46. Favoring the measure were twenty-eight Progressives, fourteen Democrats, seventeen Republicans, and one Socialist. Opposing the bill were twenty-eight Republicans, four Democrats, and one Progressive. See Saltvig, "Progressive Movement," 178–79, 307–8, 348–49.

decided to concentrate on direct action rather than individual trust to achieve its program. To that end, the committee initiated seven measures in 1914 described by one historian as "the farmers' and workers' response to the fish combine, the lumber trust, and other special interests."[47] The first was the "Blue Sky" law that had previously been rejected by the legislature. However, the proposal was so loosely written as to invite future litigation and would probably have improved actual conditions little. A second measure would have abolished the State Bureau of Supervision and Inspection of Public Offices and transferred those duties to the state auditor, whereas a third would have eliminated the State Tax Commission and shifted those duties to the Public Service Commission. Apparently intended to trim needless state bureaucracy, the move actually sought to eliminate what was, in the opinions of most, a highly effective Bureau of Supervision and Inspection and made no allowances for the increased burden placed on either of the assuming agencies. Critics labeled the second proposal a "spite" measure put forth by groups that felt they had been too closely scrutinized. The fourth item was the employment-fee measure, also previously rejected by the legislature. Designers of the proposal regarded the fees as a form of extortion and felt that such costs should be either assumed by employers or provided for free by state-run agencies. The fifth proposition sought to amend the Industrial Insurance Act of 1911 and require employers to provide "first aid" care to workers injured on the job. The proposal targeted a glaring omission in the law, but lacked details as to the kind of treatment or length of care required and placed the burden of expense on unhappy employers. Item 6 required all able-bodied prison inmates be put to work on public highways. The proposal, designed to reduce highway appropriations and, ideally, spending and pork barrel, would have upset the state's newly enacted comprehensive road-construction plan and rendered existing labor programs (a prison jute mill) useless. The last of the so-called Seven Sisters sought to regulate and tax fisheries.

Joining these propositions on the ballot were several other proposals. Two were initiatives. The first was a universal eight-hour law sponsored by the Socialist Party but actively supported by organized labor. Farmers, however, opposed the law, even with the inclusion of an exemption that allowed two extra hours a day for work that involved "farm management." E. P. Marsh had pledged to obtain an eight-hour workday without a strike, but less than 36 percent of the voters supported the initiative. The second was a statewide prohibition measure sponsored by the Anti-Saloon League

47. Schwantes, *Radical Heritage*, 198.

that won voter approval. Rounding out the ballot propositions were two spending measures referred by the legislature that involved creating a retirement system for teachers and constructing an elaborate and extremely expensive irrigation project, and a confusing legislative amendment that revised the state law governing alien landownership.[48]

More significant perhaps than the individual ballot measures was the controversy that developed surrounding them. At the start of the signature-gathering process, the Stop-Look-Listen League, funded by manufacturers' and employers' associations, circulated a forty-eight-page pamphlet attacking the measures in an attempt to persuade voters not to sign the petitions. The Stop-Look-Listen League refused to reveal the names of its members, but the *Seattle Star* pointed to E. H. Sims, the Republican floor leader in the House in 1913, as the individual directing the organization. Sims, the owner of four fish canneries and a logging company, had reason to feel threatened by several of the initiated measures. When the league realized that it had not acted quickly enough to deter enough signers, it worked to convince signers that they had made a mistake and to ask that their names be removed from the petitions. The state's secretary of state not only willingly complied with their wishes, but even proceeded to remove other names that he believed to be fraudulent or forged as well as any that certifying officials had initialed in pencil instead of ink as set in the statute. When he finished only three of the original seven propositions had enough signatures to qualify for the ballot.

The sponsors of the original measures immediately appealed to the state supreme court. Deciding that the secretary of state's duties were simply ministerial and that the law empowered him to reject only the names that appeared more than once on a petition, the court ordered that all other signatures be restored. As a result, five of the seven proposals survived to qualify for the ballot. Piqued by all the political maneuvering and legal challenges surrounding the initiatives, voters turned out in large numbers (the average vote in initiated measures was more than 80 percent) but rejected all but two of the propositions: to establish statewide prohibition and to abolish private employment agencies. Although supporters of the Temporary Joint Legislative Committee might have claimed a victory at the polls, they had actually suffered a defeat. In concentrating their attention on legislation rather than pledging candidates, the committee had unwittingly allowed reactionary politicians to gain new ground, as voters re-

48. See Johnson, "Initiative and Referendum," 31–33; *Equity* 16 (October 1914): 190–91; Shippee, "Washington's Experiment," 237–44; H. A. Crawford, *Washington State Grange,* 177; Saltvig, "Progressive Movement," 349–50; and "Washington," King Papers, Library of Congress.

turned enough regular Republicans to allow that party to continue its hold on the legislature.[49]

The reactionary nature of that new majority was made evident as soon as the 1915 legislative session got under way. The legislature, which C. B. Kegley characterized as being controlled by liquor, lumber, and fish interests, quickly enacted statutes that rendered the initiative and referendum ineffective, obstructed the recall, and weakened the state's direct primary system. Also included in the list of reactionary measures was an antipicketing law designed to weaken the trade union movement. The revised direct legislation law, misleadingly titled "An Act to Facilitate the Operation of the . . . Initiative and Referendum," required voters to sign initiative petitions in the office of a registration official who would accept signatures on Fridays and Saturdays from six to nine at night for a period of ninety days and made it a misdemeanor for any individual to solicit petition signatures within one hundred feet of a registration office. Democratic governor Ernest Lister vetoed all three of the measures, but the Republican majority in the legislature overrode his vetoes. Shocked by the tactics of the opposition, the joint committee, in cooperation with the Democratic and Progressive Parties' leaders, began a campaign to contest the assault on direct democracy via the referendum. By election time successful challenges had been made on the initiative and referendum, recall, direct primary, and antipicketing laws and on three other legislative enactments that voters also deemed to be pernicious.[50]

At the election in 1916, the electorate sent the legislature a strong rebuke. They rejected all seven referred measures by majorities of three or four to one, voted down a proposed constitutional amendment that would have required a property qualification to vote on bond issues or on proposals that would incur "public obligations," and elected a legislature less reactionary than the previous one. Voters reelected Governor Lister, who had actually signed three of the objectionable measures, including the antipicketing law, but only after he publicly admitted the "error of his ways" and campaigned in favor of the referenda. From a rather complacent regard

---

49. See Saltvig, "Progressive Movement," 351; Johnson, "Initiative and Referendum," 33–36; *Equity* 17 (January 1915): 59; Shippee, "Washington's Experiment," 244–53; H. A. Crawford, *Washington State Grange,* 175–79; and "Washington," King Papers, Library of Congress.

50. The other three referred items included measures to require new public utilities to get approval from the Public Service Commission, reorganize the management of the Port of Seattle, and prohibit municipalities from using funds for purposes other than those originally designated. See Johnson, "Initiative and Referendum," 36–37; H. A. Crawford, *Washington State Grange,* 180–82; and "Washington," King Papers, Library of Congress.

for the initiative and referendum in 1912 and a cautious attitude toward their use in 1914, Washington's voters enthusiastically embraced those reforms to discipline a legislature that seemed to insidiously threaten their prerogatives and arrogantly misrepresent their views in 1916.[51]

51. Also on the ballot in 1916 were two measures that sought to modify the 1914 prohibition statute by allowing for the manufacture and sale of 4 percent beer and permitting the restricted sale (in hotels and restaurants) of liquor. Voters overwhelmingly defeated both measures. A new organization, the Non-Partisan League, attempted to secure signatures for four other initiative measures: to add a first-aid amendment to the industrial insurance law that would create a state fund from which workers could receive emergency medical treatment, to levy a royalty tax on commercial fishermen, to allow municipalities to regulate public utilities rather than a state board, and, most important to the sponsors, to establish nonpartisanship in all state, county, and municipal elections. However, bickering over the scope of the nonpartisanship measure and disinterest among farmers prevented all four propositions from qualifying for the ballot. See Johnson, "Initiative and Referendum," 36; H. A. Crawford, *Washington State Grange*, 185–88; Saltvig, "Progressive Movement," 379–81; *Equity* 17 (April 1915): 125–26; 17 (July 1915): 192; 19 (January 1917): 41; "Washington," King Papers, Library of Congress; and Schwantes, *Radical Heritage*, 199.

8

Michigan and North Dakota

MICHIGAN

The Republican Party controlled state politics in Michigan during the 1890s much as it did in neighboring Ohio. The party governed in close alliance with big business and showed no interest in the concerns of reformers. When popular Detroit reform mayor Hazen Pingree conducted a successful campaign for governor of Michigan in 1896 on the Republican ticket, he won with the support of party conservatives and influential businessmen who thought his reform reputation could help the national ticket by drawing voters away from William Jennings Bryan in favor of William McKinley. The by-product of this strategy, the election of a reform governor, seemed of little concern to the leaders of the state's Republican Party. They were confident that conservative Republicans who controlled the state senate could block any Pingree-sponsored reform program. They were not disappointed. The state legislatures of 1893, 1895, 1897, and 1899 overwhelmingly opposed reform of any sort. When Governor Pingree attempted to get the legislature to enact railroad rate regulation, corporate (that is, railroad) tax reform, meaningful factory inspection, protective labor legislation for women and children, pure-food laws, and state regulation of banks and insurance companies, and requested that they repeal the special charter privileges of the Michigan Central Railroad, intransigent state senators rebuffed him. To frustrated dissenters in Michigan, it was as if they had no political voice.[1]

1. Pingree had won the support of Detroit's consumers and taxpayers (and alarmed businessmen) by attacking the city's system of taxation that assessed homes at a higher rate than factories and downtown business buildings, the gas company for charging almost twice as much for gas as other cities, and the street-railway company for refusing to electrify its line and for paying the city nothing for its franchise privilege. During the panic of 1893 Pingree enhanced his popularity by permitting the unemployed to use vacant city land to plant gardens and grow their own vegetables. As mayor, Pingree succeeded in getting the gas company to lower its rates, established a municipal

Organized labor generated the earliest discussion of direct legislation in Michigan, with the Detroit trade unions under the direction of John R. Morrissey taking the lead. The *Labor Day Souvenir,* published by the Trades and Labor Council of Detroit, reprinted and distributed ten thousand copies of a direct legislation amendment being proposed in New Jersey in 1893. The Democratic Campaign Committee also discussed the topic in serial form in its labor "sheet" edited by trade unionists in 1894. Similarly involved was Miller G. Moore, secretary of the Street Railway Employees' Union, who introduced a referendum amendment in the Michigan legislature in 1895 as a member of the lower house. The plan, which failed to pass, would have allowed ten members of the legislature to call for a referendum on legislation.[2]

The stirrings for direct legislation took on an added dimension in Michigan in the fall of 1895. Following an address by J. W. Sullivan in Detroit, a group led by two local physicians, Dr. George F. Sherman and Dr. David Inglis, formed a Direct Legislation Club and immediately set to work drafting a constitutional amendment. Their initial proposal allowed for voters to initiate statutes and constitutional amendments as well as refer laws passed by the legislature based on petition of 5 percent of the electorate. The initiative and referendum would be extended to each county, township, and municipal corporation under the same percentages. On May 1, 1896, the club began publication of a four-page monthly newsletter titled *Direct Legislation* and claimed to have a list of nearly one thousand subscribers. Encouraged by the growth of other local clubs in the state (there were fifteen to twenty by September) and the inclusion of direct legislation in the state platforms of the Prohibitionist and Populist Parties, Michigan's small band of advocates hoped to gain the support of Detroit mayor Hazen Pingree. In his seventh annual message as mayor of that city, Pingree publicly acknowledged that there was a growing feeling on the part of the public, "due to apprehension that the encroachments of private interests upon legislative bodies may influence those bodies to surrender public rights to even a more serious degree in the future than has marked the past," that the adoption of a system of direct legislation might provide a remedy for the problem. However, the mayor refused to "go to the limit of advocacy"

---

lighting plant, and persuaded another group to construct a rival streetcar line that offered consumers lower fares. Pingree, however, found that state law often blocked changes he wanted to make and was certainly a factor in his interest in the governorship. See Willis Frederick Dunbar, *Michigan: A History of the Wolverine State,* 532. For information on Michigan politics during the 1890s, see ibid., 531–36; Bruce A. Rubenstein and Lawrence E. Ziewacz, *Michigan: A History of the Great Lakes State,* 116–18; and Melvin G. Holli, *Reform in Detroit: Hazen S. Pingree and Urban Politics,* 195–205.

2. See *Direct Legislation Record* 1 (July 1894): 43; and 2 (June 1895): 12.

regarding direct legislation and held himself to the modified position that the issuing of franchises should be decided by popular vote.[3]

By the spring of 1898, the campaign for direct legislation in Michigan seemed to be making headway. George Sherman had been named to the executive committee of the National Direct Legislation League, and the initial Detroit "club" had grown into the Michigan Direct Legislation League with David Inglis, a professor at the Detroit Medical College, as president. Continuing the policy of working for the inclusion of direct legislation in the various party platforms, the league convinced the Democratic Party at its state convention to include a plank favoring the initiative and referendum in 1898. Inglis also announced that the league was taking the novel approach of illustrating the idea behind direct legislation by tying it to two current local option proposals—in method of taxation (single tax) and in method of granting franchises—that could be decided by popular vote.[4]

The real accomplishment of the league, though, according to state secretary G. R. Weikert, was in the respectability that the movement for direct legislation had gained. Said Weikert:

> Two years ago, when we organized, the idea of Direct Legislation was known to but a few individuals in this commonwealth; to-day it is not only known, but understood and appreciated by a majority of the members of labor organizations. . . . Then a . . . partisan who wished to introduce Direct Legislation into the platform of his party was decried a crank, 'a wild-eyed, long-haired Populist,' . . . ; the idea itself was not even considered, much less discussed. . . . Then the press was a unit in its silence on the subject . . . ; now there is hardly a paper in the State that does not . . . draw the attention of its readers to the subject, and, though the press is by no means a unit in its favor, it is invariably discussed earnestly, without sneers or ridicule, as a business proposition for the people to consider earnestly.

Weikert also noted that the major reason for the transformation were the letters and articles written, meetings arranged, and assemblies addressed by members of the league.[5]

Optimists within the Michigan league might have thought their moment of triumph had finally arrived in 1898. Buoyed by the endorsement of the Democratic Party, the league pushed ahead with its campaign to get leg-

---

3. Pingree quoted in *Direct Legislation Record* 3 (March 1896): 12. See also *Direct Legislation Record* 2 (December 1895): 27; and 3 (June 1896): 19–20.

4. See *Direct Legislation Record* 3 (September 1896): 27; 5 (May 1898): 26; and 5 (September 1898): 54.

5. Weikhert, "Direct Legislation in Michigan," *Direct Legislation Record* 5 (June 1898): 44.

islative candidates to pledge themselves to support direct legislation in the legislature. The league again drew up a proposed amendment, printed it with petitions and circulars, and distributed it to between twelve thousand and thirteen thousand voters. The league then managed to get its amendment introduced in the legislature, secured hearings on it, and lobbied vigorously for it, but lost. The explanation seemed clear. As long as the Republican Party refused to endorse the initiative and referendum, and as long as Michigan's conservative electorate continued to sustain Republican majorities in the state legislature, political progress would be difficult.[6]

Disappointed, Inglis announced that the league would adopt a more aggressive political approach. The plan called for the league to map the state, targeting legislators who had voted against their amendment. In districts where the election promised to be close, the league would send speakers, disseminate literature, and hold mass meetings in an attempt to defeat unsupportive legislators. The league also attempted to prod the Democratic Party into taking a stronger stance on direct legislation and seeing it as the issue that could bring them electoral success. To that end, the leaders of the two organizations composed a circular letter that was signed by sixty-seven Democrats from around the state indicating their intention of making direct legislation the issue in the next state political campaign, in 1902. Despite the organizing, publicity, campaigning, and lobbying efforts of the Direct Legislation League, the increased willingness on the part of many of the state's Democrats to embrace the initiative and referendum, and endorsements from the Michigan State Grange and various labor organizations, proponents were still unable to break the impasse at the state capitol.[7]

In 1906, however, it looked like there might be an opportunity to obtain an amendment by a means other than overturning Republican control of the legislature. At a special election held that year, voters cast their ballots in favor of calling a convention to revise the state's constitution. However, either unconvinced that such a convention would automatically include direct legislation in a new constitution or apprehensive concerning the character of that inclusion if delegates were left to their own devices, propo-

6. See Eltweed Pomeroy, "A Michigan D.L. Campaign," *Direct Legislation Record* 6 (June 1899): 26. Direct legislationists did win one victory during the 1899 legislative session when legislators approved the Eikhoff Bill that allowed citizens in Detroit to amend their charter by initiative petition (five thousand voters could force the submission of a charter amendment). See *Direct Legislation Record* 6 (September 1899): 68.

7. See *Direct Legislation Record* 6 (June 1899): 26; and 8 (December 1901): 59. The *Record* noted that "Organized Labor" declared for the initiative and referendum at its annual convention in 1902 and that the chairman of its legislative committee, Matthew J. Lynch, editor of the *Port Huron Labor Leader,* was a strong advocate. See *Direct Legislation Record* 10 (March 1903): 3.

nents pushed hard during the 1907 legislative session to secure an amendment prior to the convention. Despite support from voters who mailed thousands of letters and petitions to the legislature, which the *Lansing Journal* declared was indicative of the campaign in which "two hundred thousand intelligent men and women are actively engaged . . . in this state," the legislature refused to report the amendment, with the explanation that it should be considered by the constitutional convention scheduled to convene later that year.[8]

At the constitutional convention, in which all but eight of the delegates were Republican, conservatives made just enough concessions to the adherents of progressive reform to ensure ratification. Women taxpayers were allowed to vote on bond issues (woman suffrage was rejected). Cities were given home rule and allowed to own and operate public utilities. In addition, the legislature was granted the authority to enact laws limiting hours of work for women and children in factories and regulating the conditions under which they worked. Beyond these revisions, there were only minor changes. The topic of direct legislation generated more interest and discussion than any other, and, according to one observer, delegates divided into three distinct clusters. One group ("a considerable number, but distinctly less than a majority") favored the Oregon model. A second group favored the general idea, but wanted a plan that would prevent hasty and ill-conceived measures. A third group ("comprising almost half the delegates") opposed the initiative and referendum in any form. Realizing the impossibility of gaining an amendment along the lines of the Oregon example, proponents agreed to a limited and restrictive proposal in committee that allowed for the initiative only on constitutional amendments upon petition of 20 percent of those who had voted in the previous election. An affirmative vote of not less than one-third of the votes cast in the election was necessary for adoption.

During the debate before the entire convention, however, opponents encumbered the amendment with additional restrictions: signatures to petitions would have to be verified by registration or election officials, and initiated amendments could appear on the ballot only after they had been approved by a majority vote of the legislature in joint session. Proponents were confronted with the choice of accepting a law that excluded the statutory initiative and referendum, imposed a prohibitive signature requirement, and included a legislative veto that contradicted the theory behind direct popular democracy, or arguing against any law at all. Without the

8. The proposed amendment provided for the initiation of statutes and constitutional amendments upon petition of thirty thousand voters, the referendum upon petition of the same number, and the recall of state officials upon petition of fifty thousand. See *Equity* 9 (April 1907): 13.

votes to defeat the measure, aware that the opportunity afforded by the calling of a constitutional convention would not soon come again, and perhaps wishfully hoping that the ineffectiveness of the current law could be remedied by future legislative action, proponents saw little alternative other than to acquiesce. Voters approved the state's revised constitution with its unworkable direct legislative feature in November 1908 by a vote of 244,705 to 130,783.[9]

Between 1910 and 1912 the spirit of reform that had taken hold of national and state politics began to show itself in Michigan as well. Voters elected Republican Chase S. Osborn governor in 1910 on a progressive platform, and in his message to the legislature in 1911 he included a request for a more liberal initiative and referendum amendment. Under Osborn's leadership the legislature passed a number of major reforms—regulation of railroads, expanded state authority over business, revision of the state tax structure, a state primary law, and a workmen's compensation act—but declined to enact the initiative and referendum. His successor, Governor Woodbridge N. Ferris, a progressive Democrat, repeated the request after his election in 1912 and won a favorable response from the legislature. Designed to replace the restrictive direct legislation clause in the constitution (the provision had never been employed) were two amendments. The first allowed for the direct initiative on constitutional amendments and lowered the signature requirement to 10 percent. The second allowed for the indirect initiative (with a requirement of 8 percent) and referendum (requiring only 5 percent) on statutes. Proposed laws first had to be submitted to the legislature for approval or rejection. The legislature could propose a substitute measure on the same topic, in which case both the original and the substitute would appear on the ballot. Voters approved the constitutional initiative (204,796 to 162,392), the indirect statutory initiative, and the referendum (219,057 to 152,388) at the spring election in 1913.[10]

The fact that a workable system of direct legislation had finally been adopted in Michigan did not mean, however, that it signaled an abandonment of the state's traditional conservative political tendencies. In fact, voters considered only four initiated amendments between 1914 and 1918 (no voter-initiated statutes and no voter-initiated referenda appeared on the ballot). In 1914 and again in 1916 voters considered propositions relating to the incorporation, regulation, and supervision of fraternal benefit and insurance societies. Ironically, the interesting feature in these rather minor

9. See John A. Fairlie, "The Referendum and Initiative in Michigan," *Annals of the American Academy* 43 (September 1912): 150–54, 158; James K. Pollock, *The Initiative and Referendum in Michigan,* 3; *Equity* 10 (April 1908): 37–39; and Dunbar, *Michigan,* 538.

10. See Pollock, *Initiative and Referendum,* 3–5; Rubenstein and Ziewacz, *Michigan,* 189–90; and *Equity* 15 (July 1913): 189.

measures was the proposed application of the principles of the initiative and referendum to the operation of those associations. Under the proposals, promoted by the New Era Mutual Insurance Association, such societies would have been required to submit to state regulation and operate more democratically by providing the opportunity to change their constitutions upon petition of 10 percent of the membership or to recall officers of an organization by majority vote if 15 percent of the membership so demanded. The idea was vigorously opposed by a majority of the state's other fraternal benefit and insurance societies, and voters rejected it on both occasions by decisive majorities.

In 1916 voters were asked to decide two liquor questions. The first proposal, for statewide prohibition, was supported by the Anti-Saloon League of Michigan and opposed by the Michigan Home Rule League, a "wet" campaign organization. Voters decided it was time to go "dry" and approved the amendment. A second proposal, sponsored by the Michigan Home Rule League and opposed by the Anti-Saloon League of Michigan, called for local option by "cities, villages and townships" in place of the existing county option method. Voters rejected this limited alternative to a statewide ban.[11]

In assessing Michigan's limited record on ballot propositions from the perspective of 1940, one historian of Michigan's electoral behavior concludes:

> No proposition has ever been presented which would have vitally changed the structure of government; no issue has come up which would seriously disturb vested economic interest; and many issues which are raised in other states with apparent ease have not appeared in Michigan. This failure to resort to the initiative and referendum appears to indicate the Michigan voter's apathy toward, or satisfaction with, his general governmental arrangements.[12]

That verdict is perhaps too harsh. In addition to the few initiated measures on the ballot, voters were asked to consider twenty-one constitutional amendments passed by the Michigan legislature between 1910 and 1918. Among the important political topics included in that list were woman suffrage (defeated in 1912 and 1913, approved in 1918), liberalizing the use of the initiative and referendum (approved in 1913), and the recall of public officials (approved in 1913).

11. For a listing of Michigan's use of direct legislation to 1918, see Pollock, *Initiative and Referendum,* app. 3; *Equity* 16 (October 1914): 180; and George Judson King Papers, Library of Congress, Manuscripts Division, Washington, D.C.

12. Pollock, *Initiative and Referendum,* 42–43.

NORTH DAKOTA

Another state controlled by a single party staunchly opposed to any reform agenda was North Dakota. As mentioned earlier, the late 1880s was a difficult time for farmers in Dakota Territory. They complained that wheat prices were well below production costs and that buyers unfairly graded their grain. When markets continued to be depressed, farmers increasingly talked of market manipulation. From their point of view, the marketing system for grain was severely flawed. Millers, centered in Minneapolis, had formed an association to eliminate competition in purchasing wheat. In cooperation with the major railroads, they controlled lines of grain elevators at one end and the terminal market at the other. Such an arrangement forced out independent elevator operators and left the wheat producer at the mercy of a monopoly.[13]

Through the newly organized (in 1885) Dakota Territorial (Farmers') Alliance, farmers demanded reform. Specifically, they urged the legislature to pass laws that would force the railroads to end discrimination in the selection of grain elevator sites and require them to provide an adequate supply of freight cars at harvest time. They called for an "elected" board of railroad commissioners with power to set maximum rates, regulate storage facilities, and standardize grain-grading practices. They also demanded that the legislature tax corporate property on a par with other property, and that it pass a maximum interest-rate law.

In spite of their complaints, farmers had little to show for their efforts. The territorial assembly of 1885 passed the Free Market Act, but the law granted only supervisory powers to the Board of Railroad Commissioners and left it virtually powerless to fix rates or enforce its recommendations. The 1887 legislature approved a maximum interest-rate law, but rendered it virtually useless by allowing rates above 7 percent to be set by mutual consent of lender and borrower. It also successfully delayed any vote on railroad legislation. When the last territorial legislature met in 1889, the alliance controlled a majority in the lower house. Nonetheless, it still could not get its program passed. A bill to provide an adequate supply of freight cars at harvest time was ineffective, and a maximum interest-rate bill was "lost" or "stolen" as the legislature came to a close. Other alliance-sponsored bills were either "sidetracked" or "vetoed." Five years of political campaigning had left the grain elevator, railroad, and banking interests virtually unscathed.[14]

13. See D. Robinson, *History of South Dakota,* 1:294–325; E. B. Robinson, *History of North Dakota,* 203–4. For an excellent account of economic problems facing Dakota farmers during the 1880s and early 1890s, see Glenn Lowell Brudvig, "The Farmers' Alliance and Populist Movement in North Dakota, 1884–1896," 1–33.

14. See E. B. Robinson, *History of North Dakota,* 204–7; and Brudvig, "Farmers' Al-

Political reform for farmers in North Dakota was made especially difficult by the unique political situation in the state. Not only was North Dakota dominated by a single political party, the GOP, but the party itself was controlled by a political machine run by "Boss" Alexander McKenzie as well. McKenzie's power came from his corporate connections. He acted as "agent" for railroad, insurance, banking, line, and terminal elevator companies headquartered outside the state. His highest priority was to make sure that legislation adversely affecting the interests of those corporations was defeated. McKenzie's management of corporate-sponsored campaign funds and free railroad passes ensured his control over party-nominating conventions as well as legislative caucuses and committee assignments. He could not prevent the passage of all reform legislation, but his control over the state administration rendered enforcement ineffectual. Minneapolis grain merchants, distant railroad corporations, and eastern bankers controlled the economic life of North Dakota, and Alexander McKenzie personified that control.[15]

Statehood seemed to generate a new sense of civic responsibility, and the first state legislature, which met in 1890, passed numerous measures regulating transportation and the trade in grain. The Board of Railroad Commissioners was granted power to regulate railroads and grain elevators, to fix "reasonable" railroad rates, and to determine grades for North Dakota wheat. Railroads could not discriminate in the location of their storage facilities, freight car availability, or rates. Grain elevator operators could not fix prices, allocate trade, or mix grades of grain. Elevators had to be licensed, operators had to be bonded, and elevators had to adhere to set charges for the storage of grain. Even banking did not escape state regulation. Normal interest rates were set at 7 percent, with an absolute limit of 12 percent by mutual consent of lender and borrower. Farmers appeared to have gotten everything for which they had campaigned, and the McKenzie machine appeared to have deferred to a stronger popular will. According to historian Elwyn Robinson, though, "the laws were so faultily drawn, so complicated, and so contradictory that they were a failure."[16]

Legislative disappointments, coupled with a severe drought during the summer of 1890, led farmers to organize a new political party. The Inde-

---

liance," 34–68, 101–34. Brudvig notes that the leaders of the alliance in North Dakota were nearly all highly successful farmers. For the role of the alliance in Dakota politics prior to 1890, see Larry Remele, "'God Helps Those Who Help Themselves': The Farmers' Alliance and Dakota Statehood," 22–33.

15. See Raymond V. Anderson, "Adoption and Operation of Initiative and Referendum in North Dakota," 32–35; Charles N. Glaab, "The Revolution of 1906: N.D. vs. McKenzie," 101–2; Bruce Nelson, *Land of the Dacotahs*, 253; and David B. Baglien, "The McKenzie Era: A Political History of North Dakota, 1880–1920."

16. E. B. Robinson, *History of North Dakota*, 220–21. See also Lewis F. Crawford, *History of North Dakota*, 378.

pendent Party, organized in September, chose Walter Muir, a Cass County
farmer and former president of the North Dakota Alliance, as its nominee
for governor. The late start hampered the new party electorally, though.
Muir received only 13 percent of the vote in the fall election, and voters
elected only eight Independents to the legislature. Loyalty to the Republican Party, in North Dakota as in South Dakota, proved difficult to break.
The 1891 legislature did pass a number of reform bills: an Australian ballot
law, an antiusury law, and a "platform law" that allowed farmers to bypass
local elevators and sell their wheat to track buyers who used loading platforms. However, when Governor Andrew Burke vetoed a bill that would
have designated all warehouses and grain elevators as public facilities and
placed them under strict regulatory control, farmers once again felt betrayed.[17]

Falling wheat prices, Governor Burke's unpopular veto of the elevator-
warehouse bill, and general dissatisfaction with the national Republican
Party, gave the Independent Party a chance in 1892. At their state convention in Valley City, they embraced the Populist Party platform and nominated a full slate of candidates. Independents-Populists, alliance men, and
Democrats then combined forces to elect Independent Eli Shortridge as
governor. Shortridge, a farmer and recent president of the Farmers' Alliance, had campaigned on an anticorporation platform and promised to
build a state-owned terminal elevator somewhere on the Great Lakes. In
addition to the governorship, the Independents-Populists captured every
state office except secretary of state, but the Republicans controlled the legislature. As a result, the legislature failed to enact any major reforms. According to Governor Shortridge, "[E]very bill brought before the Legislature . . . that was not satisfactory to the corporations, and could not be
otherwise defeated, was either stolen, mutilated, or destroyed in some way
to prevent them from becoming laws of the State." As a result, the Shortridge administration was a failure. Excessive spending bankrupted the
state treasury, and the panic of 1893–1894 further reduced farm prices and
destroyed any plans for a state-owned grain elevator. With Populism dis-
credited, the Republicans were able to win back farmer loyalty and sweep
the election in 1894. Populism, at least the 1890s version, never recovered
in North Dakota. When William Jennings Bryan brought his "free silver"
campaign to the state in 1896, disillusioned voters decisively rejected it.[18]

17. See E. B. Robinson, *History of North Dakota,* 204, 221–22; L. F. Crawford, *History of
North Dakota,* 378; and Brudvig, "Farmers' Alliance," 135–70.

18. Shortridge quoted in E. B. Robinson, *History of North Dakota,* 225 (see also 222–
25). See also L. F. Crawford, *History of North Dakota,* 380–82; D. Jerome Tweton, "North
Dakota in the 1890s: Its People, Politics, and Press," 112–18; and Brudvig, "Farmers' Alliance," 171–91.

One individual who sympathized with the farmer was Lars A. Ueland. Born in Wisconsin in 1855, Ueland spent the first twenty years of his life on a farm. He eventually left home to attend Luther College in Decorah, Iowa, and farmed in Iowa for nearly ten years. He came to Dakota Territory in 1887 and homesteaded near Edgeley in La Moure County. Ueland became successful as a wheat farmer, horticulturist of fruit trees, and raiser of prime beef stock. Ueland actively promoted farming in North Dakota as a member of the Grain Growers' Association. He was also an astute businessman, reinvesting his profits in additional land (farming almost one thousand acres by 1909), banks, and other business ventures.[19]

Ueland, as a practical farmer, observed the political economy in North Dakota with a great deal of concern. During the late 1880s and early 1890s, Ueland joined the earliest efforts to bring about economic improvement for Dakota farmers. He soon became prominent in the local Farmers' Alliance in Edgeley and active in the Dakota Territorial Alliance. He also took an active interest in politics, and gained election to the first legislative assembly of 1889–1890 as a Republican. Ueland quickly realized, however, that agrarian reforms would not be forthcoming from a party controlled by corporate and financial interests. After his first term in office, he severed his ties to the Republican Party. During 1892 he contributed an editorial column to the *Edgeley Mail* titled "Alliance Department." He used his column to try to convince others that the policies of the Republican Party were becoming increasingly antagonistic to the interests of farmers and that an independent political course was necessary. As a leader of the political opposition, Ueland won election as chairman of the central committee of the newly formed Independent-Populist Party of La Moure County. He followed this with nomination as a state representative on that ticket and election to the legislature in 1892.[20]

Ueland's political thinking took an important turn in 1892. While attending the Populist Party convention in Omaha, Nebraska, he became acquainted with the idea of direct legislation. The Populist Party platform had "commended" two novel reform ideas—the initiative and referendum—to the "thoughtful consideration of the people and the reform press," and Ueland was struck with a sense of their value. He began to give these ideas serious consideration as a member of the legislature in 1893, and actually introduced the first measures for the initiative and referendum in North Dakota during that session. Ueland had no hope for the passage of

19. See "Representative Ueland," *North Dakota Magazine* 1 (February 1907): 111–12; North Dakota, *Legislative Manual, 1907,* 380; *Edgeley Mail,* September 24, 1909; and Anderson, "Adoption and Operation," 29–30.

20. See *Bismarck Daily Tribune,* November 21, 1889; *Edgeley Mail,* March 25, April 1, September 2, 20, 1892; and Anderson, "Adoption and Operation," 35–38.

his bills, but said that he felt it was important to introduce them as "educational" measures. House Bills 142 and 148 called for the statewide referendum based on a petition of 5 percent of the qualified voters, and the statewide initiative based on a similar 10 percent petition. Ueland's bills were lost in a legislative session dominated by debates over the selection of a U.S. senator, woman suffrage, and resubmission of the prohibition clause of the state constitution. Nevertheless, Ueland had at least started the discussion of alternative legislative methods. The *Bismarck Daily Tribune* commented that Ueland's proposals had provided "food for thought," and the newspaper's founder, Colonel Clement A. Lounsberry, stated: "Two more men like Ueland would revolutionize legislation." Perhaps most important, though, Ueland seemed to have convinced himself that the initiative and referendum could supply the means to improve popular self-government.[21]

During the next several years the initiative and referendum made little progress in North Dakota. The dominating presence of the McKenzie-controlled Republican Party and the general weakness of the Populists worked against the success of the initiative and referendum. The McKenzie machine regarded direct legislation as a threat both to its political control and to the special interests it protected. As long as the McKenzie machine went unchallenged, most newspapers in the state followed its lead and either ignored the initiative and referendum or dismissed the reforms as a "passing hobby." North Dakota Populists added a direct legislation plank to their platform in 1894, and the national Populist Party took a similar step in 1896. The effect of this in North Dakota was to link the reforms even more strongly to radical third-party demands. Populist, or "fusionist," representatives continued to introduce bills for the initiative and referendum in the legislative sessions of 1895, 1897, and 1899. These measures were referred to the appropriate subcommittee and then indefinitely postponed.[22]

Another element inhibiting support for the initiative and referendum was the influence of the prohibition lobby in North Dakota. The Women's Christian Temperance Union (WCTU) had been active in Dakota Territory

21. Lounsberry quoted in Anderson, "Adoption and Operation," 40 (see also 38–40). See also *House Journal of the Third Session of the North Dakota Legislative Assembly, 1893,* 573–75, 647–48; and *Valley City Times-Record,* October 29, 1908.

22. There were reportedly 163 newspapers in the state in 1900, 146 of which were Republican. See Anderson, "Adoption and Operation," 41–48; and E. B. Robinson, *History of North Dakota,* 230. For brief descriptions of the initiative and referendum proposals and an extensive listing of page references, see *Senate Journal of the Fourth Session of the North Dakota Legislative Assembly, 1895; House Journal of the Fifth Session of the North Dakota Legislative Assembly, 1897;* and *Senate Journal of the Sixth Session of the North Dakota Legislative Assembly, 1899.*

since 1882, and a prohibition amendment had been approved with the state constitution in 1889. Because the initial vote on prohibition had been so close (18,552 to 17,393), temperance advocates were constantly on guard against efforts to reintroduce liquor into the state. This was especially true after 1895 when the neighboring state of South Dakota repealed the prohibition amendment to its state constitution. As a result, the WCTU kept an active presence in Bismarck whenever the legislature was in session. President Elizabeth Preston Anderson took personal charge of lobbying efforts and utilized telegrams, letters, and petitions from her tightly knit, well-organized union to defeat each legislative challenge. With the appearance of the initiative and referendum, prohibitionists were even more alarmed. The initiative could bring prohibition to a popular vote and provide a short-cut method of subverting the constitutional amendment process, whereas existing law required approval of two consecutive legislatures before submission to the electorate. In states that did not have prohibition amendments, temperance advocates usually supported direct legislation. In North Dakota, they tended to be against it.[23]

In spite of the unfavorable political climate, Lars Ueland continued to work to publicize the merits of the initiative and referendum. He contributed articles to newspapers in La Moure County and to the *North Dakota Independent*, and continued an active interest in politics. However, Ueland found political office elusive, suffering defeat as a Populist-Democratic candidate for lieutenant governor in 1894, for state representative in 1896 and 1898, and for U.S. congressman in 1902. Ueland did, however, gain modest recognition as a delegate to the organizing convention of the National Direct Legislation League in St. Louis on July 21, 1896. Those in attendance elected vice presidents for every state and territory who would act as organizing officers in their districts. Ueland, who had already established a reputation as a spokesperson for the initiative and referendum, was chosen to represent North Dakota. He was also one of seven individuals se-

23. The political influence of the WCTU, supported by a significant number of Republicans, Norwegian Americans, and Protestant churches, was not lost on the McKenzie machine. When bills were introduced that threatened the status quo of railroads or related businesses, the machine could, on occasion, use the threat of resubmission to block such legislation. If the WCTU would help defeat such regulatory measures, the machine would kill any resubmission resolution. For information on the goals and tactics of the prohibition forces in North Dakota, see Robert P. Wilkins, "Alexander McKenzie and the Politics of Bossism"; Bill G. Reid, "Elizabeth Preston Anderson and the Politics of Social Reform," 28, 183–202; Elizabeth Preston Anderson, "The Story of Fifty Years," "Under the Prairie Wind," and "New Year's Letter," Elizabeth Preston Anderson Papers, North Dakota State University, North Dakota Institute for Regional Studies, Fargo; Anderson, "Adoption and Operation," 53–61; and E. B. Robinson, *History of North Dakota*, 258–59.

lected to serve on the executive committee of the new organization, and soon became an active contributor of articles to the *Direct Legislation Record*, the official publication of the Direct Legislation League.[24]

Ueland was unable, however, to transfer organizational enthusiasm to North Dakota, even after neighboring South Dakota adopted a direct leg- islation amendment to its constitution in 1898. The state was still without a local direct legislation league in 1900, and all work for direct legislation was done solely by individuals. Katherine V. King, active in the Social Re- form Union, an organization dedicated to broadening the discussion of the basic principles of democracy and supportive of direct legislation, stated: "The present movement for Direct Legislation in North Dakota is unique in that it has behind it no popular demand and is not the result of any po- litical propaganda." King attempted to fill the void in 1902 with the orga- nization of the North Dakota Referendum League (an affiliate of the Peo- ple's Sovereignty League of America), but the organization was ineffective. It was not until August 1906 that a branch of the National Federation of People's Rule (the result of a merging of the People's Sovereignty League and the National Direct Legislation League) took root in the state and ef- fectively aided the cause of direct legislation.[25]

The initiative and referendum began to gain respectability in North Dakota when George B. Winship, the influential reform editor and pub- lisher of the *Grand Forks Herald,* added those reforms to his political agen- da. Winship had been critical of Boss McKenzie's control of Republican pol- itics and his obvious connections to eastern corporate interests as far back as the 1880s. However, Winship, a Republican editor, had chosen to con- demn the McKenzie machine while remaining loyal to the Republican Par- ty. In 1897, however, Winship decided to break with the party, and called upon all North Dakota voters to throw out the "gang politicians." Win- ship's action triggered a split in the state Republican Party between west- ern "stalwarts" (McKenzie men) and eastern "insurgents" (that is, reform- ers) that ultimately came to a head in the Progressive revolt of 1906. By 1899 Winship was openly advocating giving voters a stronger voice in govern- ment, and his specific proposals had broadened to include the direct elec- tion of senators and the initiative and referendum. During one six-week period in early 1900 Winship devoted more than thirty columns of his newspaper to a discussion of direct legislation. According to one observer, this was having an effect. "As [Winship] is frequently mentioned for Gov-

24. See Anderson, "Adoption and Operation," 40–48; and *Direct Legislation Record* 3 (September 1896): 25–28.

25. King quoted in *Direct Legislation Record* 7 (March 1900): 13. See also *Direct Legis- lation Record* 7 (December 1900): 68; and Anderson, "Adoption and Operation," 49. For biographical information on King, see *Direct Legislation Record* 10 (June 1903): 40.

ernor, his course is attracting widespread attention, even outside the State."
The reform faction of the Republican Party nominated Winship for governor at its state convention in 1900, but the McKenzie machine successfully
defeated him.[26]

By 1902 the campaign for direct legislation in North Dakota appeared to
be making progress. Katherine King organized the first Referendum League
that September. The new organization worked at generating a membership
list that could be used to support a league-backed initiative and referendum bill in the 1903 legislature. The Referendum League questioned candidates for the legislature in each of the forty districts in the state to get their
position on direct legislation, and distributed a large amount of information supplied by the National Federation for Majority Rule. Support was
also forthcoming from the state Democratic Party, which declared itself in
favor of a law that would "enable the people to initiate and control legislation." The Grand Forks County Republican Convention, undoubtedly inspired by George Winship, also endorsed direct legislation.[27]

Two more attempts to pass direct legislation measures took place in the
1903 and 1905 sessions of the legislature. Senator Charles W. Plain, a Democrat from Cavalier County, introduced the 1903 bill. Plain's measure, actually drafted by Ueland, allowed for the initiative and referendum based
on petitions of 5 percent of the voters, whereas 15 percent of the voters
could petition to propose a constitutional amendment. The Senate approved the bill by the surprising vote of twenty-three to ten, with fourteen
Republicans joining nine Democrats in the majority. The real debate, however, occurred after the measure had been sent to the House. Supporters
argued that direct legislation would diminish the influence of lobbyists,
prevent bad legislation, and promote good legislation. Many insurgent Republicans hoped that direct legislation might speed the passage of a direct
primary law, which they thought was necessary to break machine control
over the nominating process. Opponents continued to link the measure to
Populist radicalism, and argued that the 15 percent petition would endanger the constitutional amendment process. Opponents used this last point
to rally the powerful prohibition lobby.

Many prohibitionists regarded the measure as a scheme on the part of
resubmissionists. The *White Ribbon Bulletin,* the official publication of the
WCTU in North Dakota, warned its readers to take heed: "[T]here is little

26. Winship quoted in D. Jerome Tweton, "Sectionalism in North Dakota Politics: The
Progressive Republican Revolt of 1900," 22 (see also 21–28); "Other observer" quoted
in *Direct Legislation Record* 7 (March 1900): 13. See also E. B. Robinson, *History of North
Dakota,* 263–64; and Edward C. Blackorby, "George B. Winship: Progressive Journalist
of the Middle Border," 5–17.
27. See *Direct Legislation Record* 9 (September 1902): 45; and 9 (December 1902): 67.

question but that the first amendment proposed will be to repeal that clause of the constitution prohibiting the manufacture and sale of intoxicating liquor."[28] As a result, the WCTU lent its considerable support to the opposition, and the Plain Bill was defeated. Senator Alex MacDonald, a Republican, introduced a measure identical to the Plain Bill late in the 1905 session, and gained a favorable report from the judiciary committee. This time the machine used its control of the steering committee to delay the bill until the rush of legislative business at the end of the session prevented its full consideration. Nevertheless, advocates of direct legislation took solace from the fact that they were making progress. The issue had gained a hearing, interest seemed to be increasing, and newspapers seemed generally more favorable. At the same time there were signs of incipient rebellion within the ranks of the Republican Party.[29]

The dissension that had been stirring within the Republican Party since 1897 finally turned into open rebellion in 1906. Late in 1905 Republican insurgents, denied a comprehensive direct primary law by the machine, organized the Good Government League of North Dakota with George Winship as its president. Utilizing the support of insurgent newspapers such as the *Grand Forks Herald*, they began a campaign to end corporate-machine control of state government. As Winship reminded his readers in the *Herald*: "There is just one issue before the people of North Dakota this year; and that is whether the people are ready to take charge of their government."[30]

The insurgents received a tremendous boost with the appearance of the first installment of Rex Beach's "Looting of Alaska" in *Appleton's* magazine in January 1906. As sensational as the best of the current muckraking exposés, the article described a scheme on the part of Alexander McKenzie to gain control of gold claims in Alaska. Caught up in the gold fever of 1900, McKenzie had organized the Alaskan Mining Company as a means for speculation. When U.S. law prohibited his access to claims in the area, McKenzie used his influence with the McKinley administration to get a personal friend, Alfred H. Noyes, appointed judge of Alaska's Second Judicial District (where the disputed properties were located). Noyes then made McKenzie receiver of all contested claims. When McKenzie boldly violated a federal injunction and proceeded to work the claims for himself,

28. WCTU quoted in Anderson, "Adoption and Operation," 60. See also *White Ribbon Bulletin* 10 (March 1903): 2.

29. See Anderson, "Adoption and Operation," 50–53, 59–62; *Senate Journal of the Eighth Session of the North Dakota Legislative Assembly, 1903*, 57, 63, 335–37, 428–29; *House Journal of the Eighth Session of the North Dakota Legislative Assembly, 1903*, 655, 732–33; *Direct Legislation Record* 10 (March 1903): 5; 5 (June 1903): 29; and *Senate Journal of the Ninth Session of the North Dakota Legislative Assembly, 1905*, 367, 534.

30. Winship quoted in Charles N. Glaab, "John Burke and the Progressive Revolt," 57.

though, he was arrested, convicted of contempt of court, and sentenced to a year in jail. The incident added new urgency to the demand that voters end the era of "McKenzieism" in North Dakota.[31]

The final break between insurgents and stalwarts came at the Republican State Convention in 1906. When stalwarts again refused to yield control of the convention and proceeded to nominate machine candidates, insurgents abandoned their party and supported John Burke, a progressive Democrat, for the governorship. Burke also won the support of Protestant church groups and prohibitionists who liked his emphasis on honest government and law enforcement. Back from the brink of extinction in 1904, when their candidate for governor lost the election by a three-to-one margin and they could count only five senators and one representative in the statehouse, the Democrats rallied around an attractive candidate and a liberal-reform platform to elect Burke and a clear majority to the lower house of the legislature in 1906. The Democratic program included an expanded direct primary law, tax equalization, child labor legislation, the enforcement of laws regulating railroads and prohibition, and the initiative and referendum.[32]

Progressive Republicans and Democrats rallied behind two reform measures—a more extensive direct primary law and the initiative and referendum—in 1907 in hopes that voters could gain direct control over the political process for the first time. Appropriately, Lars Ueland, elected to the House as a Democrat in 1906, introduced the direct legislation amendment. Ueland modeled his bill after the existing Oregon law, and had corresponded with the leading direct legislation advocates in that state. As initially proposed, the bill called for a 5 percent petition for the referendum, and an 8 percent petition for both the statutory and the constitutional initiatives. In an obvious attempt to placate prohibitionists, Ueland qualified the use of the constitutional initiative by stipulating that the same constitutional amendment could not be proposed more often than once every ten years.[33]

The debate over the Ueland Bill was a heated one. Ueland, speaking for the Democrats and many progressive Republicans, argued that direct legislation simply meant majority rule. "It stands for a simple and effective means of getting a popular expression, which in turn will prevent corruption, bribery, graft and bossism in politics, and the encroachment of corporate powers on the rights and liberties of the people." Ueland admitted that

31. See ibid., 55–56; Glaab, "Revolution of 1906," 103–5; and E. B. Robinson, *History of North Dakota*, 265–66.

32. See Glaab, "Progressive Revolt," 50; and Glaab, "Revolution of 1906," 105–8.

33. See E. B. Robinson, *History of North Dakota*, 266; Anderson, "Adoption and Operation," 68–69; and *Bismarck Daily Tribune*, January 25, 1907.

the voters of North Dakota were not as well informed about the merits of direct legislation as they were in some states, but argued that they were quickly being educated by events. "They are coming to see that there is no hope for reform under the existing system of voting."[34] Lending further support, but providing grist for the opposition at the same time, were the resubmissionists, who thought the Ueland Bill offered the opportunity for a vote on prohibition.

Leading the opposition were the machine Republicans who took the position that the Ueland Bill was socialistic in principle and populist in sentiment. When Ueland's bill came up for a vote, many progressive Republicans deserted him and joined with the stalwarts in an unlikely coalition. Some opposed the measure because it included the constitutional initiative and would diminish the importance of deliberative bodies in modifying the constitution. More pointedly, others did so because they either supported prohibition or represented a strong prohibition constituency. When a vote to indefinitely postpone the bill carried by a vote of fifty to forty-seven, Ueland agreed to drop the constitutional initiative provision. The House then passed the modified Ueland Bill by the decisive vote of seventy-two to seventeen.[35]

Passage of the amended Ueland Bill in the House meant that it then had to gain approval in the stalwart-controlled Senate. When the bill got to the Senate it was referred to the judiciary committee, chaired by an ardent resubmissionist. There the bill was again revised and the clause relating to constitutional amendments reinserted. As expected, outraged prohibitionists raised a storm of protest when the bill reached the Senate floor. They accused resubmissionists of manipulating the measure solely for the purpose of overturning prohibition. Ueland was forced to defend his bill by stating that it "was not demanded by the resubmissionists as such, nor given any particular enthusiastic support by them until the natural opponents of direct legislation and a few over zealous prohibitionists had whipped them in by the cry of resubmission." The balance of power in this contest was held by the stalwarts, who, ultimately, joined with the resubmissionists (possibly as a payback for the desertion of prohibitionists in 1906) and approved the bill. It was then up to the House to accept essentially the same bill it had previously rejected. In the end, due primarily to the persistent lobbying of Ueland, the House reversed itself and passed the initiative and referendum measure by a vote of fifty-three to forty. Under North Dakota law the proposed amendment still had to pass the next session of the legislature, in 1909, before being submitted to a

34. *Valley City Times-Record*, April 4, 1907.
35. See ibid. and Anderson, "Adoption and Operation," 68, 70–73.

popular vote. Everyone expected the ensuing campaign to be hotly contested.[36]

The campaign for the Ueland Bill began as soon as the legislative session ended. Looking to broaden the popular base of support for the initiative and referendum statewide, supporters of the Ueland Bill organized the North Dakota Direct Legislation League in the summer of 1907. Apparently hoping to mute the prohibitionist challenge, organizers of the new league elected H. H. Aaker, the Prohibition Party candidate for governor in 1904, as their president. Ueland was chosen secretary and press agent. Both Ueland and Aaker wrote extensively for the cause, their articles appearing in daily and weekly newspapers throughout North Dakota. The league intensified its fund-raising activities to support the publication of printed material and to sponsor Ueland on a speaking tour of the state. When Ueland delivered an especially effective speech at Valley City on January 13, 1908, the Direct Legislation League had ten thousand copies of the address printed for distribution throughout the state. President George H. Shibley of the National Direct Legislation League presented a copy to Senator Robert L. Owen of Oklahoma, who had it memorialized to Congress. Senator Owen then used his franking privilege to have sixty thousand copies of the speech mailed in North Dakota.[37]

Having worked to improve their organization, the advocates of direct legislation sought to strengthen their political position as well. Supporters of direct legislation made a special effort to undermine the prohibitionist argument. Leading prohibitionists like Aaker argued that prohibition and direct legislation were not incompatible, and that the principle of majority rule was too important to be denied for any reason. Said Aaker: "I believe in government by the people and I cannot afford to take the . . . position that because it makes it easier to get a vote on resubmission, I must therefore oppose." The suggestion that prohibitionists in North Dakota were hypocritical was supported from the pulpit as well. The Reverend J. H. Batten, pastor of the Plymouth Congregational Church in Grand Forks, in a sermon titled "Direct Legislation and the Prohibitory Law," argued: "To oppose this principle [direct legislation] in North Dakota in the interest of prohibition, while supporting it in almost every other state . . . in the interest of prohibition, is short sighted selfishness and essentially dishonest." Oth-

36. Ueland quoted in Anderson, "Adoption and Operation," 78. The legislature also passed the more extensive direct primary law (see 74–78). See also *House Journal of the Tenth Session of the North Dakota Legislative Assembly, 1907*, for H.B. 26; and *Senate Journal of the Tenth Session of the North Dakota Legislative Assembly, 1907*, for S.B. 41. A copy of the Ueland Bill is printed in *Equity* 9 (July 1907): 7–8.

37. See Anderson, "Adoption and Operation," 78–97; "Majority Rule or the Initiative and Referendum," address delivered by Ueland in Valley City, January 13, 1908; and *Valley City Times-Record*, July 25, 1907, February 27, July 2, 1908.

ers took a softer line and suggested that prohibitionists had nothing to fear. They argued that after living for twenty years under prohibition, it would be difficult for a majority to vote to bring back the saloon. Besides, it was apparent to many that prohibition was marching forward as a national issue rather than backward.[38]

Opponents of the Ueland Bill wasted little time in organizing their own campaign. Elizabeth Preston Anderson summarized the position of her organization at the WCTU Institute held during the Chautauqua assembly at Devil's Lake on July 6, 1907. Temperance people, said Anderson, favored the initiative and referendum, but only if applied to statutory as opposed to constitutional matters. It was absurd, she argued, to make the constitution as easy to alter as statutory law. The provision preventing the same amendment from being proposed more often than once in ten years was meaningless, because resubmissionists would simply modify the bill to get around the law. The result would be a prohibition vote every four years; a flood of money into the state from national brewers, distillers, and liquor dealers (Ueland, a prohibitionist himself, was accused of having his travel expenses paid by the liquor interests); and, ultimately, local temperance forces being overwhelmed in an unfair contest.

To add emphasis to their campaign, the WCTU adopted resolutions against the bill, as did the State Enforcement League, the Scandinavian Total Abstinence Society, the State Sunday School Association, and the Annual Conference of the Methodist Episcopal Church. The WCTU distributed literature, kept members informed through the *White Ribbon Bulletin,* and worked to secure the nomination of candidates who would vote against the Ueland Bill. With twenty years of lobbying experience, and with more than two thousand members and 150 local unions, the WCTU easily overmatched the Direct Legislation League. When Governor Burke lent support to the opposition by making several speeches against the provisions of the Ueland Bill that applied to constitutional amendments, it began to look as though the measure would be defeated. Finally, as if a portent of things to come, Ueland himself was defeated in his bid for reelection by C. H. Sheils, a staunch prohibitionist.[39]

38. Aaker quoted in *Valley City Times-Record,* July 25, 1907; Batten quoted in ibid., February 27, 1908. See also Anderson, "Adoption and Operation," 78–97.

39. See Anderson, "Adoption and Operation," 78–97; *White Ribbon Bulletin,* August 1907, January 1909; *Report of the Nineteenth Annual Meeting of the Woman's Christian Temperance Union of North Dakota,* 29; and *Valley City Times-Record,* February 13, November 19, December 3, 1908. Ueland's defeat was part of the Republican sweep of 1908. Ueland came within thirteen votes of defeating his Republican opponent in a county that voted two to one for Taft over Bryan. Ueland actually received nearly one hundred votes more than Governor Burke, who was reelected. See *Valley City Times-Record,* November 19, December 3, 1908; and North Dakota, *Legislative Manual, 1909,* 212, 244, 285.

The fight over direct legislation in 1909 proved to be demoralizing for most supporters. Martin Thoreson of Barnes County reintroduced the Ueland Bill in the House in 1909. Ueland, who went to Bismarck to lobby for it, found himself powerless to save it, though. The House formally sent the bill to the judiciary committee, which killed it with the recommendation that the measure be indefinitely postponed. The debate, however, was not yet finished. Representative Bardi G. Skulason of Grand Forkes, chairman of the judiciary committee and floor leader of the progressive Republicans, introduced a substitute measure. The Skulason Bill, which passed the House after amendment, dropped the constitutional initiative, increased the signatures required for initiative petitions to 20 percent and for referendum petitions to 15 percent, and required that such figures be met by voters in one-half of the counties in the state.

Senator Plain introduced a competing bill in the Senate. The Plain Bill, which the Senate passed after amendment, complicated matters further when it added the constitutional initiative, changed the petition requirements for both the initiative and the referendum to 10 percent of the voters in at least three-fifths of the counties in the state, and excluded laws relating to appropriations from the referendum. The result was a legislative impasse that allowed prohibitionists to claim victory once again. The stalwart-controlled Senate refused to approve the prohibition-supported Skulason Bill, while the progressive-controlled House refused to approve the prohibition-opposed Plain Bill. Neither of the measures, with their onerous signature requirements, was acceptable to direct legislation purists. Ueland apparently decided to abandon his dream. He sold his farm in Edgeley in 1909 and moved to the West Coast the following year. He eventually settled in Roseburg, Oregon, one of the most active direct legislation states.[40]

Both major parties ran on strong reform-oriented programs in 1910, and the platforms of each included planks favoring the initiative and referendum. Governor Burke gained reelection, while progressives completed defeat of the McKenzie machine by securing control of all important state offices and both houses of the legislature. When Governor Burke made the initiative and referendum a legislative priority in his message to the legislature in 1911, it looked as though some type of direct legislation measure would be enacted. But what type?

The legislature actually considered four measures. To please the prohi-

40. See Anderson, "Adoption and Operation," 98–104; *House Journal of the Eleventh Session of the North Dakota Legislative Assembly, 1909*, for H.B. 93, 80, 270; and *Senate Journal of the Eleventh Session of the North Dakota Legislative Assembly, 1909*, for S.B. 82. For information on Ueland's move, see *Edgeley Mail*, September 24, 1909, February 20, 1947; and *Valley City Times-Record*, March 17, 1910.

bitionists, Senator H. J. Bessesen of Wells County introduced a bill that allowed for only statutory use of the initiative and referendum (on petitions
of 10 percent of the legal voters in a majority of the counties in the state).
To please resubmissionists, Senator A. S. Gibbens of Towner County introduced a bill that allowed for only the initiative on constitutional amendments (on petitions of 25 percent of the legal voters in not less than one-half
of the counties in the state). Senator Plain introduced a third measure,
which appealed to the more conservative advocates of direct legislation.
The bill allowed for both the statutory initiative and referendum (on petitions of 10 percent of the legal voters in at least one-half of the counties in
the state) and the constitutional initiative (on petitions of 15 percent of the
legal voters in at least one-half of the counties in the state). The more liberal advocates of direct legislation in the House, however, were not satisfied
with the Plain Bill and supported a fourth measure sponsored by Representatives John J. Doyle of McIntosh County and Frank E. Ployhar of Barnes
County. Known as the Doyle-Ployhar Bill, it provided for both the statutory initiative and referendum (on petitions of 8 percent or twenty thousand
legal electors for the initiative and 5 percent or ten thousand electors for the
referendum) and the constitutional initiative (on petitions of 15 percent of
the legal voters in at least one-half of the counties in the state). The Doyle-
Ployhar Bill also extended the initiative and referendum to counties and
municipalities, and added the recall of elective public officials as well. In
the end, the legislature passed all four bills and left responsibility for making the final decision on direct legislation to the 1913 legislature.[41]

In spite of the progressive-reform climate in the state in 1913, the legislative
battle over direct legislation proved to be more acrimonious than in 1911. All
four bills from 1911 were resubmitted. Senator W. B. Overson of Williams
County reintroduced the Bessesen Bill, and Senators Plain and Gibbens again
submitted their measures. The Doyle-Ployhar Bill was reintroduced as the
Ployhar-Blakemore Bill.[42] It soon became evident that the House and the Senate were far apart on the question of what constituted an acceptable direct legislation law. The House, despite charges that the liberal Ployhar-Blakemore
Bill was an attempt to bring about resubmission of the liquor question, passed
the measure by an overwhelming majority. The Senate passed the conservative Overson statutory bill and the restrictive Gibbens constitutional bill,
and defeated the Plain Bill. When the Senate finally considered the liberal

41. See Anderson, "Adoption and Operation," 106–22; and *Equity* 13 (April 1911): 81.
In addition to the initiative and referendum, the legislature also passed a list of other
progressive measures, including a corrupt-practices act, antipass legislation, regulation
of lobbying, and a presidential preference primary.
42. Robert Blakemore, a Democrat from Cass County, was acknowledged to be the
champion of the direct legislation purists.

Ployhar-Blakemore measure, the vote resulted in a tie, twenty-four to twenty-four. It was up to Lieutenant Governor Anton Kraabel, a progressive Republican, to break the tie, and he voted against the bill! In defense of his position, Kraabel stated that he objected to the provision of the bill applying to counties and municipalities in that it offered no safeguard to prevent local districts from granting licenses to sell liquor. It was then up to the House either to accept the Gibbens and Overson Bills or to begin the prolonged amendment process again in 1915. In the end the House relented and accepted what many progressives classified as "makeshift" legislation. Voters approved the Overson amendment by a vote of 48,783 to 19,964 and the Gibbens amendment by a vote of 43,111 to 21,815 in the general election of 1914.[43]

Prohibitionists were, in fact, tested under the new laws. Relying on the heavily populated German sections in the resubmission areas of the state, the liquor interests managed to obtain signatures from 10 percent of the legal voters in a majority of the counties in the state to refer a measure known as the Bootlegging Bill, House Bill 141. This law had been passed to enhance enforcement of the existing prohibition law by making it easier to apprehend bootleggers. Voters decided to stick with the prohibitionists, however, and upheld the law by a vote of 51,673 to 42,956 at the general election in 1916.

Successful in mounting a petition drive under the referendum, the liquor interests also circulated petitions to resubmit the prohibition question under the constitutional initiative. Spearheading the petition drive was the Personal Liberty League of the German-American Alliance of North Dakota. To counter this effort, the North Dakota Enforcement League, the WCTU, and the Scandinavian Total Abstinence Society conducted a campaign warning voters not to sign the petitions. The petition drive ultimately failed, defeated more by the 25 percent signature requirement (in at least one-half the counties in the state) than anything else.

Proposals to make the constitutional amending process more workable (requiring the action of only one legislature before a proposed amendment could be submitted to the people, and reducing the number of signatures required for a constitutional initiative from 25 to 15 percent) were introduced in the 1915 legislature but never given serious consideration. During the period 1915–1918 various groups attempted to refer fifteen laws and initiate two constitutional amendments. Only two of these efforts (both referenda) ever gained enough signatures to appear on the ballot. The statutory initiative was never used. In reality, North Dakota's initiative and referendum laws were virtually useless.[44]

43. See Anderson, "Adoption and Operation," 125–43.
44. See ibid., 157–58, 161–62, 167–68, 191.

Advocates of direct legislation had seen their reforms become law (though not in the form they might have wanted) and were well aware that they were indebted to the larger progressive reform impulse in the state. The overall accomplishments of the progressives toward creating a more responsive government in North Dakota were indeed impressive. They had not only defeated the authoritarian control of the McKenzie machine, but also enacted a model program of political and social reform between 1907 and 1913. Voters could now create their own laws (initiative and referendum), select their own candidates (direct primary), and indicate preferences for national senators and president (senatorial and presidential preference primaries). They could also look to a day when voting would be even more democratic (with improved voter registration), when local government would be more efficient (a commission form of government), and when it would be more difficult for money to corrupt the democratic political process (through corrupt-practices acts). In addition, North Dakota progressives took steps in the direction of governmental regulation by enacting pure-food and drug legislation, establishing a juvenile court system, and restricting child labor.

However, North Dakota was a state of farmers, and though farmers supported the progressive reform program, they felt slighted by its achievements. To farmers, the progressives failed where they had succeeded. Their political and social agenda had largely ignored economic reforms, especially those aimed at redressing the economic problems that had plagued North Dakota farmers since the mid-1880s. In the final accounting, the persistent and agonizing problems of prohibitory and discriminating railroad rates, farm credit, and the Minneapolis grain-marketing monopoly remained. Farmers again felt betrayed. Their solution was simple. Either state government would have to generate an economic program that would address chronic farm problems or farmers would have to control state government. Farmers soon realized that the political reforms of the progressives could help them gain control. The direct primary provided them with an avenue to power, whereas the initiative and referendum offered an expeditious means of implementing their program. In the end, however, voters also received a lesson in how the tools of direct democracy could be exploited for partisan political advantage.[45]

Organized in North Dakota in 1907, the American Society for Equity led the next attempt by farmers to confront the Minneapolis grain-marketing monopoly. The Equity program was simple: withhold wheat from market

---

45. See Glaab, "Revolution of 1906"; Charles N. Glaab, "The Failure of North Dakota Progressivism"; Glaab, "Progressive Revolt"; and Louis G. Geiger, "Conservative Reform and Rural Radicalism."

until the price reached one dollar a bushel. The response in North Dakota was enthusiastic. Some ten thousand North Dakota farmers pledged to withhold a million bushels of wheat, and thousands joined the Society of Equity. The following year Equity organized its own cooperative exchange in Minneapolis in an attempt to market and purchase commodities independent of the Minneapolis Grain Exchange. Equity also made plans to erect a state-owned terminal elevator (first suggested in the early 1890s) in Minneapolis, St. Paul, or the ports of Duluth, Minnesota, and Superior, Wisconsin, on Lake Superior. The idea of a state-owned elevator was so popular that voters approved constitutional amendments allowing state funds to be used for such purposes in 1912 and 1914. All that remained was for the State Board of Control to recommend the best method for state action. However, when the Board of Control, motivated by fiscal considerations and doubts concerning the soundness of the plan, recommended against the appropriation of state funds for the project, the legislature killed the idea in 1915. To farmers, it once again appeared as if the will of the majority had been denied.[46]

As the Society of Equity looked for a political means to establish its economic program, it found itself ideologically close to the North Dakota Socialist Party. Socialists, sensing an opportunity, hoped to attract Equity members to their banner and adopted a program that called for state-owned grain-marketing facilities. To facilitate recruitment, the Socialist Party created an affiliated organization department. Disenchanted farmers could join and receive literature without having to subscribe to Marxist doctrine or be required to carry the red membership card. Led by Arthur C. Townley and the farm-by-farm recruiting efforts of some able organizers, the Organization Department did well. The doctrinaire Marxists within the party soon became embarrassed by Townley's success and cut off funds for his efforts, though. When Townley and his organizers refused to quit, the party fired them. Townley and an associate, Albert E. Bowen, then decided to create their own independent nonpartisan organization.[47]

From the separate efforts of Equity and the Townley-led Organization Department of the Socialist Party came the Nonpartisan League. The Society of Equity had proved the popularity of the idea of a state-owned terminal elevator, and Townley had proved that farmers were receptive to cooperation and organization. The formal organization of the league oc-

46. See Theodore Saloutos, "The Rise of the Nonpartisan League in North Dakota, 1915–1917," 44; Larry Remele, "Power to the People: The Nonpartisan League," 68; E. B. Robinson, *History of North Dakota,* 272–78; L. F. Crawford, *History of North Dakota,* 418; and Nelson, *Land of the Dacotahs,* 258.

47. See Saloutos, "Rise of the Nonpartisan League," 45–48; and Remele, "Power to the People," 69–70.

curred shortly after the convention of the Society of Equity in February 1915. At the convention Townley renewed a friendship with F. B. Wood, a highly regarded Equity leader, and they, along with Bowen, sketched the outlines of the new league. The program was simple and straightforward: state ownership of terminal elevators, flour mills, packing plants, and cold-storage facilities; state inspection of grain and grain dockage; exemption of farm improvements from taxation; state hail insurance; and rural credit banks. The familiar story of the league's rise need not be retold here. League organizers established their own newspaper, the *Nonpartisan Leader,* worked within the dominant Republican Party, used the direct primary to gain control of the party, and then used control of the Republican Party to gain control of the governorship, the House of Representatives, and the state supreme court in 1916.[48]

Leaders of the Nonpartisan League realized that the state's constitution would have to be amended before they could establish their program. To achieve this goal as quickly as possible, league organizers boldly attempted to have the 1917 legislature approve an entirely new state constitution by simple legislative action. The measure, known as House Bill 44, passed easily in the House but failed in the Senate where twenty-four holdover senators blocked its way. Before the legislature adjourned, however, the league's leadership decided upon an alternative plan and announced that it intended to use the initiative to place constitutional amendments on the ballot in 1918 as a means of implementing its industrial program. The proposed amendments would allow for the exemption of personal property from taxation, raise the debt limit, permit the taxation of land for a state hail-insurance fund, and allow the state to engage in industries, enterprises, or businesses. The league began its petition drive in March 1918. Using league organizers to obtain signatures in the field, and printing petitions in newspapers that voters could clip, circulate, and return to the league, the petition drive was an overwhelming success.[49]

The election of 1918 was another Nonpartisan League victory. The league gained control of both houses of the legislature. More important, voters ap-

48. See Remele, "Power to the People," 70–79; E. B. Robinson, *History of North Dakota,* 327–37; and Saloutos, "Rise of the Nonpartisan League," 48–53.

49. Involved in this political maneuvering was a complicated legal battle as well. In an attempt to stifle the league's radical program, a conservative, antileague state supreme court had ruled in *State ex rel. Linde v. Hall* (1916) that the existing constitutional initiative amendment was not self-executing and, therefore, ineffectual until the legislature passed enabling legislation to give the law effect. After the league's success in electing three of its partisans to the court in 1916, the previous court's decision was overturned in *State ex rel. Twichel v. Hall* (1918). See E. B. Robinson, *History of North Dakota,* 337–38; L. F. Crawford, *History of North Dakota,* 425–26, 430; Saloutos, "Rise of the Nonpartisan League," 55–56; and Anderson, "Adoption and Operation," 165–80.

proved all the league-sponsored constitutional amendments. Included in the list of voter-approved initiatives were two substantive revisions to the existing initiative and referendum amendment. League officials had persuasively argued that such modifications were necessary to give the people the effective power to govern themselves. The league had campaigned vigorously for the changes through the league press and had distributed leaflets and pamphlets directly to voters. League officials had also recruited nationally known authorities on direct legislation either to speak at mass meetings or to contribute letters of endorsement. The new law, far more liberal than the one approved in 1914, allowed ten thousand electors "at large" to initiate any law, whereas seven thousand electors "at large" could refer any measure enacted by the legislature. An additional revision changed the petition requirement for constitutional amendments to twenty thousand electors "at large." If a majority of the voters approved a proposed amendment, it became law independent of any action by the legislature. Voters approved the proposals to revise the initiative and referendum amendments by a vote of 47,447 to 32,598. The vote on the measure to revise the method for proposing constitutional amendments was 46,329 for and 33,572 against.[50]

The 1919 legislature completed the league's triumph by enacting the heart of its program. Legislators created the Industrial Commission to manage all state-run enterprises and the Bank of North Dakota to provide low-cost rural credits and finance state industries. They also established the North Dakota Mill and Elevator Association to perfect a system of state-run warehouses, elevators, flour mills, and factories and a Home Building Association to facilitate the construction and sale of houses. League officials praised the work of the legislature as a new day in North Dakota.[51]

Opponents did not agree. To the Independent Voters Association (IVA), an organization created to oppose the league and led by conservative businessmen, conservative editors, and disaffected league organizers, the league program appeared as a radical anticapitalist experiment in state socialism. IVA leaders charged the league's leadership with "bossism" and "bolshevism" and declared that the league's centralization of power would inevitably lead to corruption by appointed officials. They emphasized that the liberalized initiative and referendum laws would destroy the constitution of the state, and allow cranks to secure petitions "for or against anything under the sun." As they waited for the league to self-destruct, the leaders of the IVA began a petition campaign to submit the new legislation

50. See L. F. Crawford, *History of North Dakota*, 430–31; and Anderson, "Adoption and Operation," 181–90.

51. See L. F. Crawford, *History of North Dakota*, 434–35; and E. B. Robinson, *History of North Dakota*, 342–43.

to the people under the revised referendum law! Nevertheless, in a special election held on June 26, 1919, voters stuck by the league and upheld all the referred measures.[52]

The task ahead of the league was to sustain its momentum even after its program had been implemented, and to prove that it could govern as well as organize. It failed on both counts. Soon, the warnings of the IVA began to ring true. The Industrial Commission never showed itself as an agency of wise management. The Bank of North Dakota, inadequately capitalized from the start, exhibited favoritism toward certain banks in the depositing of state funds and suffered from instances of fraud. The North Dakota Mill and Elevator Association lost money and proved unable to sell the bonds necessary to expand its facilities. The Home Building Association recklessly overextended itself in construction and credit. Intraparty fighting also hampered league efforts, and the IVA missed no opportunity to attack the league simultaneously on a number of fronts. Farmers, now the victims of the agricultural depression following World War I, grew increasingly receptive to charges of mismanagement and machine rule.

Looking to tap the negative popular reaction that seemed to be building against league officials, the IVA used the initiative to place five measures on the ballot in 1920 that restricted actions of the league. In the election of 1920 the IVA saw all of its initiative measures approved, and was able to gain control of the lower house of the legislature. Sensing its new strength, the IVA then decided to subject three members of the Industrial Commission (including Governor Lynn Frazier) to a recall petition for gross mismanagement of state-run enterprises.[53] Realizing that it confronted a legislative impasse in 1920, but still hoping to dismantle the league program, the IVA again used the initiative to propose seven laws aimed at either limiting or curtailing state-run industries. At a special election held on October 28, 1921, voters dismissed the Industrial Commission, but, surprisingly, rejected all the IVA-sponsored initiatives. Voters had lost confidence in league officials, but not in the essence of the league's program. Ironically, state ownership, the key issue in the debate, actually continued in North Dakota under conservative management after 1921. Between 1916, when the Nonpartisan League first rose to power, and 1922, when the Independent Voters Association was able to regain control of both houses of the legislature, North Dakota voters cast ballots on fifteen constitutional amend-

52. See Remele, "Power to the People," 86–88; and E. B. Robinson, *History of North Dakota,* 345–46. For a thorough account of IVA efforts, see D. Jerome Tweton, "The Anti-League Movement: The IVA."

53. An amendment allowing for the recall of public officials had appeared on the ballot at the presidential primary in 1920. Voters approved the measure by a count of 29,262 to 17,255. See Anderson, "Adoption and Operation," 553.

ments proposed by the legislature, eight initiated constitutional amendments, nineteen statutory initiatives, and thirteen referenda.[54]

Unlike in neighboring South Dakota, serious discussion of the initiative and referendum did not take place in North Dakota until Lars Ueland discovered the ideas at the Populist Party convention in 1892. The North Dakota Populist Party added a direct legislation plank to its platform in 1894, but its influence in the state was already on the wane. After a brief, ineffective moment in power in 1893–1894, Populism was never really a factor in North Dakota politics. Instead, political control rested in the hands of a political machine directed by Alexander McKenzie. The McKenzie machine, supported by powerful corporations and a strong prohibition lobby, both of which saw their interests threatened by the initiative and referendum, effectively derailed efforts to gain adoption of those reforms for years. The absence of an effective reform organization and the apparent lack of overwhelming popular support made the task doubly difficult for advocates of direct legislation. Lonely crusaders like Lars Ueland faced the control of the McKenzie machine and the powerful prohibition lobby with almost no organizational or editorial support. Regardless, Ueland doggedly kept the issue alive, continued to argue for it, made it the topic of legislative discussion, and ultimately convinced progressive Republicans and Democrats to add direct legislation to their political agenda.

When the legislature finally passed the initiative and referendum, however, following the successful revolt of the progressives and the subsequent defeat of the McKenzie machine, the influential prohibition lobby was still able to encumber the laws with burdensome petition requirements. For direct legislationists, the victory was bittersweet. They had capped a twenty-year effort with legislative victory, but they had failed to get the initiative and referendum adopted on their terms. Support from progressives had been essential to success, but commitment from progressives was never strong enough to overcome resistance from a special interest group with tremendous popular appeal in the state. Direct legislation purists could only hope that the laws would be liberalized in the future (perhaps after passage of a national prohibition amendment).

Politics unexpectedly took a radical turn in North Dakota when the Nonpartisan League captured partial control of power in a political whirlwind in 1916. Holdover senators, however, successfully impeded the implementation of the league's industrial reform program. In reaction, the league

54. See E. B. Robinson, *History of North Dakota,* 343–51; L. F. Crawford, *History of North Dakota,* 442–47; Remele, "Power to the People," 88; Tweton, "Anti-League Movement," 93–122; and Anderson, "Adoption and Operation," 552–55.

used its popular support to establish the legal basis for its industrial program via the initiative, and then used its control of the legislature in 1918 to implement its program and revise the direct legislation statutes. Contrary to the argument of direct legislation purists that the initiative and referendum would allow voters to consider issues without regard to party affiliation, however, they had, in fact, become tools of partisanship. As the Independent Voters Association mobilized in opposition, they too used the initiative and referendum successfully to restrict actions of the league. North Dakotans, however, demonstrated that there were limits to the partisan uses of those reforms by sustaining the Nonpartisan League's program in 1921 despite tremendous pressure to terminate it.

9

Massachusetts and Nebraska

MASSACHUSETTS

The only eastern state other than Maine to adopt both the statewide initiative and the referendum as an amendment to its state constitution was Massachusetts in 1918.[1] At first glance, the reluctance with which Massachu-

---

1. Maryland adopted the referendum only in 1915. Reformers had created a direct legislation league in the state as early as 1900 with A. G. Eichelberger of Baltimore as president, but the organization could not sustain itself. A new league was created in 1910 with Jackson H. Ralston of Hyattsville as president. One year later the league claimed to have one thousand "active working members." An amendment calling for the statewide initiative and referendum gained a favorable report from the Committee on Constitutional Amendments and a hearing in the Maryland House of Delegates in 1912, but was defeated by a vote of thirty-five to forty-one. Jackson Ralston accepted blame for the defeat: "[T]he vote obtained in the House this year was the result rather of the forward pressure of the times than of the work we did. . . . We, the friends of the measure, are but just coming to know each other, and to know the strength of the movement." With the endorsement of the state's Republican and Progressive Parties and supported by a petition favoring the submission of a direct legislation bill signed by ten thousand people, the Maryland Direct Legislation League backed an amendment sponsored by William J. Ogden of Baltimore calling for the statewide initiative and referendum in 1914. The legislature, however, amended the measure by removing its initiative provision. Legislative acts could be referred based on petitions signed by ten thousand voters of whom not more than one-half could be residents of Baltimore or any other county. Local ordinances could also be referred based on petitions of 8 percent of the registered voters in any city or district. Excluded from the referendum were any measures concerning the sale or manufacture of intoxicating liquors and "emergency" measures so declared by a three-fifths majority of both houses of the legislature. Voters adopted the referendum amendment by a vote of 33,150 to 10,022 in 1915. In 1916 the Maryland Direct Legislation League urged the legislature to approve a statewide initiative amendment. The measure passed the Senate with only six dissenting votes. After being delayed in House committee until the last day of the session, legislators voted to table the measure by a vote of sixty-six to twenty-seven and effectively killed it. Lobbyists against the bill made effective use of the argument that the city of Baltimore would gain legislative advantage from the initiative and succeeded in intimidating a sufficient number of county delegates. See *Direct Legislation Record* 7 (December 1900): 64; 8 (February 1901): 4; *Equity* 12 (April 1910): 60–61; 13 (January 1911): 26; 14 (April 1912): 77–78; 15 (October 1913): 218; 16 (January 1914): 33–34; 16 (April 1914): 89–90; 16 (July 1914): 136; 18 (January 1916): 28–31; and 18 (July 1916): 142–43.

setts joined other states in adopting these measures is surprising. By the turn of the century Massachusetts had already achieved a record of progressive reform in public health, education, civil service, and protection of women and child workers that placed it ahead of other states. However, the reform impulse in Massachusetts did not derive primarily from radical or populist demands for change. Instead, as one historian has noted, it derived from a conservative impulse, rooted in the state's tradition of social responsibility that "worked continually to readjust the state's laws and institutions so as to preserve the state's traditional standards of social behavior in the face of the challenges of industrialism."[2] The state's conservative political leadership was willing to accept moderate change, but it was not conditioned to move quickly or to adopt "radical" panaceas.

Not everyone in Massachusetts found the conservative-dominated political order to their liking. During the last decade of the nineteenth century and the first decade of the twentieth century good government–minded reformers grew increasingly impatient with the pace of legislative action as it related to modernization of state and local government, the elimination of tax inequities, and the willingness to curb the influence of political machines and special interests. According to one recent study of the period, the "obstruction of such legislation was blamed on alliances of 'practical politicians' in the General Court [the Massachusetts legislature] with city bosses, county courthouse political rings, and financial interests with a vested advantage in the status quo." Joining the chorus was organized labor that complained about the antilabor attitudes of the Republican majorities in both houses of the state legislature and charged that "legislation beneficial to the working people was being watered down, ignored or sabotaged by reason of the influence on the political process of lobbyists representing financial institutions, manufacturers and public utilities before the General Court."[3] When these critics suggested that the influence of large corporations on representative government should be curbed, that direct participation by voters in both the electoral and the legislative processes should be established, and that the bounds of government intervention to achieve greater economic and social justice in society should be expanded, they served only to unnerve the conservative power structure.

Also threatening the traditional order of things in the Bay State and serving to intensify conservative political tendencies were the social transformations that accompanied rapid industrialization—the rising tide of im-

2. Richard M. Abrams, *Conservatism in a Progressive Era: Massachusetts Politics, 1900–1912*, x.

3. Quoted in Massachusetts, *Report Relative to Revising Statewide Initiative and Referendum Provisions of the Massachusetts Constitution*, House no. 5435, February 4, 1975, 55–56.

migration and persistent labor unrest. For the state's tradition-bound culture, it was easy to become alarmed about the increase in "undesirable" social elements, especially the non-Yankee wage-earning classes. In 1890 the foreign born and their native-born offspring accounted for roughly 50 percent of the state's total inhabitants. By 1900 that figure had increased to almost 62 percent, and by 1910 to 66 percent of Massachusetts's population. From 1880 to 1900 the Massachusetts Bureau of Labor Statistics recorded an average of nearly one hundred labor disturbances involving approximately thirty-nine thousand workers per year. Massachusetts ranked third in the nation in that respect. Labor unrest in the state would persist throughout the Progressive Era. This uneasiness intensified as the immigrant and working masses became more vocal in demanding legislation to help them guard against the insecurities caused by industrialization and in advocating changes in political methods that would allow their demands to be more effectively heard.[4]

Controlling the legislature, and seeing itself as sort of a guardian at the gate, was the dominant Republican Party. The party tended to draw its leadership primarily from the so-called Brahman class—self-conscious colonial descendants with a strong sense of superiority and self-righteous paternalism. They tended to distrust human nature, revere private property, and favor a government led by a responsible minority. The individual perhaps most representative of this worldview was Henry Cabot Lodge. Throughout the period under review, the Massachusetts senator stood as the righteous defender of the Constitution, of representative government, and of an independent judiciary. He assailed any proposals that would allow voters to overrule the legislature in matters of law, create their own laws, modify the state's constitution directly, or possibly allow for the recall of judges as revolutionary in nature and tending to promote anarchy and despotism.[5] Getting the initiative and referendum passed in Massachusetts would be difficult.

The torturous process by which Massachusetts became the twenty-second state to accept direct legislation dates from the early 1890s. Discussion of the idea began, as it had in New Jersey, among intellectuals, inspired primarily by the writings of W. D. McCrackan. While in Europe in 1890, McCrackan wrote a series of letters on the topic of direct legislation as practiced in Switzerland that were published by the *New York Evening Post*. His article on the initiative and referendum that appeared in *Arena* in 1891 was the first of its type. Years later editor B. O. Flower recalled that the oppor-

4. See Abrams, *Conservatism in a Progressive Era*, 28–29, 228–31, 273–76.

5. For an extended discussion of Lodge's views, see *Senate Document No. 122*, "The Constitution and Its Makers: An Address Delivered before the Literary and Historical Association of North Carolina at Raleigh, November 28, 1911, by Henry Cabot Lodge."

tunity for the publication came about after Hamlin Garland (a special contributor to the magazine) brought McCrackan to the *Arena* office. "Flower," said Garland, "I have found the very man you want to tell the people how they can get the government back into their hands. . . . This is W. D. McCrackan, who has recently returned from Switzerland, where he has been for five years studying political and social conditions and writing a comprehensive history of the Swiss Republic. He is a Single-Taxer, a graduate of Trinity College, Hartford, a careful thinker, and a fine man." As a result of this interview, Flower "arranged for a series of papers dealing with the democratic innovations in Switzerland, and these were the first series of papers on Direct Legislation published in a leading magazine of opinion devoted to general discussions."[6] The following year McCrackan published *The Rise of the Swiss Republic*, a history of the workings of the idea in Switzerland. Fascinated with McCrackan's writings (as others were with those of J. W. Sullivan), reformers in Massachusetts began to take an interest in the idea. McCrackan continued to sharpen their interest by actively lecturing on the subject before various clubs and societies.

It was not long, however, before various labor societies showed an interest in the topic and quickly became the driving force behind the movement in the state. The Boston Central Labor Union incorporated direct legislation in its platform of legislative demands in 1892, and the state branch of the American Federation of Labor circulated petitions on behalf of the idea that same year. The State Federation of Labor agreed to concentrate its efforts on securing legislative recognition of the principle of direct legislation, and instructed its legislative committee at its annual convention to push the issue in the legislature. Workingmen's Political Leagues of Boston and elsewhere also joined labor's lobbying campaign.

Other organizations soon became involved and helped the movement gather momentum. Assisting labor's efforts was the Direct Legislation League, organized in Boston in 1893. Led by its president, William N. Osgood, a lawyer, the league held several public meetings to discuss the topic, distributed informational leaflets and pamphlets, and successfully prodded the press into devoting more attention to the subject. At the urging of a committee composed of representatives of the State Federation of Labor and President Osgood of the Direct Legislation League, the platform committees of both the Democratic and the Republican Parties added planks in support of direct legislation to their party platforms.

When the 1893–1894 session of the Massachusetts General Court convened, proponents hoped to see some sort of direct legislation amendment adopted. Early in the session, Republican representative R. Neil of West-

6. Flower, *Progressive Men, Women, and Movements of the Past Twenty-five Years*, 62–63.

field introduced a bill calling for the statewide referendum on legislative acts and the statewide initiative for both statutes and amendments to the state constitution. Neil's proposal was in response to a petition signed by labor reformer Frank K. Foster and others demanding legislation allowing for a popular referendum on legislative decisions. The bill was referred to the committee on constitutional amendments, which held public hearings. Among those making presentations before the committee in support of the measure were Edwin D. Mead, editor of the *New England Magazine;* W. D. McCrackan; and numerous representatives from organized labor. The bill, however, appeared to most members of the General Court to be too radical a departure from standard practice, and they rejected it. Republican representative Richard W. Irwin of Northampton introduced a more modest direct legislation measure that applied only to cities, but it too failed to win approval. Irwin concluded that legislators refused to support the idea because they did not fully understand it. "Unwillingness to leave the beaten paths of precedent and enter the field of reform," said Irwin, "actuated many members."[7]

Despite Irwin's attempts to revive his measure in succeeding sessions of the General Court, mention of direct legislation in the political platforms of the Populist, Prohibition, and Democratic Parties (the Republicans dropped the idea in 1895), and support from Massachusetts single taxers who favored the adoption of direct legislation as a means by which towns and counties could try Henry George's tax ideas as a form of local option, enthusiasm for the initiative and referendum lagged until 1900.[8] In January of that year, Henry Sterling, editor of the *Leader* (a monthly newspaper devoted to direct legislation and labor issues) and a member of the legislative committee of the State Federation of Labor (Sterling was a member of the International Typographical Union), rekindled interest in the idea with a paper he read before the Central Labor Union of Boston. Encouraged by the response, he, along with William Osgood of the Direct Legislation League, urged legislative consideration of a new direct legislation bill. Submitted by Representative Martin P. Higgins of Charlestown (later president of the International Pressmen's Union), the bill authorized voters to initiate constitutional amendments upon petition of fifty thousand registered voters. Once again, the measure failed to win approval.

7. Irwin, "In the Massachusetts Legislature," *Direct Legislation Record* 1 (July 1894): 34 (see also 33–35). See also Foster, "Direct Legislation in Massachusetts," *Direct Legislation Record* 1 (July 1894): 35, 38–39; and 1 (August 1894): 48–49.

8. Delegates from Massachusetts took part in the organizational meeting of the National Direct Legislation League held in St. Louis on July 21, 1896. They elected Richard W. Irwin, Edward Bellamy (author of *Looking Backward*), and B. O. Flower (editor of the *Arena*) as vice presidents representing their state. See *Direct Legislation Record* 3 (September 1896): 26; and 6 (December 1899): 86.

Undeterred, Sterling succeeded in getting a revised version of his proposal resubmitted the following year (the General Court in Massachusetts met annually), increasing the petition requirement to seventy-five thousand signatures "in deference to conservative sentiment." The committee on constitutional amendments again held public hearings on the proposal, accepted supporting petitions from approximately twenty-five hundred individuals and more than thirty labor unions, and listened to presentations from forty to fifty speakers, including Sterling and Professor Frank Parsons, author of *The City for the People* and the president of the Massachusetts Direct Legislation League. Supporters were of the general opinion that such a measure was necessary, as legislation in Massachusetts was "usually unfavorable to the masses and favorable to the classes." One labor spokesman asserted that "80 per cent of the people were dissatisfied with results under the present system." Still reluctant to accept the new idea, legislators rejected the proposal by a vote of 92 to 102.[9]

In its fight for direct legislation, organized labor received some unexpected support from the Public Franchise League, headed by Louis Brandeis and organized for the purpose of maintaining public control over franchise grants. The group was fearful that municipal governments might commonly grant franchise privileges to public service corporations without adequate compensation or oversight (there had been heated debates concerning franchise extensions for the West End Street Railway Company of Boston in 1899 and the Boston Elevated Railway Company in 1901) and looked to attach the referendum to all public franchise grants and extensions as a safeguard. The Public Franchise League addressed letters to all state political candidates demanding to know whether they favored a popular referendum as a check on "questions involving the use of public franchises by public service corporations." The league threatened to work to defeat those individuals who opposed the referendum on franchise matters as an aspect of local home rule. Both major political parties incorporated statements favoring the idea in their platforms, with the minority Democratic Party going so far as to state that "the domination of the people and usurpation of political authority by irresponsible and selfish interests is a serious menace to popular government."[10]

Buoyed by the increase in the popular discussion of direct legislation and by comments from newspapers such as the *Boston Post* that "the great principle of reference to the people is rapidly gaining ground," Henry Sterling

9. See *Direct Legislation Record* 2 (September 1895): 18; 2 (December 1895): 26–27; 4 (March 1897): 20; 8 (June 1901): 23; 8 (December 1901): 61–62; and 10 (September 1903): 59.

10. See *Direct Legislation Record* 6 (December 1899): 83; 7 (March 1900): 5; 8 (September 1901): 47–48; and 8 (December 1901): 61.

again petitioned the General Court to consider a proposal by which fifty thousand registered voters could initiate an amendment to the state constitution. More than four hundred trade unions endorsed the measure, and the Joint Committee on Direct Legislation, representing the State Federation of Labor, the Central Labor Union of Boston, and the Boston Building Trades Council, actively lobbied for it. As an indication that labor's interest had intensified, the usual public hearing turned into a public demonstration with more than fifteen hundred wage earners in attendance. In the face of such organized popular support, the committee on constitutional amendments unanimously reported in favor of the bill. The House approved the measure by a vote of 111 to 64, but it still failed to gain the necessary two-thirds majority required of amendments to the constitution. In assessing the reasons for the defeat, Professor Frank Parsons concluded that it "was not due to partisanship or to any special opposition on the part of any corporative or monopolistic interests, but rather to apathy and old fogyism and a dislike of anything that might make the Legislature less omnipotent."[11]

Failing to win in 1902, direct legislationists opted for a different approach in 1903. Using the rationalization that the gradual development of the principle in even a weak bill was preferable to no bill at all, they agreed to a proposal calling for a modified form of the direct initiative on constitutional amendments. The measure allowed fifty thousand qualified voters (not more than twenty-five thousand to come from any one county) to petition the General Court for an amendment. Approval required the votes of fifteen members of the Senate (there were forty in all) and one-half of those in the House. Organized labor again actively supported the bill, led by the indefatigable Henry Sterling and the petitions of 570 labor organizations. Adding its voice to that of organized labor for the first time was the Referendum Union, a rural society that furnished each legislator with copies of two supportive tracts: "Direct Legislation" and "The Referendum Opinions of Prominent People." The secretary of the Referendum Union also mailed these arguments, along with letters and petition blanks, to various branches of the State Grange. The bill, almost punitive when compared to other states that required only the filing of a petition with the proper percentage of voters as sufficient to send an amendment to the voters, won both Senate (23 to 10) and House (155 to 22) approval in 1903. However, in Massachusetts, as in Oregon and North Dakota, constitutional amend-

11. Parsons, "The Referendum Movement in Massachusetts," *Direct Legislation Record* 9 (June 1902): 33. See also *Direct Legislation Record* 9 (March 1902): 2–3, 16; 9 (June 1902): 33; and B. O. Flower, "Organized Labor and Direct Legislation," *Arena* 27 (May 1902): 535–36.

ments had to pass two consecutive sessions of the legislature before they could be presented to the voters for ratification.[12]

Hoping to rally popular support and influence voters in their selection of candidates to the 1904 General Court, the Joint Committee on Direct Legislation distributed thousands of copies of the text of the proposed amendment, supportive arguments, and the names of the 155 representatives and 23 senators who had voted for it. The committee also issued separate editions of their "Report" with two different arguments—one for more conservative and another for more radical organizations. The Public Information Society in Boston even mailed voters the voting records of legislators up for reelection. Nevertheless, once again all effort was for naught. The House showed only a narrow majority (105 to 103) for the bill, whereas the measure never even came to a vote in the Senate. Supporters blamed class antagonisms, a silent or disapproving press, and corporate lobbyists for their defeat. Hoping to salvage the principle, Henry Sterling petitioned for a law allowing an advisory vote on questions of public policy based on petitions signed by 3 percent of registered voters. Unwilling to compromise on the question, legislators rejected versions of Sterling's modest "Public Opinion Bill" in 1906, 1907, and 1908. The direct legislation movement in Massachusetts seemed to have lost its momentum.[13]

Direct legislationists reorganized in 1909 as the Massachusetts Direct Legislation League and continued to petition to have an initiative and referendum amendment passed in each session of the General Court from 1909 to 1916. The various proposals received solid majorities in almost every instance, but never the necessary two-thirds House majority required for constitutional amendments. Supporters also organized the Equity League in 1909 to push for favorable legislation through a campaign of public education. Assisting that process, the Direct Legislation League placed Henry Sterling in the field as a traveling advocate to stir up labor unions and other organizations (a role similar to that performed by Silas Moser in Missouri). Senators Robert L. Owen of Oklahoma and Jonathan Bourne Jr. of Oregon, both nationally known advocates of direct legislation, aided the educational work being done by speaking in the state, while the Massachusetts Direct Legislation League continued its statewide distribution of informational literature.[14]

The movement received a boost in 1910 with the election of Eugene Foss

12. See *Direct Legislation Record* 10 (June 1903): 26; and 10 (September 1903): 45.
13. See *Direct Legislation Record* 10 (December 1903): 74; *Equity* 8 (July 1906): 25–28; 9 (January 1907): 14; 9 (April 1907): 12; and 10 (April 1908): 49.
14. See *Equity* 11 (April 1909): 54–55; 11 (October 1909): 131; 12 (January 1910): 27; 12 (July 1910): 107; 13 (April 1911): 76; 13 (October 1911): 177; 14 (July 1912): 107; 15 (July 1913): 188; 16 (July 1914): 136; 17 (April 1915): 117; and 18 (April 1916): 89.

as the state's first Democratic governor in more than fifteen years. Using his inaugural address as a reform manifesto, the governor acknowledged a crisis confronting representative government. "The people of all sections of the country," said Foss, "have lost confidence in many of their public servants. The dictatorship by political bosses and by representatives of special interests is hotly resented, for these men desire to control public servants and to direct legislation to their own ends." Foss's recommended cures for this "usurpation of power" were the direct primary, the recall, and the initiative and referendum. The governor's rhetoric captured the spirit of political change then taking hold in Massachusetts and elsewhere across the country. Over the next three years the General Court enacted a broad program of progressive legislation and moved Massachusetts a little closer to adoption of the initiative and referendum. Among those measures expanding the bounds of popular democracy were the direct primary and presidential preference primary laws, a constitutional amendment granting the General Court the authority to refer laws to the people for acceptance or rejection at the polls, and the Public Opinion law. The last measure allowed voters in any state senatorial or representative district to petition to have placed on the ballot any question relating to public policy. The popular vote recorded thereon would serve as a nonbinding instruction to legislators from that district. Proponents of direct legislation used the new law to conduct "straw polls" on the initiative and referendum in a number of legislative districts in 1914, 1915, and 1916.[15]

Direct legislationists won a second "victory" when Democrat David I. Walsh succeeded Foss as governor in 1913. The platforms of both the Democratic Party and the upstart Progressive Party, whose candidate for governor came in second in the three-way contest, had endorsed the initiative and referendum as well as a call for a constitutional convention.[16] Many direct legislationists looked upon a constitutional convention as a means to overcome the seemingly insurmountable two-thirds majority rule that had stymied any initiative and referendum amendment and bring about its inclusion in a revised document. Governor Walsh had indicated his support for direct legislation during the campaign. "The strongest argument in favor of direct legislation," said Walsh, "lies in the fact that every dishonest politician, every selfish public utility corporation and every self-seeking interest is against it." Believing that direct legislation was "the great Demo-

15. Foss quoted in *Equity* 13 (January 1911): 26 (see also 26–27). See also Abrams, *Conservatism in a Progressive Era*, 259–60; and Massachusetts, *Report Revising Provisions*, 57–58.

16. A measure calling for a constitutional convention required only a majority in each chamber in one legislative session and ratification by a majority of the electorate for approval.

cratic movement of the age," Walsh broke precedent and appeared, along with Progressive Party leader Joseph Walker, before a legislative committee to urge favorable action on the initiative and referendum amendment. Despite the governor's efforts and Democratic and Progressive strength in the General Court, an obdurate Republican minority again prevented the amendment from obtaining a two-thirds majority in the House, with a vote of 141 to 85. Defections from both Democratic and Progressive ranks also caused the defeat of the constitutional convention bill by a vote of 90 to 106. Republican gains in the election of 1914 signaled defeat for both measures when they were resubmitted the following year.[17]

Direct legislationists regarded the election of Republican Samuel W. McCall over David I. Walsh in 1915 as a setback for the initiative and referendum. Unable to capitalize on the insurgent spirit in the state since 1910, it appeared as if direct legislationists had lost their best opportunity to obtain an amendment. However, the victory of the Republican ticket did not come without one concession being made to reformers, namely, the party's endorsement of an amendment calling for a convention to revise the state's constitution. Direct legislationists again succeeded in having an initiative and referendum bill introduced in the General Court, but agreed not to press the issue in view of the Republican majority's pledge to revise the state's fundamental law. A measure calling for a constitutional convention passed the legislature by a nearly unanimous vote in 1916, and voters ratified the proposition at the November election (217,293 to 120,979). Also on the ballot in thirty-seven districts (and winning an affirmative vote in each one) was a test vote initiated under the Public Opinion law instructing representatives to support the adoption of the initiative and referendum.[18]

In an effort to arouse voters to the importance of the opportunity at hand, supporters of increased popular government (primarily Democrats, Progressives, and Socialists) organized as the Union for a Progressive Constitution. The committee issued a pamphlet listing reasons for favoring the initiative and referendum and the "pitfalls" to be avoided, and included the text of a model amendment they hoped would form the basis of discussion at the convention. Voters elected 320 delegates to the constitutional convention at a special election in May 1917. The convention, which

17. Walsh quoted in *Equity* 16 (January 1914): 35 (see also 34–35). See also *Equity* 16 (April 1914): 90–91; 16 (July 1914): 136–37; and 17 (April 1915): 117. At the November 1914 election there was a "straw poll" on the initiative and referendum in at least four districts under the new Public Opinion law. Where they were given the opportunity, voters overwhelmingly endorsed the idea. See *Equity* 16 (October 1914): 179–80; and 17 (January 1915): 47.

18. See *Equity* 18 (January 1916): 31; 18 (April 1916): 89; 18 (July 1916): 141–42; 19 (January 1917): 32; and Massachusetts, *Report Revising Provisions*, 58.

promised a lengthy and heated discussion of the pros and cons of the initiative and referendum, opened in Boston the following month.[19]

As expected, the debates in the constitutional convention and in the election campaign that followed proved to be acrimonious. The lengthy presentations and numerous proposed amendments ran to more than one thousand printed pages and formed one separate volume of a four-volume record of the proceedings of the convention. Discussion of the proposed initiative and referendum amendment consumed forty-five days between August 7 and November 28, 1917. Delegate Joseph Walker of Brookline, who had served as Speaker of the House of Representatives from 1909 to 1911 and head of the Union for a Progressive Constitution, and former governor David I. Walsh led those in favor of the measure. They had the support of a strong group of labor and reform delegates and appeared to have numbers sufficient to ensure the adoption of some type of initiative and referendum amendment. Former state attorney general Albert E. Pillsbury and noted railroad counsel Charles F. Choate led conservative delegates in opposition.[20]

During the debate that followed, proponents and opponents quickly discovered that there was little they could agree on. Supporters of the initiative and referendum claimed that the devices would serve as a means of defense against the influence of special interests that one delegate referred to as the "invisible government." They argued that a special minority controlled the legislative process, making representative government unrepresentative. They asserted that powerful corporations, especially public utility companies, used their influence to obtain legislative preferment and that important legislation involving taxation and labor law had been blocked, emasculated, and ignored by political machines and well-organized special interests. In addition, proponents charged that because legislators failed to remove themselves from consideration of measures that came before their committees in which they had a vested interest, they further contributed to making government in Massachusetts less than fairly representative. Believing that voters possessed a high degree of political literacy and that they were able to express an informed opinion on public issues, proponents denied that voters were, by nature, extremists out to establish mob rule

19. For the full text of the model Massachusetts plan, see *Equity* 19 (April 1917): 84–87. Of the 320 delegates, 16 were to be elected at large, 4 selected by each of the sixteen congressional districts, and the remainder, 240, chosen from existing legislative districts by the same proportion as representation in the General Court; candidates were to be nominated by petition and elected by nonpartisan ballot (*Equity* 18 [July 1916]: 141–42). See also *Equity* 19 (April 1917): 83–84; and Augustus P. Loring, "The Fourth Constitutional Convention (1914–1919)," 633.

20. See Massachusetts, *Report Revising Provisions,* 59.

or to tyrannize the majority. Instead, they argued that voters, empowered with the initiative and referendum, could separate issues from personality or party and freely consider political questions based on their merits.[21]

Opponents contested the arguments of the direct legislationists at every point. They rejected the notion of minority government and praised the progressive record of the Massachusetts General Court. They dismissed any projected "benefits" that might accrue from direct legislation as unrealistic and asserted that the existing system of annual elections offered an adequate means by which to remove corrupt or unresponsive legislators. Repeating Senator Lodge's well-known arguments, they asserted that the initiative and referendum would destroy deliberative representative government, undermine the system of checks and balances, and precipitate harmful or ill-conceived legislative proposals. Allowing the legislature no real check on popular action, the initiative and referendum would trample minority rights and, in effect, establish a tyranny of the majority. Believing that voters possessed a low level of political literacy, opponents argued that the initiative and referendum would confuse voters with technical questions, overburden them with a multiplicity of ballot propositions, and make them increasingly susceptible to demagogues who pandered to popular prejudice or narrow self-interest. They regarded the petition process with suspicion and argued that it would actually aid political machines and special interests with the funds and personnel to solicit signatures. Using data that suggested a history of low voter turnout on ballot propositions, opponents argued that a small minority of the electorate could ultimately determine important legislation affecting the majority.[22]

Prior to the general discussion, the fifteen-member Committee on the Initiative and Referendum had prepared a draft amendment for consideration by the convention's 320 delegates. The proposal called for an indirect constitutional and statute initiative based on forty thousand and twenty thousand petition signatures, respectively. Any proposed measure would have to be presented to the General Court for consideration and deliberation in two successive legislative sessions. If either house failed to approve the measure, supporters were then required to secure additional signatures (ten thousand for the constitutional and five thousand for the statute initiative) to finally bring the matter to a popular vote. A referendum could be invoked on legislation (statutes involving state appropriations and those affecting only a single municipality were excluded) if fifteen thousand voters petitioned for it. To discourage direct legislation that did not have broad

21. See ibid., 67–77.
22. See ibid. For a verbatim transcript of the debates, see "The Initiative and Referendum," in *Debates in the Massachusetts Constitutional Convention, 1917–1918*, 15–622.

appeal, not more than 25 percent of the petition signatures could come from any one county. A voter information pamphlet containing the text and explaining the arguments for and against each initiative and referendum proposal would be distributed to each voter prior to the election.[23]

After prolonged discussion, those delegates who still had reservations about the proposal or who felt that additional safeguards were necessary managed to win approval of several amendments. As a concession to conservatives, the convention agreed to expand the list of subjects excluded from the initiative and referendum. The list included laws affecting religious practices and religious institutions, the reversal of judicial decisions and the removal of judges, and any measures relating to freedom of speech, press, and assembly. Another concession allowed the General Court to propose "legislative substitutes" to laws and amendments proposed by initiative petition. Delegates also agreed to expand the role of the legislature by requiring approval of at least 25 percent of the members of the legislature in joint session before a proposed constitutional initiative could proceed to the ballot and allowing a three-fourths majority of the legislature, again sitting as a unicameral body, to amend any proposed constitutional initiative. Proponents managed to preserve the contested provision allowing a mere majority of those voting on any measure to approve it, but were forced to agree that any majority favoring a measure would have to include at least 30 percent of the total number of ballots cast in the state election to validate the law. In accepting added encumbrances, however, proponents were able to win two major concessions. The convention agreed to reduce signature requirements from forty thousand to twenty-five thousand for constitutional initiatives and to eliminate the requirement that an additional ten thousand signatures be obtained to bring constitutional initiatives to a vote if rejected by the General Court. The constitutional convention finally approved the complicated and cumbersome amendment establishing the initiative and referendum on November 27, 1917, by a vote of 163 to 125.

Before voters were given an opportunity to ratify the proposed new constitution, both proponents and opponents of the initiative and referendum organized committees that continued to press their respective positions to the voting public. Sixty prominent individuals made up the committee in favor of the new constitution, which spent a modest sum of just over three thousand dollars to cover expenses. Thirty individuals, mostly bankers and businessmen, contributed various amounts to a fund that eventually totaled more than eighty-eight thousand dollars in one final attempt to derail ratification. Expounding their position in public meetings and debates

23. See Massachusetts, *Report Revising Provisions*, 60–61; and *Debates in the Convention*, 3–6.

and in private interviews, and supporting their arguments with a well-edited pamphlet, opponents hoped to undermine support for any expansion of popular democracy. Despite their last-ditch efforts, however, voters narrowly ratified the amendment by a vote of 170,646 to 162,103 at the general election in 1918.

Unfortunately, the passage of the initiative and referendum in Massachusetts came just as the Progressive Era was winding to a close. Distracted by the war and the economic and social dislocation that followed, Massachusetts's voters made only limited use of direct legislation during the next two years. They invoked the referendum for the first time in 1919, upholding a statute regulating monthly interest payable on savings deposits in banks. The first use of the initiative occurred the following year when voters approved a law defining cider and beer as nonintoxicating liquors.[24]

NEBRASKA

The movement to establish direct legislation in Nebraska started out as it had in several other states: as a Populist-endorsed idea, championed by a small but energetic group of activists and supported occasionally by a marginalized Democratic Party and an assortment of minor third parties. The Populists and Democrats added the initiative and referendum to their platforms for the first time in 1894. The Nationalist, Socialist-Labor, and Prohibition Parties joined them two years later. Opposition to the proposed reforms came primarily from the state's Republicans, who dismissed the ideas as socialistic experimentation and argued that their adoption would lead to the destruction of the Constitution.[25]

Leading the drive for the adoption of these new reforms in Nebraska were Walter Breen and John O. Yeiser. Having emigrated from London, England, to Nebraska at age seventeen, Breen finally settled in Omaha where he became a successful real estate salesman and secretary of the Omaha Philosophical Society. He was one of the organizers of the Populist Party in Nebraska and an early advocate of direct legislation. He eventually became secretary of the Omaha Direct Legislation League, served as a member of the executive committee of the National Direct Legislation League, and worked as an active correspondent to the *Direct Legislation Record*. In as-

24. See Massachusetts, *Report Revising Provisions*, 61–67, 86–89; *Equity* 20 (January 1918): 47–49, 52–59; and Loring, "Fourth Constitutional Convention," 656. For discussion of the amendments and the final text of the law, see *Debates in the Convention*, 623–1062.

25. See Adam C. Breckenridge, "Nebraska as a Pioneer in the Initiative and Referendum," 218.

sessing the progress of the effort to obtain the initiative and referendum in Nebraska in March 1896, Breen was glowingly optimistic: "Fully 70 per cent to 80 per cent of the Populists," he estimated, "are alive to the subject, and perhaps about 5 per cent to 10 per cent of the old party men." Yeiser moved to Nebraska from Kentucky and studied law in Red Cloud, Nebraska, before being admitted to the bar and eventually opening a law practice in Omaha. When the Farmers' Alliance and Independent movements began to break up the established parties in the state, Yeiser abandoned his Republican Party affiliation for the People's Party. Winning election to the state legislature in 1896 as a Populist, he quickly became an advocate of direct legislation.[26]

Encouraged by the numerous political endorsements and emboldened by a Populist near majority in the legislature in 1897, Representative A. E. Sheldon of Dawes County introduced a measure drafted by Representative Yeiser of Douglas County calling for the extension of the initiative and referendum to local government.[27] During the debate over the measure, proponents referred to the Swiss model and argued that the use of direct legislation had made that country a well-governed democracy responsive to public sentiment. To support their case, proponents distributed copies of J. W. Sullivan's *Direct Legislation* to every member of the House and Senate. Representative J. M. Snyder of Sherman County argued that the application of the reforms to local government was not only appropriate but also timely, stating that "the abuse of city rule under the government of city councils" was numerous. Opponents, primarily Republicans, argued that the Swiss experiment had not conclusively proved that direct voter methods worked as well as claimed, doubted their applicability to the United States, and argued that because only a minority of the voters actually voted on ballot propositions the result was government by minorities. Merrick County representative Charles Wooster's stated reason for opposing the measure was more direct. He simply could see no popular demand for it: "If you ask the majority of farmers what the initiative and referendum is, they will reply, 'what the devil is that.'" Looking back on the debate years later, A. E. Sheldon called it "one of the hardest fought battles of the session." Despite the differences of opinion, though, the bill passed by a vote of sixty to twenty-six in the House and eighteen to seven in the Senate, with Republicans unanimous in their opposition.[28]

26. Breen quoted in *Direct Legislation Record* 3 (March 1896): 9. See also *Direct Legislation Record* 3 (September 1896): 26; and 4 (June 1897): 36, 75.

27. Sheldon had apparently been asked to take such action by Yeiser because his seat was being contested.

28. Yeiser remembered the measure passing the Senate by only one vote ("How the

The law itself, the first such measure to provide for direct legislation for general use in cities in the United States, allowed for proposing (initiative) and challenging (referendum) ordinances in any city or other municipal subdivision on petitions signed by 15 percent of the voters. However, the law required the voters of any given locality to vote to enable the law before it could become effective. Municipalities were free to use the reforms or not, but the 15 percent petition requirement (20 percent in a special election) needed to bring the question before the voters proved too difficult. The first cities in the state to enable the initiative and referendum were Omaha and Lincoln, but not until 1907![29]

With the help of Populist and Democratic legislative majorities, proponents of direct legislation had at least made it possible for Nebraska voters to utilize the initiative and referendum in local governance in 1897. They were able to go no further, though. Although the Democratic and Populist Parties continued to support direct legislation, the balance of power in Nebraska state politics shifted in favor of the Republicans, who were able to reestablish secure majorities in the legislative sessions of 1899, 1901, and 1903. Beginning in 1905, however, there were indications that the political climate in Nebraska was about to change once again in the direction of reform. Reflecting the shift in national politics to progressive reform as advocated by Theodore Roosevelt, political discourse in Nebraska increasingly focused on new themes. Central to this discussion was the need for the increased regulation of business (employer liability, railroad-rate regulation, guaranteed bank deposits, and food inspection), the further expansion of popular democracy (direct primary, direct election of U.S. senators, and the initiative and referendum), and controlling morality (prohibition). It was this last issue that gripped Nebraska politics most firmly and directly affected the outcome of renewed demands for direct legislation.[30]

Temperance had been an issue in Nebraska since the 1850s. Lawmakers enacted the state's first prohibition law in 1855 only to repeal it three years later. In the late 1870s Nebraska legislators passed the Slocumb law that required saloons to pay a stiff yearly license fee of five hundred dollars and allowed for local option whereby towns could banish saloons entirely. Dissatisfaction with the Slocumb law, however, reenergized the temperance

---

Nebraska Law Was Passed," *Direct Legislation Record* 4 [June 1897]: 23–24). Quoted comments are from Breckenridge, "Nebraska as a Pioneer," 218–20.

29. Opposition to the automatic use of the plan was so great in 1897 that Sheldon agreed to amend his bill so that the law would not take effect until voted on by the people (Breckenridge, "Nebraska as a Pioneer," 222 n. 22 [see also 220–22]). See also *Direct Legislation Record* 4 (December 1897): 66; and 5 (December 1898): 76.

30. See Robert W. Cherny, *Populism, Progressivism, and the Transformation of Nebraska Politics, 1885–1915*, 83, 107, 109–10.

movement during the 1880s, but enthusiasm again fell off after voters rejected an amendment calling for statewide prohibition in 1890.

When temperance reform again emerged in the late 1890s, it did so as a branch of the Anti-Saloon League organized in 1895. Dr. John B. Carns, a Methodist minister from Grand Island, headed the Nebraska branch, created in 1897. Functioning as an arm of the national body, the Carns-led Nebraska league worked to unite all antiliquor forces into a single political bloc. Although the organization remained nonpartisan, its greatest strength lay in the Republican Party, the home of many temperance-minded, pietistic religious groups. The league published literature, hired speakers, polled candidates, advised voters, and provided legal counsel to prosecute cases involving violations of existing liquor laws. Results proved encouraging. By 1900, 75 towns in Nebraska had voted to become "dry." Three years later the league reported that 375 towns in the state had organized local chapters of the Anti-Saloon League. By 1908 that number had risen to 450.

Organizational advances seemed to be generating legislative gains as well. In 1905, Nebraska's legislators prohibited saloons within five miles of a labor camp where twenty-five or more workers were employed. They continued the process in 1907, enacting a number of antiliquor measures. The list included requiring conspicuous labeling on intoxicants, prohibiting liquor licensing within two and one-half miles of a military post, empowering the governor to remove any public official who refused to enforce local option laws, and forbidding brewers from holding financial interests in saloons.

The liquor debate intensified in 1907 when Republican governor George L. Sheldon went beyond proposals aimed at strengthening local option and boldly called for a county option liquor law. County option promised to reduce law enforcement problems and allow temperance to gradually spread as it gained strength. Many temperance advocates hoped, and undoubtedly most brewers and distributors feared, that county option would serve as a short, quick step toward statewide prohibition. Sheldon's call prompted the liquor industry to take immediate action by reorganizing the Personal Liberty League, which had campaigned successfully against the 1890 prohibition amendment. Brewers and saloon owners strengthened their ties to the more personal liberty–oriented Democratic Party and seemingly found a kindred spirit in Ashton C. Shallenberger, the Democratic nominee for governor in 1908, who promised to veto county option if elected.

The battle came to a head during the 1909 session of the legislature with the antiprohibition forces winning the greater victory by defeating not only county option but a measure calling for the statewide initiative and referendum as well. If county option posed a threat to the liquor industry, so too did direct legislation. If voters could make laws directly, they could circumvent the power of the liquor lobby. As the editor of the state's Anti-Saloon League newspaper summed it up: "[L]iquor interests oppose the adoption of any form of the initiative and referendum because they are afraid the people will use it to settle the saloon question."[31] Looking to defuse the liquor debate by appeasing the Anti-Saloon League, the Democratically controlled legislature approved a minor bill closing saloons on election days. But the House Judiciary Committee amended the measure to include prohibiting the sale of alcohol from eight at night to seven in the morning daily and all day on Sunday. After heated debate, the legislature approved the so-called daylight-saloon law as amended. Responding to pressure from the Anti-Saloon League, Governor Shallenberger reluctantly signed it.[32]

Convinced that the "whiskey representatives" in the legislature had killed the initiative and referendum in 1909, direct legislationists decided to generate an organized political response. The result was the formation of the new Nebraska Direct Legislation League in March 1910. J. H. Mockett Jr. of Lincoln acted as president, supported by six vice presidents representing districts in all parts of the state. The list included E. C. Clark of Syracuse, Ross Hammond from Fremont, H. E. Sackett of Beatrice, C. Hildreath of Franklin, J. A. Donahoe from O'Neill, and John O. Yeiser of Omaha, whose participation indicates that his enthusiasm remained strong after thirteen years. The strategy adopted by league officials was to work to see that proinitiative and -referendum candidates won election to the next legislature. To that end, the executive committee prepared a circular letter to the people of Nebraska explaining the aim of the league and asking for their assistance in making it a reality.[33]

The league also received some assistance in publicizing the issue of direct legislation from William Jennings Bryan. Bryan supported the adoption of the initiative and referendum politically and used the editorial pages of the *Commoner* to advocate it. He had also traveled to several other states to lend his voice and popularity to the cause. Bryan, who blamed the brewery interests for having contributed to his presidential defeat in 1908, saw the Nebraska legislature's refusal to submit the question of direct legislation to the voters and its defeat of county option in 1909 as a stark example of how one powerful interest group had debauched the democrat-

31. Burton W. Folsom, "Tinkerers, Tipplers, and Traitors: Ethnicity and Democratic Reform in Nebraska during the Progressive Era," 58. The liquor interests generally opposed woman suffrage for the same reason.

32. See Robert E. Wenger, "The Anti-Saloon League in Nebraska Politics, 1898–1910," 268–83; Burton W. Folsom Jr., *No More Free Markets or Free Beer: The Progressive Era in Nebraska, 1900–1924,* 14–15, 45, 49–50; and Cherny, *Nebraska Politics,* 110.

33. See *Equity* 12 (April 1910): 61–62.

ic system. In Bryan's mind, the political fight to expand popular democracy had become linked with a moral crusade against the liquor interests.

Bryan realized, however, that the same close correlation between support for the initiative and referendum and county option did not exist among many Nebraska voters. In May 1909 at the close of one of his speeches in Omaha, Bryan requested standing votes from those present on the initiative and referendum and on county option. When asked, all but one in the audience rose in favor of direct legislation, but less than half stood in support of county option. Although his form of polling was crude and his urban sample biased, Bryan sensed an important political dynamic. As he would later warn his opponents: "Those who stand back of the liquor traffic are very short-sighted when they oppose the initiative and referendum." In other words, if the liquor interests continued to use their political clout to defeat direct legislation in order to block prohibition, they would risk generating a backlash among voters who would resent being disfranchised. His advice to his fellow Democrats was to divorce themselves from the special interests (namely, the liquor lobby) and adopt a platform that stood in favor of county option and the initiative and referendum.[34]

As the 1910 political campaign heated up, direct legislationists pressed their case. The league mailed letters to every candidate for the state legislature asking them to sign the following statement: "I am in favor of submitting to a vote of the people the question of adopting the statewide Initiative and Referendum in Nebraska. If elected a member of the next Nebraska Legislature, I will vote to submit an effective Initiative and Referendum amendment to the constitution of the state."[35] By August 279 legislative candidates had signed the pledge, and planks favoring the initiative and referendum had been adopted by both the Democratic (the party also endorsed the daylight-saloon law but not county option) and the Republican State Conventions. With the two major parties publicly on record in support of the reforms, the chances that some sort of direct legislation amendment might win approval in the next legislature, in 1911, looked promising.[36]

The Democratically controlled legislature of 1911 adhered to that party's platform positions. It rejected county option, but approved an initiative and referendum amendment. Direct legislationists were less than jubilant with the result, however, as the legislature continued to reflect the power of the liquor lobby and burdened the measure with prohibitive percentage requirements and burdensome signature restrictions. Petition require-

34. Bryan quoted in Paolo E. Coletta, "The Nebraska Democratic Campaign of 1910," 369 (see also 359–79).
35. *Equity* 12 (October 1910): 154.
36. See ibid. and Coletta, "Campaign of 1910," 374.

ments for the use of the constitutional initiative were set at 15 percent and those for the statutory initiative and referendum at 10 percent. Two-fifths (that is, thirty-six) of the state's ninety-three counties had to each supply a quota of 5 percent toward all petitions. A majority of those voting on a measure would decide the question, but amendments to the constitution required a favorable vote of 35 percent of the total votes cast in the election. Despite its deficiencies, voters adopted the proposed amendment at the general election in 1912 by a vote of 189,200 to 15,315.[37]

Nebraska voters made only limited use of the initiative and referendum at the elections of 1914, 1916, and 1918, but grappled with significant political, social, and economic issues nonetheless. In 1914 voters initiated a woman suffrage amendment (defeated) and referred two bills passed by the legislature: a workmen's compensation law (approved) and an appropriation bill for a new armory (rejected). In 1916 voters finally settled the liquor debate by approving an initiated amendment spearheaded by the Nebraska Dry Federation (a consolidation of all the state's temperance forces) calling for statewide prohibition. They rejected, however, a second initiated amendment authorizing the governor to appoint a food and drug commissioner.[38]

Two propositions appeared on the ballot in 1918. One was a legislative amendment limiting the franchise to full citizens, the other a legislative referendum on the question of calling a constitutional convention. Prior to 1918, the state permitted new immigrants to vote as soon as they applied for citizenship. However, World War I triggered nativistic feelings in Nebraska that focused on the perceived threat of German American disloyalty. The 1918 ballot measure reflected this paranoia. As one editor commented: "There is no reason why a man who is still, technically, a subject of the German kaiser, should have the right to help elect the officials of Nebraska and the United States." Nebraska voters not only overwhelmingly approved the amendment, but also acquiesced as an overly patriotic legislature partially repealed the state's open primary law and enacted a restrictive voter registration statute. To many politicians, such as Nebraska's new Republican governor Sam McKelvie, the direct primary system, espe-

37. See *Equity* 13 (April 1911): 78; 14 (July 1912): 97; and 15 (January 1913): 46. The large majority can be explained by the fact that constitutional amendments were placed on the ballot in the column for candidates and received all straight party votes unless a voter deliberately crossed out the amendment.

38. In 1913 the Voters' Legislative League sought a referendum on a building appropriations measure for a new armory at Nebraska City. The petition requirement for such a referendum was 10 percent, or 25,100 signatures. To come up with that amount within the allotted ninety days, the organization was forced to spend seven hundred dollars to hire solicitors to obtain the last 10,000 signatures. See *Equity* 16 (April 1914): 83–84; 16 (October 1914): 185; 17 (January 1915): 52; and 19 (January 1917): 35.

cially one that allowed voters to cross party lines in the primaries, reck-lessly allowed minority (that is, antiwar) candidates to win nomination to key offices. "As these minorities become better organized," said the gover-nor, "it at once becomes possible for them to practically dominate the elec-tion of principle public officials. Such a system is . . . dangerous." The vot-er registration law was a response to a similar fear, as it sought to limit the voting strength of German Americans who might support political candi-dates opposed to the war. The statute required all rural voters (Nebraska's German population was heavily rural) living in towns of fewer than eight thousand inhabitants to register and declare a party affiliation thirty days before an election in order to be eligible to vote. The law would prevent vot-ers from crossing party lines in a primary to vote for the other party's mi-nority, that is, antiwar, candidate. Ironically, as the wartime hysteria sub-sided, Nebraska voters reexamined their reactionary wartime decisions and approved voter-initiated measures to restore the direct primary in 1920 and repeal the voter registration law in 1922.[39]

Voters also approved the referendum calling for a constitutional con-vention in 1918. After concluding their deliberations in 1920, delegates to that convention submitted forty-one amendments for ratification by the voters at a special election held September 21, 1920. One of the measures that won approval was a revision of the initiative and referendum amend-ment. The new law reduced petition requirements from 15 to 10 percent for the constitutional initiative, from 10 to 7 percent for the statutory initiative, and from 10 to 5 percent for the referendum. The original county distribu-tion requirements, however, remained a part of the new law.[40]

39. Quotations are from Folsom, "Tinkerers, Tipplers, and Traitors," 70, 69. For a help-ful discussion of political activities in Nebraska during World War I and an argument that direct democracy (broadly defined) was more accurately a manipulative technique rather than an uncompromising principle, see 61–72. For an expanded discussion of the same argument, see Folsom, No More Free Markets.

40. For a list of the amendments and the votes recorded on each, see Nebraska, Ne-braska Blue Book, 1974–1975, 99–101.

Conclusion

In 1915 Benjamin Parke DeWitt, an astute contemporary observer of the American political scene, published an important book titled *The Progressive Movement*. DeWitt acknowledged that there was "widespread political agitation" in the country, and argued that this activity was rooted in three popular tendencies. The first of these was the general insistence that "special, minority, and corrupt influence in government—national, state, and city—be removed." The second was a popular demand that the structure of government (then "admirably adapted to control by the few") be altered so that it would be more difficult for "the few" and easier for "the many" to control. The third was that the current functions of government were too restrictive and that they needed to be expanded to address problems of social and economic hardship. These trends, said DeWitt, were "manifested in the political changes and reforms" that were being advocated and enacted at every level of government, and, because of "their universality and definiteness, they may be said to constitute the real progressive movement."[1]

Although historians of the period have since gone well beyond DeWitt in providing subtlety, nuance, and scope to the complexities of progressivism, there is much in DeWitt's analysis that helps to explain the motivations behind the campaigns to establish direct legislation in this country. Activists in New Jersey worried about falling farm prices, feared the consequences of governmental monetary policy, and bemoaned the failure of the dominant political parties to address real issues or confront fundamental social problems. South and North Dakotans confronted monopoly-controlled transportation, warehouse, and marketing agencies; partisan, single party–dominated state government; and, in North Dakota, a corporate-controlled political machine led by Boss McKenzie. In both states

1. DeWitt, *The Progressive Movement*, 4–5.

demands for the regulation of transportation (namely, railroad) rates; the storage, grading, and weighing of grain; the equal taxation of real property; and the enactment of a maximum-interest-rate law fell on deaf ears. "Reform" legislation, when it came, was incredibly disappointing. Laws were poorly drawn, complicated, contradictory, unworkable, or subject to gubernatorial veto. Oregonians rankled under a political system dominated by political bosses and political machines influenced by corporate power, tainted by political corruption, and stymied by legislative gridlock. Voters in Washington State complained of machine-controlled and railroad-influenced politics, discriminatory railroad rates, tax inequities, and wasteful expenditures. Californians felt subservient to the Southern Pacific machine, Montanans to the mining magnates and cattle barons, and Arizonans to the railroad and mining interests. Workers in each of these states felt blocked by a general unwillingness on the part of special interest–controlled legislators to enact any meaningful protective labor legislation.

The situation was the same in other states as well. Coloradans used the terms *Lobby* to denounce corporate influence over state politics and *Big Mitt* or *cabal* to assail the political control and economic dominance of Denver's telephone, water, gas, electric, and streetcar monopolies. Missourians understood the influence of special interests as the "Big Cinch" or "Combine" in St. Louis and the "Lobby" in Jefferson City and could talk knowingly about "boodle" and bribery in politics at the local and state levels. Oklahomans complained of banking and transportation monopolies, corporate tax dodging, and autocratic territorial governors and patronage-driven politics that ignored issues vital to workers and farmers. Voters in Arkansas decried legislative irresponsibility in spending and blanched at legislative corruption, whereas those in Michigan and Ohio chafed under single-party domination of state politics and machine control of local politics that stifled any reform agenda. Voters in Maine resented tax inequities and the power of corporation lobbyists, whereas those in Massachusetts were increasingly critical of a conservative-dominated political order that allowed prolabor legislation to be watered down, sabotaged by corporate lobbyists, or ignored. They bristled as legislators refused to modernize state and local governments, address the problem of tax inequities, or take action to curb the influence of political machines and special interests.

In each state studied, frustrated voters were eventually driven to conclude that they had become economically dependent and politically powerless. Convinced that their elected representatives had failed to respond to changes that affected their lives as taxpayers, citizens, workers, or farmers, and that they had allowed a disproportionate share of political power to be held by special interests, voters concluded that the nature of political participation would have to be redefined. If the political economy was to be fundamentally changed and the spirit of the Declaration of Independence enacted, voters would have to be empowered.

When intellectuals first began to discuss direct legislation or the initiative and referendum in the late 1880s, they optimistically believed, as would later progressives, that they could transform the American political system by adopting modern methods of reform. It was possible, they hypothesized, to eliminate divisive partisanship, autocratic legislative power, and special interest–dominated politics if voters had the power to make law and veto legislation. J. W. Sullivan likened this vision to a "peaceful revolution."[2] To many Americans increasingly dissatisfied with the developing political economy, direct legislation merited serious consideration.

The adoption of these new political techniques did not seem all that extraordinary. Voters in almost every state had been ratifying state constitutions or amendments to those documents and deciding by popular vote where they wanted to locate their state capitols or universities. They had been voting on whether to raise their debt or taxation limits, issue charters, expand the electoral franchise, or allow for the sale of alcoholic beverages. To advocates of direct democracy, this process was not only natural but also beneficial. The "sphere" of every citizen, said Sullivan, would be enlarged. Participation would enhance interest in the political economy, this interest would generate education, and education would facilitate decisions designed to promote the public welfare. Advocates also applied a democratic slant to enlightened self-interest. All interest groups could gain at least a hearing with direct legislation. Labor unions, farm groups, prohibitionists, woman suffragists, and single taxers would have a voice, and voters would have a needed forum for the popular debate of important political issues. Controversial topics would no longer be ignored.

Reenforcing this sentiment among advocates of direct legislation was the general conclusion that state legislatures had proved incapable of diligent governance through either waste and inefficiency, excessive partisanship, subservience to special interests, or outright corruption. The consensus among late-nineteenth- and early-twentieth-century reformers was that legislative power should be restrained. For this to be done effectively, it would have to be done piecemeal. Civil service regulations could reduce patronage, corrupt-practices acts could limit the influence of money in political campaigns, nonpartisan state and local elections could reduce partisanship, and home rule for cities could reduce state control over local governments. Similarly, the direct election of U.S. senators could remove the power of political election from partisan and special interest influence, and

2. Sullivan, *Direct Legislation by the Citizenship through the Initiative and Referendum,* 95–120.

the direct primary could allow voters to wrest the nomination process from party control. Woman suffrage not only would empower women, but could, conceivably, force the consideration of an entirely new set of gender-based issues as well. The initiative and referendum would force legislators to share power with voters by allowing them to create law and veto legislation directly, whereas the recall would allow voters to immediately discipline irresponsible officials. With these new reforms—arguably the most significant political changes of the Populist-Progressive Era—voters could potentially break the power of the political establishment, destroy special privilege, and capture the power to directly influence the making of policies.

When reformers in New Jersey formed the first practical organization for the promotion of direct legislation in 1892, they did so with the clear intention of assuming a nonpartisan political posture and encouraging cooperation among different interest groups. Although New Jersey's direct legislationists were unsuccessful in their own state campaign, they developed an organizational blueprint for others to follow. The key elements here, as in progressive reform efforts in general, were education and publicity. They held public meetings, interrogated political candidates about their position on the initiative and referendum, and organized a speaker's bureau. They encouraged prominent labor organizations, farm associations, and municipal and civic leagues to pass resolutions in support of direct legislation, and they drew up model bills, lobbied legislators, and encouraged supporters to create or join direct legislation leagues. The first formal steps toward the creation of a national movement centered on publicity, organization, and mobilization. J. W. Sullivan and Eltweed Pomeroy began publication of the *Direct Legislation Record* in 1894. Pomeroy issued the call that led to the creation of the National Direct Legislation League and the election of an executive committee in St. Louis in 1896, and delegates to the founding convention began the process of appointing the first state and territorial organizers at that same meeting.

The leaders in the National Direct Legislation League formally adhered to a nonpartisan position when it came to identification with any single political party. In reality, though, those same leaders knew that the Populists, with their emphasis on political independence and curtailing the power of large corporations, promised to be their strongest allies. They were not disappointed. The Populist Party added a plank to its platform "commending" the initiative and referendum in 1892 and specifically endorsed those measures in 1896. Although not included as part of their platform in 1896, the recall, or "imperative mandate," was widely discussed in Populist circles. The enactment of direct legislation in South Dakota in 1898 was most certainly a Populist triumph. Additionally, many leaders in the direct legislation movement had Populist connections, and the early organizational efforts behind direct legislation in Nebraska, Oklahoma, North Dakota, Montana, Oregon, and Colorado owed their advances to activists who were or had been Populists. It was not totally ironic that organizers in several states chose to bring in William Jennings Bryan to provide Populist symbolism and rhetoric to boost their direct legislation campaigns at crucial junctures.

This particular Populist connection to progressivism is an important one. Historians Arthur Link and Richard McCormick note that progressivism in the Great Plains and the Far West "borrowed from . . . the Populist heritage." They have also found that the western variety of progressive reform often grew out of "factional cleavages" in many state Republican Parties (an observation confirmed by this study). After the turn of the century, political "outs" proved quite resourceful at using anticorporate and antimachine rhetoric to displace the "ins." Some of this, they argue, "was political opportunism." They quickly add, however, that "it could not have succeeded without tapping deeply felt political and economic grievances among voters," and that the targets of their ire were most often the railroads, mining and timber corporations, and public utility companies. The most distinctive aspect of western progressivism identified by Link and McCormick, however, and underscored in this study, "was its passion for the more democratic, anti-institutional political reforms, such as the initiative, the referendum, and the recall."[3]

Progressive control of state government was key to winning legislative approval of these measures. Important to this process was the leadership provided by reform governors such as John Burke in North Dakota, George Hunt in Arizona, John Shafroth in Colorado, Hiram Johnson in California, and George Donaghey in Arkansas, who pressed for legislative enactment of that agenda. The roles performed by progressive governors as leaders in the campaign to expand popular democracy, however, were only the more highly visible and well-publicized parts of the story. In almost every state, the effort to win legislative approval of the initiative and referendum was led by individuals of common vocations who possessed uncommon abilities. Eltweed Pomeroy plied his trade as a small ink manufacturer. Henry Loucks and George Winship were newspaper editors. Robert W. Haire was a Roman Catholic priest and Herbert Bigelow a Congregational minister. J. Warner Mills was a lawyer, William U'Ren an itinerant blacksmith and public interest lobbyist. John R. Haynes and William Preston Hill were physicians, Silas Moser a business manager, and Judson King a paid organizer. Lars Ueland was a wheat farmer, cattle raiser, and horticulturist.

3. Link and McCormick, *Progressivism*, 33–34.

C. B. Kegley was a Granger, and J. W. Sullivan and Henry Sterling were printers. Interestingly, nearly a majority of those listed (Pomeroy, U'Ren, Moser, Hill, Bigelow, Sullivan, and Mills) were known to be ardent single taxers. Taken together, they were critical thinkers, brilliant organizers, savvy political tacticians, and indefatigable campaigners. They generated enthusiasm and engendered optimism with their own energy and fortitude. They were idealistic, determined visionaries, and the success of the direct legislation movement is a testament to their efforts. Deserving of Lincoln Steffens's classic designation, they were "Upbuilders."[4]

Direct legislation was, as historian Carlos Schwantes has so aptly put it, a "protean reform" that united labor, farmers, and the middle class.[5] Perhaps this is not surprising, as direct legislation simply offered the best means to correct political, economic, and social abuses as defined or prioritized by each particular group. In every state studied a combination of middle-class reformers, trade unionists, and farm organizers entered into loose political coalitions to direct grassroots campaigns designed to gain passage of statewide initiative and referendum statutes. Although the relative strength of the various groups, the effectiveness of the leadership, and the overall cohesion of the coalitions varied from state to state, each group demonstrated a willingness or understood the need to cooperate to obtain direct legislation. In many ways, the effectiveness of that cooperation determined the success of state campaigns to enact the initiative and referendum. But let me reiterate. There was more than just a shared sense of common self-interest that brought these seemingly oppositional interest groups together. What really made them willing to speak, lobby, and work together was quite simply a sense of overwhelming frustration with the "system" as they knew it.

The struggle to obtain the initiative and referendum in the United States was not an easy one. In every state, conservative defenders of the status quo fought mightily to block passage of those reforms. In some states political partisanship, expressed as the dominant party's desire to maintain its hold on power, provided the force of greatest resistance. In other states it might be the boss or the political machine, corporate lobbyists, or legislators who felt their prerogatives threatened who worked to undermine the reform effort. In some states it was a dominant interest group that felt threatened, such as the liquor industry in Nebraska that feared prohibition or, conversely, the prohibition lobby, the Women's Christian Temperance Union, in North Dakota that worried that voters would demand resub-

---

4. See Steffens, *Upbuilders*.

5. Schwantes, *Radical Heritage: Labor, Socialism, and Reform in Washington and British Columbia, 1885–1917*, 93.

mission of the liquor question. In Arkansas resistance came from a coalition of conservative interests that included the Arkansas Bar Association, the Arkansas Supreme Court, and the *Arkansas Gazette*. Even more formal associations such as the State Board of Commerce in Ohio (supported by the state's public utility corporations) or the Stop-Look-Listen League in Washington (a manufacturers' and employers' association) campaigned to derail enactment.

As part of their opposition to direct legislation, opponents in every state mounted a vigorous intellectual critique of the idea, often masking threatened self-interests in the process. On a philosophical level they challenged the assumption that voters could be trusted or that they were qualified to make informed decisions on complex issues. Direct legislation, they argued, was really a nondeliberative democracy that would weaken the principle of representative government as they defined it. Broadening the legislative process would leave voters susceptible to demagogues who would pander to popular prejudice or narrow self-interest. The result would be tyranny of the majority. Those who opposed the initiative and referendum offered numerous practical objections as well. Direct legislation would clutter the ballot with trivial or confusing propositions, make it too easy to amend state constitutions, and allow heavily populated urban areas to dominate sparsely populated rural ones. Critics especially abhorred the initiative, seeing it as a tool of radicals and cranks that would open the door for the single tax or other wild-eyed measures. At worst, they charged that direct legislation was communistic or socialistic.

Supporters of direct legislation also had to contend with a long list of imperfections that opponents embedded in the system at the time of adoption as well as numerous difficulties that appeared once the new methods were put to use. In many instances legislators burdened the reforms with numerous restrictions and encumbrances. They often attached and then abused emergency clauses that exempted certain legislation from the initiative and referendum, denied the application of the initiative to constitutional amendments, and demanded prohibitive percentages on petitions. They also set onerous geographic distribution requirements that had to be met in a specified number of counties or congressional districts, occasionally required legislative approval before propositions could even appear on the ballot, and imposed nearly impossible supermajority requirements for passage.

Reformers also failed to anticipate how the new reforms could be manipulated. Governors might use the initiative to push their own pet projects in specially called elections, moneyed interests could hire paid petition circulators, and moral purists and religious fundamentalists could use the initiative for restrictive or illiberal purposes. Reformers also failed to anticipate the effectiveness of what might be called "counterreform" campaigns conducted by the ideological Right and Left. In both Oregon and Arizona, employers' associations mounted spirited initiative campaigns to enact anti-labor statutes. In North Dakota the Non-Partisan League used the initiative to circumvent the legislature and enact a radical economic program, and then watched as the Independent Voters Association attempted to use the referendum to overturn that same program.

Examined nationally, the initiative and referendum laws enacted during the Progressive Era revealed imperfections that critics then and now have used to argue that the process itself is a failure.[6] However, those same critics often overlook or trivialize the significance of what happened at that historical moment. Despite the numerous structural flaws mentioned above and the embarrassments associated with superfluous or spiteful ballot propositions, voters used the new tools to enact provisions and build protections that had previously been denied them. Included in this list of voter-initiated accomplishments are woman suffrage, direct primary laws, the recall, corrupt-practices acts and antipass legislation, workmen's compensation, child labor and eight-hour laws, public utilities regulation, and modifications to existing tax statutes, to name but a few. Although they may not have fully realized the reform potential longed for by some advocates, voters demonstrated that they at least expected their government to be more accountable and more responsive. The ratification of the statewide initiative or referendum or both in twenty-two states between 1898 and 1918, and the consideration of more than four hundred ballot propositions under those laws, offers an indication that voters had gained a voice. That in itself has an importance that should not be diminished.

6. For a recent account that argues that moneyed interests have co-opted the initiative process to further their own special interests, see David S. Broder, *Democracy Derailed: Initiative Campaigns and the Power of Money.*

Appendix

Measure	Origin	Yes	No	Majority For	Majority Against
1912					
1. Miners' Lien Law	Ref. Stat.	13,551	5,804	7,747	
2. Full Train Crew Law	Ref. Stat.	11,123	7,635	3,488	
3. Electric Headlight Law	Ref. Stat.	11,286	7,408	3,878	
4. Law Requiring Railroad Engineers and Conductors to Be Experienced Men	Ref. Stat.	10,921	7,956	2,965	
5. Car Limit for Trains	Ref. Stat.	10,709	8,228	2,481	
6. Law Reducing Passenger Rates to 3 Cents per Mile	Ref. Stat.	14,823	4,835	9,988	
7. Semimonthly Payday for State Employees	Ref. Stat.	13,350	5,986	7,364	
8. Game License Law	Ref. Stat.	13,121	6,334	6,787	
9. Woman Suffrage	Init. Amend.	13,442	6,202	7,240	
10. Recall of Judges	Leg. Amend.	16,272	3,705	12,567	
11. Giving the State and Municipalities the Right to Engage in Industrial Pursuits	Leg. Amend.	14,928	3,602	11,326	
12. Giving Legislature Right to Regulate Tax Assessment	Leg. Amend.	15,967	2,283	13,684	
13. Increasing Bonded Indebtedness of School Districts for Education	Leg. Amend.	15,358	2,676	12,682	

Measure	Origin	Yes	No	Majority For	Majority Against
1914					
1. Statewide Prohibition	Init. Amend.	25,887	22,743	3,144	
2. Limiting Prohibition Elections to Eight-Year Periods	Init. Amend.	16,059	26,437		10,378
3. A $5 Million Highway Bond Issue	Init. Amend.	13,215	23,499		10,284
4. Creating a State Reclamation Service	Init. Amend.	14,701	17,994		3,293
5. Depriving the Governor and Legislature of the Right to Veto Initiative or Referendum Measures Approved by the Voters	Init. Amend.	16,567	16,484	83	
6. To Create a State Board of Pardons and Paroles	Ref. Stat.	15,425	13,554	1,871	
7. Fixing a Maximum Passenger Intrastate Railroad Rate	Ref. Stat.	20,968	12,210	8,758	
8. Relating to the Creation of New Counties	Ref. Stat.	10,756	21,152		10,396
9. Changing County Seats	Ref. Stat.	14,255	17,740		3,485
10. To Abolish the Death Penalty	Init. Stat.	18,129	19,381		1,252
11. As to Semiannual Payment of Taxes	Init. Stat.	13,842	15,934		2,092
12. Prohibiting Blacklisting	Init. Stat.	18,207	17,444	763	
13. Old Age and Mothers' Pensions	Init. Stat.	25,827	12,394	13,433	
14. Appropriation for Participation in Panama Exposition	Init. Stat.	10,995	22,434		11,439
15. Requiring that 80 Percent of Employees Must Be American Citizens	Init. Stat.	25,017	14,323	10,694	
16. Enabling Property Owners to Assess Their Own Property, the State Reserving Right to Take Over Any Property	Init. Stat.	13,023	21,277		8,254
17. Regulating the Erection of Electric Poles, Wires, etc.	Init. Stat.	18,871	12,256	6,615	
18. To Establish a Contract System on All State Construction	Init. Stat.	16,754	15,853	901	
19. Creating Miami County	Init. Stat.	5,878	30,055		24,177

Measure	Origin	Yes	No	Majority For	Majority Against

1916

Measure	Origin	Yes	No	Majority For	Majority Against
1. Requiring a Majority of Total Votes Cast to Pass Initiative and Referendum Measures	Leg. Amend.	18,356	18,961		605
2. Tax Exemptions for Widows	Leg. Amend.	14,296	16,882		2,586
3. Prohibiting Importation of Liquor	Init. Amend.	28,473	17,379	11,094	
4. Legislative Redistricting	Init. Amend.	15,731	17,921		2,190
5. To Allow Local Option	Init. Amend.	13,377	29,934		16,557
6. Abolishing State Senate	Init. Amend.	11,631	22,286		10,655
7. Workmen's Compensation	Init. Amend.	18,061	21,255		3,194
8. Abolishing Death Penalty	Init. Stat.	18,936	18,784	152	
9. Creating Department of Labor	Init. Stat.	13,798	21,492		7,694
10. Creating Office of State Architect	Init. Stat.	10,010	25,960		15,950
11. Fish and Game Law	Init. Stat.	17,518	16,849	669	
12. Extending the Grounds for Divorce	Init. Stat.	13,564	18,097		4,533

1918

Measure	Origin	Yes	No	Majority For	Majority Against
1. Workmen's Compensation	Init. Amend.	12,873	27,177		14,304
2. Legislative Redistricting	Init. Amend.	17,564	10,688	6,876	
3. Legislative Control of Public Land Leases	Init. Amend.	16,372	10,867	5,505	
4. To Limit Lease of Public Lands	Init. Amend.	14,379	11,179	3,200	
5. To Abolish the Contract System on All State Construction	Leg. Ref.	13,297	11,658	1,639	
6. Antigaming Law	Ref. Stat.	10,736	10,066	670	
7. Red-Light Abatement	Ref. Stat.	19,102	8,990	10,112	
8. Restoration of Capital Punishment	Init. Stat.	20,443	10,602	9,841	
9. Against Compulsory School Vaccination	Init. Stat.	16,9411	3,411	3,530	
10. Amending the Land Code	Init. Stat.	10,239	10,975		736

ARKANSAS
INITIATIVE AND REFERENDUM, 1910

Measure	Origin	Yes	No	Majority For	Majority Against
1912					
1. Revision of Tax Laws, etc.	Ref. Stat.	57,176	79,899		22,723
2. Prohibition	Init. Stat.	69,390	85,358		15,968
3. Amending Election Laws	Init. Stat.	57,192	72,879		15,687
4. State Textbook Commission	Init. Stat.	64,898	73,701		8,803
5. Limiting Legislative Sessions to Sixty Days	Init. Amend.	103,246	33,397	69,849	
6. Recall of Elective Officials	Init. Amend.	71,234	57,860	13,374	
7. Municipal Bonds Authorization	Init. Amend.	76,660	53,098	23,562	
8. Education Qualification for Voting	Leg. Amend.	51,334	74,950		23,616
9. To Exempt Cotton Mills from Taxation for Seven Years	Leg. Amend.	66,919	51,469	15,450	
1914					
1. Child Labor	Init. Stat.	72,313	25,300	47,013	
2. Using Newspaper Publicity for Public Measures or Acts	Init. Stat.	55,519	40,725	14,794	
3. Municipal Bond Authorization	Init. Amend.	54,802	40,430	14,372	
4. To Fix Salaries of Legislators	Leg. Amend.	43,916	49,098		5,182
5. To Define Duties of Lieutenant Governor	Leg. Amend.	46,567	45,206	1,361	
1916					
1. Primary and State Election Law	Leg. Stat.	93,790	46,696	47,094	
2. Local Option	Leg. Stat.	58,064	109,697		51,633
3. School District Tax Increase	Leg. Amend.	108,173	52,175	55,998	
4. Improved Initiative and Referendum Provision	Init. Amend.	69,817	73,782		3,965
5. Good Roads Tax	Leg. Amend.	82,753	67,656	15,097	
1918					
1. Municipal Bond Authorization	Init. Amend.	25,059	24,191	868	
2. Increase Number of Supreme Court Justices	Leg. Amend.	20,721	28,888		8,167
3. State Farm Loans	Leg. Amend.	22,741	27,571		4,830

CALIFORNIA
INITIATIVE AND REFERENDUM, 1911

Measure	Origin	Yes	No	Majority For	Majority Against
1912					
1. Law Making Office of County Registrar Appointive	Ref. Stat.	145,924	255,051		109,127
2. Permitting Consolidation of Municipalities	Init. Amend.	174,076	280,465		106,389
3. To Prohibit Bookmaking and to Authorize a State Racing Commission	Init. Stat.	149,864	353,070		203,206
4. For Home Rule in Taxation	Init. Amend.	169,321	243,959		74,638
5. For Free Textbooks in Public Schools	Leg. Amend.	343,443	171,486	171,957	
6. Deposit of Moneys Belonging to the State	Leg. Amend.	307,199	128,411	178,788	
7. To Regulate Salaries and Fees of Officers in Third-Class Counties	Ref. Stat.	135,303	254,327		119,024
8. To Change the Law on Officers of Counties	Ref. Stat.	142,729	246,818		104,089
1914					
1. Calling Convention for Revision of Constitution	Leg. Res	180,111	442,687		262,576
2. Prohibition	Init. Amend.	355,536	524,781		169,245
3. Eight-Hour Law	Init. Stat.	282,692	560,881		278,189
4. Red-Light Abatement	Ref. Stat.	402,629	352,821	49,808	
5. Investment Companies Act	Ref. Stat.	343,805	288,084	55,721	
6. Water Commission Act	Ref. Stat.	309,950	301,817	8,133	
7. Local Taxation Exemption	Leg. Amend.	267,618	375,634		108,016
8. Exempting Vessels from Taxation	Leg. Amend.	359,176	301,969	57,207	
9. Regulating Investment Companies	Init. Stat.	249,500	353,812		104,312
10. Abolition of Poll Tax	Init. Amend.	405,375	374,487	30,888	
11. University of California Building Bond Act	Init. Stat.	413,020	239,332	173,688	
12. Constitutional Conventions	Leg. Amend.	271,896	274,325		2,429
13. Qualification of Voters at Bond Elections	Init. Amend.	312,193	337,951		25,758

Measure	Origin	Yes	No	Majority For	Majority Against
14. Voting by Absent Electors	Init. Stat.	244,855	390,333		145,478
15. Deposit of Public Moneys	Init. Amend.	236,573	324,558		87,985
16. Condemnation for Public Purposes	Leg. Amend.	259,192	307,155		47,963
17. Exposition Contribution by Alameda County	Leg. Amend.	390,835	202,128	188,707	
18. Nonsale of Game	Ref. Stat.	353,295	361,446		8,151
19. Consolidation of City and County, and Limited Annexation of Contiguous Territory	Init. Amend.	293,019	287,185	5,834	
20. Prohibiting Prizefights	Init. Stat.	413,741	327,569	86,172	
21. City and County Consolidation and Annexation with Consent of Annexed Territory	Init. Amend.	248,112	318,224		70,112
22. Land Title Law	Init. Stat.	359,757	224,846	134,911	
23. Elections by Plurality, Preferential Vote, and Primary	Leg. Amend.	240,600	294,265		53,665
24. Assembly Payroll Expenses	Leg. Amend.	87,315	494,272		406,957
25. Adoption and Amendment of Municipal Charters	Leg. Amend.	285,338	226,679	58,659	
26. Legislative Control of Irrigation, Reclamation, and Drainage Districts	Leg. Amend.	335,047	216,865	118,182	
27. County Charters	Leg. Amend.	261,219	225,530	35,689	
28. Regulation of Public Utilities	Leg. Amend.	291,665	260,589	31,076	
29. Incorporation of Municipalities	Leg. Amend.	284,757	214,312	70,445	
30. Irrigation Districts Controlling International Water Systems	Leg. Amend.	349,684	185,168	164,516	
31. Valuation of Condemned Public Utilities by Railroad Commission	Leg. Amend.	291,836	244,379	47,457	
32. Election of U.S. Senators	Leg. Amend.	404,283	190,969	213,314	
33. Public Utilities in Municipalities	Leg. Amend.	231,724	278,129		46,405
34. Taxation of Public Property	Leg. Amend.	344,433	216,612	127,821	
35. Sacramento State Building Bonds	Leg. Stat.	294,928	267,717	27,211	

Measure	Origin	Yes	No	Majority For	Majority Against
36. San Francisco State Building Act	Leg. Stat.	300,028	257,119	42,909	
37. State Fairgrounds Bonds	Leg. Stat.	259,721	301,764		42,043
38. Los Angeles State Building Bonds	Init. Stat.	285,796	320,302		34,506
39. Suspension of Prohibition Amendment	Init. Amend.	448,648	226,688	221,960	
40. Extra Sessions of District Courts of Appeal	Leg. Amend.	203,674	322,891		119,217
41. Miscarriage of Justice	Leg. Amend.	378,237	182,073	196,164	
42. Place of Payment of Bonds and Interest	Leg. Amend.	306,195	206,479	99,716	
43. Exempting Educational Institutions from Taxation	Leg. Amend.	331,599	293,721	37,878	
44. Minimum Wage	Leg. Amend.	379,311	295,109	84,202	
45. One Day of Rest in Seven	Init. Stat.	290,679	457,890		167,211
46. Creating Board Regulating Drugless Practice	Init. Stat.	223,217	462,355		239,138
47. No Prohibition Elections for Eight Years	Init. Amend.	355,394	435,701		80,307
48. San Francisco Harbor Improvement Act of 1913	Leg. Stat.	408,633	167,589	241,044	

1915*

Measure	Origin	Yes	No	Majority For	Majority Against
1. Direct Primary	Ref. Stat.	112,681	156,967		44,286
2. Form of Ballot	Ref. Stat.	106,377	151,067		44,690
3. Term of Superior Judges	Leg. Amend.	47,229	213,067		165,838
4. Term of Judges Filling Vacancies	Leg. Amend.	124,610	125,124		514
5. Rural Credits	Leg. Amend.	124,247	132,320		8,073
6. Deposit of Public Moneys	Leg. Amend.	92,981	151,845		58,864
7. Revising Initiative and Referendum	Leg. Amend.	121,210	127,160		5,950
8. Condemnation for Public Purposes	Leg. Amend.	92,048	155,786		63,738
9. Taxation	Leg. Amend.	42,158	205,597		163,439
10. Exempting Property from Taxation	Leg. Amend.	94,460	168,171		73,711
11. County Charters	Leg. Amend.	85,571	152,097		66,526

*Special election

Measure	Origin	Yes	No	Majority For	Majority Against
1916					
1. Statewide Prohibition	Init. Amend.	436,639	538,200		101,561
2. Prohibition in Public Houses	Init. Amend.	461,039	505,783		44,744
3. State Highway Bond Issue	Leg. Stat.	542,239	137,107	405,132	
4. Direct Primary	Ref. Stat.	319,559	349,723		30,164
5. Home Rule in Taxation	Init. Amend.	260,332	576,533		316,201
6. Ineligibility	Init. Amend.	414,208	230,360	183,848	
7. State Highway	Leg. Stat.	483,151	152,910	330,241	
1918					
1. "Liquor Control": Permitting Wines and Beer	Init. Stat.	256,778	341,897		85,119
2. Usury Law	Init. Stat.	231,147	212,207	18,940	
3. County and School Tax Limitations	Init. Stat.	167,049	227,953		60,904
4. To Ease Dental Licensing Requirements	Init. Stat.	200,475	314,713		114,238
5. "Bone Dry" Prohibition	Init. Stat.	275,643	306,488		30,845
6. Land Value Taxation (Single Tax)	Init. Amend.	118,088	360,334		242,246
7. To Limit Tax Increase to 5 Percent Annually	Ref. Stat.	127,634	259,626		131,992
8. Deposit of Public Money	Leg. Amend.	239,203	180,856	58,347	
9. Absentee Voters	Leg. Amend.	189,845	252,387		62,542
10. Organization within County of Consolidated City and County Government	Leg. Amend.	195,998	183,610	12,388	
11. Court Authority	Leg. Amend.	86,132	274,231		188,099
12. Los Angeles County Funds	Leg. Amend.	183,994	178,970	5,024	
13. University of California Administration	Leg. Amend.	249,886	148,305	101,581	
14. Appellate Court Divisions	Leg. Amend.	188,243	169,803	18,440	
15. Borough Government Permanency	Leg. Amend.	179,627	171,735	7,892	
16. Exempting Cemeteries from Taxation	Leg. Amend.	170,296	302,325		132,029
17. Reimbursing Cities for Revenue Losses from Taxation Exemptions for Military Service	Leg. Amend.	115,727	262,421		146,694

Measure	Origin	Yes	No	Majority For	Majority Against
18. Condemnation of Right-of-Way for Public Use	Leg. Amend.	212,011	179,976	32,035	
19. Taxation Exemptions	Leg. Amend.	166,486	290,573		124,087
20. State Budget Board	Leg. Amend.	96,820	261,311		164,491
21. City of Venice Indebtedness	Leg. Amend.	188,349	167,647	20,702	
22. Health Insurance	Leg. Amend.	133,858	358,324		224,466
23. Workmen's Compensation	Leg. Amend.	229,974	224,517	5,457	
24. Stockholder's Liability	Leg. Amend.	178,355	196,948		18,593
25. Eminent Domain	Leg. Amend.	138,131	228,324		90,193

COLORADO
INITIATIVE AND REFERENDUM, 1910

Measure	Origin	Yes	No	Majority For	Majority Against
1912					
1. Statewide Prohibition	Init. Amend.	75,877	116,774		40,897
2. Providing a Special Fund for the State Immigration Bureau	Init. Amend.	30,359	54,272		23,913
3. Granting Home Rule to Cities and Towns	Init. Amend.	49,596	44,778	4,818	
4. Providing for the Recall of Officials from Office, Including Judges	Init. Amend.	53,620	39,564	14,056	
5. Regulating the Submission of Proposed Constitutional Amendments	Init. Amend.	33,413	40,634		7,221
6. Regulating Proceedings for Contempt of Court and Allowing Jury Trials for Contempt in Certain Cases	Init. Amend.	31,850	41,855		10,005
7. To Create a Public Utilities Court	Init. Amend.	27,534	51,820		24,286
8. Providing for Wider Use and Control of Schools by the People	Init. Amend.	38,318	55,691		17,373
9. Giving the People the Right to Overrule Decisions of the Supreme Court Declaring Laws Unconstitutional	Init. Amend.	55,416	40,891	14,525	

Measure	Origin	Yes	No	Majority For	Majority Against
10. Designating Mining and Smelting as Affected with the Public Interest	Leg. Amend.	35,997	37,953		1,956
11. Creating a State Tax Commission in Lieu of the State Board of Equalization	Leg. Amend.	32,548	40,012		7,464
12. Substitution of Fixed Salaries for Official Fees	Leg. Amend.	28,889	41,622		12,733
13. To Enlarge Limitation on County Debts for Highway and Other Purposes	Leg. Amend.	29,741	47,284		17,543
14. Authorizing Bonded Debt for Construction and Improvement of Public Highways	Leg. Amend.	36,636	53,327		16,691
15. Search and Seizure Laws to Enforce Prohibition	Init. Stat.	64,616	79,190		14,574
16. Eight-Hour Law for Women in Injurious Occupations	Init. Stat.	108,959	32,019	76,940	
17. Regulation of Public Service Corporations	Init. Stat.	30,347	64,138		33,791
18. To Establish a State Fair (a Gambling-Legalization Law)	Init. Stat.	49,102	52,462		3,360
19. To Reduce Costs of Publishing Arguments for and against Initiated Measures and Referred Laws	Init. Stat.	39,551	50,635		11,084
20. Amending Election Laws	Init. Stat.	37,616	38,537		921
21. Providing for a Headless Ballot	Init. Stat.	43,390	39,504	3,886	
22. Mothers' Compensation Act and Aid to Dependent and Neglected Children	Init. Stat.	82,337	37,870	44,467	
23. Civil Service Regulation Bill	Init. Stat.	38,426	35,282	3,144	
24. Limiting Hours in Mines, Smelters	Init. Stat.	52,525	48,777	3,748	
25. Establishing a State Highway Commission	Init. Stat.	44,568	45,101		533
26. Eight-Hour Law for Miners	Ref. Stat.	69,489	30,992	38,497	
27. Concerning the Branding and Marking of Live Stock	Ref. Stat.	37,387	37,740		353

Measure	Origin	Yes	No	Majority For	Majority Against
28. Regulating the Custody and Management of Public Funds	Ref. Stat.	20,968	44,322		23,354
29. Establishing Teachers' Summer Normal Schools	Ref. Stat.	23,521	63,266		39,745
30. Concerning Examination of Teachers	Ref. Stat.	25,369	54,086		28,717
31. Regulating Irrigation	Ref. Stat.	22,931	47,614		24,683
32. Construction of Tunnel through James Peak	Leg. Ref.	45,800	93,183		47,383

1914

Measure	Origin	Yes	No	Majority For	Majority Against
1. Proposing a Six-Year Interval for Resubmission of an Initiated Proposition	Init. Amend.	55,667	112,537		56,870
2. Statewide Prohibition	Init. Amend.	129,589	118,017	11,572	
3. Providing for a Three-fourths Jury Verdict in Civil Cases and Permitting Women to Serve on Juries	Init. Amend.	67,130	77,488		10,358
4. Enabling 25 Percent of Voters to Demand a Special Election for Submission of Measures Under the Initiative and Referendum and Authorizing Governor to Call Such Election	Init. Amend.	40,643	80,977		40,334
5. To Codify Laws Relating to Women and Children	Init. Stat.	68,242	72,122		3,880
6. Permitting Probation for Minors and First Offenders	Init. Stat.	62,561	68,512		5,951
7. For Better Roads	Init. Stat.	117,146	54,844	62,302	
8. Making Newspapers Public Utilities	Init. Amend.	35,752	91,426		55,674
9. Creating a Public Utilities Commission	Ref. Stat.	39,703	65,182		25,479
10. Licensing Commission Merchants	Ref. Stat.	39,448	67,454		28,006
11. Relieving Workmen of Industrial Risk	Ref. Stat.	69,006	60,298	8,708	
12. Concerning the Appointment of Peace Officers	Ref. Stat.	49,116	66,836		17,720
13. To Regulate Public Utility Corporations	Ref. Stat.	37,633	63,603		25,970

Measure	Origin	Yes	No	Majority For	Majority Against
14. Municipal Indebtedness	Leg. Amend.	38,589	65,206		26,617
15. Enlarging Powers of the State Board of Equalization	Leg. Amend.	55,987	55,275	712	
16. Concerning Publication of Constitutional Amendments and Initiated and Referred Laws	Leg. Amend.	48,301	56,259		7,958

1916

Measure	Origin	Yes	No	Majority For	Majority Against
1. Regulating the Practice of Medicine	Ref. Stat.	96,879	82,317	14,562	
2. Civil Service	Init. Amend.	62,458	96,561		34,103
3. Manufacture and Sale of Beer	Init. Amend.	77,345	163,134		85,789
4. Care of Insane	Init. Stat.	164,220	39,415	124,805	
5. To Abolish State Tax Commission	Init. Stat.	80,362	84,011		3,649
6. Regulating the Running of Stock at Large	Init. Stat.	85,279	155,134		69,855
7. Providing for the Investment of School Funds	Init. Stat.	102,956	66,058	36,898	
8. Holding Constitutional Convention	Leg. Ref	53,530	69,579		16,049

1918

Measure	Origin	Yes	No	Majority For	Majority Against
1. Concerning Publication of Constitutional Amendments and Initiated and Referred Laws	Leg. Amend.	98,715	12,237	86,478	
2. Limiting Time for Introduction of Legislative Bills from Twenty-five to Fifteen Days	Leg. Amend.	67,693	19,901	47,792	
3. Placing State Civil Service in the Constitution	Init. Amend.	75,301	41,287	34,014	
4. "Bone-Dry" Prohibition Law	Init. Stat.	113,636	64,740	48,896	
5. Relief of Adult Blind	Init. Stat.	131,469	9,440	122,029	

IDAHO
INITIATIVE AND REFERENDUM, 1912
ENACTING PROVISIONS PASSED BY LEGISLATURE IN 1915 BUT VETOED BY GOVERNOR

MAINE
INITIATIVE AND REFEREDUM, 1908
NO CONSTITUTIONAL INITIATIVE

Measure	Origin	Yes	No	Majority For	Majority Against
1910					
1. To Establish a Uniform Standard for Percentage of Alcohol in Intoxicating Liquor	Ref. Stat.	31,093	40,475		9,382
2. To Divide the Town of York	Ref. Stat.	19,692	34,722		15,030
3. Authorizing Reconstruction of the Portland Harbor Bridge	Ref. Stat.	21,251	29,851		8,600
1911*					
1. Direct Primary Law	Init. Stat.	65,810	21,774	44,036	
2. Repeal of Prohibition	Leg. Amend.	60,095	60,853		758
3. To Move the State Capitol from Augusta to Portland	Leg. Amend.	41,294	59,678		18,384
4. Increasing Debt Limit of Cities	Leg. Amend.	39,242	38,712	530	
1912					
1. To Provide for a Uniform Ballot Box and Preservation of Ballots	Ref. Stat.	72,816	33,884	38,932	
2. State Bond Issue for Highways	Leg. Amend.	80,619	21,454	59,165	
1913					
1. Classification of Property for Tax Purposes	Leg. Amend.	18,060	8,157	9,903	
2. To Simplify the Amending Feature of the State Constitution	Leg. Amend.	16,746	6,741	10,005	
1914					
1. To Create a Public Utility Commission	Ref. Stat.	67,365	37,008	30,357	
1916					
1. State and County Aid in Building Highway Bridges	Ref. Stat.	96,677	14,138	82,539	

Measure	Origin	Yes	No	Majority For	Majority Against
2. To Establish a Fifty-four-Hour Week for Women and Minors	Ref. Stat.	95,591	40,252	55,339	

1917*

1. Woman Suffrage	Leg. Amend.	20,604	38,838		18,234
2. Removal of Sheriffs	Leg. Amend.	29,584	25,416	4,168	
3. Permission for Towns to Create Local Polling Places	Leg. Amend.	22,588	24,593		2,005
4. Relating to the State Militia	Leg. Amend.	20,585	23,912		3,327
5. Apportionment of Representatives in Merger of Towns and Cities	Leg. Amend.	22,013	21,719	294	

*Special election

MARYLAND
REFERENDUM ONLY, 1915

MASSACHUSETTS
INITIATIVE AND REFERENDUM, 1918

MICHIGAN
INITIATIVE AND REFERENDUM, 1908; REVISED 1913

Measure	Origin	Yes	No	Majority For	Majority Against
1910					
1. To Limit the Bonded Indebtedness of Counties	Leg. Amend.	137,147	128,729	8,418	
1911					
1. Apportionment of Primary School Interest Money	Leg. Amend.	246,167	118,391	127,776	
1912					
1. Woman Suffrage	Leg. Amend.	247,375	248,135		760

Measure	Origin	Yes	No	Majority For	Majority Against
2. Relating to the Amendment of Charters of Villages and Cities	Leg. Amend.	285,373	137,972	147,401	

1913

Measure	Origin	Yes	No	Majority For	Majority Against
1. Woman Suffrage	Leg. Amend.	168,738	264,882		96,144
2. Relating to the Initiative and Referendum on Constitutional Questions	Leg. Amend.	204,796	162,392	42,404	
3. Relating to the Initiative and Referendum on Legislative Questions	Leg. Amend.	219,057	152,388	66,669	
4. Relating to Relief, Insuring, and Pensioning of Members of Fire Departments	Leg. Amend.	179,948	206,204		26,256
5. Relating to the Recall of Elective Officers	Leg. Amend.	237,743	145,412	92,331	

1914

Measure	Origin	Yes	No	Majority For	Majority Against
1. Issuing Bonds for Road Improvements	Leg. Amend.	164,333	202,087		37,754
2. Issuing Bonds for Construction of Drains and Improvement of Agricultural Lands	Leg. Amend.	165,290	199,873		34,583
3. Relating to Right of Absentee Voting	Leg. Amend.	190,510	175,948	14,562	
4. Incorporation and Regulation of Beneficiary Societies	Init. Amend.	92,392	291,776		199,384

1915

Measure	Origin	Yes	No	Majority For	Majority Against
1. Permitting Drainage Districts to Issue Bonds for Drainage Purposes	Leg. Amend.	191,337	198,553		7,216

1916

Measure	Origin	Yes	No	Majority For	Majority Against
1. Prohibition	Init. Amend.	353,378	284,754	68,624	
2. Providing for Local Option	Init. Amend.	256,272	378,871		122,599

Measure	Origin	Yes	No	Majority For	Majority Against
3. Permitting the Legislature to Repeal Local or Special Acts of the Legislature without a Vote of the District Affected	Leg. Amend.	283,823	275,701	8,122	
4. Relating to the Regulation of Beneficiary Societies	Init. Amend.	225,220	349,810		124,590

1917

Measure	Origin	Yes	No	Majority For	Majority Against
1. Permitting Drainage Districts to Issue Bonds for Drainage Purposes	Leg. Amend.	198,918	139,027	59,891	
2. Relating to the Elective Franchise	Leg. Amend.	216,270	114,594	101,676	
3. Authorizing the State to Acquire, Hold, and Dispose of Railroad Property	Leg. Amend.	242,969	100,722	142,247	
4. Relating to the Salaries of State Officers	Leg. Amend.	148,625	193,119		44,494
5. Relating to the Construction and Maintenance of Highways	Leg. Amend.	209,559	126,871	82,688	

1918

Measure	Origin	Yes	No	Majority For	Majority Against
1. Requiring All Proposed Amendments to Be Printed on One Ballot	Leg. Amend.	317,070	90,744	226,326	
2. Woman Suffrage	Leg. Amend.	229,790	195,284	34,506	

MISSOURI
INITIATIVE AND REFERENDUM, 1908

Measure	Origin	Yes	No	Majority For	Majority Against
1910					
1. Statewide Prohibition	Init. Amend.	207,281	425,406		218,125
2. Tax Levy to Support State University	Init. Amend.	181,659	344,274		162,615
3. Police Pensions	Leg. Amend.	132,354	384,774		252,420
4. Teachers' Pension Fund	Leg. Amend.	122,063	389,647		267,584
5. Tax Levy Road Fund	Leg. Amend.	170,847	347,561		176,714

Measure	Origin	Yes	No	Majority For	Majority Against
6. Method of Amending City Charter, St. Louis	Leg. Amend.	138,942	349,147		210,205
7. New State Capitol Building	Leg. Amend.	188,259	332,858		144,599
8. Permitting Increase of County Debt	Leg. Amend.	150,174	337,984		187,810
9. Increase Per Diem of Legislature	Leg. Amend.	95,045	385,765		290,720
10. To Install Voting Machines	Leg. Amend.	133,569	352,915		219,346
11. To Allow Increase City Tax Rate Limit	Leg. Amend.	110,283	374,942		264,659

1912

Measure	Origin	Yes	No	Majority For	Majority Against
1. Graduated Tax on Land Values	Init. Amend.	86,647	508,137		421,490
2. Establishing State Tax Commission	Init. Amend.	96,911	475,151		378,240
3. Giving Grand Juries Right to Investigate Election Frauds	Init. Amend.	197,643	348,495		150,852
4. For a Tax Levy to Support Public Education	Init. Amend.	154,952	401,843		246,891
5. Extending Age Limit of Admission to Public Schools	Leg. Amend.	207,298	367,032		159,734
6. Increasing Debt Limit of St. Louis for Sewers, etc.	Leg. Amend.	140,611	402,473		261,862
7. Changing Tax Rates	Leg. Amend.	121,794	401,918		280,124
8. Changing Time of Legal Residence before Citizen Can Vote	Leg. Amend.	172,140	378,263		206,123
9. To Authorize Registration of Voters in Counties	Leg. Amend.	151,694	385,698		234,004

1914

Measure	Origin	Yes	No	Majority For	Majority Against
1. To Amend Initiative and Referendum Law to Restrict the Submission of Single Tax or Other Taxation Measures	Leg. Amend.	138,039	334,310		196,271
2. To Increase Kansas City Debt Limit	Leg. Amend.	123,596	312,651		189,055
3. Ten-Cent Tax on $100 Property Assessment for Good Roads	Leg. Amend.	112,497	346,995		234,498

Measure	Origin	Yes	No	Majority For	Majority Against
4. To Change Basis of Payment for Members of Legislature from Per Diem to $1,000 Annual Salary	Leg. Amend.	89,629	355,326		265,697
5. To Increase Debt Limit for Cities of More Than 100,000 Population	Leg. Amend.	117,197	316,959		199,762
6. To Authorize Voters of a District to Increase the Road Tax by Majority Vote	Leg. Amend.	117,041	333,576		216,535
7. To Authorize the Pensioning of the Blind	Leg. Amend.	214,951	255,717		40,766
8. To Authorize Easier Amendment of Charters of Certain Cities	Leg. Amend.	140,475	290,562		150,087
9. Requiring Railroads to Employ Full Crews of Trainmen	Ref. Stat.	159,892	324,384		164,492
10. Making Counties the Sole Units in Local Option Elections	Ref. Stat.	172,909	311,285		138,376
11. Abolishing Office of Excise Commissioners in Cities of 300,000 Population and Having a Bipartisan Board Appointed	Ref. Stat.	134,449	303,757		169,308
12. Abolishing Office of Police Commissioner in Cities of 300,000 Population and Having Bipartisan Board Appointed	Ref. Stat.	131,382	306,942		175,560
13. Woman Suffrage	Init. Amend.	182,257	322,463		140,206
14. A $50 Million Highway Bond Issue	Init. Amend.	76,574	378,530		301,956
15. To Levy Taxes or Issue Bonds for Road Building	Init. Amend.	80,935	373,302		292,367

1916

Measure	Origin	Yes	No	Majority For	Majority Against
1. Creation of State Land Bank	Init. Amend.	296,964	346,443		49,479
2. Statewide Prohibition	Init. Amend.	294,288	416,826		122,538
3. Pensions for the Blind	Leg. Amend.	385,627	272,908	112,719	

Measure	Origin	Yes	No	Majority For	Majority Against
1918					
1. Revision of Tax Rate for School Purposes	Leg. Amend.	90,637	297,118		206,481
2. Affecting Revenue for School Purposes	Leg. Amend.	93,392	289,269		195,877
3. Special Tax Levy	Leg. Amend.	94,142	287,488		193,346
4. Special Road Tax	Leg. Amend.	81,610	293,101		211,491
5. Extending Limits of Municipal Debt in Cities of 2,000 to 30,000	Leg. Amend.	88,246	286,886		198,640
6. Prohibition	Leg. Amend.	223,618	297,582		73,964
7. To Establish a Homestead Loan Fund	Init. Amend.	102,452	290,207		187,755
8. To Establish a Version of the Single Tax	Init. Amend.	80,725	373,220		292,495
9. Authorizing Cities of More Than 100,000 to Frame Special Charters	Init. Amend.	95,197	280,839		185,642

MONTANA
INITIATIVE AND REFERENDUM, 1906
NO CONSTITUTIONAL INITIATIVE UNTIL 1972

Measure	Origin	Yes	No	Majority For	Majority Against
1908					
1. Create State Depository Board	Leg. Amend.	29,273	10,653	18,620	
2. Raise State Tax Rate	Leg. Amend.	14,083	25,706		11,623
3. University Bonds	Leg. Ref.	24,809	12,910	11,899	
1910					
1. Extend State Mill Tax Levy Limit	Leg. Amend.	34,481	17,883	16,598	
1912					
1. Law Providing for State Militia	Ref. Stat.	21,195	41,749		20,554
2. Corrupt-Practices Act	Init. Stat.	44,337	13,645	30,692	
3. Presidential Primary Law	Init. Stat.	46,241	12,144	34,097	
4. Popular Election of U.S. Senators	Init. Stat.	45,620	12,442	33,178	

Measure	Origin	Yes	No	Majority For	Majority Against
5. Direct Primary Law	Init. Stat.	46,437	12,879	33,558	
6. Insane Asylum Bonds	Leg. Ref.	34,235	30,461	3,774	

1914

Measure	Origin	Yes	No	Majority For	Majority Against
1. Establishing a Commission to Regulate Boxing Contests	Ref. Stat.	34,440	42,581		8,141
2. Compensation for Industrial Accidents	Init. Stat.	36,979	44,275		7,296
3. To Loan State Funds on Farmland Security	Init. Stat.	45,162	27,780	17,382	
4. Consolidation of Educational Institutions	Init. Stat.	30,465	46,311		15,846
5. Woman Suffrage	Leg. Amend.	41,302	37,788	3,514	
6. Increase in School Tax Levy	Leg. Ref.	28,703	46,265		17,562

1916

Measure	Origin	Yes	No	Majority For	Majority Against
1. Equalize State Property Tax	Leg. Amend.	74,257	60,839	13,418	
2. Religious Properties Tax Exemption	Leg. Amend.	48,656	83,198		34,542
3. State Prison Twine Factory Bond Issue	Leg. Ref.	68,059	79,158		11,099
4. Prohibition	Leg. Ref.	102,776	73,890	28,886	
5. Legalize Boxing	Init. Stat.	72,162	76,510		4,348

1918

Measure	Origin	Yes	No	Majority For	Majority Against
1. Regulating Practice of Chiropractors	Init. Stat.	46,302	39,320	6,982	
2. Tax Exemption for Mortgages	Leg. Amend.	55,296	30,614	24,682	
3. State Grain Elevator Bonds	Leg. Ref.	54,215	29,630	24,585	

NEBRASKA
INITIATIVE AND REFERENDUM, 1912; REVISED 1920

Measure	Origin	Yes	No	Majority For	Majority Against

1914

Measure	Origin	Yes	No	Majority For	Majority Against
1. To Consolidate State University and Agricultural College on Common Site	Leg. Ref.	66,883	148,110		81,227

Measure	Origin	Yes	No	Majority For	Majority Against
2. Workmen's Compensation	Ref. Stat.	92,513	85,777	6,736	
3. Appropriation to Construct Armory at Nebraska City	Ref. Stat.	40,520	133,457		92,937
4. Woman Suffrage	Init. Amend.	90,738	100,842		10,104
5. Eliminating the Rule of Uniformity in Taxation	Leg. Amend.	88,068	82,136	5,932	
6. Permitting Three-fourths Jury Verdict in Civil Cases	Leg. Amend.	102,891	63,596	39,295	
7. Raising Salaries for State Officers	Leg. Amend.	89,385	76,013	13,372	
1916					
1. Statewide Prohibition	Init. Amend.	146,574	117,132	29,442	
2. Authorizing Governor to Appoint Food and Drug Commissioner	Init. Amend.	91,215	105,993		14,778
1918					
1. Suffrage, Limited to Full Citizens	Leg. Amend.	123,292	51,600	71,692	

NEVADA
REFERENDUM ONLY, 1904
INITIATIVE, 1912

Measure	Origin	Yes	No	Majority For	Majority Against
1904					
1. To Establish the Initiative and Referendum	Leg. Amend.	4,404	794	3,610	
1906					
1. Relating to Taxation	Leg. Amend.	5,450	1,359	4,091	
1908					
1. Police Bill	Ref. Stat.	9,954	9,078	876	

Measure	Origin	Yes	No	Majority For	Majority Against
1910					
1. Poll Tax Collections to Be Used for Maintenance and Betterment of Roads	Leg. Amend.	8,231	2,870	5,361	
1912					
1. To Introduce a General Initiative for Constitutional Amendments and Laws	Leg. Amend.	9,956	1,027	8,929	
2. To Subject All Public Officers, State and Local, to Recall	Leg. Amend.	9,636	1,173	8,463	
3. All Property Given for Education to Be Pledged for Education, with Provisions for Investment	Leg. Amend.	8,418	1,683	6,735	
4. To Make Women Eligible for Offices of School Superintendent and Notary Public	Leg. Amend.	8,603	2,241	6,362	
5. Amendment of Provision about Indictment for Crime and Depriving of Property without Due Process of Law	Leg. Amend.	8,259	1,504	6,755	
1914					
1. Woman Suffrage	Leg. Amend.	10,936	7,258	3,678	
2. Changing Form of Official Oath of Office	Leg. Amend.	10,161	7,258	2,903	
1916					
1. Relative to Investment of School Moneys	Leg. Amend.	17,492	5,167	12,325	
2. Raise Limit of State Debt to 1 Percent of Assessed Valuation	Leg. Amend.	16,368	6,752	9,616	
1918					
1. Statewide Prohibition	Init. Stat.	13,248	9,060	4,188	

NEW MEXICO
REFERENDUM ONLY, 1911
LEGISLATIVE AMENDMENT DATA FOR 1916 AND 1918 NOT INCLUDED
NEW MEXICO DID NOT MAKE USE OF THE POPULAR REFERENDUM UNTIL 1930

Measure	Origin	Yes	No	Majority For	Majority Against
1912					
1. To Abolish Provision Requiring State Officials to Know English	Leg. Amend.	26,663	13,678	12,985	
2. State Highway Bond Issue	Leg. Ref.	26,333	17,338	8,995	
1914					
1. Regulating Terms of Office for County Officials	Leg. Amend.	20,282	18,468	1,814	
2. Revising State Tax and Revenue System	Leg. Amend.	18,468	13,593	4,875	
3. Regulating Terms of Office for State Officials	Leg. Amend.	18,474	12,257	6,217	

NORTH DAKOTA
INITIATIVE AND REFERENDUM, 1914; REVISED 1918

Measure	Origin	Yes	No	Majority For	Majority Against
1916					
1. To Establish Dickenson Normal School	Leg. Amend.	60, 582	43,334	17,248	
2. To Establish a State Hospital for the Insane	Leg. Amend.	49,001	44,356	4,645	
3. Repeal of Mill Tax for Terminal Elevators	Ref. Stat.	51,889	47,035	4,854	
4. Defining the Crime of Bootlegging	Ref. Stat.	51,673	42,956	8,717	
1918					
1. Voting Privileges Cooperative Corporations	Leg. Amend.	49,392	32,053	17,339	
2. Number Judges to Declare Law Unconstitutional	Leg. Amend.	52,687	28,846	23,841	

Measure	Origin	Yes	No	Majority For	Majority Against
3. Hail Insurance	Leg. Amend.	52,475	30,257	22,218	
4. Amending Provisions Governing the Initiative and Referendum	Init. Amend.	47,447	32,598	14,849	
5. Defining Emergency Measures	Init. Amend.	46,121	32,507	13,614	
6. Revising Procedure for Submitting Constitutional Amendments	Init. Amend.	46,329	33,572	12,757	
7. Taxation	Init. Amend.	46,833	33,921	12,912	
8. Hail Insurance	Init. Amend.	49,878	31,586	18,292	
9. Raise the Debt Limit	Init. Amend.	46,275	34,235	12,040	
10. Authorize State to Engage in Business	Init. Amend.	46,830	32,574	14,256	

OHIO
INITIATIVE AND REFERENDUM, 1912

Measure	Origin	Yes	No	Majority For	Majority Against
1913					
1. Short Ballot for State Officers	Leg. Amend.	239,126	461,555		222,429
2. Short Ballot for County and Township Officers	Leg. Amend.	217,875	449,493		231,618
3. State and Local Bond Tax Exemption	Leg. Amend.	312,232	340,570		28,338
4. Eligibility of Women to Hold Official Positions in Institutions Caring for Females and Children	Leg. Amend.	435,222	255,036	180,186	
5. Smaller Legislature (Sponsored by "Wets" to Force Consolidation of Rural Counties and Reduction of Voting Strength of "Drys" in Legislature)	Init. Amend.	240,237	418,114		177,877
6. Prohibiting Shipment of Liquor into "Dry" Territory	Init. Stat.	360,534	455,099		94,565
1914					
1. Home Rule on the Subject of Intoxicating Liquors (Sponsored by "Wets" to Repeal Existing County Option Law)	Init. Amend.	559,872	547,254	12,618	

Measure	Origin	Yes	No	Majority For	Majority Against
2. Classification of Property and Limitation on General Property Tax	Init. Amend.	223,873	551,760		327,887
3. Woman Suffrage	Init. Amend.	335,390	518,295		182,905
4. Statewide Prohibition	Init. Amend.	504,177	588,329		84,152

1915

1. Statewide Prohibition	Init. Amend.	484,969	540,377		55,408
2. To Limit Elections on Twice-Defeated Initiative Proposals (Submitted by "Wets" to Forestall Annual Submission of Prohibition)	Init. Amend.	417,384	482,275		64,891
3. Fixing Terms for All County Officers	Init. Amend.	207,435	604,463		397,028
4. Exempting Bonds from Taxation	Leg. Amend.	337,124	401,083		63,959
5. To Decentralize Control of Liquor Licensing	Ref. Stat.	242,671	355,207		112,536
6. Congressional Redistricting	Ref. Stat.	271,987	329,095		57,108

1917

1. Statewide Prohibition	Init. Amend.	522,590	523,727		1,137
2. Allowing Women to Vote for Presidential Electors	Ref. Stat.	420,166	564,972		144,806

1918

1. Granting Voters the Use of the Referendum on Amendments to the United States Constitution Ratified by the State Legislature	Init. Amend.	508,282	315,030	193,252	
2. Statewide Prohibition	Init. Amend.	463,654	437,895	25,759	
3. That the State Legislature Shall Classify Property for Tax Purposes	Init. Amend.	336,616	304,399	32,217	
4. Allowing for the Passage of Laws to Prevent Double Taxation	Leg. Amend.	479,420	371,176	108,244	

OKLAHOMA
INITIATIVE AND REFERENDUM, 1907

Measure	Origin	Yes	No	Majority For	Majority Against
1908					
1. Liquor Agency Bill	Leg. Amend.	105,392	121,573		16,181
2. Torrens Land System	Leg. Amend.	114,394	83,888	30,506*	
3. Location of State Capitol	Leg. Amend.	120,352	71,933	48,419*	
4. "New Jerusalem" Plan (Advisory)	Leg. Ref.	117,441	75,792	41,649	
5. Sale of School Lands	Init. Stat.	96,745	110,840		14,095
1910					
1. Permitting Railroad Consolidation	Init. Amend.	53,784	108,205		54,421**
2. Location of State Capitol	Init. Stat.	96,448	64,522	31,926	**
3. "Grandfather Clause" to Disfranchise Black Voters	Init. Amend.	135,443	106,222	29,221	**
4. Woman Suffrage	Init. Amend.	88,808	128,928		40,120
5. Prescribing Distribution of Taxes	Leg. Amend.	101,636	43,133	58,503*	
6. Permitting Railroad Consolidation	Leg. Amend.	83,169	55,175	27,994*	
7. To Enact Local Option Liquor Law	Init. Amend.	105,041	126,118		21,077
8. Bryan Election Law	Ref. Stat.	80,146	106,459		26,313
9. "New Jerusalem" Plan	Init. Stat.	84,366	118,899		34,533
1911**					
1. Permitting Railroad Consolidation	Leg. Amend.	41,768	46,662		4,894
1912					
1. Direct Election of U.S. Senators	Init. Stat.	139,844	23,400	116,444	**
2. To Move State Capitol to Guthrie	Init. Amend.	86,549	103,106		16,557
3. School Aid	Leg. Amend.	100,042	65,436	34,606*	
4. Creating Board of Agriculture	Init. Amend.	164,530	63,586	100,944	

Measure	Origin	Yes	No	Majority For	Majority Against
1913**					
1. Permitting Railroad Consolidation	Leg. Amend.	59,437	35,115	24,322	
2. Mining Bill	Ref. Stat.	73,345	21,559	51,786	
3. Prescribing Distribution of Taxes	Leg. Amend.	63,330	30,295	33,035	
4. Allowing Voters to Call for an Election to Create a Township	Leg. Amend.	50,634	39,690	10,944	
5. Creating Board of Agriculture	Leg. Amend.	67,367	25,087	42,280	
1914					
1. School Aid	Leg. Amend.	89,653	56,916	32,737*	***
2. To Repeal Antigambling Bill	Ref. Stat.	68,878	76,495		7,617***
3. To Repeal Anti–Slot Machine Bill	Ref. Stat.	67,562	73,770		6,208***
4. Direct Taxation	Init. Stat.	88,994	45,232	43,762*	***
5. Drunkenness Cause for Impeachment	Init. Amend.	114,833	31,659	83,174	
6. To Reduce Number of Appellate Courts	Init. Amend.	105,529	64,782	40,747*	
7. To Reduce Maximum State Tax Levy	Init. Amend.	117,675	57,120	60,555*	
8. Mine Production Tax	Init. Amend.	107,342	62,380	44,962*	
9. To Reduce Legislature to One Body	Init. Amend.	94,686	71,742	22,944*	
1916					
1. To Create State Tax Commission	Leg. Amend.	50,656	146,130		95,474***
2. Literacy Test	Leg. Amend.	90,605	133,140		42,535***
3. Prescribing Distribution of Taxes	Leg. Amend.	76,093	127,525		51,432***
4. Reducing Salary of Supreme Court Clerk	Leg. Amend.	58,933	134,963		76,030***
5. Limiting Municipal Debt	Leg. Amend.	44,687	147,933		103,246***
6. To Establish System of Compulsory Compensation in Case of Death or Disability	Leg. Amend.	50,998	139,132		88,134***
7. To Consolidate Appellate Courts	Leg. Amend.	42,896	149,272		106,376***

Measure	Origin	Yes	No	Majority For	Majority Against
8. To Reduce Number of Jurymen in District Court	Leg. Amend.	49,954	142,333		92,379***
9. To Abolish County Court	Leg. Amend.	47,194	157,284		110,090***
10. To Allow for Equal Tripartite Representation on Election Boards	Init. Amend.	147,067	119,602	27,465*	
11. To Require That Changes to Election Laws Be Submitted to Popular Approval via the Initiative	Init. Amend.	140,366	114,824	25,542*	

1918

1. Woman Suffrage	Leg. Amend.	106,909	81,481	25,428	

*Failed to receive a majority of all votes cast
**Special election
***Primary election

OREGON
INITIATIVE AND REFERENDUM, 1902

Measure	Origin	Yes	No	Majority For	Majority Against

1904

1. Local Option Liquor Law	Init. Stat.	43,316	40,198	3,118	
2. Direct Primary	Init. Stat.	56,205	16,354	39,851	
3. Authorizing Legislative Assembly to Regulate Office of State Printer	Leg. Amend.	45,334	14,031	31,303	

1906

1. Amending Local Option Liquor Law	Init. Stat.	35,297	45,144		9,847
2. General Appropriation for State Institutions	Ref. Stat.	43,918	26,758	17,160	
3. Antipass Bill	Init. Stat.	57,281	16,779	40,502	
4. State Ownership of a Toll Road	Init. Stat.	31,525	44,527		13,002
5. Tax on Gross Earnings of Sleeping and Refrigerator Car Companies and Oil Companies	Init. Stat.	69,635	6,441	63,194	

Measure	Origin	Yes	No	Majority For	Majority Against
6. Tax on Gross Earnings of Express, Telegraph, and Telephone Companies	Init. Stat.	70,872	6,360	64,512	
7. Woman Suffrage	Init. Amend.	36,902	47,075		10,173
8. Applying the Referendum to Acts of Legislature Affecting Constitutional Conventions and Amendments	Init. Amend.	47,661	18,751	28,910	
9. To Give Cities and Towns Exclusive Power to Enact and Amend Their Charters	Init. Amend.	52,567	19,852	32,715	
10. To Allow the State Printing, Binding, and Printers' Compensation to Be Regulated by Law	Init. Amend.	63,749	9,571	54,178	
11. Extending the Initiative and Referendum to Localities	Init. Amend.	47,678	16,735	30,943	

1908

Measure	Origin	Yes	No	Majority For	Majority Against
1. Giving Sheriffs Control of County Prisoners	Ref. Stat.	60,443	30,033	30,410	
2. Requiring Railroads to Grant Public Officials Free Passes	Ref. Stat.	28,856	59,406		30,550
3. Appropriating Funds for Construction of Armories	Ref. Stat.	33,507	54,848		21,341
4. Increasing Appropriation for the University of Oregon	Ref. Stat.	44,115	40,535	3,580	
5. Regulating Fishing on Columbia River in Favor of Fish-Wheel Operators	Init. Stat.	46,582	40,720	5,862	
6. Regulating Fishing on Columbia River in Favor of Gill-Net Operators	Init. Stat.	56,130	30,280	25,850	
7. Instructing Legislature to Vote for Popular Choice for U.S. Senators	Init. Stat.	69,668	21,162	48,506	
8. Corrupt-Practices Act Governing Elections	Init. Stat.	54,042	31,301	22,741	
9. To Create Hood River County	Init. Stat.	43,948	26,778	17,170	
10. Woman Suffrage	Init. Amend.	36,858	58,670		21,812

Measure	Origin	Yes	No	Majority For	Majority Against
11. Giving Cities Exclusive Powers to Regulate Liquor Selling, Theaters, Race Tracks, Pool Rooms, etc.	Init. Amend.	39,442	52,346		12,904
12. Providing for a Modified Single Tax	Init. Amend.	32,066	60,871		28,805
13. Recall Power on Public Officials	Init. Amend.	58,381	31,002	27,379	
14. Authorizing Proportional Representation	Init. Amend.	48,868	34,128	14,740	
15. Requiring Indictment to Be by Grand Jury	Init. Amend.	52,214	28,487	23,727	
16. To Increase Salary of Legislators	Leg. Amend.	19,691	68,892		49,201
17. To Permit Location of State Institutions at Places Other Than the State Capitol	Leg. Amend.	41,975	40,868	1,107	
18. To Reorganize System of Courts and Increase Number of Supreme Court Judges	Leg. Amend.	30,243	50,591		20,348
19. Changing Date of Regular Elections from June to November	Leg. Amend.	65,728	18,590	47,138	

1910

Measure	Origin	Yes	No	Majority For	Majority Against
1. To Increase Salary of Circuit Judge	Ref. Stat.	13,161	71,503		58,342
2. Statewide Prohibition	Init. Stat.	42,651	63,564		20,913
3. Home Rule for Municipalities Regarding Liquor Control	Init. Amend.	53,321	50,779	2,542	
4. Regulating Employers' Liability	Init. Stat.	56,258	33,943	22,315	
5. For an Employers' Liability Commission	Init. Stat.	32,224	51,719		19,495
6. Appropriation for Monmouth Normal	Init. Stat.	50,191	40,044	10,147	
7. Appropriation for Weston Normal	Init. Stat.	40,898	46,201		5,303
8. Appropriation for Ashland Normal	Init. Stat.	38,473	48,655		10,182
9. Creating Nesmith County	Init. Stat.	22,866	60,951		38,085
10. Creating Otis County	Init. Stat.	17,426	62,016		44,590

Measure	Origin	Yes	No	Majority For	Majority Against
11. Annexing Part of Clackamas County to Multnomah County	Init. Stat.	16,250	69,002		52,752
12. Creating Williams County	Init. Stat.	14,508	64,090		49,582
13. Creating Orchard County	Init. Stat.	15,664	62,712		47,048
14. Creating Clark County	Init. Stat.	15,613	61,704		46,091
15. Annexing Part of Washington County to Multnomah County	Init. Stat.	14,047	68,221		54,174
16. Creating Des Chutes County	Init. Stat.	17,592	60,486		42,894
17. Regulating Fishing in Rogue River	Init. Stat.	49,712	33,397	16,315	
18. Regulating Creation of New Counties	Init. Stat.	37,129	42,327		5,198
19. Providing for Presidential Primary Elections	Init. Stat.	43,353	41,624	1,729	
20. Judiciary Reform, Three-fourths' Jury Verdict in Civil Cases	Init. Amend.	44,538	39,399	5,139	
21. Providing That an Official State Gazette Be Mailed to All Registered Voters	Init. Stat.	29,955	52,538		22,583
22. Statewide Prohibition	Init. Amend.	43,540	61,221		17,681
23. For County Local Option System of Taxation	Init. Amend.	44,171	42,127	2,044	
24. Woman Suffrage	Init. Amend.	35,270	59,065		23,795
25. Increasing County Indebtedness for Road Improvements	Init. Amend.	51,275	32,906	18,369	
26. Proportional Representation	Init. Amend.	37,031	44,366		7,335
27. New Insane Asylum for Eastern Oregon	Leg. Stat.	50,134	41,504	8,630	
28. Calling Constitutional Convention	Leg. Stat.	23,143	59,974		36,831
29. Creating Separate Legislative Districts	Leg. Amend.	24,000	54,252		30,252
30. Repealing Uniform Tax System	Leg. Amend.	37,619	40,172		2,553
31. For Classified Property Tax System	Leg. Amend.	31,629	41,692		10,063
32. Permitting State to Build Railroads	Leg. Amend.	32,884	46,070		13,186

1912

Measure	Origin	Yes	No	Majority For	Majority Against
1. Woman Suffrage	Init. Amend.	61,265	57,104	4,161	
2. To Create Office of Lieutenant Governor	Leg. Amend.	50,562	61,644		11,082

Measure	Origin	Yes	No	Majority For	Majority Against
3. To Divorce Local and State Taxation	Leg. Amend.	51,852	56,671		4,819
4. Permitting Different Tax Rates on Classes of Property	Leg. Amend.	52,045	54,483		2,438
5. To Repeal County Tax Option	Leg. Amend.	63,881	47,150	16,731	
6. To Require a "Majority of All Votes Cast in the Election" for the Approval of Constitutional Amendments	Leg. Amend.	32,934	70,325		37,391
7. To Provide for Double Liability of Bank Stockholders	Leg. Amend.	82,981	21,738	61,243	
8. To Require a "Majority of All Votes Cast in the Election" for Approval of All Initiated Measures	Init. Amend.	35,721	68,861		33,140
9. Limiting State Indebtedness for Roads	Init. Amend.	59,452	43,447	16,005	
10. Limiting County Indebtedness for Roads	Init. Amend.	57,258	43,858	13,400	
11. Permitting Taxation of Incomes	Init. Amend.	52,702	52,948		246
12. Granting Home Rule to Counties in Matter of Indebtedness for Roads	Init. Amend.	38,568	63,481		24,913
13. For Extensive Reorganization of the Legislature	Init. Amend.	31,020	71,183		40,163
14. For a Modified Single Tax on Land Values	Init. Amend.	31,534	82,015		50,481
15. Statewide Public Utilities Regulation	Ref. Stat.	65,985	40,956	25,029	
16. To Create Cascade County	Init. Stat.	26,463	71,239		44,776
17. To Levy a Millage Tax to Support the State University and the Agricultural College	Init. Stat.	48,701	57,279		8,578
18. Authorizing the Issue of County Bonds for Roads	Init. Stat.	49,699	56,713		7,014
19. To Create a State Highway Department	Init. Stat.	23,872	83,846		59,974
20. Adjusting Salary of the State Printer	Init. Stat.	34,793	69,542		34,749
21. Creating the Office of Hotel Inspector	Init. Stat.	16,910	91,995		75,085
22. Providing for an Eight-Hour Day on Public Works	Init. Stat.	64,508	48,078	16,430	

Measure	Origin	Yes	No	Majority For	Majority Against
23. Protecting Investors: "Blue Sky Law"	Init. Stat.	48,765	57,293		8,528
24. Regulating the Employment of State Prisoners	Init. Stat.	73,800	37,492	36,308	
25. Regulating the Employment of County and City Prisoners	Init Stat.	71,367	37,731	33,636	
26. Creating a State Road Board and Authorizing the Issue of State Road Bonds	Init. Stat.	30,897	75,590		44,693
27. To Issue County Bonds for Roads	Init. Stat.	43,611	60,210		16,599
28. To Establish a Method for the Consolidation of Cities and the Creation of New Counties	Init. Stat.	40,199	56,992		16,793
29. Exempting Household Goods from Taxation	Init. Stat.	60,357	51,826	8,531	
30. Exempting All Debts from Taxation	Init. Stat.	42,491	66,540		24,049
31. To Revise the Inheritance Tax Law	Init. Stat.	38,609	63,839		25,230
32. To Regulate Freight Rates	Init. Stat.	58,306	45,534	12,772	
33. To Abolish Capital Punishment	Init. Stat.	41,951	64,578		22,627
34. To Prohibit Boycotts and Pickets	Init. Stat.	49,826	60,560		10,734
35. Prohibiting the Use of Streets, etc., for Public Assembly or Speechmaking without a Permit	Init. Stat.	48,987	62,532		13,545
36. Appropriation for the University of Oregon	Ref. Stat.	29,437	78,985		49,548
37. Appropriation for the University of Oregon	Ref. Stat.	27,310	79,376		52,066

1913*

Measure	Origin	Yes	No	Majority For	Majority Against
1. State University Building Repair Fund	Ref. Stat.	56,659	40,600	16,059	
2. Building Appropriation for University of Oregon	Ref. Stat.	53,569	43,014	10,555	
3. Sterilization of Habitual Criminals	Ref. Stat.	41,767	53,319		11,552
4. Increasing Number of District Attorneys	Ref. Stat.	54,179	38,159	16,020	

Measure	Origin	Yes	No	Majority For	Majority Against
5. Creating an Industrial Accident Commission	Ref. Stat.	67,814	28,608	39,206	

1914

Measure	Origin	Yes	No	Majority For	Majority Against
1. Requiring Voters to be U.S. Citizens	Leg. Amend.	164,879	39,847	125,032	
2. Creating Office of Lieutenant Governor	Leg. Amend.	52,040	143,804		91,764
3. Permitting the Consolidation of Cities and Counties	Leg. Amend.	77,392	103,194		25,802
4. Authorizing State Indebtedness for Irrigation and Power Projects	Leg. Amend.	49,759	135,550		85,791
5. Abolishing Requirement for Equal and Uniform Taxes	Leg. Amend.	59,206	116,490		57,284
6. Changing Rules of Taxation as to Uniformity	Leg. Amend.	52,362	122,704		70,342
7. To Establish State Normal School at Ashland	Leg. Stat.	84,041	109,643		25,602
8. Permitting Merger of Adjacent Cities	Leg. Amend.	96,116	77,671	18,445	
9. To Establish State Normal School at Weston	Leg. Stat.	87,450	105,345		17,895
10. Increasing Pay of Legislators	Leg. Amend.	41,087	146,278		105,191
11. To Establish a Universal Eight-Hour Workday	Init. Amend.	49,360	167,888		118,528
12. Providing for an Eight-Hour Day for Women Workers	Init. Stat.	88,480	120,296		31,816
13. Providing for Nonpartisan Nomination of Judicial Officers	Init. Stat.	74,323	107,263		32,940
14. $1,500 Tax Exemption	Init. Amend.	65,495	136,193		70,698
15. Public Docks and Water Frontage	Init. Amend.	67,128	114,564		47,436
16. Municipal Wharves and Docks	Init. Stat.	67,110	111,113		44,003
17. Statewide Prohibition	Init. Amend.	136,842	100,362	36,480	
18. Abolishing Death Penalty	Init. Amend.	100,552	100,395	157	
19. Personal Graduated Extra Tax	Init. Amend.	59,186	124,943		65,757
20. Consolidating Corporation and Insurance Departments	Init. Stat.	55,469	120,154		64,685
21. Regulating Licensing of Dentists	Init. Stat.	92,722	110,404		17,682
22. Extending Terms of County Officers	Init. Amend.	82,841	107,039		24,198

Measure	Origin	Yes	No	Majority For	Majority Against
23. For a Tax Code Commission	Init. Stat.	34,436	143,468		109,032
24. Abolishing Desert Land Board	Init. Stat.	32,701	143,366		110,665
25. Proportional Representation	Init. Amend.	39,740	137,116		97,376
26. Abolish State Senate	Init. Amend.	62,376	123,429		61,053
27. To Establish a Department to Give Work to the Unemployed and Establish an Inheritance Tax for Its Maintenance	Init. Amend.	57,859	126,201		68,342
28. To Amend the Presidential Primary Law	Init. Stat.	25,058	153,638		128,580
29. To Amend the Uniform Tax Law	Init. Amend.	43,280	140,507		97,227

1916

1. Single-Item Veto	Leg. Amend.	141,773	53,207	88,566	
2. Ship Tax Exemption	Leg. Amend.	119,652	65,410	54,242	
3. Negro Suffrage	Leg. Amend.	100,027	100,701		674
4. Single Tax	Init. Amend.	43,390	154,980		111,590
5. Location of Normal School at Pendleton	Init. Amend.	96,829	109,523		12,694
6. Anticompulsory Vaccination	Init. Stat.	99,745	100,119		374
7. Repeal of Sunday Closing Law	Init. Stat.	125,836	93,076	32,760	
8. Permitting Manufacture and Regulating Sale of 4 Percent Malt Liquors	Init. Amend.	85,973	140,599		54,626
9. Prohibition	Init. Amend.	114,932	109,671	5,261	
10. Rural Credits	Init. Amend.	107,488	83,887	23,601	
11. Tax and Debt Limit	Init. Amend.	99,536	84,031	15,505	

1917*

1. Authorizing Ports to Create Limited Indebtedness to Encourage Water Transportation	Leg. Amend.	67,445	54,864	12,581	
2. Limiting Number of Bills Introduced and Increasing Pay of Legislators	Leg. Amend.	22,276	103,238		80,962
3. Declaration against Implied Repeal of Constitutional Provisions by Amendments Thereto	Leg. Amend.	37,187	72,445		35,258

Measure	Origin	Yes	No	Majority For	Majority Against
4. Uniform Tax Classification	Leg. Amend.	62,118	53,245	8,873	
5. Requiring Election of City, Town, and State Officers at the Same Time	Leg. Amend.	83,630	42,296	41,334	
6. Tax Levy for a New Penitentiary	Leg. Stat.	46,666	86,165		39,499
7. State Road Bond Issue	Leg. Stat.	77,316	63,803	13,513	

1918

Measure	Origin	Yes	No	Majority For	Majority Against
1. Delinquent Tax Notice	Init. Stat.	66,652	41,594	25,058	
2. Fixing Compensation for Publication of Legal Notice	Init. Stat.	50,073	41,816	8,257	
3. Establishing and Maintaining Southern and Eastern Oregon Normal Schools	Leg. Amend.	49,935	66,070		16,135
4. To Establish a Dependent, Delinquent, and Defective Children's Home	Leg. Stat.	43,441	65,299		21,858
5. Prohibiting Seine and Set-Net Fishing in the Rogue River	Ref. Stat.	45,511	50,227		4,716
6. Closing a Portion of the Willamette River to Commercial Fishing	Ref. Stat.	55,555	40,908	14,647	
7. Authorizing Increase in Amount of Levy of State Taxes for Year 1919 (Submitted by State Tax Commission under Chapter 150, Laws 1917)	Ref. Stat.	41,364	56,974		15,610

*Special election

SOUTH DAKOTA
INITIATIVE AND REFERENDUM, 1898

Measure	Origin	Yes	No	Majority For	Majority Against

1908

Measure	Origin	Yes	No	Majority For	Majority Against
1. Action for Divorce	Ref. Stat.	60,208	38,794	21,414	
2. Protection of Quail	Ref. Stat.	65,340	32,374	32,966	
3. Against Sunday Performances	Ref. Stat.	48,378	48,007	371	

Measure	Origin	Yes	No	Majority For	Majority Against
4. Local Option Liquor	Init. Stat.	39,075	41,405		2,330
5. Revise Taxation Articles	Leg. Amend.	34,915	47,732		12,817
6. Attorney General's Salary	Leg. Amend.	43,908	52,437		8,529

1910

Measure	Origin	Yes	No	Majority For	Majority Against
1. Electric Headlights for Locomotives	Ref. Stat.	37,914	49,938		12,024
2. Removal of State and Local Officers	Ref. Stat.	32,160	52,153		19,993
3. Embalmers' Licenses	Ref. Stat.	34,560	49,496		14,936
4. Congressional Districts	Ref. Stat.	26,918	48,884		21,966
5. Militia	Ref. Stat.	17,852	57,440		39,588
6. County Local Option Liquor	Init. Stat.	42,406	55,372		12,966
7. School Land Use	Leg. Amend.	48,212	44,220	3,992	
8. Attorney General's Salary	Leg. Amend.	35,932	52,387		16,455
9. Woman Suffrage	Leg. Amend.	35,290	57,709		22,419
10. Add to Debt for School Construction	Leg. Amend.	32,613	52,243		19,630
11. Change State Tax Structure	Leg. Amend.	29,830	52,943		23,113
12. Popular Approval of New Institutions	Leg. Amend.	36,128	47,625		11,497

1912

Measure	Origin	Yes	No	Majority For	Majority Against
1. Electric Headlights for Locomotives	Ref. Stat.	77,172	21,180	55,992	
2. Damages for Trespass of Animals	Ref. Stat.	57,601	30,273	27,328	
3. Regulating Location of County Seats	Ref. Stat.	49,498	27,909	21,589	
4. Richards Primary Election Law	Init. Stat.	58,080	32,118	25,892	
5. Taxation of Corporations	Leg. Amend	70,686	31,110	39,576	

1914

Measure	Origin	Yes	No	Majority For	Majority Against
1. Woman Suffrage	Leg. Amend.	39,605	51,519		11,914
2. Relating to the Sale of School Lands	Leg. Amend.	45,554	35,102	10,452	
3. Superintendent of Schools' Term	Leg. Amend.	32,092	45,733		13,641
4. To Apply the Initiative and Referendum to Municipalities	Leg. Amend.	28,226	43,162		14,936

Measure	Origin	Yes	No	Majority For	Majority Against
5. Change in State Institution Boards	Leg. Amend.	29,601	44,107		14,506
6. Four-Year Legislative Terms	Leg. Amend.	29,746	44,951		15,205
7. Supreme Court Judges Disqualification	Leg. Amend.	36,317	36,543		226
8. State Control and Promotion of Irrigation	Leg. Amend.	32,958	40,457		7,499
9. Local Option Liquor	Init. Stat.	38,000	51,779		13,779
10. Coffey Primary Election Law	Init. Stat.	37,106	44,697		7,591
11. Fixing Course of Study at Aberdeen Normal School	Ref. Stat.	27,538	49,382		21,844
12. To Call Constitutional Convention	Leg. Res.	34,832	51,585		16,753

1916

Measure	Origin	Yes	No	Majority For	Majority Against
1. State Supply Coal; Build and Maintain Roads	Leg. Amend.	75,922	33,521	42,401	
2. State Construction and Maintenance of Irrigation	Leg. Amend.	58,775	44,238	14,537	
3. State Revenue and Finance Structure	Leg. Amend.	43,793	55,568		11,775
4. To Establish a System of State-Operated Rural Credits	Leg. Amend.	57,569	41,957	15,612	
5. Number of Members to Constitutional Convention	Leg. Amend.	35,377	56,432		21,005
6. Woman Suffrage	Leg. Amend.	53,432	58,350		4,808
7. Prohibition	Leg. Amend.	65,334	53,371	11,963	
8. Lease Limit on School Land	Leg. Amend.	41,379	61,798		20,419
9. To Increase State Salaries	Leg. Amend.	39,169	61,223		22,054
10. Richards Primary Election Law	Init. Stat.	52,410	52,733		323
11. Issuance of Liquor Permits	Ref. Stat.	49,174	54,422		5,248
12. To Create Department of Banking and Finance	Init. Stat.	47,715	52,205		4,490
13. To Create a State Banking Board	Init. Stat.	47,925	50,226		2,301
14. Five-sixths of Jury to Render Verdict in Civil Cases	Ref. Stat.	49,601	51,529		1,928

1918

Measure	Origin	Yes	No	Majority For	Majority Against
1. Supreme Court Judges Replacement	Leg. Amend.	41,646	24,798	16,848	

Measure	Origin	Yes	No	Majority For	Majority Against
2. Woman Suffrage	Leg. Amend.	49,318	28,934	20,384	
3. Down Payment—Sale of School Lands	Leg. Amend.	45,809	21,785	24,024	
4. Graduated Individual Income Tax	Leg. Amend.	50,970	25,047	25,923	
5. State Works of Internal Improvement	Leg. Amend.	42,097	24,424	17,673	
6. State Debt for State Development	Leg. Amend.	34,821	27,886	6,935	
7. State Development and Supply Water Power	Leg. Amend.	41,658	24,429	17,229	
8. State Manufacture and Sell Cement	Leg. Amend.	38,103	25,702	12,401	
9. Increase State Salaries	Leg. Amend.	26,784	42,779		15,995
10. State to Enter Hail Insurance Business	Leg. Amend.	40,762	25,896	14,866	
11. State to Build and Operate Grain Elevators	Leg. Amend.	41,292	25,545	15,747	
12. State to Mine and Sell Coal	Leg. Amend.	40,632	24,922	15,710	
13. Richards Primary Election Law	Init. Stat.	47,981	34,705	13,276	

UTAH
INITIATIVE AND REFERENDUM, 1902
ENACTING LEGISLATION NOT PASSED UNTIL 1917
NO CONSTITUTIONAL INITIATIVE

WASHINGTON
INITIATIVE AND REFERENDUM, 1912
NO CONSTITUTIONAL INITIATIVE

Measure	Origin	Yes	No	Majority For	Majority Against
1914					
1. Statewide Prohibition	Init. Stat.	189,840	171,208	18,632	
2. To Protect Investors in Securities: "Blue Sky" Law	Init. Stat.	142,017	147,298		5,281
3. Abolishing Bureau of Inspection of Public Offices	Init. Stat.	117,882	167,080		49,198
4. To Abolish Private Employment Agencies	Init. Stat.	162,054	144,544	17,510	

Measure	Origin	Yes	No	Majority For	Majority Against
5. Requiring Employers to Provide First Aid for Injured Workmen	Init. Stat.	143,738	154,166		10,428
6. Providing for Convict Road Work	Init. Stat.	111,805	183,726		71,921
7. To Establish the Universal Eight-Hour Day	Init. Stat.	118,881	212,935		94,054
8. To Establish Teachers' Retirement System	Leg. Ref.	59,051	252,356		193,305
9. To Borrow $40 Million for Quincy Valley Irrigation Project	Leg. Ref.	102,315	189,065		86,750
10. Prohibiting Alien Landownership	Leg. Amend.	55,080	212,542		157,462

1916

Measure	Origin	Yes	No	Majority For	Majority Against
1. To Facilitate (Actually Obstruct) the Operation of the Initiative and Referendum	Ref. Stat.	62,117	196,363		134,246
2. To Facilitate (Actually Obstruct) the Operation of the Recall	Ref. Stat.	63,646	193,686		130,040
3. To Strengthen Party Conventions and Weaken Direct Primary	Ref. Stat.	49,370	200,499		151,129
4. To Severely Restrict Picketing during Labor Disputes	Ref. Stat.	85,672	183,042		97,370
5. To Require New Public Utilities to Get Approval of Public Utilities Commission	Ref. Stat.	46,820	201,742		154,922
6. To Reorganize the Management of the Port of Seattle	Ref. Stat.	45,264	195,253		149,989
7. To Require Local Governments to Adopt a Budget System	Ref. Stat.	67,205	181,833		114,628
8. To Permit Restricted Liquor Sales	Init. Stat.	48,354	263,390		215,036
9. To Permit Manufacture of 4 Percent Beer	Init. Stat.	98,843	245,399		146,556
10. To Include Property Ownership as a Qualification for Voting on Bond Issues	Leg. Amend.	88,963	180,179		91,216

1918

Measure	Origin	Yes	No	Majority For	Majority Against
1. To Authorize $30 Million in Bonds to Improve State Roads	Ref. Stat.	96,100	54,322	41,778	

Measure	Origin	Yes	No	Majority For	Majority Against
2. To Call a Constitutional Convention	Leg. Ref.	55,148	58,713		3,565

Sources: **(AZ)** Office of the Secretary of State, *General Election Returns, 1912–1918;* George Judson King Papers, Library of Congress, Manuscripts Division, Washington, D.C. **(AR)** *Equity* 15 (January 1913): 43; 17 (January 1915): 39; 19 (January 1917): 27; *Biennial Report of the Secretary of State for the Years 1909–10–11–12,* 411, 415; *Biennial Report of the Secretary of State for the Years 1913–1920,* 340, 352, 364; *Biennial Report of the Secretary of State for the Years 1924–1926,* 211, 213, 229–31. **(CA)** Office of the Secretary of State, *Statement of Vote in the State of California for the General Election Held on:* November 5, 1912; November 3, 1914; October 26, 1915 (special election); November 7, 1916; November 5, 1918. **(CO)** Charles H. Queary, *The Initiative and Referendum in Colorado; Direct Legislation in Colorado: A Report by the Special Committee on Direct Legislation of the City Club,* 24–29; Richard E. Cushman, "Analysis of the Popular Vote on Constitutional and Legislative Proposals in the General Election of 1914," 20–21. **(ME)** Lawrence Lee Pelletier, "The Initiative and Referendum in Maine," 26, 28, 31, 33; King Papers, Library of Congress. **(MA)** Massachusetts, *Report Relative to Revising Statewide Initiative and Referendum Provisions of the Massachusetts Constitution,* February 4, 1975, p. 89. **(MI)** James K. Pollock, *The Initiative and Referendum in Michigan,* app. 3; King Papers, Library of Congress. **(MO)** *Equity* 15 (January 1913): 42; 17 (January 1915): 50; *Official Manual of the State of Missouri, 1913–1914,* 1108–10; *Official Manual of the State of Missouri, 1917–1918,* 484–85; *Official Manual of the State of Missouri, 1919–1920,* 424–29; N. D. Houghton, "The Initiative and Referendum in Missouri" (master's thesis), 48–61. **(MT)** Ellis L. Waldron and Paul B. Wilson, *Atlas of Montana Elections, 1889–1976.* **(NE)** *Nebraska Blue Book, 1974–1975,* 103, 107; Cushman, "Analysis of the Popular Vote," 25. **(NV)** Office of the Secretary of State, *Political History of Nevada,* 1996, 10th ed., on-line at http://dmla.clan.lib.nv.us/docs/nsla/archives/political/main.htm; A. Lawrence Lowell, *Public Opinion and Popular Government,* 379–80. **(NM)** New Mexico Legislative Council Service; Lowell, *Public Opinion,* 380; Cushman, "Analysis of the Popular Vote," 25. **(ND)** Raymond V. Anderson, "Adoption and Operation of Initiative and Referendum in North Dakota,"app. 2. **(OH)** Virginia Graham, *A Compilation of Statewide Initiative Proposals Appearing on the Ballots through 1976,* 147–48; *Annual Statistical Report of the Secretary of State for the Year Ending:* November 15, 1913 (300–305); November 15, 1914 (277–78); June 30th, 1915 (226–30); June 30, 1918 (261–62); June 30, 1919 (253–54); June 30, 1920 (312, 315–16); Hoyt Landon Warner, *Progressivism in Ohio, 1897–1917,* 395, 416–17, 437–38, 476, 492. **(OK)** John H. Bass, "The Initiative and Referendum in Oklahoma," 137–44; *Directory and Manual of the State of Oklahoma,* 179–85. **(OR)** *Oregon State Blue Book,* on-line at http://www.sos.state.or.us/bluebook/1999_2000/state/elections/elections06.htm **(SD)** C. Kenneth Meyer, *Direct Democracy in South Dakota: The People Conducting Their Own Business;* Cushman, "Analysis of the Popular Vote," 28. **(WA)** Claudius O. Johnson, "The Initiative and Referendum in Washington," 54–56; King Papers, Library of Congress.

Bibliography

MANUSCRIPT COLLECTIONS

Historical and Philosophical Society of Ohio, Cincinnati
    Herbert S. Bigelow Papers
Library of Congress, Manuscripts Division, Washington, D.C.
    William Jennings Bryan Papers
    George Judson King Papers
    Robert L. Owen Papers
    Eltweed Pomeroy Papers
North Dakota State University, North Dakota Institute for Regional Studies, Fargo
    Elizabeth Preston Anderson Papers
Ohio Historical Society, Columbus
    Robert Crosser Papers, MSS 281
Oklahoma Historical Society, Oklahoma City
    Peter Hanraty Papers
South Dakota Historical Society, Pierre
    Doane Robinson Papers
University of Arkansas Libraries, Special Collections, Fayetteville
    David Yancey Thomas Papers
University of California at Los Angeles Research Library, Special Collections
    John Randolph Haynes Papers
University of Colorado, Western Historical Collections, Boulder
    Edward P. Costigan Papers
University of Missouri, Western Historical Manuscript Collection, Columbia
    N. D. Houghton Papers
University of Oklahoma, Western History Manuscripts, Norman
    Oklahoma State Federation of Labor Collection

NEWSPAPERS

Bismarck Daily Tribune
Dakota Ruralist
Denver Rocky Mountain News
Edgeley (N.D.) Mail
Guthrie Oklahoma State Capital
Little Rock Arkansas Democrat
Little Rock Arkansas Gazette
Los Angeles Express
Los Angeles Record
Los Angeles Times
Newark Evening News
New York Herald
New York Times
Oklahoma City Daily Oklahoman
Oklahoma City Labor Signal
Oklahoma City Oklahoma Pioneer
Poteau (Okla.) Journal
St. Louis Post-Dispatch
St. Louis Wetmore's Weekly
Tecumseh (Okla.) Leader
Tulsa Democrat
Valley City (N.D.) Times-Record
Vermillion (S.D.) Plain Talk
White Ribbon (N.D.) Bulletin

GOVERNMENT DOCUMENTS

Arizona. Office of the Secretary of State. *General Election Returns, 1912–1918.* Phoenix: Department of Archives.
Arkansas. *Biennial Report of the Secretary of State for the Years 1909–10–11–12.* Little Rock: Tunnah and Pittard Printers, 1913.
———. *Biennial Report of the Secretary of State for the Years 1913–1920.* Little Rock: H. G. Pugh, 1921.
———. *Biennial Report of the Secretary of State for the Years 1924–1926.* Little Rock: Russellville Printing, 1926.
———. *Brickhouse et al. v. Hill.* In *Southwestern Reporter*, 268:865–80. St. Paul: West Publishing, 1925.
———. *Hildreth v. Taylor.* In *Southwestern Reporter*, 175:40–45. St. Paul: West Publishing, 1915.

———. *Hodges v. Dawdy*. In *Southwestern Reporter*, 149:656–62. St. Paul: West Publishing, 1912.

———. *State ex rel. City of Little Rock et al. v. Donaghey et al.* In *Southwestern Reporter*, 152:746–52. St. Paul: West Publishing, 1913.

California. Office of the Secretary of State. *Statement of Vote in the State of California for the General Election Held on November 5, 1912.* Sacramento: California State Printing Office, 1912.

———. *Statement of Vote in the State of California for the General Election Held on November 3, 1914.* Sacramento: California State Printing Office, 1914.

———. *Statement of Vote in the State of California for the Special Election Held on October 26, 1915.* Sacramento: California State Printing Office, 1915.

———. *Statement of Vote in the State of California for the General Election Held on November 7, 1916.* Sacramento: California State Printing Office, 1916.

———. *Statement of Vote in the State of California for the General Election Held on November 5, 1918.* Sacramento: California State Printing Office, 1918.

Colorado. *House Journal of the General Assembly.* 9th extra sess. Denver: Smith-Brooks Printing, 1894; 10th sess. (1895); 17th sess. (1909); 17th extra sess. (1910).

———. *The Initiative and Referendum in Colorado.* Denver: Legislative Reference Office, 1938.

———. *Laws Passed at the Extraordinary Session of the Seventeenth General Assembly of the State of Colorado.* Denver: Western Newspaper Union, 1915.

———. *Senate Journal of the General Assembly.* 10th sess. Denver: Smith-Brooks Printing, 1895; 15th sess. (1905); 17th sess. (1909); 17th extra sess. (1910).

Massachusetts. *Report Relative to Revising Statewide Initiative and Referendum Provisions of the Massachusetts Constitution.* House no. 5435. Boston: Legislative Research Council, 1975.

Missouri. *Official Manual of the State of Missouri, 1895–1896.* Jefferson City: Tribune Printing, 1896.

———. *Official Manual of the State of Missouri, 1903–1904.* Jefferson City: Tribune Printing, 1904.

———. *Official Manual of the State of Missouri, 1905–1906.* Jefferson City: Tribune Printing, 1906.

———. *Official Manual of the State of Missouri, 1907–1908.* Jefferson City: Tribune Printing, 1908.

———. *Official Manual of the State of Missouri, 1909–1910.* Jefferson City: Tribune Printing, 1910.

————. *Official Manual of the State of Missouri, 1911–1912.* Jefferson City: Tribune Printing, 1912.

————. *Official Manual of the State of Missouri, 1913–1914.* Jefferson City: Tribune Printing, 1914.

————. *Official Manual of the State of Missouri, 1915–1916.* Jefferson City: Tribune Printing, 1916.

————. *Official Manual of the State of Missouri, 1917–1918.* Jefferson City: Tribune Printing, 1918.

————. *Official Manual of the State of Missouri, 1919–1920.* Jefferson City: Tribune Printing, 1920.

————. *Official Manual of the State of Missouri, 1921–1922.* Jefferson City: Tribune Printing, 1922.

Nebraska. *Nebraska Blue Book, 1974–1975.* Lincoln: Nebraska Legislative Council, 1975.

North Dakota. *House Journal of the Third Session of the North Dakota Legislative Assembly, 1893.* Bismarck, 1893.

————. *Senate Journal of the Fourth Session of the North Dakota Legislative Assembly, 1895.* Bismarck, 1895.

————. *House Journal of the Fifth Session of the North Dakota Legislative Assembly, 1897.* Bismarck, 1897.

————. *Senate Journal of the Sixth Session of the North Dakota Legislative Assembly, 1899.* Bismarck, 1899.

————. *House Journal of the Eighth Session of the North Dakota Legislative Assembly, 1903.* Bismarck, 1903.

————. *Senate Journal of the Eighth Session of the North Dakota Legislative Assembly, 1903.* Bismarck, 1903.

————. *Senate Journal of the Ninth Session of the North Dakota Legislative Assembly, 1905.* Bismarck, 1905.

————. *House Journal of the Tenth Session of the North Dakota Legislative Assembly, 1907.* Bismarck, 1907.

————. *Legislative Manual, 1907.* Bismarck: Tribune Printing, 1907.

————. *Senate Journal of the Tenth Session of the North Dakota Legislative Assembly, 1907.* Bismarck, 1907.

————. *House Journal of the Eleventh Session of the North Dakota Legislative Assembly, 1909.* Bismarck, 1909.

————. *Legislative Manual, 1909.* Bismarck: Tribune Printing, 1909.

————. *Senate Journal of the Eleventh Session of the North Dakota Legislative Assembly, 1909.* Bismarck, 1909.

Ohio. *Amendment and Legislation: Proposed Constitutional Amendments, Initiated Legislation, and Laws Challenged by Referendum, Submitted to the Electors.* Comp. Arthur A. Schwartz and J. Kenneth Blackwell. Columbus: Office of the Secretary of State, 1999.

———. *Annual Statistical Report of the Secretary of State for the Year Ending November 15, 1912.* Springfield, Ohio: Springfield Publishing, 1913.

———. *Annual Statistical Report of the Secretary of State for the Year Ending November 15, 1913.* Springfield, Ohio: Springfield Publishing, 1914.

———. *Annual Statistical Report of the Secretary of State for the Year Ending November 15, 1914.* Springfield, Ohio: Springfield Publishing, 1915.

———. *Annual Statistical Report of the Secretary of State for the Year Commencing November 16th, 1914 and Ending June 30th, 1915.* Springfield, Ohio: Springfield Publishing, 1916.

———. *Annual Statistical Report of the Secretary of State for the Year Ending June 30, 1916.* Springfield, Ohio: Springfield Publishing, 1917.

———. *Annual Statistical Report of the Secretary of State for the Year Ending June 30, 1918.* Springfield, Ohio: Springfield Publishing, 1919.

———. *Annual Statistical Report of the Secretary of State for the Year Ending June 30, 1919.* Springfield, Ohio: Springfield Publishing, 1920.

———. *Annual Statistical Report of the Secretary of State for the Year Ending June 30, 1920.* Springfield, Ohio: Springfield Publishing, 1921.

Oklahoma. *Directory and Manual of the State of Oklahoma.* Oklahoma City: n.p., 1961.

———. *Journal of the Council, Proceedings of the Third Legislative Assembly of the Territory of Oklahoma, 1895.* N.p., n.d.

———. *Journal of the House, Proceedings of the Third Legislative Assembly of the Territory of Oklahoma, 1895.* N.p., n.d.

———. *Session Laws of 1907–1908 Passed at the First Session of the Legislative Assembly of the State of Oklahoma.* Guthrie: Oklahoma Printing, 1908.

———. *Session Laws of 1910 Passed at the Extraordinary Session of the Second Legislature of the State of Oklahoma.* Guthrie: State Capital, 1910.

South Dakota. *Biographical Directory of the South Dakota Legislature, 1889–1989.* Pierre: South Dakota Legislative Research Council, 1989.

———. "Initiative and Referendum in South Dakota." Pierre: Division of Legislative Reference, 1916.

———. *Journal of the House of Representatives of the South Dakota Legislature.* 5th sess. Pierre: Carter Publishing, 1897.

———. *Journal of the Senate of the South Dakota Legislature.* 5th sess. Pierre: Carter Publishing, 1897.

———. "South Dakota Constitutional Convention of 1885." In *Constitutional Debates,* 1:113. Pierre: n.p., 1907.

U.S. Congress. Senate. "The Constitution and Its Makers." 62d Cong., 2d sess., 1911, doc. no. 122.

———. "Memorial of State Referendum League of Maine Concerning Initiative and Referendum." 60th Cong., 1st sess., 1908, doc. no. 521.

————. "New Dangers to Majority Rule." 62d Cong., 2d sess., 1912, doc. no. 897.

————. "Popular v. Delegated Government." Washington, D.C.: Government Printing Office, 1910.

————. "The Public Opinion Bill." 60th Cong., 1st sess., 1907, doc. no. 114.

————. "The State-Wide Initiative and Referendum." 64th Cong., 2d sess., 1917, doc. no. 736.

OTHER SOURCES

Abbott, Carl. *Colorado: A History of the Centennial State.* Boulder: Colorado Associated University Press, 1976.

Abrams, Richard M. *Conservatism in a Progressive Era: Massachusetts Politics, 1900–1912.* Cambridge: Harvard University Press, 1964.

Adams, Sir Francis Ottiwell. *The Swiss Confederation.* London: Macmillan, 1889.

Albertson, Ralph. "Montana Constitution Amended." *Arena* 37 (February 1907): 199–200.

————. "Victory in Maine." *Arena* 40 (November 1908): 511–14.

Allen, C. M. *The "Sequoyah" Movement.* Oklahoma City: Harlow Publishing, 1925.

Allswang, John M. *The Initiative and Referendum in California, 1898–1998.* Stanford: Stanford University Press, 2000.

American Newspaper Annual. Philadelphia: N. W. Ayer and Son's, 1891.

Ameringer, Oscar. *If You Don't Weaken: The Autobiography of Oscar Ameringer.* New York: Henry Holt, 1940.

Anderson, Raymond V. "Adoption and Operation of Initiative and Referendum in North Dakota." Ph.D. diss., University of Minnesota, 1962.

Arrowsmith, J. W. "Direct Legislation Movement in New Jersey." *Direct Legislation Record* 1 (May 1894): 2–3.

Baglien, David B. "The McKenzie Era: A Political History of North Dakota, 1880–1920." Master's thesis, North Dakota Agricultural College, 1955.

Baker, James, and Leroy Hafen. *History of Colorado: Biographical.* Vol. 4. Denver: Linderman, 1927.

Barnett, James D. *The Operation of the Initiative, Referendum, and Recall in Oregon.* New York: Macmillan, 1915.

Bass, John H. "The Initiative and Referendum in Oklahoma." *Southwestern Political Science Quarterly* 1 (September 1920): 125–46.

Baum, Dale. "The New Day in North Dakota: The Nonpartisan League and the Politics of Negative Revolution." *North Dakota History* 40 (spring 1973): 5–19.

Beaver, Daniel R. *A Buckeye Crusader.* Privately published, 1957.

Bellamy, Edward. *Looking Backward.* New York: Random House, 1951.

Berman, David R. *Reformers, Corporations, and the Electorate: An Analysis of Arizona's Age of Reform.* Boulder: University Press of Colorado, 1992.

Biographical Directory of the South Dakota Legislature, 1889–1989. Pierre: South Dakota Legislative Research Council, 1989.

Bird, Frederick L., and Frances M. Ryan. *The Recall of Public Officers: A Study of the Operation of the Recall in California.* New York: Macmillan, 1930.

Black, J. William. "Maine's Experience with the Initiative and Referendum." *Annals of the American Academy* 43 (September 1912): 159–78.

Blackorby, Edward C. "George B. Winship: Progressive Journalist of the Middle Border." *North Dakota Quarterly* 39 (summer 1971): 5–17.

Blaire, Diane D. *Arkansas Politics and Government: Do the People Rule?* Lincoln: University of Nebraska Press, 1988.

Bliss, William D. P. *The Encyclopedia of Social Reform.* New York: Funk and Wagnalls, 1897.

Blythe, Samuel G. "Putting the Rollers under the S. P." *Saturday Evening Post* 183 (January 7, 1911): 6–7.

Bourne, Jonathan, Jr. "Popular Government in Oregon." *Outlook* 96 (October 8, 1910): 321–30.

Braeman, John. "Albert J. Beveridge and Statehood for the Southwest, 1902–1912." *Arizona and the West* 10 (winter 1968): 313–42.

Breckenridge, Adam C. "Nebraska as a Pioneer in the Initiative and Referendum." *Nebraska History* 34 (September 1953): 215–23.

Broder, David S. *Democracy Derailed: Initiative Campaigns and the Power of Money.* New York: Harcourt, 2000.

Brown, Kenny L. "A Progressive from Oklahoma: Senator Robert Latham Owen, Jr." *Chronicles of Oklahoma* 62 (fall 1984): 232–65.

Brudvig, Glenn Lowell. "The Farmers' Alliance and Populist Movement in North Dakota, 1884–1896." Master's thesis, University of North Dakota, 1956.

Brundage, David. *The Making of Western Labor Radicalism: Denver's Organized Workers, 1878–1905.* Urbana: University of Illinois Press, 1994.

Bryant, Keith L. *Alfalfa Bill Murray.* Norman: University of Oklahoma Press, 1968.

———. "Kate Barnard, Organized Labor, and Social Justice in Oklahoma during the Progressive Era." *Journal of Southern History* 35 (May 1969): 145–64.

———. "Labor in Politics: The Oklahoma State Federation of Labor during the Age of Reform." *Labor History* 11 (summer 1970): 259–76.

Bryce, James. *The American Commonwealth.* 3d ed. New York: Macmillan, 1893.

Burbank, Garin. *When Farmers Voted Red: The Gospel of Socialism in the Okla-*

homa Countryside, 1910–1924. Westport, Conn.: Greenwood Press, 1976.

Burlingame, Merrill G., and K. Ross Toole. *A History of Montana*. Vol. 1. New York: Lewis Publishing, 1957.

Cassity, R. O. Joe, Jr. "The Political Career of Patrick S. Nagle." *Chronicles of Oklahoma* 64 (winter 1986–1987): 48–67.

Caswell, John E. "The Prohibition Movement in Oregon." *Oregon Historical Quarterly* 40 (March 1939): 64–82.

Cherny, Robert W. *Populism, Progressivism, and the Transformation of Nebraska Politics, 1885–1915*. Lincoln: University of Nebraska Press, 1981.

———. *A Righteous Cause: The Life of William Jennings Bryan*. Boston: Little, Brown, 1985.

Christensen, Lawrence O. "Missouri: The Heart of the Nation." In *Heartland*, ed. James H. Madison. Bloomington: Indiana University Press, 1988.

Clark, Blue. "Delegates to the Constitutional Convention." *Chronicles of Oklahoma* 48 (winter 1970–1971): 400–415.

Clem, Alan L. *Prairie State Politics: Popular Democracy in South Dakota*. Washington, D.C.: Public Affairs Press, 1967.

Clinch, Thomas A. *Urban Populism and Free Silver in Montana: A Narrative of Ideology in Political Action*. Missoula: University of Montana Press, 1970.

Clodius, Albert Howard. "The Quest for Good Government in Los Angeles, 1890–1910." Ph.D. diss., Claremont Graduate School, 1953.

Coletta, Paolo E. "The Nebraska Democratic Campaign of 1910." *Nebraska History* 52 (winter 1971): 359–82.

Connolly, Christopher P. *The Devil Learns to Vote: The Story of Montana*. New York: J. J. Little and Ives, 1938.

Crawford, Harriet Ann. *The Washington State Grange, 1889–1924: A Romance of Democracy*. Portland: Binfords and Mort, 1940.

Crawford, Lewis F. *History of North Dakota*. Chicago: American Historical Society, 1931.

Cree, Nathan. *Direct Legislation by the People*. Chicago: A. C. McClurg, 1892.

Crockett, Norman L. "The 1912 Single Tax Campaign in Missouri." *Missouri Historical Review* 56 (October 1961): 40–52.

Cronin, Thomas E. *Direct Democracy: The Politics of Initiative, Referendum, and Recall*. Cambridge: Harvard University Press, 1989.

Crosser, Robert. "The Initiative and Referendum Amendments in the Proposed Ohio Constitution." *Annals of the American Academy* 43 (September 1912): 191–202.

Crouch, Winston W. *The Initiative and Referendum in California*. Los Angeles: Haynes Foundation, 1950.

———. "John Randolph Haynes and His Work for Direct Government." *National Municipal Review* 27 (September 1938): 434–53.

Culbertson, Paul Thomas. "A History of the Initiative and Referendum in Oregon." Ph.D. diss., University of Oregon, 1941.

Culton, Donald R. "Charles Dwight Willard: Los Angeles' 'Citizen Fixit.'" *California History* 57 (summer 1978): 158–71.

Cushman, Robert E. "Analysis of the Popular Vote on Constitutional and Legislative Proposals in the General Election of 1914." *New Republic* 2 (March 6, 1915): supp. 4–29.

Dargan, Marion. "New Mexico's Fight for Statehood, 1885–1912." Parts 1 and 2. *New Mexico Historical Review* 14 (January 1939): 1–33; (April 1939): 121–42.

Debates in the Massachusetts Constitutional Convention, 1917–1918. Vol. 2. Boston: Wright and Potter, 1918.

DeLorme, Roland. "Turn-of-the-Century Denver: An Invitation to Reform." *Colorado Magazine* 45 (winter 1968): 1–15.

Deploige, Simon. *The Referendum in Switzerland.* London: Longmans, Green, 1898.

Destler, Chester McArthur. *American Radicalism, 1865–1901.* New York: Octagon Books, 1963.

DeWitt, Benjamin Parke. *The Progressive Movement.* New York: Macmillan, 1915.

Dibbern, John. "Who Were the Populists? A Study of Grass-Roots Alliancemen in Dakota." *Agricultural History* 56 (October 1982): 677–91.

Direct Legislation in Colorado: A Report by the Special Committee on Direct Legislation of the City Club. Denver: City Club of Denver, 1927.

Donaghey, George W. *Autobiography.* Benton, Ark.: L. B. White, 1939.

Donovan, Timothy P., Willard B. Gatewood Jr., and Jeannie M. Whayne, eds. *The Governors of Arkansas: Essays in Political Biography.* Fayetteville: University of Arkansas Press, 1995.

Dorman, Robert L. "The Tragical Agrarianism of Alfalfa Bill Murray." *Chronicles of Oklahoma* 66 (fall 1988): 240–67.

Dressner, Richard B. "William Dwight Porter Bliss's Christian Socialism." *Church History* 47 (March 1978): 66–82.

Dudden, Arthur P. *Joseph Fels and the Single Tax Movement.* Philadelphia: Temple University Press, 1971.

Dunbar, Willis Frederick. *Michigan: A History of the Wolverine State.* Grand Rapids: William B. Eerdman's, 1970.

Ellinger, Charles Wayne. "Congressional Viewpoint toward the Admission of Oklahoma as a State, 1902–1906." *Chronicles of Oklahoma* 58 (fall 1980): 283–95.

———. "The Drive for Statehood in Oklahoma, 1889–1906." *Chronicles of Oklahoma* 41 (spring 1963): 15–37.

Ellis, Albert H. *A History of the Constitutional Convention of the State of Oklahoma.* Muskogee, Okla.: Economy Printing, 1923.

Evans, Tony Howard. "Oregon Progressive Reform, 1902–1914." Ph.D. diss., University of Oregon, 1966.

Farmer, Hallie. "The Economic Background of Frontier Populism." *Mississippi Valley Historical Review* 10 (March 1924): 406–27.

Farmer, Rod. "Direct Democracy in Arkansas, 1910–1918." *Arkansas Historical Quarterly* 40 (spring 1981): 99–118.

———. "The Maine Campaign for Direct Democracy, 1902–1908." *Maine Historical Society Quarterly* 23 (summer 1983): 13–28.

Faulkner, Harold Underwood. *The Quest for Social Justice, 1898–1914.* New York: Macmillan, 1937.

Filler, Louis. *Crusaders for American Liberalism.* Yellow Springs, Ohio: Antioch Press, 1964.

Fink, Gary M. *Labor's Search for Political Order: The Political Behavior of the Missouri Labor Movement, 1890–1940.* Columbia: University of Missouri Press, 1973.

Fiske, John. *Civil Government in the United States.* Boston: Houghton Mifflin, 1890.

Flower, B. O. *Progressive Men, Women, and Movements of the Past Twenty-five Years.* Boston: New Arena, 1914.

Fogelson, Robert M. *The Fragmented Metropolis: Los Angeles, 1850–1930.* Cambridge: Harvard University Press, 1967.

Folsom, Burton W. "Tinkerers, Tipplers, and Traitors: Ethnicity and Democratic Reform in Nebraska during the Progressive Era." *Pacific Historical Review* 50 (February 1981): 53–75.

Folsom, Burton W., Jr. *No More Free Markets or Free Beer: The Progressive Era in Nebraska, 1900–1924.* Lanham, Md.: Lexington Books, 1999.

Franklin, Jimmie Lewis. *Born Sober: Prohibition in Oklahoma, 1907–1959.* Norman: University of Oklahoma Press, 1971.

Fuller, Leon W. "Colorado's Revolt against Capitalism." *Mississippi Valley Historical Review* 21 (December 1934): 343–60.

———. "A Populist Newspaper of the Nineties." *Colorado Magazine* 9 (May 1932): 81–87.

Gaboury, William Joseph. *Dissension in the Rockies: A History of Idaho Populism.* New York: Garland Publishing, 1988.

Garlock, Jonathan Ezra. "A Structural Analysis of the Knights of Labor: A Prolegomenon to the History of the Producing Classes." Ph.D. diss., University of Rochester, 1974.

Geiger, Louis G. "Conservative Reform and Rural Radicalism." *North Dakota Quarterly* 28 (winter 1960): 1–9.

Gibbs, Christopher C. *The Great Silent Majority: Missouri's Resistance to World War I.* Columbia: University of Missouri Press, 1988.

Gilbert, James H. "Single-Tax Movement in Oregon." *Political Science Quarterly* 31 (March 1916): 25–52.

Glaab, Charles N. "The Failure of North Dakota Progressivism." *Mid-America* 39 (October 1957): 195–209.

———. "John Burke and the Progressive Revolt." In *The North Dakota Political Tradition,* ed. Thomas W. Howard, 40–65. Ames: Iowa State University Press, 1981.

———. "The Revolution of 1906: N. D. vs. McKenzie." *North Dakota Quarterly* 24 (fall 1956): 101–9.

Glad, Paul W. *The Trumpet Soundeth: William Jennings Bryan and His Democracy, 1896–1912.* Lincoln: University of Nebraska Press, 1960.

Goble, Danney. *Progressive Oklahoma: The Making of a New Kind of State.* Norman: University of Oklahoma Press, 1980.

Goldman, Eric F. *Rendezvous with Destiny.* New York: Knopf, 1952.

Goodwyn, Lawrence. *Democratic Promise: The Populist Moment in America.* New York: Oxford University Press, 1976.

Graham, Virginia. *A Compilation of Statewide Initiative Proposals Appearing on the Ballots through 1976.* Washington, D.C.: Library of Congress, Congressional Research Service, 1978.

Grant, H. Roger. "The Origins of a Progressive Reform: The Initiative and Referendum Movement in South Dakota." *South Dakota History* 3 (fall 1973): 390–407.

Grantham, Dewey W. "The Contours of Southern Progressivism." *American Historical Review* 86 (December 1981): 1035–59.

———. *Southern Progressivism: The Reconciliation of Progress and Tradition.* Knoxville: University of Tennessee Press, 1983.

Gray, Alexander G., and Thomas R. Kiley. "The Initiative and Referendum in Massachusetts." *New England Law Review* 26 (fall 1991): 27–109.

Griffiths, David B. "Far Western Populism: The Case of Utah, 1893–1900." *Utah Historical Quarterly* 37 (fall 1969): 396–407.

Hanson, Bertil L. "Oklahoma's Experience with Direct Legislation." *Southwestern Social Science Quarterly* 47 (December 1966): 263–73.

Haynes, George H. "'People's Rule' on Trial." *Political Science Quarterly* 28 (March 1913): 18–33.

Haynes, John R. "The Actual Workings of the Initiative, Referendum, and Recall." *National Municipal Review* 1 (October 1912): 586–602.

Heflin, Reuben W. "New Mexico Constitutional Convention." *New Mexico Historical Review* 21 (January 1946): 60–68.

Hefner, Richard D., ed. *A Documentary History of the United States.* New York: New American Library, 1965.

Hendrick, Burton J. "The Initiative and Referendum and How Oregon Got Them." *McClure's* 37 (July 1911): 235–48.

Hendrickson, Kenneth E., Jr. "The Public Career of Richard F. Pettigrew of South Dakota, 1848–1926." Ph.D. diss., University of Oklahoma, 1962.

———. "Some Political Aspects of the Populist Movement in South Dakota." *North Dakota History* 34 (winter 1967): 77–92.

Hichborn, Franklin. *Story of the Session of the California Legislature of 1909.* San Francisco: James H. Barry, 1909.

———. *Story of the Session of the California Legislature of 1911.* San Francisco: James H. Barry, 1911.

Hicks, John D. *The Populist Revolt: A History of the Farmers' Alliance and the People's Party.* Lincoln: University of Nebraska Press, 1961.

Holli, Melvin G. *Reform in Detroit: Hazen S. Pingree and Urban Politics.* New York: Oxford University Press, 1969.

Hornbein, Marjorie. "Denver's Struggle for Home Rule." *Colorado Magazine* 48 (fall 1971): 337–54.

Houghton, N. D. "Arizona's Experience with the Initiative and Referendum." *New Mexico Historical Review* 29 (July 1954): 183–209.

———. "The Initiative and Referendum in Missouri." Master's thesis, University of Missouri, 1923.

———. "The Initiative and Referendum in Missouri." *Missouri Historical Review* 19 (January 1925): 268–99.

Hubbard, H. A. "The Arizona Enabling Act and President Taft's Veto." *Pacific Historical Review* 3 (September 1934): 307–22.

Huber, Frances A. "The Progressive Career of Ben B. Lindsey, 1900–1920." Ph.D. diss., University of Michigan, 1963.

Hurst, Irvin. *The 46th Star: A History of Oklahoma's Constitutional Convention and Early Statehood.* Oklahoma City: Semco Color Press, 1957.

Huthmacher, J. Joseph. *Massachusetts People and Politics, 1919–1933.* Cambridge: Harvard University Press, 1959.

Jaques, Janice. "The Political Reform Movement in Los Angeles, 1900–1909." Master's thesis, Claremont Graduate School, 1948.

Johnson, Claudius O. "The Adoption of the Initiative and Referendum in Washington." *Pacific Northwest Quarterly* 35 (October 1944): 291–303.

———. "The Initiative and Referendum in Washington." *Pacific Northwest Quarterly* 36 (January 1945): 29–63.

Jones, Allen W. "Political Reforms of the Progressive Era." *Alabama Review* 21 (July 1968): 173–94.

Kessler, Lauren. "The Ideas of Woman Suffrage and the Mainstream Press." *Oregon Historical Quarterly* 84 (fall 1983): 257–75.

Key, V. O., Jr., and Winston W. Crouch. *The Initiative and Referendum in California.* Berkeley and Los Angeles: University of California Press, 1939.

King, Clyde Lyndon. *The History of the Government of Denver with Special Ref-*

erence to Its Relations with Public Service Corporations. Denver: Fisher Book, 1911.

Knepper, George W. *Ohio and Its People*. Kent, Ohio: Kent State University Press, 1997.

Lamar, Howard R. *Dakota Territory, 1861–1889*. New Haven: Yale University Press, 1956.

———. *The Far Southwest, 1846–1912: A Territorial History*. New Haven: Yale University Press, 1966.

Lamm, Richard D., and Duane A. Smith. *Pioneers and Politicians: 10 Colorado Governors in Profile*. Boulder: Pruett Publishing, 1984.

Larson, Robert W. *New Mexico Populism: A Study of Radical Protest in a Western Territory*. Boulder: University Press of Colorado, 1974.

———. "Populism in the Mountain West: A Mainstream Movement." *Western Historical Quarterly* 13 (April 1982): 143–64.

———. "Statehood for New Mexico, 1888–1912." *New Mexico Historical Review* 37 (July 1962): 161–200.

Ledbetter, Calvin R., Jr. "Adoption of Initiative and Referendum in Arkansas: The Roles of George W. Donaghey and William Jennings Bryan." *Arkansas Historical Quarterly* 51 (fall 1992): 199–223.

———. *Carpenter from Conway: George Washington Donaghey as Governor of Arkansas, 1909–1913*. Fayetteville: University of Arkansas Press, 1993.

Leonard, Thomas C. *The Power of the Press: The Birth of American Political Reporting*. New York: Oxford University Press, 1986.

Leopard, Donald. "Joint Statehood, 1906." *New Mexico Historical Review* 34 (October 1959): 241–47.

Lewallen, Robert D. "'Let the People Rule': William Jennings Bryan and the Oklahoma Constitution." *Chronicles of Oklahoma* 73 (fall 1995): 278–307.

Lindell, Terrence J. "South Dakota Populism." Master's thesis, University of Nebraska, 1982.

Lindsey, Ben B., and Harvey J. O'Higgins. *The Beast*. Seattle: University of Washington Press, 1970.

Link, Arthur S. "The Progressive Movement in the South, 1870–1914." *North Carolina Historical Review* 23 (April 1946): 172–95.

Link, Arthur S., and Richard L. McCormick. *Progressivism*. Arlington Heights, Ill.: Harlan Davidson, 1983.

Lockridge, Kenneth A. *The New England Town: The First Hundred Years*. New York: W. W. Norton, 1970.

Lonsdale, David L. "The Fight for an Eight-Hour Day." *Colorado Magazine* 43 (autumn 1966): 339–53.

Loring, Augustus P. "The Fourth Constitutional Convention (1914–1919)." In vol. 5 of *Commonwealth History of Massachusetts*, ed. Albert Bushnell Hart. New York: States History, 1930.

Loucks, H. L., George A. Silsby, and W. H. Lyon. "The Initiative and Referendum: A Symposium." *Monthly South Dakotan* 1 (September 1898): 69–73.

Lowell, A. Lawrence. *Public Opinion and Popular Government.* New York: Johnson Reprint, 1969.

Maben, Michael. "The Initiative and Referendum in Oregon: An Historical Perspective." *State Constitutional Commentaries and Notes* 3 (winter 1992): 18–22.

Mabry, Thomas J. "New Mexico's Constitution in the Making: Reminiscences of 1910." *New Mexico Historical Review* 19 (April 1944): 168–84.

MacColl, E. K. "John Franklin Shafroth, Reform Governor of Colorado, 1909–1913." *Colorado Magazine* 29 (January 1952): 37–52.

———. "Progressive Legislation in Colorado, 1907–1917." Master's thesis, University of Colorado, 1949.

Mahnken, Norbert R. "William Jennings Bryan in Oklahoma." *Nebraska History* 31 (December 1950): 247–74.

Malone, Michael P., Richard B. Roeder, and William L. Lang. *Montana: A History of Two Centuries.* Seattle: University of Washington Press, 1991.

Malone, Michael P., and Dianne G. Dougherty. "Montana's Political Culture: A Century of Evolution." *Montana: The Magazine of Western History* 31 (January 1981): 44–58.

Maxwell, Amos D. *The Sequoyah Constitutional Convention.* Boston: Meador Publishing, 1953.

McClintock, Thomas C. "Seth Lewelling, William S. U'Ren, and the Birth of the Oregon Progressive Movement." *Oregon Historical Quarterly* 68 (September 1967): 197–220.

McCrackan, W. D. *The Rise of the Swiss Republic.* Boston: Arena Publishing, 1892.

McMath, Robert C., Jr. *Populist Vanguard.* Chapel Hill: University of North Carolina Press, 1975.

McNelis, Sarah. *Copper King at War: The Biography of F. Augustus Heinze.* Missoula: University of Montana Press, 1968.

Melzer, Richard. "New Mexico in Caricature: Images of the Territory on the Eve of Statehood." *New Mexico Historical Review* 62 (October 1987): 335–60.

Meredith, H. L. "The Agrarian Reform Press in Oklahoma, 1889–1922." *Chronicles of Oklahoma* 50 (spring 1972): 82–94.

———. "The 'Middle Way': The Farmers' Alliance in Indian Territory, 1889–1896." *Chronicles of Oklahoma* 47 (winter 1969–1970): 377–87.

Meyer, C. Kenneth. *Direct Democracy in South Dakota: The People Conducting Their Own Business.* Vermillion: Government Research Bureau of the University of South Dakota, 1979.

Miller, Joseph Dana, ed. *Single Tax Year Book*. New York: Single Tax Review Publishing, 1917.

Miller, Robert Worth. *Oklahoma Populism: A History of the People's Party in the Oklahoma Territory*. Norman: University of Oklahoma Press, 1987.

Mitchell, Paul J. "Progressivism in Denver: The Municipal Reform Movement, 1904–1916." Ph.D. diss., University of Denver, 1966.

Moses, Bernard. *The Federal Government of Switzerland*. Oakland: Pacific Press Publishing, 1889.

Mowry, George E. *The California Progressives*. Chicago: Quadrangle, 1963.

Moyers, David Michael. "Arkansas Progressivism: The Legislative Record." Ph.D. diss., University of Arkansas, 1986.

Munro, William Bennett. *The Initiative, Referendum, and Recall*. New York: D. Appleton, 1924.

Murray, William H. "The Constitutional Convention." *Chronicles of Oklahoma* 9 (June 1931): 126–38.

Musselman, Lloyd. "Governor John F. Shafroth and the Colorado Progressives: Their Fight for Direct Legislation, 1909–1910." Master's thesis, University of Denver, 1961.

Nelson, Bruce. *Land of the Dacotahs*. Lincoln: University of Nebraska Press, 1946.

Niswonger, Richard L. *Arkansas Democratic Politics, 1896–1920*. Fayetteville: University of Arkansas Press, 1990.

Noble, Ransom E. "Henry George and the Progressive Movement." *American Journal of Economics and Sociology* 8 (April 1949): 259–69.

Oberholtzer, Ellis Paxson. *The Referendum in America*. New York: Charles Scribner's Sons, 1900.

Omdahl, Lloyd B., ed. *Vote of the People*. Grand Forks: University of North Dakota Bureau of Governmental Affairs, 1968.

Owen, Homer L. "Oregon Politics and the Initiative and Referendum." Bachelor's thesis, Reed College, 1950.

Palsson, Mary Dale. "The Arizona Constitutional Convention of 1910: The Election of Delegates in Pima County." *Arizona and the West* 16 (summer 1974): 111–24.

Parsons, Frank. *The City for the People*. Philadelphia: C. F. Taylor, 1901.

Pease, Lute. "The Initiative and Referendum—Oregon's 'Big Stick.'" *Pacific Monthly* 17 (May 1907): 563–75.

Pelletier, Lawrence Lee. "The Initiative and Referendum in Maine." *Bowdoin College Bulletin* no. 300 (March 1951): 7–35.

Pickens, Donald K. "Oklahoma Populism and Historical Interpretation." *Chronicles of Oklahoma* 43 (autumn 1965): 275–83.

Piott, Steven L. *Holy Joe: Joseph W. Folk and the Missouri Idea*. Columbia: University of Missouri Press, 1997.

Piper, Kingsbury. "The Victorious Campaign for Direct-Legislation in Maine." *Arena* 40 (December 1908): 546–51.

Pollock, James K. *The Initiative and Referendum in Michigan.* Ann Arbor: University of Michigan Press, 1940.

Pomeroy, Earl. *The Pacific Slope.* New York: Knopf, 1965.

Pomeroy, Eltweed. "The Direct Legislation Movement and Its Leaders." *Arena* 16 (June 1896): 29–43.

Potter, Edwin S. "Letting the People Rule." *Equity* 16 (July 1914): 121–24.

Pratt, William C. "Radicals, Farmers, and Historians: Some Recent Scholarship about Agrarian Radicalism in the Upper Midwest." *North Dakota History* 52 (fall 1985): 12–25.

———. "Socialism on the Northern Plains, 1900–1924." *South Dakota History* 18 (spring–summer 1988): 1–35.

Price, Charles M. "The Initiative: A Comparative State Analysis and Reassessment of a Western Phenomenon." *Western Political Quarterly* 28 (June 1975): 243–62.

Proceedings of the Constitutional Convention of the Proposed State of Oklahoma. Muskogee, Okla.: Muskogee Printing, 1907.

Queary, Charles H. *The Initiative and Referendum in Colorado.* Denver: Legislative Reference Office, 1938.

Quint, Howard H. *The Forging of American Socialism.* Indianapolis: Bobbs-Merrill, 1953.

Reid, Bill G. "Elizabeth Preston Anderson and the Politics of Social Reform." In *The North Dakota Political Tradition,* ed. Thomas W. Howard, 183–202. Ames: Iowa State University Press, 1981.

Remele, Larry. "'God Helps Those Who Help Themselves': The Farmers' Alliance and Dakota Statehood." *Montana: The Magazine of Western History* 37 (autumn 1987): 22–33.

———. "Power to the People: The Nonpartisan League." In *The North Dakota Political Tradition,* ed. Thomas W. Howard, 66–91. Ames: Iowa State University Press, 1981.

Report of the Nineteenth Annual Meeting of the Woman's Christian Temperance Union of North Dakota, Minot, N.D., September 25–28, 1908. Bismarck: Bismarck Tribune, 1908.

Richards, W. B. *The Oklahoma Red Book.* Oklahoma City: Democrat Printing, 1912.

Ridgeway, Gordon B. "Populism in Washington." *Pacific Northwest Quarterly* 39 (October 1948): 284–311.

Roberts, Frank H. H. "The Denver Situation and the Rush Amendment." In *Proceedings of the Chicago Conference for Good City Government and the Annual Meeting of the National Municipal League, 1904,* 122–29. Philadelphia: National Municipal League, 1904.

Robinson, Doane. *History of South Dakota*. Aberdeen, S.D.: B. F. Bowen, 1904.

Robinson, Elwyn B. *History of North Dakota*. Lincoln: University of Nebraska Press, 1966.

Roeder, Richard B. "Montana in the Early Years of the Progressive Period." Ph.D. diss., University of Pennsylvania, 1971.

———. "Montana Progressivism: Sound and Fury and One Small Tax Reform." *Montana: The Magazine of Western History* 20 (October 1970): 18–27.

Rood, W. S. "James W. Sullivan: The Father of the Initiative and Referendum in the United States." *Garment Worker* 12 (March 21, 1913): 5–6.

Roush, Russell. "The Initiative and Referendum in Arizona, 1912–1978." Ph.D. diss., Arizona State University, 1979.

Rubenstein, Bruce A., and Lawrence E. Ziewacz. *Michigan: A History of the Great Lakes State*. Wheeling, Ill.: Harlan Davidson, 1995.

Rush, John A. *The City-County Consolidated*. Los Angeles: privately published, 1941.

Ryan, Frederick L. *A History of Labor Legislation in Oklahoma*. Norman: University of Oklahoma Press, 1932.

Saloutos, Theodore. "The Rise of the Nonpartisan League in North Dakota, 1915–1917." *Agricultural History* 20 (January 1946): 43–61.

Saltvig, Robert D. "The Progressive Movement in Washington." Ph.D. diss., University of Washington, 1966.

Scales, John R., and Danney Goble. *Oklahoma Politics: A History*. Norman: University of Oklahoma Press, 1982.

Schell, Herbert S. *History of South Dakota*. Lincoln: University of Nebraska Press, 1968.

Schmidt, David D. *Citizen Lawmakers: The Ballot Initiative Revolution*. Philadelphia: Temple University Press, 1989.

Schwantes, Carlos A. *Radical Heritage: Labor, Socialism, and Reform in Washington and British Columbia, 1885–1917*. Seattle: University of Washington Press, 1979.

Scott, Anne Firor. "A Progressive Wind from the South, 1906–1913." *Journal of Southern History* 29 (February 1963): 53–70.

Sheridan, Thomas E. *Arizona: A History*. Tucson: University of Arizona Press, 1995.

Shibley, George H. "The Initiative and Referendum in Practical Operation." *Arena* 40 (September 1908): 142–50.

Shippee, Lester Burrell. "Washington's First Experiment in Direct Legislation." *Political Science Quarterly* 30 (June 1915): 235–53.

Shoemaker, Floyd C. *Missouri and Missourians*. Chicago: Lewis Publishing, 1943.

Shore, Elliott. *Talkin' Socialism: J. A. Wayland and the Role of the Press in Amer-*

ican Radicalism, 1890–1912. Lawrence: University Press of Kansas, 1988.

Sitton, Tom. "California's Practical Idealist: John Randolph Haynes." *California History* 67 (March 1988): 3–17, 67–69.

———. *John Randolph Haynes: California Progressive.* Stanford: Stanford University Press, 1992.

Smith, George Martin. *South Dakota: Its History and Its People.* Chicago: S. J. Clarke, 1915.

Snodgrass, William George. "A History of the Oklahoma State Federation of Labor to 1918." Master's thesis, University of Oklahoma, 1960.

Snyder, Richard. "The Election of 1904: An Attempt at Reform." *Colorado Magazine* 45 (winter 1968): 16–26.

Speich, Virginia. "The Political Career of George H. Sheldon, 1907–1909." *Nebraska History* 53 (fall 1972): 339–79.

Sponholtz, Lloyd. "The Initiative and Referendum: Direct Democracy in Perspective, 1898–1920." *American Studies* 14 (fall 1973): 43–64.

———. "The 1912 Constitutional Convention in Ohio: The Call-up and Nonpartisan Selection of Delegates." *Ohio History* 79 (summer–fall 1970): 209–18.

Starr, Kevin. *Inventing the Dream: California through the Progressive Era.* New York: Oxford University Press, 1985.

Starr, Paul Dean. "The Initiative and Referendum in Colorado." Master's thesis, University of Colorado, 1958.

Starring, Charles R. "Hazen S. Pingree: Another Fallen Eagle." *Michigan History* 32 (June 1948): 129–49.

Steffens, Lincoln. *Upbuilders.* Seattle: University of Washington Press, 1968.

Stimson, Grace Heilman. *Rise of the Labor Movement in Los Angeles.* Berkeley and Los Angeles: University of California Press, 1955.

Stockbridge, Frank Parker. "Ohio Wide Awake." *Everybody's* 27 (November 1912): 696–707.

———. "The Single Taxers: Who They Are and What They Are Doing." *Everybody's* 26 (April 1912): 507–22.

Stone, Wilbur Fiske, ed. *History of Colorado.* Chicago: S. J. Clarke, 1918.

Stumph, Roy C. "The History of the Referendum in New Mexico." Master's thesis, University of New Mexico, 1941.

Sullivan, J. W. *Direct Legislation by the Citizenship through the Initiative and Referendum.* New York: True Nationalist Publishing, 1892.

Tallian, Laura. *Direct Democracy: An Historical Analysis of the Initiative, Referendum, and Recall Process.* Los Angeles: People's Lobby Press, 1977.

Teal, Joseph N. "The Practical Workings of the Initiative and Referendum in Oregon." In *National Conference for Good City Government: Proceedings of the Cincinnati Conference for Good City Government and the Fif-*

teenth Annual Meeting of the National Municipal League Held November 15, 16, 17, 18, 1909, ed. Clinton Rogers Woodruff, 309–25. N.p.: National Municipal League, 1909.

Thelen, David P. *The New Citizenship: The Origins of Progressivism in Wisconsin.* Columbia: University of Missouri Press, 1972.

———. *Paths of Resistance: Tradition and Dignity in Industrializing Missouri.* New York: Oxford University Press, 1986.

Thomas, David Y. "Direct Legislation in Arkansas." *Political Science Quarterly* 29 (March 1914): 84–110.

———. "The Initiative and Referendum in Arkansas Come of Age." *American Political Science Review* 27 (February 1933): 66–75.

———, ed. *Arkansas and Its People: A History, 1541–1930.* Vol. 1. New York: American Historical Society, 1930.

Thompson, Cecil T. "The Origin of Direct Legislation in Oregon: How Oregon Secured the Initiative and Referendum." Master's thesis, University of Oregon, 1929.

Thompson, John. *Closing the Frontier: Radical Response in Oklahoma, 1889–1923.* Norman: University of Oklahoma Press, 1986.

Tiffany, Burton Ellsworth. "The Initiative and Referendum in South Dakota." In *South Dakota Historical Collections*, 14:331–74. Aberdeen, S.D.: News Printing, 1924.

Tittmann, Edward D. "New Mexico Constitutional Convention: Recollections." *New Mexico Historical Review* 27 (July 1952): 177–86.

Todd, Charles Foster. "The Initiative and Referendum in Arizona." Master's thesis, University of Arizona, 1931.

Toole, K. Ross. *Twentieth-Century Montana: A State of Extremes.* Norman: University of Oklahoma Press, 1972.

Torrey, Edwin C. *Early Days in Dakota Territory.* Minneapolis: Farnham Publishing, 1925.

Tweton, D. Jerome. "The Anti-League Movement: The IVA." In *The North Dakota Political Tradition*, ed. Thomas W. Howard, 93–122. Ames: Iowa State University Press, 1981.

———. "North Dakota in the 1890s: Its People, Politics, and Press." *North Dakota History* 24 (April 1957): 113–18.

———. "Sectionalism in North Dakota Politics: The Progressive Republican Revolt of 1900." *North Dakota History* 25 (January 1958): 21–28.

Ueland, L. A. "Majority Rule or the Initiative and Referendum." Valley City, N.D.: Times-Record Printing, 1908.

Viehe, Fred W. "The First Recall: Los Angeles Urban Reform or Machine Politics?" *Southern California Quarterly* 70 (spring 1988): 1–23.

Vincent, John Martin. *State and Federal Government in Switzerland.* Baltimore: Johns Hopkins University Press, 1891.

Waldron, Ellis L., and Paul B. Wilson. *Atlas of Montana Elections, 1889–1976.* Missoula: University of Montana Press, 1978.

Warner, Hoyt Landon. "Ohio's Constitutional Convention of 1912." *Ohio State Archaeological and Historical Quarterly* 61 (January 1952): 11–31.

———. *Progressivism in Ohio, 1897–1917.* Columbus: Ohio State University Press, 1964.

Webber, Christopher L. "William Dwight Porter Bliss: Priest and Socialist." *Historical Magazine of the Protestant Episcopal Church* 38 (March 1959): 9–39.

Weed, Brian J. "Populist Thought in North and South Dakota, 1890–1900." Master's thesis, University of North Dakota, 1970.

Wenger, Robert E. "The Anti-Saloon League in Nebraska Politics, 1898–1910." *Nebraska History* 52 (fall 1971): 267–92.

Whitman, Alden, ed. *American Reformers.* New York: H. W. Wilson, 1985.

Wilkins, Robert P. "Alexander McKenzie and the Politics of Bossism." In *The North Dakota Political Tradition,* ed. Thomas W. Howard, 3–39. Ames: Iowa State University Press, 1981.

Williams, T. Harry. *Romance and Realism in Southern Politics.* Athens: University of Georgia Press, 1961.

Wilson, Terry Paul. "The Demise of Populism in Oklahoma Territory." *Chronicles of Oklahoma* 43 (autumn 1965): 265–74.

Winchester, Boyd. *The Swiss Republic.* Philadelphia: J. B. Lippincott, 1891.

Woodward, C. Vann. *Origins of the New South, 1877–1913.* Baton Rouge: Louisiana State University Press, 1951.

Woodward, Robert C. "W. S. U'Ren and the Single Tax in Oregon." *Oregon Historical Quarterly* 61 (March 1960): 46–63.

———. "William S. U'Ren: A Progressive Era Personality." *Idaho Yesterdays* 4 (summer 1960): 4–10.

———. "William Simon U'Ren: In an Age of Protest." Master's thesis, University of Oregon, 1956.

Wright, James Edward. *The Politics of Populism: Dissent in Colorado.* New Haven: Yale University Press, 1974.

Young, Arthur Nichols. *The Single Tax Movement in the United States.* Princeton: Princeton University Press, 1916.

Young, F. C. "The Single Tax Movement in Oregon." *American Economic Review* 1 (September 1911): 643–48.

Index

Note: I & R represents initiative and referendum